Understanding Expertise

Other books by Fernand Gobet

Problem gambling: Cognition, prevention and treatment (2014)

Psychologie du talent et de l'expertise (2011)

Foundations of cognitive psychology (2011)

Moves in mind: The psychology of board games (2004)

Techniques for modeling human performance in synthetic environments (2003)

Perception and memory in chess (1996)

Les mémoires d'un joueur d'échecs (1993)

Understanding Expertise

A Multi-Disciplinary Approach

Fernand Gobet
University of Liverpool

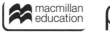

First published 2016 by
PALGRAVE

Palgrave in the UK is an imprint of Macmillan Publishers Limited,
registered in England, company number 785998, of 4 Crinan Street,
London, N1 9XW.

Palgrave Macmillan in the US is a division of St Martin's Press LLC,
175 Fifth Avenue, New York, NY 10010.

Palgrave is a global imprint of the above companies and is represented
throughout the world.

Palgrave® and Macmillan® are registered trademarks in the United States,
the United Kingdom, Europe and other countries.

ISBN 978–1–137–57205–9 hardback
ISBN 978–0–230–27624–6 paperback

This book is printed on paper suitable for recycling and made from fully
managed and sustained forest sources. Logging, pulping and manufacturing
processes are expected to conform to the environmental regulations of the
country of origin.

A catalogue record for this book is available from the British Library.

A catalog record for this book is available from the Library of Congress.

Printed in China

In memory of my brother Tobie, an expert computer programmer, for the great moments shared together.

Contents

List of Illustrations

Boxes

Preface

Writing this book, my fifth book on expertise, has been extremely challenging, but also very rewarding. My first two books on this topic were monographs on perception and memory in chess. My third book expanded the horizon somewhat and provided a systematic review on research carried out on board games. Many games were discussed (Go, checkers, awele and so on), but the focus was still on chess, since it was by far the board game having most contributed to the scientific literature. My fourth book, published in 2011 in French, was more ambitious and dealt with the whole field of the psychology of expertise. As a reflection on the evolution of my own scientific views, a considerable part of that book was devoted to the notion of talent.

The book you are holding in your hands is even more ambitious – with hindsight and considering the delay in finishing it, it was probably too ambitious. The idea was both to cover more domains of expertise than in the 2011 book (in particular, sports, music and medicine are discussed in more breadth and detail), and to address the question of expertise from multiple academic disciplines. Specifically, in addition to psychology, my own field, the book discusses expertise from the point of view of neuroscience, sociology, artificial intelligence and philosophy. Addressing these topics has required discovering entire new literatures and has taken me way beyond my comfort zone. It has also challenged some of the views I had held for decades. I had always found it surprising that nobody had written such an integrative, single-authored book before about expertise. Now, I know why... In any case, the experience has been extremely enriching.

Three intellectual tensions are omnipresent in this book. First, there is the tension between talent and practice, nature and nurture. My first intension was to downplay this aspect, but this was simply not possible. In particular, in recent years wars have been raging between the proponents of the extreme positions of the nature and nurture debate, in particular but not exclusively on the issue of deliberate practice, and this simply could not be ignored. As a student much influenced by Jean Piaget's thought on development and his middle ground approach in the nature-nurture debate, I had always thought that such extreme positions were absurd and had fully disappeared from the scientific horizon. I was right on the first point, but totally wrong on the second!

Second, some fields focus on the positive aspects of experts (superior memory, world records, inextinguishable creativity and so on) while others focus on their failings (arbitrary criteria for selection, inept predictions, lack of understanding of complex situations, arrogance and so on). In general, expertise is defined by performance in the first case and by society in the second. While there is some overlap between these two definitions, this overlap is far from being perfect.

Third, there is the tension between unlimited rationality and bounded rationality. Do humans make optimal decisions given the available information, or do they make systematic mistakes due to cognitive limits such as the limited capacity of short-term memory and the bottleneck of attention? Expertise is an ideal domain for studying this question, and the answers will clearly support the idea of bounded rationality.

A difficulty in writing this book is that there is a huge literature on expertise in each discipline, with little communication between them. For example, the literature on the sociology of expertise largely ignores the literature on the psychology of expertise, and the indifference is reciprocal. Given the amount of the material available – most of which is fairly recent – only snapshots of the relevant research can be given in this book. Inevitably, I have been biased in my selection of the material. While I have tried to provide a balanced sample, there is no doubt that I have tended to choose the topics I had researched myself directly or those that I found interesting. To compensate for this, numerous pointers to the respective literatures will be provided in the "Further Reading" sections.

As is typical of reviews or monographs on expertise, there is a fair amount of material on chess. In addition to chess being one of my topics of research, there are also scientific reasons for this. Historically, chess has dominated research into expertise. This is because it offers a relatively manageable but still complex task environment, and because it is nearly unique in expertise research in providing a reliable, quantitative, internal and thus ecologically valid measure of skill, the Elo rating (Elo, 1978). In addition, most of the phenomena identified with chess have been found to generalise to other domains. Thus, chess can be considered as a good model for expertise in general.

The economic and societal implications of a better understanding of expertise are considerable, and there are potentially serious implications for policy. One advantage – well worth the pains – of addressing expertise from the vantage point of multiple disciplines is that parallels and contradictions become evident between them. This allows one to derive some interesting prescriptions for education and other applications.

Finally, I should mention that I have carried out research on expertise for more than 20 years, mostly from the point of view of psychology. One consequence is that I tend to focus on the individual rather than on other levels such as brain structure, group or society. I think this intellectual bias is appropriate for studying expertise; ultimately, the entity being identified as an "expert" is an individual, although of course other levels of analysis are important as well. A second consequence is that I do have strong views about various aspects of expertise. I thought it would be more interesting for the reader to read a text that is personal, if sometimes opinionated, than to read an asepticised account. While I have tried to provide an objective account of divergent opinions, I have not hesitated to criticise them squarely when I thought the criticism was fair.

Acknowledgements

Over the years, I have had the pleasure and privilege to work with many colleagues and students on the psychology of expertise. In particular, I would like to thank the following people, with whom collaboration has led to publications on this topic: Erik Altmann, Merim Bilalić, James Borg, Terry Bossomaier, Mark Buckley, Christopher Connolly, Guillermo Campitelli, Neil Charness, Philippe Chassy, Gary Clarkson, André Didierjean, Adriaan de Groot, Morgan Ereku, Alessandro Guida, Zack Hambrick, Mike Harre, Kay Head, Sam Jackson, Peter Jansen, Stephen Johnston, Riekent Jongman, Peter Lane, Gerv Leyden, Daniele Luzzo, Peter McLeod, Elizabeth Meinz, Jeroen Musch, Serge Nicolas, Fred Oswald, Andrew Parton, Amanda Parker, Payal Nanik Ramchandani, Jean Retschitzki, Howard Richman, Yvan Russel, Herbert Simon, Kieran Smallbone, Richard Smith, Alan Snyder, Toby Staff, Jim Staszewski, Hubert Tardieu, Alex de Voogt, Andrew Waters, Harvey Whitehouse, Gareth Williams, David Wood, Michael Wright and Omar Yousaf. I'm grateful to Mark Addis, David Boyd and Christopher Winch for organising several seminars and workshops on the philosophy of expertise. My thanks also go to the commissioning and editorial staff at Palgrave – Isabel Berwick, Jenny Hindley, Jamie Joseph, Neha Sharma and Paul Stevens – for their support and patience.

I would also like to express my gratitude to the anonymous reviewers who commented on the book proposal or the entire manuscript, and Julian Pine who offered useful comments on the last chapter. I'm particularly grateful to Martyn Lloyd-Kelly, Guillermo Campitelli and Jim Staszewski, who provided detailed comments on the entire manuscript.

The writing of this book has been made possible by a generous Research Fellowship on "Modelling the (expert) mind" from the Economic and Social Research Council, United Kingdom.

Publisher's Acknowledgements

The publisher and the author thank the people listed below for permission to reproduce material from their publications:

American Psychological Association, for permission to reproduce and adapt Figure 3.5. From Richman, H. B., Staszewski, J. J., & Simon, H. A. (1995). Simulation of expert memory with EPAM-IV. *Psychological Review, 102*, 305–330. Copyright © 1995 by the American Psychological Association.

American Psychological Association, for permission to reproduce and adapt Figures 9.2 and 9.3. From Simonton, D. K. (1997). Creative productivity. *Psychological Review, 104*, 66–89. Copyright © 1997 by the American Psychological Association. The use of APA information does not imply endorsement by APA.

Cambridge University Press, for permission to reproduce Table 12.1. From Mieg, H. A. (2006). Social and sociological factors in the development of expertise. In K. A. Ericsson, N. Charness, P. J. Feltovich & R. R. Hoffman (Eds.), *The Cambridge handbook of expertise and expert performance* (pp. 743–760). Cambridge: Cambridge University Press. Copyright © Cambridge University Press 2006.

Harold Cohen and Gordon Bell, for permission to reproduce Figure 6.1 Meeting on Gauguin's Beach Copyright © Harold Cohen.

De Boeck, for permission to adapt Figure 7.1. From Gobet, F. (2011). *Psychologie du talent et de l'expertise*. Bruxelles: De Boeck. Copyright © De Boeck 2011.

Diana Deutsch, for permission to reproduce and adapt Figure 2.2 Deutsch's scale illusion. From Deutsch, D. I. (1987). Illusions for stereo headphones. *Audio Magazine*, March, 36–48. Copyright © 1987 Diana Deutsch.

Elsevier, for permission to reproduce Table 5.1. From Shanteau, J. (1992). Competence in experts: The role of task characteristics. *Organizational Behavior and Human Decision Processes, 53*, 252–266. Copyright © 1992 Elsevier.

Elsevier, for permission to reproduce Figure 8.1. From Hambrick, D. Z. et al. (2014). Deliberate practice: Is that all it takes to become an expert? *Intelligence, 45*, 34–45. Copyright © 2014 Elsevier.

John Wiley and Sons, for permission to reproduce Figure 3.6. From Patel, V. L., & Groen, G. J. (1986). Knowledge based solution strategies in medical reasoning. *Cognitive Science, 10*, 91–116. Copyright © 1986 John Wiley and Sons.

Psychology Press, for permission to adapt Figures 4.1 and 4.2. From Gobet, F., de Voogt, A. J., & Retschitzki, J. (2004). *Moves in mind*. Hove: Psychology Press. Copyright © 2004 Psychology Press.

Routledge, for permission to reproduce and adapt Figure 4.6. From Gobet, F. (1997). A pattern-recognition theory of search in expert problem solving. *Thinking and Reasoning, 3*, 291–313. Copyright © Routledge 1997 www.tandfonline.com.

Springer Science + Business Media, for permission to reproduce and adapt Figures 3.8 and 3.9. From Waters, A. J., & Gobet, F. (2008). Mental imagery and chunks: Empirical and computational findings. *Memory & Cognition, 36*, 505–517. Copyright © 2008 Springer Science + Business Media.

The International Research Association for Talent Development and Excellence, for permission to reproduce and adapt Figures 15.1 and 15.2. From Gobet, F. (2013). Expertise vs. talent. *Talent Development and Excellence, 5*, 75–86. Copyright © 2013 The International Research Association for Talent Development and Excellence.

University of Chicago Press, for permission to reproduce Figure 12.1. From Collins, H. M., & Evans, R. (2007). *Rethinking expertise*. Chicago: University of Chicago Press. Copyright © 2007 University of Chicago Press.

List of Abbreviations and Acronyms

ACT-R	Adaptive Character of Thought – Rational
AI	artificial intelligence
AP	absolute pitch
CHREST	Chunk Hierarchy and REtrieval STructures
DP	deliberate practice
EPAM	Elementary Perceiver and Memorizer
g	general intelligence
GPS	General Problem Solver
IQ	intelligence quotient (used as a measure of intelligence in intelligence tests)
LTM	long-term memory
LTWM	long-term working-memory theory
ms	millisecond
NSS	Newell, Shaw and Simon (chess program)
SD	standard deviation
SOS	satisfaction of search
STM	short-term memory

CHAPTER 1

Introduction

1.1 Preview of Chapter

We live in a complex environment, where new technological developments regularly challenge our wits. With the development of the Internet, the amount of information that is available has increased exponentially over the last decade. It is therefore essential that we improve our understanding of the way people learn to cope with these challenges. In the last century or so, a tremendous amount of information has been acquired regarding learning in psychology, neuroscience, education, sociology and other fields, with a substantial portion derived from research into expertise. The aim of this book is to review the most important results stemming from this line of research and to evaluate their implications for society. In particular, we will be interested in the educational methods that have benefited from expertise research and in the implications that this research has on how society can develop ways to help citizens cope with these new challenges.

A good way to start is to illustrate, with a few examples, what we mean by experts. A list of top-level experts would include Wolfgang Amadeus Mozart in music, Marie Curie in science, Magnus Carlsen in chess, Bill Gates in business and Jessica Ennis-Hill in sports. A list of more ordinary experts would include a physician, an engineer, a lawyer but also a baker, a florist and a nurse.

From the outset, we face a few central questions on the nature of expertise. The most obvious is: what is expertise? We will spend some time discussing some of the many definitions that have been proposed and evaluating the extent to which they are successful. This will lead to a working definition that we will use in most of this book. Another important question relates to the reasons why it is important to study expertise. We will see that there are both basic scientific reasons and more applied ones. However, before we address these questions, we need to clear up an important issue about the dual meaning of the word "expertise".

1.2 The Dual Meaning of the Term "Expertise"

Whatever the detail of the definitions, which we will consider in the next section, one must recognise from the outset that the term "expertise" has two basic meanings, which are not necessarily consistent with each other. For example, the *Oxford Talking Dictionary* (1998) defines expertise as "Expert opinion or knowledge; know-how, skill, or expertness in something". The first part of the definition emphasises knowledge or even opinion – *knowing-that*. The second part emphasises skill – *knowing-how*, as indeed mentioned in the definition. This is a fundamental divide reflected in several of the fields we will consider in this book. On the one hand, sociology, law and – to some extent – philosophy are more interested in the first part of the definition (knowing-that). On the other hand, psychology, neuroscience and education essentially use the second part of the definition (knowing-how). Interestingly, some languages such as French accept only the first meaning of the term "expertise" in everyday language.

These two meanings raise the irksome question as to whether they are related, and indeed whether it makes sense to devote a book to expertise as a single concept. This book will argue that this is not only a meaningful endeavour but also an important one. Bringing together traditions of research that have focused on either meaning of the word will help integrate two bodies of knowledge that have essentially evolved independently. It also raises new and important questions that will spur new research and bring about new applications.

1.3 Definitions of Expertise

Having cleared up the question of the two basic meanings of "expertise", we can consider some of the definitions of expertise that have been proposed in the literature. Note that not all definitions neatly fit with the two meanings we have just discussed.

Intuitively, the term "expertise" brings to mind individuals such as physicians, engineers, chess masters and lawyers. Most people would also consider that good examples of experts are offered by the pundits (such as academics, journalists or business consultants) who proffer their views about their area of expertise (and even sometimes well beyond) on TV/radio and in newspapers. But what about occupations such as bricklaying and cigar making, or abilities such as language and walking, which most people carry out fluently? Obviously, some activities are more likely to be labelled as "expertise" than others. Is this reasonable or is it just a reflection of the prejudices of our society?

In research papers, expertise is often defined using experience and the amount of time an individual has spent in a domain. Unfortunately, while the amount of dedicated practice predicts expertise fairly well (see Chapter 8), experience in itself is often a poor predictor of true expertise (Ericsson et al., 1993; Meehl, 1954; Richman et al., 1996). Everybody knows amateur tennis players or pianists who fall short of expert performance despite having practised their favourite activity for years. In fact, there is direct empirical evidence from research on clinical expertise (Meehl, 1954) and chess (Gobet et al., 2004) indicating that the correlation between expertise level and the number of years spent in a field is weak.

Another reasonable approach is to use diplomas: PhDs, honorary titles and certificates from official professional associations. There are at least four weaknesses with this approach. First, diplomas are often based not only on an objective measure of performance but also on sociocultural criteria. Second, diplomas often do not test the skills that will be used later, but rather test declarative knowledge. This is the case, for example, in medical schools and most fields in universities (psychology is a case in point). Thus, future medical doctors are tested on their knowledge of anatomy, biochemistry and pathology, and not on their ability to diagnose and treat patients. Third, unless detailed grades are supplied, diplomas do not provide much information about the skill level obtained. Fourth, some individuals can be experts without formal qualifications. A striking example is provided by Epstein (1996), who showed that some AIDS activists had acquired considerable knowledge about microbiology and statistics, which, added to their knowledge of AIDS culture, allowed them to make substantial contributions to research. As Gallo, who co-discovered the human immunodeficiency virus (HIV) and who was originally lukewarm to AIDS activists' work, put it: "It's frightening sometimes how much they know and how smart some of them are" (Epstein, 1996, p. 338).

Some fields offer more reliable measures of expertise, measures that are also ecological, in the sense that they are part of the culture of the domain. Researchers of business expertise can use the wealth accumulated by different individuals; students of expertise in science can use the number of citations that scientists have accrued during their career; and researchers of writing expertise can use the number of books an author has sold. While having the advantage of being quantitative, these measures have shortcomings as well. In particular, they can be sensitive to factors unrelated to expertise, such as market fluctuations in business, popularity of a specific school of thought in science and fashion in literature.

In an ideal world – at least for scientific research – experts would be rank-ordered as a function of their level of expertise, or even better, they would have their expertise quantified. When absolute measures are involved (e.g. time to run 100 metres or the amount of weight that an athlete can lift), there is no debate, barring accusations of cheating. Rank ordering is used in sports such as football, where the International Federation of Association Football (FIFA) publishes a monthly ranking of national teams, using a rather byzantine formula. Tennis uses the ranking of the Association of Tennis Professionals (ATP): the sum of the best 18 results from the immediate past 52 weeks. From the point of view of expertise research, the ATP rating has two weaknesses. First, it measures skill only over the last year, and second, it only takes points won in entire tournaments into account and ignores the strength of the opponents as well as the outcomes of specific matches.

The best available system so far is the Elo rating (Elo, 1978), developed for measuring chess skill but now also used in other domains such as Scrabble and table tennis. The Elo rating takes into account both the outcome of a game (win, loss or draw) and the skill level of the opponent. It can be used after each game or match, producing a finely graded and up-to-date measure of skill. It also has the advantage that it is based on a sound mathematical model. Having such a quantitative measure is a real bonus, and this in fact partly explains why a considerable amount of research has been carried out on chess expertise. While researchers in most other domains of expertise have to satisfy themselves with coarse comparisons between novices, intermediates and experts, chess researchers can differentiate between a grandmaster with 2,620 Elo points and another with 2,680 Elo points, and even compute the expected outcome of a game between those two players.

Some researchers emphasise that expertise is something that can only be acquired with effort and intentionally, with a clear goal in mind (Bereiter & Scardamalia, 1993). This seems an unnecessary requirement. How expertise is acquired is of course important, but it does not seem wise to include this in a definition. Similarly, whether somebody is talented or not in a specific domain should not be part of the definition of expertise, not least because there is considerable disagreement about this question. We shall take up these issues in Chapters 7 and 8.

In a similar vein, it has been proposed that the hallmark of experts is that they display fluid behaviour, requiring few conscious decisions (Dreyfus & Dreyfus, 1988; Fitts, 1964). We shall see that this description captures expertise in some but not all situations. Moreover, it should also be pointed out that almost the opposite definition of expertise has sometimes been proposed. Bereiter and Scardamalia (1993, p.11) argue that "the expert addresses problems whereas the experienced nonexpert carries out practiced routines". A similar view is shared by Ericsson et al. (1993), who argue that just performing routine actions hinders the development of expertise, and that experts must deliberatively practice selected components of their skill. We will discuss this idea in considerable detail in Chapter 8 when dealing with *deliberate practice*.

The importance of knowledge has often been emphasised, in particular when human expertise is compared to the expertise (or the lack thereof) of computers. For example, it has been proposed that expertise is made possible by the acquisition of a large number of domain-specific patterns. While this is true in many domains (see Chapters 2 and 3), it seems prudent to not include putative *mechanisms* in the definition of expertise, in part because the nature of these mechanisms is still the topic of vigorous debate. In any case, investigating expertise will require reflecting on, and questioning, long-held views about the status of knowledge in cognition. An important question will be the link between knowledge and real-time cognitive processing. In intelligence research, these two forms of cognition are called *crystallised* and *fluid* intelligence, respectively (Cattell, 1971).

Based on the seminal work of de Groot (1965), who asked chess players of various skill levels to find the best move in a given chess position, Ericsson has repeatedly emphasised (e.g. Ericsson, 1996a; Ericsson & Smith, 1991a) that expert performance should be replicable in the laboratory, when tasks representative of the domain are used. For example, when studied in the laboratory and compared to non-experts, chess experts should find better moves, physicists should provide better solutions to physics problems and medical doctors should provide better diagnoses. As we shall see in this book, this is in fact what has been found in the three examples just given, and indeed in most (although by no means all) domains of expertise. Thus, Ericsson's requirement seems a valid one, at least with domains where it is feasible to set up laboratory tasks that are ecologically valid. But this is not always possible. A counter-example is expertise in developing novel and ground-breaking scientific theories in physics; by definition, such events are rare, and thus unlikely to be captured in the laboratory.

Finally, we would be remiss to not mention some definitions where the social aspects of expertise play a central role. These definitions emphasise that "expertise" is a label that society or other groups give to individuals, sometimes irrespectively of the real competences of these individuals. Support for this view comes from the fact that selection criteria differ from one domain to the next, and indeed even differ within a domain (Sternberg, 1997). Labels can be official, such as university and professional titles, or informal, such as the label of the "local technology wizard", but this is immaterial when it comes to societal recognition. Stein (1997) argues that the term "expertise" can only be used within a specific context. According to him, it is incorrect to say that expertise resides solely in the expert: while individual knowledge and skills are obviously important, these gain their meaning only within the context provided by the social system of which the expert is a part. We will take up these issues in Chapters 11 and 12 when dealing with the social aspects of expertise and the sociology of professions.

In most of this book, we will define an expert as somebody who obtains results that are vastly superior to those obtained by the majority of the population. This definition has the advantage that it can be applied recursively and that we can define a *super-expert*: somebody whose performance is vastly superior to the majority of experts (Gobet, 2011).[1] This definition also has the advantage of providing a means to deal with domains where most individuals have a high level of natural ability (e.g. language, walking). It is still possible to identify an expert in language (e.g. somebody who possesses a large vocabulary) and an expert in walking (e.g. somebody who has won an Olympic medal in the 20 km race walking event). Indeed, even with an ability as basic as breathing, it could be argued that practitioners of hatha yoga are experts, in that they have mastered breathing techniques unknown to most people. Finally, this definition can be applied to the two meanings of "expertise" we have highlighted earlier. The application is trivial with the *know-how* meaning: we can simply observe whether an expert does better than a non-expert. Does Lionel Messi dribble more successfully than a third-division player, or does an

---

[1]A super-expert might correspond to what is sometimes called a "genius".

experienced surgeon operate better than a newcomer? The application is more delicate, but still possible, with the *know-that* meaning. The difficulty is not in testing the amount of knowledge – simple questionnaires can do this – but in the fact that knowledge itself can be of variable quality. For example, we would doubt the scientific quality of the knowledge used by an astrologer, but not by a civil engineer. This issue will be dealt with at great length in Chapter 12.

1.4 Why Study Expertise?

The study of expertise is important for society in several ways. First, it sheds important light on learning and the acquisition of knowledge, which can be used to develop better methods of instruction and training. Given the pace at which technology advances in our society, this is a significant contribution. For example, research on physics and mathematics expertise, together with other studies, has led to the development of artificial tutoring systems in mathematics that perform better than human teachers (see Chapter 8).

Second, research on expertise can lead to better ways of coaching experts. The clearest illustration of this comes perhaps from sport and music. In athletics, world records are improved every year due to better training techniques, and the difference between current and previous achievements is sometimes stunning. The winners of Olympic medals in the marathon one century ago recorded times similar to today's amateur runners. In swimming, the seven world records that earned Mark Spitz as many gold medals at the Munich Olympic Games in 1972 would not have been sufficient for qualification for the semi-finals in the 2008 Beijing Olympic Games.

Third, research on human expertise can inform the development of artificial expert systems performing at high or even human-like levels, as we shall see in Chapter 14. Expert systems are much cheaper, do not tire and do not move to other jobs – considerable advantages from the point of view of industry. Thus, expert systems can make valuable contributions to the economy.

With respect to cognitive psychology, research on expertise has shed important light on human cognition, and several general cognitive mechanisms have first been identified in expertise research. These include the role of pattern recognition in decision making and problem solving, progressive deepening and selective search. (We will discuss these mechanisms in detail in Chapter 4.) Thus, just as neuropsychology illuminates human cognition by studying a "special" population characterised by brain damage, expertise research provides critical information on cognition by focusing on individuals who go beyond the limits that mar most of us. In both cases, looking at an atypical population offers a unique window on typical cognition.

Positive psychology, which is now a very influential approach in psychology, was created from the observation that most psychology devoted all its energy to negative aspects of human psychology, such as pathology, while ignoring its more positive aspects (Linley et al., 2006; Seligman & Csikszentmihalyi,

2000). By contrast, positive psychology focuses on hope, optimism and other human virtues. It might be worth emphasising that research on expertise, which focuses on humans' creativity and their potential to achieve extraordinary performances, had unequivocally anticipated at least some of the claims of positive psychology.

1.5 Preview of Book

The following chapters deal with the psychology of expertise. Chapter 2 focuses on perception and categorisation. It shows that *perception* lies at the heart of expertise: experts literally "see" things differently compared to novices, enabling them to categorise situations and problems better. Chapter 3 argues that this superior perception is due to the vast amount of *knowledge* that has been stored in *long-term memory* (LTM) during the years of practice necessary to reach expertise. Numerous theories have been developed to explain expert memory, and this chapter reviews the main candidates.

In Chapters 4 and 5, we shall see how these differences in perception and knowledge affect *problem solving* and *decision making*. They also affect experts' *intuition*, *insight* and *creativity*, topics of Chapter 6. In all cases, non-cognitive factors are involved as well. These include *personality* and *intelligence*, which are covered in Chapter 7. This chapter examines different approaches, mostly from differential psychology, that defend the role of *talent*, and it also addresses the issue of *gender differences*. In domains such as mathematics, science and chess, men vastly outperform women; is the origin of these differences social or biological? Finally, the chapter examines the hypothesis that creativity might benefit from *psychopathologies* such as manic depression and schizophrenia. When discussing these issues, these chapters provide an overview of the *key empirical results*, the *methods* used to obtain these results, and the *main theories* developed to explain them.

Chapter 8 covers the links between expertise, learning and education. It is concerned with four broad issues. First, it addresses the implications of theories based on talent for education. Second, it discusses the role of *practice* in acquiring expertise, and what theories focusing on practice tell us about the *training of experts*. If the theories presented in Chapters 2, 3 and 4 are correct, then it should be possible to isolate the components of *knowledge* that experts must acquire and design instruction and training methods that optimise their transmission to budding experts. Suitable practice schedules can then be designed and optimal feedback can be provided. In the extreme case, aspects of coaching could be automated with *intelligent tutoring systems*. Great attention will be devoted to the *deliberate practice* framework, which has been very influential in recent years. Proponents of *deliberate practice* argue that there is no empirical evidence for the role of talent in the development of expertise, and this claim will be discussed. The third issue addressed in this chapter is that of *transfer*. Do skills acquired in one domain transfer to others?

How do some experts appear to move to a different domain of expertise seamlessly, for example from being a biochemist to university vice-chancellor, while others fail to make such transitions? Finally, the chapter addresses the question of *expert learners* and *expert teachers*. Are some individuals just better than the majority at acquiring new information? Are some individuals particularly efficient at transmitting information to others? If so, what does this tell us about education in general?

Chapter 9 covers expertise across the life span. How does expertise develop with children? What are the respective roles of knowledge (including strategies) and biological maturation? What light do *savants* throw on expertise in general? Is the talent of *gifted children* limited to a single domain? At the other side of the life span, we will consider how *ageing* affects expertise, and whether expertise acts as a moderating variable in the ageing process. We will also consider how the careers of creative people evolve across time.

Chapter 10 addresses the links between expertise, biology and neuroscience. It discusses the influential theory proposed by Geschwind and Galaburda (1987), which ties together data from psychopathology (e.g. *dyslexia* and *autism*), developmental neuroscience and expertise in a large variety of domains including mathematics, visual arts and music. Recently, important discoveries have been made with the advent of novel *brain imaging techniques* (e.g. functional magnetic resonance imaging) as well as new developments with older techniques (e.g. electro-encephalography), and this chapter reviews the most important of them. These cover a large variety of expertise domains, most notably *sports* and *music*. The key notion of *brain plasticity*, which impinges on the interpretation of some of these data, is also examined. Finally, a better understanding of the biological mechanisms underpinning expertise raises the possibility of *creating new drugs* that will speed up the development of experts and enhance their performance. How far are we from this Brave New World?

Chapters 11 and 12 deal with expertise and its place in society. In some domains, the *distinction between experts and non-experts* is obvious. If one doubts that Maryam Mirzakhani, who in 2014 was the first woman, Muslim and Iranian to win the prestigious Fields Medal, is an expert in mathematics and more specifically the symmetry of curved surfaces, one can always try to identify errors in her proofs. However, as we have just seen, there are other domains – perhaps most domains in "real life" – where the definition of expertise is controversial. More generally, there is the issue that *expertise criteria* vary from one domain to the next, and that criteria are sometimes used inconsistently within the same domain of expertise. This particularly applies to *the professions*, which are the main kind of institutionalised expertise in industrialised countries (most notably lawyers and the medical profession).

How then are experts *selected* and *labelled* by society? Are official titles (such as those awarded by universities) always necessary? To what extent do *specific contexts* create new types of expertise and new experts? Is expertise just the product of an arbitrary selection from a particular group? What are the specific practices that enable social and cultural authority? Do experts in Scientology and astrology have the same status as experts in neuroscience and astronomy? What is the *role of scientific knowledge* in validating experts? Are today's experts tomorrow's non-experts? These considerations are answered by results from sociology research.

Another key topic of these chapters concerns the *power of experts*, at least in industrialised societies. Directly or indirectly, experts played a role in the recent global financial crisis either by condoning financial practices that were – with the benefit of hindsight – too risky or failing to predict the consequences of these practices on the dynamics of markets. Similarly, experts have a considerable impact on *political decisions* (consider, for example, global warming or the 2009 swine flu pandemic), even though the science itself is a matter of dispute amongst experts. This raises complex questions about *experts' legitimacy and accountability*.

These chapters also address the extent to which it is possible to *communicate expert knowledge* – an issue that is crucial in legal settings, for example with expert testimony. Authors such as Luhmann (1995) have argued that experts essentially cannot communicate knowledge outside their constituency. This is because social communication systems each make sense of their environment using their own code. Others, such as Mieg (2001), have been more sanguine about experts' ability to do so. Finally, the chapters address the question as to how the *mass media* and more recently the *Internet* affect the way expert knowledge is communicated.

The final theme addressed in these chapters is the issue of the legal status of the expert. There are vast differences in the way experts are *defined and selected in different legal systems*. These chapters compare and contrast practices in the common law jurisdictions of Anglo–American courts with the civil law jurisdictions within continental Europe. Key questions include an analysis of current systems of *appointment of expert witnesses* and, more generally, of the designation of someone as an "expert". Another issue is that the legal coding of information will be different to that used, for example, in engineering. As a consequence, *expert opinion* will have a different meaning and significance within the legal system to those within the domain from which the expertise originated, often creating serious misunderstandings and distortions.

The discussion of the philosophy of expertise in Chapter 13 will allow us to revisit some of the central questions of this book: the question of *rationality*, the nature of *knowledge* acquired by experts (*knowing-that* and/or *knowing-how*), and the nature of *scientific knowledge*. Anticipating the following chapter, it will also address the *philosophical implications* of artificial systems emulating human experts.

A motivation for some of the research discussed in Chapters 2 and 3 was that a sound understanding of the cognitive processes underlying expert behaviour should make it possible to develop *artificial systems* that are able to perform as well as, or even better than, human experts. The field of *expert systems* is a recognised and active discipline of computer science, and there are a number of expert systems developed to the point that they are crucial to some industries (for example, banking and geology). Chapter 14 discusses *strengths and weaknesses of such systems* as well as other related issues. What are the differences between expert systems and human experts? How is knowledge elicited from experts? Can experts really communicate their perceptual and procedural knowledge? What do expert systems teach us about *human expertise and human psychology* more generally?

Finally, the conclusion weaves together several of the strands that were discussed in previous chapters. It proposes a synthesis, highlighting the issues that should be addressed in future research.

1.6 Chapter Summary

This chapter started with a discussion of the two key meanings of expertise: knowing-that and knowing-how. It then considered a number of definitions of expertise, each emphasising a different aspect (e.g. type of measurement or place in society). It was noted that many of these definitions suffer from weaknesses. A fair amount of space was devoted to the question as to why we should study expertise. The main reasons were: the development of better methods for coaching and instruction in general, the prospect of building artificial-intelligence programs that can emulate human experts and to improve our understanding of human cognition.

1.7 Further Reading

Several edited books provide worthwhile overviews of the various ways expertise has been studied. Chi et al. (1988), Ericsson and Smith (1991b), Ericsson (1996b) and Staszewski (2013a) focus on cognitive psychology, although other viewpoints are occasionally discussed. Feltovich et al. (1997) discuss both human and machine expertise, with a special interest in the role of context. Ericsson et al.'s handbook (2006) provides a comprehensive overview of the psychology of expertise, with a strong emphasis on deliberate practice. Another handbook (Simonton, 2014) focuses on extreme forms of expertise – genius.

CHAPTER 2

Perception and Categorisation

2.1 Preview of Chapter

How can experts immediately "see" the right solution to a routine problem, while non-experts fumble hopelessly? The short answer is simple, although the details are much more complicated: in nearly all domains, expertise relies considerably on perception, which allows experts to rapidly categorise a problem. This perception is not innate but the product of extensive study and practice. A considerable amount of research has been carried out on this topic, starting with de Groot's (1965) seminal research on chess players, originally published in Dutch in 1946.

The chapter covers perception and, to a lesser extent, categorisation. It starts with de Groot's studies on chess, and then covers the role of perception in medical expertise, sport and music. The concepts of holistic perception and anticipatory schemata are also discussed. Finally, the chapter briefly addresses the topics of perceptual learning, perceptual expertise and categorisation. Note that there is a fair amount of conceptual overlap between this chapter and the next on memory. Whilst somewhat artificial, devoting one chapter to "perception and categorisation" and the other to "memory" has the advantage of providing a structured presentation of the material.

2.2 De Groot's Seminal Research

Perhaps the most striking aspect of expertise is that experts, very rapidly, see the key features of a scene or a problem situation, so long as the material comes from their domain of expertise. This phenomenon was experimentally established by Adriaan de Groot in his doctoral dissertation (de Groot, 1965). In a first experiment, de Groot gave chess players of various skill levels a chess position and asked them to select what they thought was the best move whilst thinking aloud. As expected, better players tended to find better moves. However, surprisingly, an analysis of the verbal protocols did not identify clear-cut differences in the structure of search. That is, better players did not search deeper, examine more moves or display a different way of searching. However, strong players very rapidly identified promising solutions, unlike weaker players. In fact, de Groot noted that the world champion had a better understanding of the position after 5 seconds than a strong amateur after 15 minutes! Thus, the first few seconds of seeing a position are critical for its understanding. De Groot concluded that perception must be a key component of chess skill, and presumably other skills.

To test this hypothesis, de Groot designed a simple experiment that was destined to have a tremendous impact on the psychology of expertise. He presented a chess position taken from an unknown game for a short amount of time (from 2 seconds to 15 seconds), then removed it from view and asked the participant to reconstruct it; the skill effect was striking. While a top grandmaster could recall almost the entire position, a strong amateur would struggle to remember 50 per cent of the pieces. Although this experiment is classified nowadays as a *memory* experiment (see Chapter 3 for an in-depth discussion), it is important to realise that de Groot considered it as a *perception* experiment, aimed at understanding what chess masters were *seeing* during the brief presentation of a position.

In some variations of the experiment, de Groot asked his players to think aloud when seeing an unknown position for a brief amount of time (e.g. 5 seconds). The protocols were collected in three different conditions: when the position was presented, immediately after the presentation or 30 seconds after the presentation (de Groot, 1965; de Groot & Gobet, 1996). A detailed analysis of the protocols revealed that, rather than seeing individual pieces, experts see large complexes, in which perceptual and dynamic aspects are interwoven. In fact, they rarely see static constellations of pieces, but rather notice dynamic possibilities, such as threats and potential moves and even sequences of moves. We will take up this hypothesis in Section 2.4.

Skill differences in perception were later corroborated in an experiment where chess masters' and amateurs' eye movements were recorded when they were looking at a position for 5 seconds (de Groot & Gobet, 1996). As shown in Figure 2.1, masters' fixations were shorter and less variable than those of amateurs. Masters also fixated on more squares than amateurs, and tended to look more often at the important squares, as defined by a technical analysis of the positions. This last result cannot be explained away by the fact that masters looked at more squares, because the effect remains when the total number of fixated squares is controlled for statistically. Interestingly, de Groot and Gobet also found that masters fixated more on the intersection of squares, which supports the idea that they were looking at groups of pieces rather than at pieces individually. This result has been replicated by Reingold et al. (2001), who used a check detection task rather than a memory task.

In an elegant experiment, Reingold et al. (2001) tried to estimate the visual span of chess players of different skill levels. To do so, they combined the change blindness paradigm (also known as the flicker paradigm) with the gaze-contingent window paradigm. In the change blindness paradigm, a picture is repeatedly presented in alternation with a modified version of

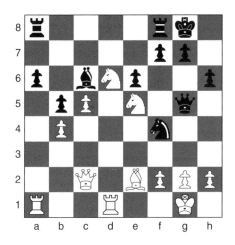

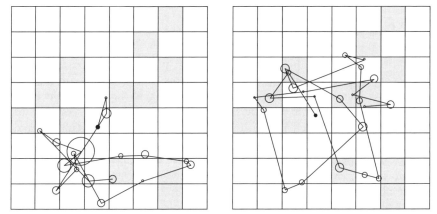

Figure 2.1 Eye movements during a 5-second presentation of a chess position. On the left, the eye movements of an amateur. On the right, the eye movements of a master. The diameter of the circles is proportional to the duration of the fixation. Important squares in the position are greyed. The first fixation is indicated by the black circle in the middle of the board.

Source: From de Groot, A. D., & Gobet, F. (1996). *Perception and memory in chess.* Assen: Van Gorcum. Copyright: F. Gobet.

this picture. Each picture is preceded by a flashed blank screen. The task is to identify the difference. This paradigm has shown that humans have great difficulties in detecting striking changes to objects and scenes (Rensink et al., 1997). In the gaze-contingent window paradigm, sophisticated eye-tracking software makes it possible to change the display in real time so that what is clearly visible to the participant (the "window") is modified as a function of what the eye fixates.

Reingold et al. used this methodology to study the extent to which randomising chess positions affects perception. After each eye movement, the window was centred on the fixation point, and grey blobs replaced chess pieces that lay outside the window. The change after the flicker modified the kind of piece located on a given square, and could happen either inside or outside the window. There were two independent variables: chess skill (novice vs. intermediate vs. expert) and configuration type (game vs. random). The dependent variable of interest was response time to detect the minor change in the position. Participants' visual span was determined by varying the size of the window after each trial and estimating the smallest window for which performance did not significantly differ in comparison to the baseline condition, where pieces outside the window were not replaced by blobs. Reingold et al. found that experts' visual spans were larger with structured positions, but not with random positions.

2.3 Medical Expertise

Eye movements have also been studied with professional experts, such as experts in radiology, a domain where a better understanding of expertise could have lifesaving implications. Radiologists take high-stake decisions, but their task is difficult as it necessitates the analysis of low-contrast and small features embedded in non-uniform backgrounds. The data collected using eye tracking have identified clear skill differences in perception between novices and experts (for reviews of literature, see Reingold & Sheridan, 2011; Taylor, 2007). Even with brief exposure times, radiologists are still able to detect a large proportion of abnormalities in an image. For instance, Kundel and Nodine (1975) found that expert radiologists could identify 70 per cent of the abnormalities when chest films were presented only for 200 ms. By comparison, with no limits in viewing time, they could identify 97 per cent of the abnormalities.[1] An important feature of brief-exposure studies is that there is not enough time for participants to make an eye movement, which means that successful identification of abnormalities requires the use of peripheral vision.

A number of studies have been interested in the pattern of eye movements when radiologists of varying skill levels scan an image. A comparison of novices' and experts' scan paths shows several important differences, which together point to more efficient scan paths for the experts and to the use of peripheral vision to guide search (e.g. Kocak et al., 2005; Krupinski, 1996; Krupinski

---

[1]The high percentage is not representative of real-life performance, where diagnosis hovers between 75 per cent and 95 per cent, which is low considering that 50 per cent is chance level (Groopman, 2007). Intra- and inter-observer variability is also high. Interestingly, the performance of automated computer diagnosis systems is around 80 per cent, but with different errors compared to humans. Computer-assisted diagnosis has tried to combine human and computer skills to reach higher-quality diagnoses.

et al., 2006; Manning et al., 2006). Experts tend to have fewer fixations, to use fewer but longer saccades, to cover a smaller portion of the image and to reach the abnormality faster, often within one second of viewing. In addition, Kundel et al. (2007) found that there is a negative correlation between first fixation of abnormality and accuracy (the participants fixating the abnormality faster tended to be more accurate). Interestingly, immediately after viewing the image, mammogram experts often display a long saccade in the direction of the abnormality. In general, expert radiologists show what Kundel and Wright (1969) call a circumferential scan pattern: they first get a general impression by scanning the image with a small number of long saccades that land in points that are wide apart in the display.

Several experiments have used the gaze-contingent window paradigm, which we have described earlier with chess. Kundel et al. (1991) compared a condition where nodules (small aggregations of cells on the lung that are about 3 cm long) could be seen only when fixated upon directly in foveal vision with a condition where they could also be seen in parafoveal and peripheral vision. The nodules were identified faster in the latter than in the former case. Moreover, an increase of the window size led to faster identification (Kundel et al., 1984). In line with these results, presenting the full image led to better performance than the presentation of segments of that image one at a time. Finally, accuracy is lower when participants are instructed to focus on one aspect or region of the image than when they receive no such instruction (free viewing). In total, these experiments support the role of peripheral vision in experts' scan of radiology images.

Two models have been proposed to explain experts' eye-movement patterns in radiology. The global-focal search model (Nodine & Kundel, 1987) proposes that, by comparing the image with their schemas of normal and abnormal radiographs, experts are able to rapidly create a landscape view of the picture. This view enables them to process information for a larger visual span than novices, and thus to scan the image more efficiently. Once deviations from the normal schemas and matches with abnormal schemas are identified, the experts scan the image in more detail with foveal vision.

The two-stage detection model (Swensson, 1980) proposes that experts have refined their perception with the acquisition of mechanisms that provide a filter to automatically point out features of the display that should be examined further. As noted by Reingold and Sheridan (2011), there is a clear similarity between these models and Chase and Simon's (1973a) chunking theory, which will be discussed at length in the next chapter.

The importance of parafoveal and peripheral information for finding relevant information has been demonstrated in other medical fields as well. Krupinski et al. (2006) provide data from telepathology, where participants examined virtual slides and had to decide which locations they would select for further analysis. Compared to medical students and pathology residents, practising pathologists moved their eye less often but had longer saccades. This was interpreted as being indicative of a more efficient scan path being used by practising pathologists. Some of the locations selected by the practising pathologists were never fixated, which strongly suggests that parafoveal and peripheral vision was used. In an experiment using tasks similar to laparoscopic surgery simulation, expert surgeons fixated fewer locations than novices (Kocak et al., 2005). Interestingly, in three basic laparoscopic tasks, experts tended to fixate the target but not the tool, which suggests that they were able to manipulate the tool with information from peripheral vision only.

2.4 Holistic Perception and Anticipatory Schemata

A classic question in psychology is whether perception is holistic – as for example argued by Gestalt psychology – or whether it can be accounted for by incremental, constructive mechanisms. Tikhomirov and Poznyanskaya (1966) argued that the eye movements of a chess player considering his next move supported the former view. By contrast, Simon and Barenfeld (1969) defended the view that these data could be explained equally well by a simulation program that was based on local aspects of the board position (e.g. relations of defence and attack between pieces). More recent simulation work with CHREST, a computer model based on the idea of chunking (see Section 3.11.4.2), is in line with Simon and Barenfeld's view. For example, Gobet and Chassy (2009) present simulations showing how the internal representation of a player can be explained by the progressive recognition of chunks and templates.

Authors such as Selz (1922) and de Groot (1965) postulated the existence of *anticipatory schemas*. These schemas comprise information that makes it possible to anticipate actions. A logical hypothesis is that these schemas should be more developed with experts, who should thus anticipate actions better. A series of experiments has tested this hypothesis with chess players (Ferrari et al., 2006), basketball players (Didierjean & Marmèche, 2005), car drivers (Blättler et al., 2010) and pilots of the French Air Force (Blättler et al., 2011). In general, these experiments support the notion of an anticipatory schema: rather than memorising a scene the way it was presented, experts tend to memorise it the way it will be in the near future. For example, in one of the driving experiments, participants were shown a video of a car driving in some direction. The video was then interrupted, and then resumed either at the point before the interruption, or at a different point. Participants' task was to estimate whether the resumption point of the video was at the same point as or at a different point than when it stopped. Both experienced and inexperienced drivers tended to remember the position of the car when the video was interrupted as being farther in the direction of movement than it actually was when the video resumed. However, the effect was stronger with experienced drivers, which supports the hypothesis that their anticipatory schemata were more developed.

2.5 Perception in Sport

Perceptual requirements vary considerably between different sports. They tend to be high in team sports and in sports such as football and badminton that include a moving object, and low in individual non-contact sports such as weight lifting, swimming and running. Perceptual requirements also vary depending on one's role in sport (Hodges et al., 2006). For example, in football, a goal-keeper, a defender and an attacker will direct their attention to different features of the game. Similarly, a player, a coach and a referee will develop different perceptual skills.

An added difficulty with sports, compared to more cognitive domains of expertise, is that perceptual skills must be linked to movements, with a few critical constraints: as time pressure is considerable, processing must be rapid, so players use only minimal cues most of the time; movements often incur a fair amount of coordination and must be executed rapidly and precisely; and players must keep in mind the possibility that their opponents might use deception tactics. As an example, consider a tennis player such as Venus Williams returning a serve. The ball travels so fast (115 mph; 185 km/h) that Williams has to decide on her response and initiate the movements before the ball is served; the movements include, at the minimum, moving to a specific location, and hitting the ball with the racket with suitable strength and spin. There is only about 300 ms between the time the ball is served and returned, and it has been estimated that the minimum time for the visual input to reach the visual cortex is 100 ms and the minimum time to initiate a motor response is 150 ms. To this, one must add the time to actually execute the movement. You can see that there is little time available for deciding which sequence of actions to carry out. Essentially, all relevant processing must happen automatically and subconsciously.

Considerable research has confirmed that elite athletes make both better and quicker decisions. Among other sports, the experimental evidence includes tennis (Wright & Jackson, 2007), football (Williams et al., 1993), cricket (Mueller et al., 2006) and badminton (Abernethy, 1988). Following de Groot's original work, experts' perceptual superiority has often been explained in the literature in terms of the knowledge they hold, and we will specify this knowledge in more detail in the chapter on memory. However, we must also deal with another plausible explanation: it could be the case that experts simply have better low-level perceptual abilities, such as static visual acuity, dynamic visual acuity and stereovision, perhaps for genetic reasons. A fair amount of research has been carried out in sport psychology between 1950 and 1980, and the answer appears to be negative: there is no correlation between skill level in sport and the underlying perceptual mechanisms with material unrelated to sport (Helsen & Starkes, 1999; Shea & Paull, 1996; Starkes et al., 1995).[2] Similarly, empirical results in sport expertise allow us to reject the hypothesis that skill differences are due to experts being generally quicker: there is no correlation between skill in sport and simple reaction times for domain-unrelated material (Goulet et al., 1988; Helsen & Starkes, 1999; Nielsen & McGown, 1985; Shea & Paull, 1996).

In general, de Groot's basic result on the importance of perception in chess has been replicated in sports such as volleyball and tennis, where the ability to use early cues rapidly to execute anticipatory responses is critical (Farrow & Abernethy, 2003). Experiments using normal video displays or matched point-light displays[3] have shown that experts can predict ball direction more precisely than novices (Abernethy et al., 2001). This allows them to act seemingly without hurry, in spite of considerable time pressure. A plausible explanation is that the perceptual patterns they have acquired during training make them more efficient at processing their opponent's body movements to extract kinematic information about the speed and likely impact location of the ball. The patterns provide automatic and rapid access to the kind of actions that should be carried out.

Competitive sport is a type of arms race, and an important part of the expertise of elite players is to try to conceal or distract from cues that the opponent can use to predict the direction of play. Not surprisingly, expert players are considerably better than novices at detecting deceptive moves in an opponent. For example, Jackson et al. (2006) studied how novice and skilled rugby players detected deceptive movement when watching a video of rugby play. The tasks consisted of predicting change of direction of players, both with and without deception. Whilst the novices were misled by the deceptive movement, this was not the case with the skilled participants. (We will take up the question of deception in Chapter 10 on neuroscience.)

A popular task for studying experts' perception is the occlusion task (Abernethy & Russell, 1987; Jones & Miles, 1978). A video showing a player carrying out an action is suddenly cut, and the task is to predict how some feature of the display will evolve. For example, Abernethy et al. (2001) used the occlusion task for studying perception in squash. The video showing a player carrying out a serve is cut just before the racket hits the ball. Participants have to predict where the ball will hit the ground. The general finding is

---

[2]There are exceptions, however. For example, Laby et al. (1996) found that baseball professionals playing for the Los Angeles Dodgers had better visual acuity, contrast sensitivity and distance stereoacuity than the general population. There were also statistically reliable differences on some visual tests between major and minor league players.

[3]Point-light displays show movement by displaying only the major joints of the body. These displays are created by attaching light markers to the body and then processing the video to remove any other information.

that experts perform better in this task than amateurs. In another condition, the racket or parts of the body are not visible any more. Hiding the racket negatively affects all players. However, hiding the movement of the body and of the arm holding the racket affects the experts, but not the beginners. Thus, only experts use this kind of information. The general conclusion is that experts use more perceptual cues than novices.

Visual search is another aspect of behaviour that has been studied in detail. To do so, researchers record participants' eye movement when they perform domain-specific tasks. This method has been used both with films depicting simulations of sport situations and more recently in real situations. A number of sports have been studied, including basketball (Vickers, 1996), shooting (Causer et al., 2010) and tennis (Singer et al., 1998).

For example, Helsen and Starkes (1999) found skill differences with detection tasks related to football. In general, experts make fewer fixations before making a decision, and fixate the important aspects of the display quicker. As with chess experts, football experts focus on more important and informative areas than novices, and are more selective in where they look. However, a limit of this kind of research for understanding basic perceptual processes, not only in sports but in expertise generally, is that visual search is influenced by a number of factors, including: the kind of sport studied, the exact nature of the task (e.g. finding the ball vs. evaluating the situation), conscious strategies, the nature of the stimuli (e.g. offensive vs. defensive situations) and emotional factors such as stress (Helsen & Pauwels, 1993; Lavallee et al., 2012).

While important, perception is not sufficient for reaching high levels of skill in sports. Obviously, sports include a motor component. In addition to a high level of fitness and specialised muscular and cardiovascular characteristics, most sports also require efficient motor programming. Schmidt's (1975) influential theory proposes that motor programs are organised using schemata. These schemata include four kinds of information: initial conditions (information about the environment, the position of the body and the circumstances surrounding the action); response specifications (e.g. parameters about speed, force and direction); sensory consequences (i.e. how the action was felt); and response outcomes (whether the action was successful or not). Schmidt also assumed that there exist two kinds of schemata: recall schemata, which contain information to execute a movement, and recognition schemata, which make it possible to compare the generated movements with what was expected.

2.6 Perception in Music

Compared to the domains we have discussed so far, where vision played an essential role, music engages an auditory modality. This poses different challenges for experts and researchers.

2.6.1 Basic Skill Differences in Perception

Musicians differ from non-musicians on a number of perceptual abilities. For example, musicians display a finer discrimination of pitch[4] and loudness (Houtsma et al., 1987) and pianists display lower tactile discriminations thresholds at the tip of their left and right index finger; these thresholds correlate with daily training (Ragert et al., 2004). Importantly, these abilities tend to be domain-specific: musicians' superior discrimination of timbres and tones did not generalise to speech sounds, except with stimuli of very short duration (Münzer et al., 2002). Similarly, Rauscher and Hinton (2003) found that percussionists with more than 30 years of experience and more than 16 years of formal instruction performed better than non-musicians on an auditory duration task, while string players with similar experience performed better than non-musicians on an auditory frequency task. Neither group performed better than non-musicians on visual duration and visual frequency tasks. Dewar et al. (1977) tested recognition memory for single notes (no context) and sequences of notes (full context) with either musical sequences or random sequences of notes. They found that musically trained participants consistently outperformed participants with little musical background. The effect was larger when no context was provided and with random sequences. Interestingly, the effect of music experience nearly disappeared in the condition where musical sequences were provided with full context.

In addition to pitch and loudness, sounds are characterised by timbre – the unique characteristics of the sound produced by an instrument. Beal (1985) studied the extent to which musicians and non-musicians were able to judge whether two musical chords were the same or different. The chords were played either with the same or a different instrument. Musicians performed better than non-musicians only when the chords were played by different instruments. However, when the chords violated the rules of tonal harmony and were played on different instruments, there were no differences between the two groups, which were uniformly poor at recognising chords. In similar research, Pitt and Crowder (1992) found that, with non-musicians, the judgement of pitch was affected by timbre, even when the same instrument was used (notes were either bowed or plucked on a cello). These authors also used a digital synthesiser to produce two timbres that differed only in harmonic structure (fundamental + harmonics 1–3 vs. fundamental + harmonics 4–6). Only musicians were able to dissociate pitch from timbre.

---

[4]Note that this skill difference is discriminating pitch is not always found. Deutsch (1999) discusses an experiment where participants had to decide whether two notes played with a 6-second silent interval were the same or different. In fifty per cent of the cases, the two notes were the same, and in the other 50 per cent, they differed by one semitone. Most of the participants were correct 100 per cent of the time. More about this experiment in the chapter on memory.

Deutsch's scale illusion

In Deutsch's (1975, 1987) scale illusion, two sequences of tones are played through headphones, one sequence on each ear (see Figure 2.2). Each sequence is characterised by sharp ups and downs, and thus by an angular contour. In spite of this, listeners tend to hear two smooth melodic lines: tones are grouped as a function of their pitch rather than the ear to which they were played. This phenomenon has been long known to composers, a classic example being the beginning of the final movement of Tchaikovsky's Sixth Symphony (*The Pathétique*), where the first and second violin alternate the notes of the theme and the accompaniment. Nonetheless, the music is not perceived the way it was written, but as one violin playing the theme and the other the accompaniment. The effect is not sensitive to large differences in the position of the first two violins in the orchestra. Interestingly, expertise can modulate this effect in some circumstances. When listening to tones with large differences in timbre (e.g. synthesised piano and synthesised saxophone) and organised to create the scale illusion, musicians were grouping the notes by pitch, while non-musicians were grouping them by timbre (Smith et al., 1982).

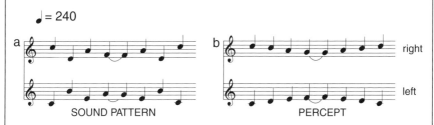

Figure 2.2 Deutsch's scale illusion. The pattern of sounds as they are played to the right and left ears (a) and as they are perceived (b).

Source: From Deutsch, D. I. (1987). Illusions for stereo headphones. *Audio Magazine*, March, 36–48. Adapted with kind permission from Diana Deutsch.

2.6.2 Absolute Pitch

Absolute pitch (AP), which is also known as perfect pitch, is the ability to correctly name or produce a pitch even when a reference note is not provided. AP is very rare; it has been estimated that less than one in 10,000 people in North America and Europe have it (Takeuchi & Hulse, 1993).

AP is categorical in nature; it enables one to correctly assign a range of pitches to a verbal label (name of the note). Importantly, AP does not make it possible to discriminate pitches categorised as the same note better (e.g. 261.6 Hz, 262.9 Hz and 260.3 Hz, all corresponding to a C). This was established in an experiment by Siegel (1974), who played two notes separated by 5 seconds, and asked music students with or without AP to estimate whether the second note was higher or lower than the first note. The two notes could differ either by one tenth of a semitone (1.3 Hz) or three-quarters of a semitone (9.7 Hz). The performance of the two groups did not differ with the one-tenth interval, but the participants with AP did better with the three-quarter interval. They could use different verbal labels in the latter case, but not in the former.

Possessing AP offers advantages, such as the ability to tune an instrument without external help, to identify a particular instrument out of tune in an orchestra, or to recognise when a choir goes slightly out of tune. It is also very useful with music that does not respect standard harmonic and melodic rules, for example contemporary atonal music (Sloboda, 1985). However, AP has disadvantages as well. Individuals with AP tend to be disturbed when a piece is played in a transposed key, and perform worse than non-AP possessors in some tone categorisation experiments (see Ward, 1999). (Admittedly, the practical relevance of these experiments is disputable.)

In fact, more so than AP, *relative pitch* is important for musical expertise (Sloboda, 1985). This concerns the ability to recognise intervals between notes that are sung or played on an instrument, or to produce the requested interval below or above a given note. It can be argued that music is more about intervals of notes rather than their absolute value, and thus having relative pitch is more profitable than having absolute pitch. In fact most of formal and informal musical training in Western countries reinforces relative rather than absolute pitch.

While a large proportion of leading composers and performers have or have had AP, such as Mozart, Beethoven and Stevie Wonder, many musicians do not have it. Most people can name colours and smells effortlessly and without specific training, so why is it that so few have AP? One possible explanation is that the Western environment in which most children grow up is not conducive to acquiring AP: most songs are sung in different keys (e.g. a female voice vs. a male voice). In addition, mastering AP possibly requires a particular vocabulary (the names of the notes) that requires some musical training.

Deutsch (2013a) presents three possible explanations to account for the rarity of AP, with no clear winner emerging. The first explanation is that AP is simply due to practice, and anybody can acquire it given sufficient commitment. This explanation has received only weak support. While it is true that many people with AP come from an environment where there was ample opportunity for practice, the fact remains that it is very difficult to acquire AP through practice in adulthood. In one of the rare studies describing such a feat, Brady (1970) reports how he used tapes to develop and refine his AP for about 60 hours. As a result, he was finally able to correctly identify pitches 65 per cent of the time, a score that rises to 97 per cent when semitone errors are allowed. Note that Brady had a considerable starting advantage compared to the average population without AP: he had begun piano training at 7 years of age and later became a musician.

A second theory is that AP is genetic, or at least innate. The evidence, whilst suggestive, is also ambiguous. The early onset of AP and the fact that AP often runs in families can also be explained by the rich musical environment present in these families. The third explanation is that there is a critical period for the acquisition of AP (e.g. Schlaug et al., 1995; Takeuchi & Hulse, 1993). According to this hypothesis, any child can develop AP if they learn music before the age of six. Early exposure to activities involving pitch recognition is not only necessary but also sufficient to fully develop the brain structures linked to perfect pitch. This explanation is supported by the negative correlation that has been documented between the starting age of musical training and possession of AP. At the same time, not all musicians who started training early have AP.

2.6.3 Laypeople's Implicit Musical Expertise

While most people do not possess AP and thus are not able to name notes, they do possess an implicit form of AP. For example, most people can notice when a familiar piece of music is played in a novel key. Deutsch (2013a) provides several kinds of data supporting the hypothesis of implicit AP, but one example will suffice here. Levitin (1994) asked participants without musical training to select two popular songs which they liked from a stack of CDs and to sing them. To make sure that the songs had always been heard in the same key, Levitin only chose songs performed by a single band. A comparison of the first notes of the original songs and of the versions produced by the participants showed that 44 per cent of them started both songs within two semitones of the original pitch.

The implicit AP hypothesis in general and Levitin's results in particular suggest that non-musicians have considerable musical expertise, even though this expertise is not declarative. While musicians do better than non-musicians in a number of tasks related to music, as reviewed above, surprisingly no differences were observed in several other tasks, in particular those related to musical structure (Bigand, 2003; Bigand & Poulin-Charronnat, 2006; Sloboda, 1985). Due to the immersion in their own musical culture, most people have implicitly acquired a considerable amount of knowledge about melody and harmony: they can be considered as experts in perceiving music.

Thus, important aspects of musical expertise are learned implicitly, and not in formal settings, and are possessed by most people. In addition, experiments have shown that individuals learn patterns that are specific to their own musical culture. For example, Americans are excellent at perceiving fine-graded pitch regularities in Western music, but not in Indian music (Castellano et al., 1984). Overall, the data discussed in this chapter provide evidence not only that a considerable amount of the knowledge used by experts is acquired implicitly but also that additional musical training can lead to improved perception.

2.6.4 Sight-Reading

When reading music, the musician translates visual input into motor actions for performance. The stimuli are analysed for musical meaning before motor commands are issued. Thus, in spite of a visual input, music reading directly taps *music* perception (Sloboda, 1984). Importantly, sight-reading competence and concert performance are two different things. Some famous pianists are poor sight-readers but excel in playing pieces that they have extensively practised and memorised, while some excellent sight-readers did not reach top levels in performing.

There is a considerable literature on sight-reading, perhaps because it makes it possible to monitor attention by recording eye movements. In general, better readers are more sensitive to structural configurations present in the stimuli and display a better visual memory for the kinds of symbols used in musical notation.

2.6.4.1 Eye movements

In an early study on pianists, Weaver (1943) found that the type of music played affected eye fixations. With contrapuntal music (where the structural units consist of melodic fragments), sequences of fixations tend to be more horizontal than vertical. The opposite pattern is found with homophonic music (where the structural units consist of chords). Whether this pattern of results is due to musical or visual factors (e.g. Gestalt law of continuity) cannot be ascertained from Weaver's results (Sloboda, 1984).

Underwood and Waters (1998) manipulated the tonal structure and the visual contour of melodic fragments, with each variable having two values (simple vs. complex). The task was to indicate whether two fragments presented in sequence were the same or not. Experts were more accurate and faster than novices, and this was particularly the case with tonally simple material. With respect to eye movements, experts used more fixations than novices in their first reading of the fragment. Surprisingly, the tonal and visual contour structure did not have any effect on experts' eye movements.

2.6.4.2 Short presentations

A number of experiments have compared novices with experienced musicians. The possible confound that novices know nothing about musical notation was addressed by using extremely simple stimuli from a musical point of view. The task was to reproduce, on an empty stave, simplified musical excerpts that were briefly presented visually (see Figure 2.3). Thus, for non-musicians, the task was simply a visual recall task. Sloboda (1976b) used presentation times of 20 ms and 2 seconds, and stimuli consisted of between one and six random notes. Musicians' performance was better in this task, but there was also an

Figure 2.3   Example of the type of stimuli used by Sloboda (1984) in visual recall tasks.

interaction. Whilst musicians were clearly superior with 2 seconds, they showed no superiority with 20 ms, where performance was very low for both groups. Interestingly, when the task was to reproduce the pattern of ups and downs between notes, rather than the exact location of the pitch symbols, Sloboda (1978) found that musicians' performance was better even with a presentation time of 20 ms. It is likely that musicians were able to take advantage of their familiarity with the visual features of the musical display. Another interesting result is that, in these experiments, musicians show a better performance even when the sequence of notes is random and thus does not have musical structure. In related research where participants also had to recall visually-presented sequences of notes, Halpern and Bower (1982) found that while non-musicians performed similarly with structured and random melodies, musicians recalled more information with the structured sequences.

These results suggest that musicians are better at coding musical stimuli, assuming that they have enough time to engage their coding mechanisms. This coding is a very robust and automated skill. To Sloboda's (1976b) surprise, none of a series of interfering tasks that participants carried out while listening to musical stimuli, including remembering a melody, had any effect on performance. Similarly, Allport et al. (1972) asked pianists to sight-read a piece of music whilst at the same time repeating out loud a passage of prose that was read to them over headphones. The performance was the same when the tasks were done together as when they were carried out individually.

In Sloboda's (1976b) experiment with an interfering task, participants first listened to a short tone sequence, then briefly saw the visual display which they tried to copy; finally, they compared the original auditory tone sequence with a new one that could differ by one note, and had to say whether the two sequences were the same or different. Halpern and Bower (1982) modified the experimental design by first presenting the visual display, then presenting the interfering task related to music (either visual or auditory), and then asking the participants to recall the visual display. With this order, Halpern and Bower found that interference impaired performance with musicians, but not with non-musicians. Sloboda (1984) explains the different results obtained in the two experiments by proposing that musicians can use their over-learnt sight-reading skills to *code* musical material, but *not to retain* it in short-term memory (STM), as it is not a task that they normally practise.

2.6.4.3 Eye-hand span

A limit of the research we have just reviewed is that it uses very simplified visual stimuli, and thus might lack ecological validity. To address this issue, a number of researchers have compared musicians of varying sight-reading ability when playing actual pieces. Bean (1938) analysed sight-reading in pianists requested to play musical extracts that were briefly presented. Pianists with more experience had a larger *span of apprehension* – they played more notes correctly. To estimate how many notes they keep in memory ahead of being played (the *eye-hand span*), Sloboda (1974, 1977) asked musicians to sight-read an unknown piece; at some unexpected point, the score sheet was removed from their view. Across a variety of musical instruments, he found that the average eye-hand span was around five to six notes, which is the same as the average *eye-voice span*, a measure of the distance between the eye and the voice when reading aloud. The eye-hand span varies as a function of expertise, with poor readers having an eye-hand span of only three to four notes.

Further results from Sloboda's research are worth mentioning. The eye-hand span correlated with sight-reading ability: musicians with a higher eye-hand span made fewer mistakes. The span was also affected by the kind of music being played; it was larger with music that followed the rules of tonal progression than with music that violated them. In line with this result, the eye-hand span tended to match phrase boundaries, although the effect was stronger with good readers (match in 72 per cent of the cases) than with poor readers (match in 20 per cent of the cases). This implies that the good readers' eye-hand span is not fixed, but increases and decreases in order to coincide with the structure of the music. Obviously, this result provides strong support to the hypothesis that musical knowledge plays an essential role in sight-reading. Sloboda (1984, p. 231) summarises this research by concluding that "good sight readers are particularly attuned to important superordinate structures within a score, structures that link notes together into musical groups. They organise their perception and performance in terms of discovering these higher order groupings, with consequential economy of coding".

2.6.4.4 The "proofreader's error"

When reading texts, skilled readers often fail to notice minor typographic mistakes, such as the omission of a letter in a word. This phenomenon is called the *proofreader's error* because it is hard for proofreaders to consciously spot spelling errors with familiar words, as these errors are automatically and unconsciously corrected. Does this kind of error occur with musicians as well? To answer this question, Sloboda (1976a) modified scores of classical music for piano by introducing misprints that displaced a note by one scale step. The resulting sequences were clearly discordant. The participants, who were competent pianists, had to sight-read each piece twice and were asked to make sure that they played the music exactly as written on the score. Very few errors were made overall (2.9 per cent and 1.7 per cent for the first and second performance, respectively). Crucially, all participants had a high level of error when playing the misprints (38 per cent and 41 per cent for the first and second performance, respectively). As expected, all the errors corrected the misprint, with pianists playing the original and correct note. A surprising result was that the number of proofreading errors increased on the second performance, although the total number of errors decreased. As noted by Sloboda, it appears that on first playing participants had picked up information on the overall structure of the piece rather than on isolated notes, which allowed them to make more inferences.

Sloboda's (1985) description of the two key differences between experts' and novices' perception of music provides a fitting conclusion to this section. The first difference concerns the structural features used to represent music, both with respect to number, complexity and hierarchical structure. The second difference is about the extent to which the listener is aware of the kind of structures used: while laypeople have good implicit knowledge of music, as we have seen, only musicians are able to refer to this knowledge explicitly.

2.7 Perceptual Learning, Perceptual Expertise and Categorisation

Most of the research reviewed so far in this chapter roughly fits into the framework of the *"classic" study of expertise*, started by de Groot (1965). However, the study of expert perception has given rise to at least three other substantial fields. The field of *perceptual learning*, influenced by Gibson and Gibson (1955), studies how perception changes as a function of experience and how these changes help the organism to adapt to the environment, through learning and acquisition of knowledge (among other things). Differentiating perceptual knowledge is seen as a key learning mechanism. More recently, *perceptual expertise*, carried out mostly in neuroscience (e.g. Gauthier et al., 2009), has addressed similar issues (we will discuss this line of research in more detail in the chapter on neuroscience). Questions related to perceptual expertise have also been addressed in a third field, *categorisation*, also known as *concept learning* or *concept formation* (e.g. Murphy, 2002). Unfortunately, these four fields of research have shown little communication and cross-fertilisation, although the overlap in interest is obvious. This lack of interaction might be due to the fact that the classic study of expertise has been primarily interested in top levels of expertise, while the other three approaches have focused on learning at lower levels of expertise (e.g. behavioural changes after a training of 10 hours of practice rather than 10 years) or have addressed domains where nearly everybody is an "expert", such as object recognition or face recognition. Thus, their interests in expertise are much more diffuse than in the case with the classic approach, as they essentially address the entire fields of learning and perception.

While such broad issues are clearly beyond the scope of this book, it might be worth mentioning some of the phenomena that have been identified in these fields. Research into perceptual learning and perceptual expertise (Gauthier et al., 2009; Goldstone, 1998) has uncovered phenomena such as: as a result of training, a visual search that was originally serial is carried out in parallel; stimuli that were originally confusable become discriminable with practice; unlike novices, experts are sensitive to irrelevant changes in an unattended part of an object; inverted faces are recognised more poorly than upright faces; people tend to show stronger behavioural effects with faces from their own racial group; and experts in recognising artificial objects are sensitive to configural changes, just like with face processing.

Similarly, several phenomena related to perceptual expertise have been identified with the field of categorisation: experts categorise objects quicker than novices (Johnson & Mervis, 1997); the basic level of a category changes as a function of expertise; experts' reaction times are equally fast at subordinate and basic levels, unlike novices'; and the salience of the constituent features of a concept changes with learning (Gauthier & Tarr, 1997; Goldstone, 1994; Schyns, 1998; Tanaka & Taylor, 1991).

2.8 Chapter Summary

De Groot's (1965) seminal research tried to understand how chess masters select moves. It showed that perception, memory and decision making are tightly intertwined. Chess masters' perceptual advantage and their superiority in recalling domain-specific material have been replicated in many other domains of expertise, including sports, music and medical expertise. In these domains, eye-movement studies have confirmed that perception plays a central role in expertise. In several domains (e.g. driving and aviation), experts memorise not the actual scenes, but the way they will be in the near future. This is explained by the presence of anticipatory schemata, which help when preparing for action. In music, absolute pitch describes the very rare ability to correctly name a pitch without a reference note. Three explanations have been proposed for its existence – practice, innate origin and critical period – without any clear winner.

2.9 Further Reading

De Groot and Gobet (1996) present quantitative and qualitative data on chess players' eye movements, and discuss the links between perception, cognition and intuition. Research on sport perception and memory is discussed in Starkes and Ericsson (2003), and the corresponding research on music can be found in Sloboda (1985). Perception in music is discussed in great detail in several chapters of Deutsch (2013b).

CHAPTER 3

Memory

3.1 Preview of Chapter

What are the memory limits that experts can transcend and those that they must abide by? What is the role of knowledge in categorisation and expertise in general? What are the strategies that experts use? These are the questions that this chapter aims to answer.

We have seen earlier that de Groot (1965) used a memory task to study perception. This emphasises the fact that the boundary between perception and cognition is fuzzy, and perhaps primarily useful for cataloguing research results and writing textbooks on cognitive psychology! In any case, de Groot's task has been extensively used in psychology for studying both perception and memory, and some of the theories that have been developed for explaining the results actually provide mechanisms explaining how perception and memory interact (see Section 3.11.4). While de Groot's explanation for his results is insightful, it is essentially descriptive and was not couched in the language of information-processing that dominated psychology starting from the late 1960s.

More than de Groot's study, it is Chase and Simon's work that has motivated most of the research on expert perception and memory. In three classic papers (Chase & Simon, 1973a, b; Simon & Chase, 1973) that built on de Groot's research, Chase and Simon provided both convincing empirical analyses and a new theory. Therefore, we first present their research before discussing the main findings of research on expert memory.

3.2 Chase and Simon's Research

Chase and Simon (1973a, b) built upon de Groot's (1965) perception task but also extended it in important ways. These extensions allowed them to infer the perceptual and memory structures – they are hypothesised to be the same – used by chess players, and how they are affected by the degree of expertise. Chase and Simon used two experimental paradigms: a recall task and a copy task.

3.2.1 The Key Empirical Results

The *recall task* is essentially the same as the perception task developed by de Groot (1965), the main difference being that Chase and Simon did not use concurrent or retrospective protocols. Participants were shown a chess constellation for 5 seconds, before it was removed from view, and subsequently tried to reconstruct it as much as they could. Just like de Groot (1965), Chase and Simon found that stronger players memorised the chess constellation better. The *copy task*, which was the key addition, gave crucial insights about the mechanisms underpinning experts' perceptual and memory superiority. In this task, the stimulus board remained in view while participants reconstructed it onto an empty board. The participants' behaviour is videotaped for further analysis. To infer the memory structures held by players, Chase and Simon used the fact that the stimulus and the reconstruction boards could not be fixated simultaneously. Thus, the glances between the boards could be used to detect the *chunks* that players presumably hold in memory. A chunk can be defined as "a collection of elements having strong associations with one another, but weak associations with elements within other chunks" (Gobet et al., 2001, p. 236). In chess, chunks are collections of pieces.

The differences in the distribution of between-glance placements and within-glance placements supported Chase and Simon's hypothesis. While only a fraction of the between-glance placements was less than 2 seconds, 80 per cent of the within-glance placement latencies were below this threshold. Chase and Simon also compared the distributions of latencies between the placement of two pieces in the recall and copy tasks. They found that they were largely similar. Using this similarity between the distributions, and assuming that glances on the board offered a means to define chunks in the copy task, they proposed an operational definition for the concept of a chunk: if two pieces are placed with less than 2 seconds' interval, they belong to the same chunk; if pieces are placed with an interval of more than 2 seconds, they belong to two different chunks.

Chase and Simon also investigated the semantics that underlie chunks. They tallied the number of chess relations (colour, defence, attack, proximity and kind) shared by two pieces placed successively. A strong support for the concept of chunk came from the fact that the number of relations correlated with the latency between the placement of two pieces, both in the recall and copy tasks. That is, if two successive pieces belong to a chunk, they share more chess relations on average than if they belong to two different chunks, and the inter-piece latency tends to be short. This result has been replicated by Gobet and Simon (1998a; see Figure 3.1).

However, two results were not predicted by Chase and Simon. First, while better players had larger chunks, the chunks used by their strongest player (a master) were not particularly large (a maximum of five to six pieces). Second, better players replaced more chunks. Although the number of chunks was still within the limits of STM, this result contradicted the assumption that all players had the same STM capacity.

3.2.2 Chunking Theory

Chase and Simon's (1973a, b) *chunking theory* provided a neat explanation for de Groot's (1965) two central results: chess experts' ability to see good moves

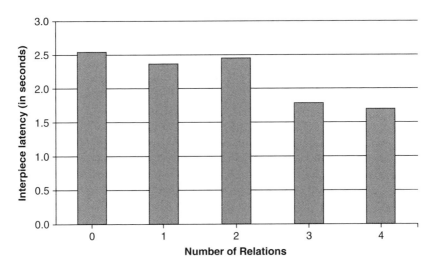

Figure 3.1 Relation between inter-piece latencies and the number of relations shared by two pieces successively placed (data from the recall task pooled over type of position and skill levels).

Source: Data from Gobet and Simon (1998a).

rapidly and their excellent memory for positions taken from chess games. The theory makes three key assumptions: (a) chunks are a single storage unit of both meaning and perception, and are retrievable from LTM in a single act of recognition; (b) STM is limited to about seven items (Miller, 1956), both for experts and non-experts; and (c) players of all skill levels learn new information at a relatively slow rate: Simon (1969) estimated that it takes about 8 seconds to create a new chunk in LTM and 2 seconds to add information to an existing chunk. Where experts differ is that they have acquired, through extended practice and study, not only more chunks, but also larger chunks.

Chunks are accessed through a discrimination network, which tests for critical features of perceptual stimuli (see Figure 3.2, for an example with learning how to spell in English). The advantage of this kind of organisation is that it allows perceptual stimuli to be rapidly recognised and categorised. Hence, experts can extract the salient elements of a scene quickly. Chunks are also linked to other useful information, such as what kind of action to carry out given the presence of a specific pattern in the environment.

Using computer simulations and mathematical extrapolations, Simon and Gilmartin (1973) estimated that a chess master must have learnt between 10,000 and 100,000 chunks, and proposed 50,000 chunks as a first approximation. The sheer size of this number, which is equivalent to the average number of words in the vocabulary of an American university student, would then explain why it takes 10 years or 10,000 hours to become an expert in chess, or in any other domain (Simon & Chase, 1973).

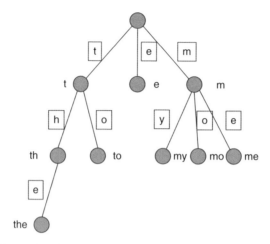

Figure 3.2 Example of a discrimination network built when learning how to spell in English. The open squares indicate which letter is being tested, and the closed circles indicate nodes.

Chase and Simon (1973a) also speculated over the properties of the mind's eye, properties that are important for problem solving. Their model emphasised the role of pattern recognition through chunks in expert perception, and provided mechanisms as to how players anticipate and visualise board positions during look-ahead search. As shown by de Groot, chess experts are able to literally "see" good moves automatically. In addition to being linked to potential moves, LTM chunks are associated to information that makes it possible to reconstruct configurations of pieces in the mind's eye. As just described, patterns on the external board activate some LTM chunks. These chunks suggest suitable moves, which are stored in STM, so that they can be analysed further. This is typically done by carrying out the candidate moves in the mind's eye using mental imagery, so that the position is updated. This process then continues recursively: new moves can be recognised by pattern recognition in the position imagined in the mind's eye, which activates new potential moves or plans. This sequence of recognition-action cycles makes selective search possible. In effect, we have here an example of a production system[1] (Newell & Simon, 1972): a chunk acts as a *condition,* which can be satisfied by recognising a specific pattern on the board, and the *action* consists of evoking the move(s) or plan(s) associated with this chunk. For example, in chess the presence of a weak square on the opponent's side of the board could activate a production such as "IF a square is weak, THEN try to place a knight on it".

In summary, chunking explains de Groot's two key results. With respect to the memory task, chunks make it possible for experts to encode stimuli with a smaller number of units than non-experts, as their units encode more

---

[1]Productions are rules of the type [IF condition THEN action]. For example: IF the light is red, THEN stop.

information. Stronger chess players perceive a position as a collection of familiar configurations rather than a collection of individual pieces, as novices do, and can thus memorise an entire position in spite of the limited capacity of their STM. As for the speed with which good players identify potentially good moves, this is explained by the fact that chunks allow experts (a) to rapidly recognise patterns on a position and (b) to automatically access information linked to these patterns, such as potential moves.

Until this day, Chase and Simon's theory has been very influential in the study of expertise, and numerous experiments have been carried out to test its predictions. After briefly commenting on the generality of experts' advantage in recall tasks, we review the main results using the four main questions that Chase and Simon's theory raised: (a) Is knowledge structured as chunks? (b) What is the number of chunks in LTM? (c) Does randomisation eliminate experts' superiority? and (d) Is the capacity of STM limited and are LTM encoding times slow? We then consider research on expert memory that has addressed topics less connected to chunking theory, such as the role of schemas and the intermediate effect in medicine.

3.3 Generalisability of Experts' Superiority in Recall Tasks

The linear relationship between expertise level and memory for meaningful material taken from the domain of expertise has been found in a number of domains. These include electronics (Egan & Schwartz, 1979); programming (Mc Keithen et al., 1981; Schneiderman, 1976), games such as Go and gomuku (Eisenstadt & Kareev, 1977; Reitman, 1976), Othello (Wolff et al., 1984), draughts (Gobet & De Voogt, submitted) and card games (bridge: Charness, 1979; Engle & Bukstel, 1978; skat: Knopf et al., 1995), along with sports and music (see sections below).

It turns out that the superior performance of experts in memorising domain-specific material remains despite considerable variations in the exact experimental methodology used. For example, in chess, experts' superiority remains with presentation times as short as 1 second and as long as 60 seconds (Gobet & Simon, 2000a). We will consider a few more variations below. Surprisingly, as we shall also see in a later section, experts maintain some advantage even with *random*, but domain-specific material. Their superiority however disappears when experts are tested with material not belonging to their domain. For example, Waters et al. (2002) found that chess players were no better than the general population at memorising geometrical shapes.

3.4 Is Knowledge Structured as Chunks?

Three sources of evidence have supported Chase and Simon's claim that chunks are the memory structures mediating experts' superior performance.

First, their study has been replicated with a larger number of participants and a better methodology. Second, other methods have been used to operationalise the concept of a chunk. Third, some experiments have directly manipulated the presence or absence of chunks in positions. We review these three sources of evidence in turn below.

In spite of its impact on the field, the original Chase and Simon study had several weaknesses: the number of participants was low (only three players: a master, an amateur and a beginner), and the estimated size of chunks might have been affected by the use of physical chess pieces and boards and, in particular, the limited capacity of the hand to hold pieces. Other criticisms were levelled at the way chunks were defined and operationalised (Freyhoff et al., 1992; Gold & Opwis, 1992; Holding, 1985; Reitman, 1976): it is unclear whether chunks can only be defined using latencies; the method did not allow for identification of chunks that overlapped or that were organised hierarchically; the assumption that chunks are completely recalled in one operation is questionable; and it is difficult to determine to what chunk erroneously replaced pieces belong. These weaknesses and criticisms led to further work on the identification of chunks.

In a replication of the original study, Gobet and Simon (1998a) used a computer program to show the positions and allow players to reconstruct them. They replicated the key original findings: the shape of latency distribution, the correlation between number of chess relations and latencies, and the large difference between the distributions of within-glance latencies and between-glance latencies in the copy task. With respect to the last point, and consistent across the three skill levels used, 79.5 per cent of the within-glance placement latencies (against only 1.11 per cent of the between-glance placement latencies) were shorter than 2 seconds.

However, an important difference between the old and new study should be noted. Gobet and Simon found that the largest chunks used by the masters (19 pieces, on average) were much bigger than what had been estimated by Chase and Simon (five or six pieces). This is obviously a considerable difference. According to Gobet and Simon, this discrepancy can be explained by the different modes of presentation (standard chess pieces and board for Chase and Simon, and computer display for Gobet and Simon). The small size of the chunks found in the original experiment seems to be an artefact of the limited number of pieces that the hand can hold. This hypothesis was directly tested by Gobet and Clarkson (2004): using a within-subject design, participants carried out both the copy and the recall task, both with physical pieces and boards and with the computer display. The same results were found as in the previous study: small chunks with physical display, and large chunks with computer display. It must also be noted that other sources of evidence support the presence of large chunks. In particular, analysis of verbal protocols recorded in memory tasks (either retrospectively or in parallel) indicates that players use high-level concepts, which sometimes refer to the whole position (Cooke et al., 1993; de Groot, 1965; de Groot & Gobet, 1996; Gruber & Ziegler, 1990). Thus, these two replications support the psychological reality of chunks, but also indicate that their size was underestimated by Chase and Simon.

Other paradigms have provided converging evidence for the existence of chunks in chess, as defined either by latency in placement or by number of relations between pieces (see Gobet & Simon, 1998a, for additional details). These techniques include sorting tasks (Gruber & Ziegler, 1990), guessing tasks (de Groot & Gobet, 1996; Gruber, 1991) and hierarchical cluster analysis of piece placements (Gold & Opwis, 1992). While these studies in general support the notion of a chunk, several of them also point to the involvement of higher-level knowledge in chess. In particular, when explicit reports are used, skilled players tend to mention high-level, abstract knowledge more often than the kind of chunks proposed by Chase and Simon.

Several variants of the *partitioning technique* have also been used to study this question. With positions from the game of Go, Reitman (1976) asked participants to separate positions into clusters by circling groups of pieces that they feel belong together. The results suggest that the master she studied tended to see the position as overlapping clusters, and not as a hierarchy of chunks as proposed by Chase and Simon.

In a chess study with children and adults, Chi (1978) carried out both a recall and a partitioning task. This allowed her to study whether the latencies in the recall task between the placements of two pieces were affected by whether or not the pieces belonged to the same cluster in the partitioning task. The results indicated that, on average, participants took longer to place pieces that cross cluster boundaries (about 3 seconds) than pieces belonging to the same cluster (about 1.5 seconds). Chi also found, just like Reitman, that some clusters overlapped. Freyhoff et al. (1992) carried out an experiment where participants were required to partition chess positions into meaningful groupings that did not intersect. Then, they were asked to combine groups into bigger ones and also to divide them into smaller ones. Thus, positions could be represented as a hierarchy of clusters. Freyhoff et al. found that masters used larger groupings at the three levels of partitioning. They also found that more typical positions led to larger clusters.

The chunk hypothesis has also been tested, and supported, by experiments in which chunks were directly manipulated. Charness (1974) dictated chess positions verbally, at the pace of 2.3 seconds per piece. (Chess has a standard notation for positions, which makes this task natural for chess players.) The key manipulation of the experiment concerned the order with which pieces were presented. There were three conditions: (a) pieces were grouped in chunks, as defined by Chase and Simon; (b) pieces were presented column by column; and (c) pieces were dictated in a random order. The results showed that recall performance was the best when the pieces were presented as chunks, followed by the performance with column-by-column presentation. The weakest recall was obtained with the presentation with random order. Charness (1974) found similar results when he presented the pieces visually.

Whereas only one piece at a time was available to the participants in Charness's (1974) experiment, Frey and Adesman (1976) used a cumulative mode of presentation. They showed slides containing a group of four new pieces, while the pieces shown in the previous slides were kept in view. Each slide was shown for 2 seconds. The results indicated that a presentation by chunks yielded better memory than a presentation by columns. Surprisingly, players recalled the position better when it was incrementally presented by chunks than when it was shown entirely for the same amount of time (12 seconds). A possible explanation for this counter-intuitive result is that chunk presentation makes it easier for players to identify chunks in the position – a direct support for the chunking hypothesis.

3.5 How Many Chunks Are Stored in LTM?

We have seen earlier that, according to Simon and Gilmartin (1973), about 50,000 chunks are necessary for reaching the recall of a chess master. This estimate was criticised by Holding (1985, 1992), who suggested that masters' recall performance can be accounted for by at most 2,500 chunks. He argued that it is not necessary for players to encode the exact location of chunks, as proposed by Simon and Gilmartin. Rather, players can encode the semantic relations between pieces (e.g. a bishop attacks a knight from one square away). If such an encoding is used, then the same chunk can be used to encode several instantiations on the board of the same configuration. For example, configurations with white and black pieces or configurations shifted horizontally or vertically on the board could be encoded by a single chunk. Thus, according to Holding, the information about location is not stored in LTM chunks, but is rather picked up during the perception of a position.

Two experiments tested the opposing predictions of Holding and chunking theory. Saariluoma (1994) modified positions by switching two quadrants of a position, while Gobet and Simon (1996a) distorted positions by using mirror images around different axes of symmetry. Both experiments found that these modifications affected recall performance, thus supporting Simon and Gilmartin's hypothesis. Both studies then led to the conclusion that chess players' chunks encode the exact location of pieces. While this seems a waste of resources at first sight, as argued by Holding, encoding location has the advantage that pattern recognition can be swift, as there are no variables to instantiate. Thus, the number of chunks estimated by Simon and Gilmartin seems reasonable. As a matter of fact, more recent computational modelling with CHREST (see Section 3.11.4.2) suggests that this number is an underestimate: computer simulations show that at least 300,000 chunks are needed for the program to reach the recall performance of a grandmaster (Gobet & Simon, 2000a).

In spite of the rather clear results, not everybody was convinced by these two experiments, and the criticism of the assumption of location coding has since regularly cropped up in the literature (e.g. Linhares & Freitas, 2010;

McGregor & Howes, 2002), mainly because it seems to neglect the semantic aspects of chess. In fact, there is a very *semantic* reason why location coding is advantageous, which is discussed at length in Lane and Gobet's (2011) reply to Linhares and Freitas's critique: in chess, the meaning of patterns changes depending on their location. For example, a typical castling formation consists of three pawns on the second row, in front of the king. This set up is *defensive*. When the same set of pieces is shifted five squares upwards (the pawns are now on the seventh row), this set up is now very *offensive*, because pawns are now close to being promoted into a queen. Similarly, tactical and strategic possibilities are different when a pattern is located in the centre of the board or near its edges. The same is actually fairly common in other human activities such as sports.[2] In basketball, the meaning of a configuration of players changes depending on whether they are located in the middle of the field or under the basket.

Whether location coding is important in most domains can only be settled empirically, by collecting new data. A possibility is that it is important in domains where space is relatively small, because wherever one is on the field, one is close to its edges, which act as boundary conditions and play a special role strategically. It is less important in domains enjoying large spaces, such as the Asian game of Go with its large board (19 × 19 squares), because proportionally fewer squares are close to the edges of the board.

3.6 Does Randomisation Eliminate Experts' Superiority?

A classic myth in cognitive psychology is that, while experts enjoy a better recall performance with meaningful material taken from their domain of expertise, they do not with randomised material (see Figure 3.3). This myth, which initiated from Chase and Simon's research on chess, can be found in numerous research articles and textbooks. It is intuitively appealing: experts can use their knowledge only when stimuli have structure. However, two studies by Gobet and Simon (1996a, b) have shown that reality is more complex. A meta-analysis of chess studies in which random positions were used in the recall task found a reliable skill effect even with these positions, although the effect was much smaller than with game positions (see Figure 3.4). In 13 studies in which random positions were used as a control task, only one (the one carried out by Chase and Simon!) did not show this pattern. However, in most studies, the skill effect was not statistically significant because of the small number of participants used. When the samples are larger, the difference in skill becomes reliable (Gobet & Waters, 2003; Gold & Opwis, 1992). It is interesting to note that this apparently counter-intuitive result was suggested by the computer model CHREST,

---

[2]But there are exceptions as well. As we saw in the previous chapter, in music the pattern of relations between notes is much more important than their absolute pitch.

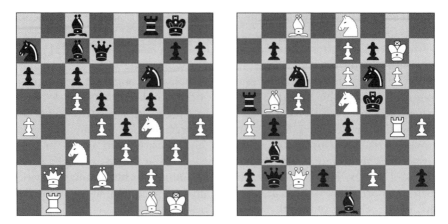

Figure 3.3 A position taken from a master game, on the left, and a random position, on the right.

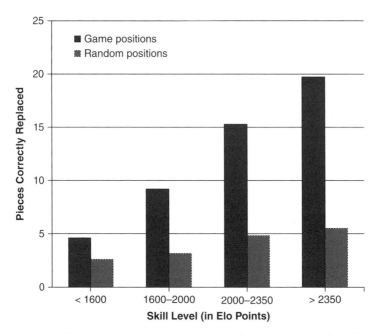

Figure 3.4 Mean number of pieces placed correctly as a function of type of positions (game or random) and skill level. The data are averaged across thirteen experiments.

Source: Data from Gobet and Simon (1996b).

which stubbornly predicted that masters should recall random positions better than novices, in spite of all textbooks!

Chess masters' superiority with random material is a robust result, which generalises to different types of random positions. In most chess research, random positions are created by taking a game position and haphazardly reallocating the pieces on the board. This has the consequence that information is maintained about the distribution of pieces (e.g. at most only one white king). Following a suggestion by Vicente and Wang (1998), Gobet and Waters (2003) created *truly random positions* in which all pieces had the same likelihood of being present. A reliable skill effect was found, although it was smaller than with standard random positions. Skill effects were also found in positions in which the proportion of randomisation was varied.

Experts' superiority with random material, albeit not always statistically significant due to lack of statistical power, has been found in other domains as well, such as the games of Go (Reitman, 1976) and Othello (Wolff et al., 1984). In some domains, the skill effect is considerable, for example with memory for sequences of notes (Sloboda, 1976b), sequences of dance steps (Allard & Starkes, 1991) and board positions in the African game of awele (Retschitzki, 1990).

This skill difference with random material is theoretically important. First, contrary to what Chase and Simon argued, chunking theory predicts a skill effect with random positions, as shown by the CHREST simulations. As chess masters have many more chunks in LTM than weaker players, they are more likely to recognise some of them by chance, even in random positions. Why Chase and Simon missed this simple probabilistic fact is better left for historians of science. Second, this result is difficult to explain with theories not based on chunking mechanisms, as we shall see in the last section of this chapter. The reason is that most theories postulate that expertise is underpinned by relatively high-level memory structures, while the reason why chunking theory explains the skill effect with random positions is that it assumes the presence of small memory structures (Gobet, 1998b).

3.7 Is STM Capacity Limited and Are LTM Encoding Times Slow?

Two strong assumptions of chunking theory are that STM has a strongly limited capacity and is therefore sensitive to interferences, and that the encoding of information in LTM is relatively slow. An obvious way to test these assumptions is to interpolate a task between the presentation of a chess position and its recall. According to chunking theory, the interfering task should erase the STM symbols pointing to LTM chunks. Thus, there should be an important loss of information in this experiment, as compared to the standard task without interference. This is in fact what was found in memory experiments using visual or verbal material with which participants were not familiar (Charness, 1976; Kintsch, 1970). Charness (1976), along with Frey and Adesman (1976), carried out a chess experiment with this paradigm. Contrary to prediction, the interfering task caused only small decrease in recall (only about 10 per cent). Interestingly, this was the case even when interfering tasks with chess material were used, such as finding the best move in a novel position.

An extreme form of interference would be to ask players to memorise not only one briefly-presented position, but a sequence of such positions. The later positions can be seen as interfering tasks for the recall of the first position, and the same applies to the other positions (e.g. with three boards, boards 1 and 2 interfere with the recall of board 3). Cooke et al. (1993) as well as Gobet and Simon (1996a) found that the task was essentially impossible for amateurs, but that masters could do it, even though they encountered serious difficulties with more than five boards.

Other important research on this issue was carried out in the 1980s on mnemonists. Studies were performed on memory for restaurant orders (Ericsson & Polson, 1988) and mental calculation (Staszewski, 1988, 1990). But by far the most influential research was on the digit span task. It is a classic finding in cognitive psychology that most people can only memorise around seven digits, if dictated rapidly (the famous "seven plus or minus two" magic number; Miller, 1956). To alleviate this limitation, which was more of a handicap when no paper, books or computers were available, humans developed *mnemonics* – systems that facilitate learning and improve memory. For example, in Greek antiquity orators invented the *method of loci* (Yates, 1966). In this method, one first learns a list of places (e.g. living room, garden, kitchen and so on). Then, when one has to learn new material (e.g. the ideas to discuss in a speech or more prosaically a list of grocery items to buy), one simply makes an association between each place in the pre-learnt list of places and each item in the new list.

While mnemonics have less practical use nowadays, they still form the basis of methods aimed at improving one's memory (e.g. Higbee, 1988; Hu et al., 2009; Worthen & Hunt, 2011). Experimental research has confirmed that these techniques work and can improve memory considerably, even with a relatively short training duration (Atkinson & Raugh, 1975). In general, mnemonics work by using LTM as a means to compensate for the limited capacity of STM, by creating what is known as *retrieval structures*. Retrieval structures are sets of LTM elements that are organised to optimise encoding of new information. Once these structures are learnt, it is possible to associate novel material to them. New material is then easier to learn, because one does not have to spend time organising incoming information: the retrieval structure provides such organisation. Note that the retrieval structures are consciously learnt, with the specific goal of improving one's memory.

The research by Ericsson et al. (Chase & Ericsson, 1982; Ericsson et al., 1980; Ericsson & Staszewski, 1989) showed that the use of suitable mnemonics by otherwise unremarkable college students could lead to stunning results – performance equivalent to the best mnemonists worldwide. Two students, SF and DD, volunteered for an experiment aimed at improving their performance in the digit span task; both had a normal digit span capacity before the experiment. Their practice was carried out in the laboratory. It was intensive, but also relatively short (about 250 hours in 2 years for SF, and about 800 hours for DD, in slightly more than 3 years). At the end of their training, SF and DD were able to memorise 84 and 106 digits, respectively. Each digit was dictated at the pace of one digit per second. You can try this at home – it is not dangerous but incredibly hard.

According to Ericsson et al., the extraordinary performance of these two students is explained by two factors. First, before starting the experiment, both had an extensive knowledge of running times. In addition to this, they had considerable knowledge of numbers, including dates, arithmetic results and historical dates. With some practice, this knowledge enabled them to group digits into chunks of three or four digits rapidly and automatically. For example, the sequence 3,492 would be encoded by DD as "3 minutes, 49.2 seconds", which is a near world record for running one mile (Ericsson & Staszewski, 1989). Incidentally, the knowledge SF and DD had about numbers means that their real training time is much longer than 250 and 800 hours, respectively.

Second, both students had acquired retrieval structures. These structures were not the kind of general mnemonic we described earlier, but were tailor-made to the demands of the digit span task, which is probably one of the reasons for their efficiency. As noted above, retrieval structures force the incoming stimuli to be organised in a specific way, which facilitates associations with known information. As part of the information has already been stored in LTM (the retrieval structure), the costs of encoding new information are relatively low.

Figure 3.5 depicts the retrieval structure used by DD with 25-, 50-, 75- and 100-digit lists, as inferred by Richman et al. (1995). The bottom level encodes digits; the second level consists of mnemonic codes (e.g. running times); the third level consists of super-groups, which encodes the location of several groups of digits of equal size; finally, the fourth level consists of super-group clusters, which combine several super-groups. This hierarchical structure has been confirmed by the analysis of pauses during recall (Richman et al., 1995).

Two sources of evidence support the hypothesis of LTM encoding. First, there is of course SF's and DD's ability to remember lengthy sequences of digits, which at the time was close to the world record.[3] Second, when free recall tests were done at the end of a session where several lists were learnt, SF and DD could remember the groups that were used for encoding each of the lists memorised during the session.

---

[3]The world record is currently held by Clemens Mayer, with 198 digits.

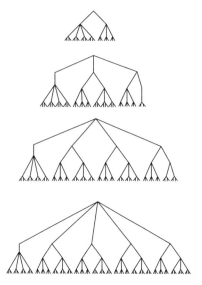

Figure 3.5 The retrieval structure used by DD for 25-, 50-, 75- and 100-digit lists.

Source: From Richman, H. B., Staszewski, J. J., & Simon, H. A. (1995). Simulation of expert memory with EPAM-IV. *Psychological Review, 102*, 305–330. Copyright © 1995 by the American Psychological Association. Adapted with kind permission.

The results reviewed in this section clearly indicate that Chase and Simon's model underestimates experts' memory ability, and suggest that, in recall tasks, information is not only stored in STM. As a consequence, LTM encoding is faster than proposed by Chase and Simon. As we shall see in Section 3.11, a number of theories have tried to improve on Chase and Simon's by attempting to explain these, and other results, on expert perception and memory.

Schemas and organisation of knowledge

Chase and Simon's theory emphasised the importance of acquiring a large number of chunks. By contrast, and partly in response to this theory, other theories emphasised the way information is organised in LTM (Chi et al., 1981; Patel & Groen, 1986; see Section 3.11). The notion of a schema has played a central role in this research and two main approaches have been used to study how experts' knowledge is structured. First, researchers have carried out an analysis of a problem situation and tried to infer the knowledge that experts should employ to solve it. For example, in a task where participants have to diagnose a septic shock, medical textbooks on physiology and pathology will be examined and knowledge about the condition extracted from them. This information is then used to infer the schemas used by experts. Incidentally, a similar approach has been used by researchers developing expert systems (see Chapters 13 and 14).

Second, verbal protocols are recorded when experts solve a problem (e.g. when making a diagnosis). The information obtained by the analysis of the protocols is then used to hypothesise the structure of the schemas used as well as the way they are interconnected. In practice, these two methods are often combined. Good examples of the joint use of these methodologies are offered by research on expertise in physics (Larkin et al., 1980a, b; Simon & Simon, 1978) and medicine (Boshuizen & Schmidt, 1992; Patel & Groen, 1986). An example of the kind of schema obtained with this type of research is shown in Figure 3.6. In some cases, it is possible to make predictions from the properties of the schemas under study. These predictions can then be tested experimentally. An example of this approach was provided in Section 2.4, when we talked about the role of anticipatory schemas in perception.

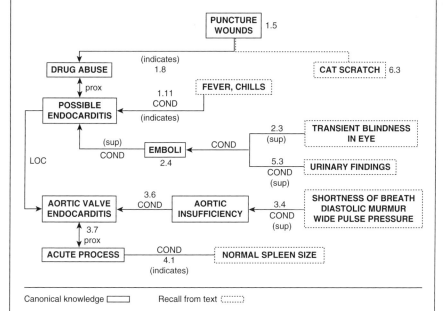

Canonical knowledge ▭   Recall from text ▭

Figure 3.6 Example of an expert's schema in medicine. The figure shows the relational structure of the pathophysiology of a patient suffering from endocarditis (inflammation of the inner lining of the heart). The numbers refer to the propositions in the verbal protocol. The arrows show directionality. PROX: Proximity relation; SUP: Supports; LOC: Locative; and COND: Conditional relation.

Source: From Patel, V. L., & Groen, G. J. (1986). Knowledge based solution strategies in medical reasoning. *Cognitive Science, 10*, 91–116. Reprinted with kind permission from John Wiley and Sons.

3.8 The Intermediate Effect in Medicine

We have seen that, in most domains of expertise, there is a linear relationship between performance in the recall task and level of expertise. There is an exception, however. With expertise in internal medicine (e.g. cardiology, pulmonology), it has been repeatedly shown that individuals with an intermediate level of expertise (e.g. students in their last year of study) outperform both novices and experts (e.g. Boshuizen & Schmidt, 1992; Patel & Groen, 1986; Rikers et al., 2000; Schmidt & Boshuizen, 1993). This is despite the fact that medical experts perform better than less expert individuals in a diagnosis task. A similar finding has been observed in dental medicine (Eberhard et al., 2009) and physiotherapy (Gobet & Borg, 2011; see Figure 3.7). In this type of experiment, participants read a case description for about one minute and are then asked to produce a diagnosis. At the end, they are asked to remember as much as they can about the case study.

The *intermediate effect* is one of the very few cases where there is not a linear, but an inverted performance U-curve as a function of expertise level. This counterintuitive result has important theoretical implications (Schmidt & Rikers, 2007) because it challenges theories, such as Chase and Simon's, that assume that expertise mainly consists in the accumulation of knowledge.

The standard explanation for the intermediate effect was proposed by Schmidt and Boshuizen (1993) and is predicated on the encapsulation of knowledge and the large differences that exist between the knowledge of experts and non-experts. During their curriculum, medical students first acquire biomedical knowledge – that is, knowledge about anatomy, physiology,

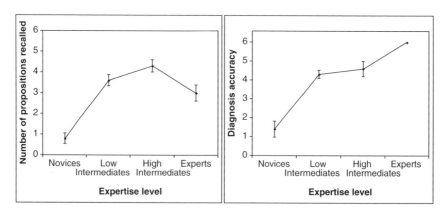

Figure 3.7 Example of the intermediate effect in physiotherapy. Memory performance follows an inverted U-curve (left panel), but diagnosis accuracy is a linear function of expertise (right panel). Error bars indicate standard errors of the mean.

Source: Data from Gobet and Borg (2011).

biochemistry, pathology and pathophysiology. Clinical knowledge, which concerns how pathologies are apparent in patients, is developed later. With the Dutch medical students studied by Schmidt et al., clinical knowledge only starts developing after around 4 years of theoretical training when students are first exposed to real patients, and its acquisition lasts for several years during which students practise in particular fields.

During clinical training and exposure to patients, medical students' biomedical knowledge becomes progressively re-structured and encapsulated under a limited number of concepts that are clinically relevant. This leads to the formation of scripts (narrative structures). Scripts possess only a limited amount of information about pathophysiological causes, but they offer a large amount of clinical information about symptoms, complaints and the factors likely to be associated with the disease. These concepts and scripts have the same explanatory power as more complete biomedical explanations, but have the advantage that they can be retrieved and processed more quickly. This process of encapsulation takes place only when students interact with patients for considerable amounts of time.

An important point in Schmidt and Boshuizen's (1993) account is that experts differ from non-experts not only with respect to the proportion of biomedical and clinical knowledge, but also with respect to the way their knowledge base is qualitatively constructed. Because concepts become subsumed ("encapsulated") under higher-level concepts, experts do not process symptoms independently, but as integrated wholes. Thus, in a recall task, experts do not remember the case as a detailed set of concrete information, but as an encapsulated concept that subsumes this information.

As medical expertise develops, biomedical knowledge is progressively integrated and encapsulated into clinical knowledge (Boshuizen & Schmidt, 1992; Rikers et al., 2002). Experts normally rely on their clinical knowledge for making routine decisions, but can also use biomedical knowledge if necessary. This would be the case if they had to justify their diagnosis, or if they face complex cases that cannot be solved by clinical knowledge alone.

When diagnosing routine cases, clinical knowledge, being mostly encapsulated, allows experts to skip intermediate steps and take shortcuts. By doing so, expert physicians use little biomedical knowledge and do not encode much of the details of the case at hand. By contrast, intermediate individuals, who lack clinical knowledge, must use their biomedical knowledge. They must then pay more attention to the details of the case study and encode more information in LTM. Thus, intermediates should perform better in the recall task than experts, as has been actually observed. Another prediction of the theory is that limiting the time to process the case study (e.g. to 30 seconds) should lead to a disappearance of the intermediate effect, as intermediate individuals now lack time for processing and storing the information. This prediction has been supported by empirical data (van de Wiel et al., 1998).

While the pioneering research of Schmidt et al. has uncovered an important phenomenon, several limitations should also be noted (see Gobet & Borg,

2011, for a more detailed discussion). First, the level of expertise is defined using the number of years that individuals have spent in the field. However, we have seen in the introductory chapter that this is a weak definition. Second, and related to the first point, experts are always older than medical students, and thus age is a confounding variable. This is a serious concern: the critical task measures memory recall, and it is known that memory declines with age, starting from the early twenties (Birren & Schaie, 1996). Third, exposure time is much longer than in other studies of expert memory (e.g. games and sports). While there is a good reason for this (the case studies have to be read), this makes comparisons between studies somewhat difficult.

Finally, Schmidt and Rikers (2007) argue that working with patients early is one of the key factors facilitating the integration of biomedical and clinical knowledge, and thus encapsulation of knowledge. However, Gobet and Borg's (2011) musculoskeletal physiotherapy experiment found an intermediate effect even though the intermediate participants had worked with a variety of patients during their training. This suggests that other crucial factors, beyond early and frequent contacts with patients, contribute to the development of clinical expertise.

3.9 Memory in Sports

Experts' superior memory for domain-specific material has also been documented in sports, which is particularly interesting, since sports are rarely considered as cognitive activities. De Groot's paradigm – brief presentation of domain-specific material followed by a recall task – has been used in several sports, with consistent expert superiority. Examples include snooker (Abernethy et al., 1994), basketball (Allard et al., 1980), football (Williams et al., 1993) and volleyball (Allard & Starkes, 1980). For instance, with basketball, Allard et al. (1980) presented participants with configurations of play during four seconds and then asked them to indicate players' positions on a diagram of the court. Experts obtained better recall performance than non-experts with structured situations, but not with unstructured situations. Overall, these results can be taken as support for Chase and Simon's chunking hypothesis.

Similar results have been found with recognition tasks. Here, a series of slides or films is presented, and the participants' task is to indicate, as quickly and accurately as possible, which slides or films had already been presented and which are new. This experimental paradigm has been used in a number of sports, including basketball (Allard et al., 1980), football (Williams et al., 1993), American football (Garland & Barry, 1991) and field hockey (Starkes, 1987). The results typically indicate an advantage for experts only with structured play configurations.

An important result in sport expertise is that perceptual chunks and other memory structures have been shown to be directly important for the tasks at hand, in particular with respect to decision making (Tenenbaum, 2003). In particular, memory recall depends on the role that individuals have in a sport.

For example, Allard et al. (1993) showed that, in basketball, officials were the best at remembering fouls and rule violations, and players at recalling real and random play situations. Similarly, strong correlations have been found between recall performance and decision quality (e.g., for football, Helsen & Starkes, 1999). The explanation is that perceptual patterns are used both in memory tasks but also, and more importantly, in real play, where they provide information helping players to anticipate the intentions of their opponents, and, when time allows, to plan future actions.

3.10 Memory in Music

We have seen in the previous chapter that Deutsch (1999), in an experiment on memory for individual notes, did not find any difference between musicians and non-musicians in a task where two notes were played 6 seconds apart and participants were asked to judge whether they were the same or different (when different, the two notes differed by one semitone). In that condition, which served as a control condition, the 5-second interval was filled by silence and the participants' performance was close to 100 per cent correct. In a second condition, the 5-second interval was filled by a spoken number, which the participants were instructed either to recall or to ignore. In either case, accuracy was again close to 100 per cent correct. However, when the 5-second interval was filled by random notes belonging to the same octave as the target notes, performance decreased to 68 per cent correct, even though the participants were told to ignore these notes. The effect was particularly large when the interpolated notes were close to the target notes. This result might seem surprising, given that musicians can remember entire pieces, where notes are obviously separated by other notes. However, as noted by Sloboda (1985), what Deutsch's experiments lack, but normal pieces of music offer, is a powerful organisation at several levels, including harmony, melody and time.

While musicians and non-musicians can identify well-known pieces even when they are played in a different key than the original, it is interesting that timbre makes things harder, at least with Western contemporary and tonal music. Poulin-Charronnat et al. (2004) changed the instrumentation and thus the timbre of a piece written by Reynolds (*The Angel of Death*). In a first phase, participants listened to nine excerpts of the piece that were played either by the piano or by the orchestra. In the second phase, they listened to 18 excerpts: the nine excerpts that were played in the first phase and nine new excerpts. The task was to recognise which excerpts were played in the first phase. Musicians were negatively affected by the change of instrumentation, unlike non-musicians whose performance was poor overall. However, musical style also played a role. When the stimuli were excerpts from a symphonic poem by Liszt (*Symphonic Poem no 3, Les préludes*), the change of instrumentation hampered performance with both musicians and non-musicians. The authors explain this result by noting that Liszt's piece was written in a style more familiar to non-musicians than Reynolds's piece.

3.11 Theoretical Accounts

In this chapter, we have offered an overview of the substantial literature on experts' memory. It is now time to review and evaluate the theories that have been proposed to explain (part of) the empirical data.

3.11.1 Chase and Simon's Chunking Theory

Chunking theory, which we have used as framework to organise this chapter, has had a substantial impact, not only on the psychology of expertise, but also on cognitive psychology in general (Charness, 1992; Gobet et al., 2004). Several strengths of the theory can be highlighted. It explains numerous aspects of experts' behaviour – be it with respect to perception, memory and problem solving – with a single theory; it makes both quantitative and qualitative predictions and parts of the theory have been specified in great detail, as they have been implemented as computer programs (e.g. Simon & Gilmartin, 1973). In addition, it should be pointed out that it is a general theory, both because the mechanisms underpinning chess expertise are used in other domains of expertise and because they are used by people who are not experts. These mechanisms are basic mechanisms that enable remarkable performances because experts push their use to extremes. Clearly, then, chunking theory is not only a theory of expertise but also a theory of cognition in general.

Opinions diverge as to how well chunking theory accounts for the empirical data. Ericsson and Kintsch (1995), Holyoak (1991), Holding (1985) and Vicente and Wang (1998) argue that it has essentially been refuted. It is worth mentioning that some of their criticisms are incorrect (for a detailed discussion, see Gobet & Simon, 1998b; Simon & Gobet, 2000). For example, we have seen in Section 3.5 that, while often criticised, the assumption of location encoding has been supported empirically, as has the assumption that a large number of chunks need to be encoded in LTM. In contrast with these negative evaluations, Gobet (1998b) argues that chunking theory does a good job overall at explaining the empirical data, although he agrees that the theory fails to account for some of them. In particular, as we have seen in this chapter, the data show that chunking theory overestimates the role of STM and underestimates the speed at which experts can store new information in LTM. In addition, experts also represent information at a level of abstraction higher than that of perceptual chunks, as proposed by chunking theory. As we shall see below, these weaknesses have been corrected in two modifications of chunking theory: EPAM-IV[4] and template theory. These augment the original chunking theory with the idea of a retrieval structure.

---

[4]EPAM stands for Elementary Perceiver and Memorizer.

3.11.2 Skilled Memory Theory

Skilled memory theory (Chase & Ericsson, 1982; Ericsson & Staszewski, 1989) was developed in reaction to chunking theory, in particular due to the difficulty the latter theory had in explaining the remarkable memory shown by some individuals in the digit span task. Skilled memory theory proposes that experts' memory can be explained by three principles: (a) use of memory cues, making it possible to associate new information with previous knowledge; (b) presence of retrieval structures (as seen above, these are pre-learnt domain-specific LTM structures enabling a rapid storage in LTM); and (c) decrease of the time required to store and retrieve LTM information, thanks to intensive practice.

As seen earlier, the method of loci is a good example of a retrieval structure. When material is presented, associations are made between the known places (the *slots*) and items to learn. Skilled memory theory proposes that essentially the same mechanism was used by SF and DD, with the qualification that they used a retrieval structure optimised for the recall of digits.

This theoretical proposal has generated much interest in cognitive psychology, as it is not clear how a theory based on chunking only could explain the memory performance of SF and DD without postulating the learning of a very large number of chunks. Indeed, all the theories (skilled memory, long-term working memory and EPAM-IV) that have tried to explain the digit span results have used the notion of retrieval structure, although the details differ from one theory to another.

Two aspects of the kind of retrieval structures used in skilled memory theory merit some comments. First, the structure can encode only one type of material. Thus, it is difficult to use the retrieval structure in a new domain (e.g. from digit span memory to memory for colours) and transfer will be difficult, which is in line with the empirical data. Second, experts must activate their retrieval structures before the presentation of the material. This means that it will be hard to use the retrieval structure when the material has little structure or is difficult to categorise. This last point limits the domains of application for the theory. In fact, the theory has been used mainly to explain mnemonists' memory. An exception is mental calculation, where memory for digits is not the main aim but develops as a side effect of performing calculations rapidly and correctly.

The main weakness of the theory is that it lacks detail and is rather descriptive. In addition, the three principles of the theory are, logically, at different levels of explanation. Principles 1 (association of novel information with existing knowledge) and 2 (presence of retrieval structures) concern memory mechanisms, whilst principle 3 (decrease in encoding and retrieval times) is merely a description of the empirical data.

3.11.3 Long-Term Working Memory

Ericsson and Kintsch (1995) have expanded skilled memory theory with their long-term working-memory theory (LTWM), to the point that the new theory can be seen as a general theory of expertise. The theory makes a systematic use of schemas and retrieval structures, which enables it to cover more domains than skilled memory theory and go beyond expert memory. The new domains include reading and problem solving in chess. According to the theory, cognitive processes can be seen as a sequence of stable states that represent final products of processing. Memory skills make it possible for these final products to be stored in LTM. Encoding is mediated either by a retrieval structure or by a structure elaborating and associating items to other items or to the context.

As an illustration, consider the case of chess. Ericsson and Kintsch propose that chess players acquire a retrieval structure isomorphic to the 64 squares of a chess board. Each of these mental squares can encode a chess piece. Moreover, the squares are connected to one another so that they form a hierarchical structure, where schemata and patterns can be encoded. Ericsson and Kintsch argue that this mechanism explains a number of phenomena linked to chess expertise. These include how chess players can carry out look-ahead search, play blindfold chess (a variant of chess where a player cannot see the board and the pieces) and how they can memorise several briefly-presented chess boards.

Whereas LTWM provides reasonable explanations for mnemonists, it is weaker when it comes to explaining data where experts' memory performance is not a goal in itself. Thus, it suffers from similar weaknesses to skilled memory theory (Gobet, 1998b, 2000a, b, c). (For a more positive evaluation of the theory, see Ericsson & Kintsch, 2000; Ericsson et al., 2000; Guida et al., 2009.) First, key terms such as schemas and patterns are not defined. Similarly, the retrieval structure used by chess players is assumed to be hierarchical, but no details are provided. Second, the theory has problems with the recall of random material: it proposes mechanisms that should enable experts to memorise such material easily, but the data show that individuals, including experts, cannot do it. Third, some of the theoretical predictions are not supported by the empirical data. A case in point is Ericsson and Kintsch's proposal that retrieval structures make it possible to memorise material perfectly, even when the natural structure of the material is destroyed by the way it is dictated. These authors cite data from chess (Frey & Adesman, 1976), where the location of pieces were dictated in a random order, and medicine (Coughlin & Patel, 1987), where the description of a patient did not respect the temporal order of the symptoms. However, what the data actually show is that distorting the natural structure of the material impairs recall performance (see Section 3.4 for a discussion of the chess data).

In conclusion, the retrieval structures proposed by Ericsson and Kintsch offer a suitable explanation when experts consciously and deliberately aim to improve their memory, but not when memory improvement is a side effect of acquiring expertise – most of the domains of expertise. The issue with the kind of retrieval structures hypothesised by LTWM is that they are *generic*; they can be used with any material within the domain of expertise. However, the data suggest that, in many cases, experts must first retrieve a schema or a retrieval structure that is consistent with the incoming information (e.g. in football, the description of an attacking set up) before this information can be rapidly stored. For example, when listening to the description of an experiment's design, experimental psychologists must first retrieve the appropriate schema (e.g. a repeated-measure design or a factor-analysis design) in order to use it to encode information. They do not use a generic description of an experiment. Likewise, in chess, players must first identify the type of position at hand before a schema or a retrieval structure can be used. In other words, detailed memory structures can only be used if the players have acquired the relevant structures for this specific subset of chess positions. In chess, this analysis is strongly supported by two empirical results. First, as we have seen in Section 3.6, randomising positions seriously affects recall performance, even though stronger players keep a small advantage over weaker players. Second, Bilalić et al. (2009) found that chess players' performance was much better in positions in which they were specialised, both in memory and problem-solving tasks. This study used the fact that, in chess, players specialise in a small number of openings (first moves in the game). Crucially, these two results should not have been observed if players had acquired generic retrieval structures, which can be used both with random positions and with positions outside of a players' domain of specialisation.

To summarise, LTWM keeps the strengths of skilled memory with respect to domains where improving one's memory is the deliberate goal. However, the empirical support for the theory is weaker when it is applied to domains where memory improvement is not the primary objective. In addition, the key mechanisms and structures it proposes lack specification. Finally, the postulated retrieval structures are generic, which does not fit the empirical data in several domains.

3.11.4 Revisions of Chunking Theory

Two theories (EPAM-IV and template theory) were developed to improve on the two main weaknesses of chunking theory (over estimation of the importance of STM and underestimation of LTM storage speed). Both theories add mechanisms for explaining how experts are able to store information rapidly in LTM. In this respect, they were influenced by skilled memory. The idea of retrieval structure plays an important role in both theories. We have seen that chunking theory assumes that it takes about 8 seconds to create a new chunk. The addition of retrieval structures explains how experts can reduce this time to a few hundred milliseconds. However, the cost for this decrease is that it takes dozens of hours to learn these structures.

The two theories have been implemented as computer programs, the predictions of which have been compared in detail with the empirical data in several domains of expertise. Importantly, they have also been used to explain phenomena beyond expertise, such as concept formation, acquisition of first language, implicit learning and verbal learning (Gobet et al., 2001).

3.11.4.1 EPAM-IV

Richman et al. (1995) proposed EPAM-IV, an extension of EPAM (Feigenbaum & Simon, 1962; Feigenbaum & Simon, 1984). The earlier versions of EPAM used a mechanism similar to chunking to simulate several phenomena in the literature of verbal learning. This field of research, very influential in the first half of the twentieth century, studies basic learning mechanisms, such as those used when people learn pairs of nonsense syllables (such as XIJ – BOJ, RAK – XEM) or sequences of such syllables. Compared to these previous versions, EPAM-IV implements the concept of retrieval structures. The theory accounts in detail for the behaviour of DD, one of the mnemonists specialised in the digit span task and studied by Ericsson and Staszewski (see Section 3.7), using retrieval structures that are fairly close to those used in skilled memory theory. However, a key contribution of the theory is that these structures are now implemented in a computer model. This means that they are specified formally in great detail.

EPAM-IV presents a fairly detailed picture of STM and LTM. STM is divided into visual and auditory components. The visual component consists of two subsystems that are interlinked: the first subsystem temporarily maintains a limited number of chunks, and the second subsystem generates a visuospatial representation of the information contained in these chunks. Similarly, the auditory component consists of a subsystem keeping a limited number of verbal chunks and a subsystem repeating this information. This mechanism is similar to the articulatory loop proposed by Baddeley (1986). LTM consists of a semantic component and a procedural component. It also contains retrieval structures and schemas, which are learned deliberately.

Since the theory is specified as a computer program, it is possible to detail how chunks and retrieval structures are acquired, and how these structures are used when storing and retrieving digits in the digit span task. All cognitive processes have a time cost associated with them, which makes it possible to simulate how the digits are recalled by the model and to make predictions about how behaviour unfolds over time. EPAM-IV was able to simulate DD's behaviour in detail, both quantitatively and qualitatively.

3.11.4.2 Template theory and CHREST

Template theory assumes that expertise results from three main sources: (a) a large number of chunks, organised by a discrimination net; (b) a large amount of LTM knowledge, encoded as productions and schemata; and (c) a link between perceptual chunks and LTM knowledge. It also proposes that the chunks in the discrimination network can be accessed by different routes, which increases the robustness of the system. Several learning mechanisms are postulated: in addition to chunks, already present in chunking theory, productions and schemas must be learnt, as well as the links connecting them together. The construction of such networks explains why the acquisition of expertise takes about 10 years in domains that are semantically rich.

Template theory is implemented as a computer program with CHREST (Chunk Hierarchy & REtrieval STructures; Gobet, 1993a, b; Gobet & Simon, 2000a; Gobet et al., 2001), which was originally developed to explain chess players' perception and memory. CHREST incorporates mechanisms for learning and using chunks, managing STM and LTM, and directing attention through eye movements (see Figure 3.8). Altogether, this enables unsupervised acquisition of perceptual, semantic and procedural knowledge. In particular, the chunks learned by CHREST are automatically created with information gathered from simulated eye movements. While EPAM-IV accounts for data in a task where memory improvement is deliberated (the digit span task), CHREST explains how memory improves in a domain where there is no deliberate intention to improve one's memory. Just like with EPAM-IV, CHREST combines the

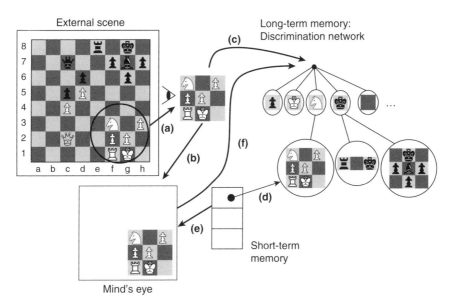

Figure 3.8 CHREST consists of four components: a simulated eye, a discrimination network giving access to LTM, an STM and a mind's eye. The simulated eye selects a portion of the external display (the *visual field*), shown by (a) in the figure. This information is sent both to the mind's eye (b) and LTM (c). If the information is recognised in LTM by accessing a node (i.e., a chunk), a pointer to this chunk is put in STM (d), and the information is unpacked in the mind's eye (e). In turn, the information in the mind's eye can be used to access a node in LTM (f). Note that LTM chunks encode information about location (e.g. the two white pieces on the 1st row would be encoded as rook on f1 and king on g1).

Source: From Waters, A. J., & Gobet, F. (2008). Mental imagery and chunks: Empirical and computational findings. *Memory & Cognition, 36*, 505–517. Reprinted with kind permission from Springer Science + Business Media.

mechanism of chunking with the use of retrieval structures. However, unlike EPAM-IV and skilled memory theory, the creation and use of these structures is performed unconsciously.

The key idea of template theory is that some chunks, which are used frequently in a given domain, lead to the acquisition of more complex data structures, known as templates. These structures are similar to schemata, with the qualification that they come with well-defined mechanisms for learning and use (all details have to be fully defined in a computer program!). This is important, since schemata have a somewhat bad press in the psychological literature for the rather vague way in which they are typically defined (Gobet, 2000c; Lane et al., 2000). Templates consist of two parts. The *core* is made of stable information and is essentially similar to a chunk; thus, it imposes a condition that must be satisfied for a template to be used. The *slots* are made of variable information and make it possible to encode information that occurs often but with some variation. For example, in the schema of a *room*, the core consists of the fact that rooms have walls, a floor and a ceiling, while slots would encode the number of doors and windows, which are variable. To give another example, this time from chess, a slot could be created for a square that is important in a given type of position and that can be occupied by different kinds of pieces. The values in the slots can be updated rapidly – Gobet and Simon (2000a) estimated a time of about 250 ms. This explains how experts are able to encode domain-specific information rapidly, without overloading STM.

Recall that the retrieval structures used by EPAM-IV (Richman et al., 1995) and skilled memory theory (Chase & Ericsson, 1982) are consistent with a general schema that is repeatedly used by the expert to encode domain-specific material. So long as this material belongs to the elected domain, and independently to its fine-grained characteristics, it can be encoded by the retrieval structure. By contrast, the templates in CHREST theory can be used by experts only when the conditions imposed by the template core are met. A consequence of this is that there exists some material belonging to the domain of expertise for which no template can be found. In chess and in other domains, randomised material would be a good example. This is an important difference compared to skilled memory and EPAM-IV. Another important difference is that the core of the template provides information that does not need to be stored in the slots. With the retrieval structure postulated by skilled memory and EPAM-IV, no default values are provided and each slot of the retrieval structure must always encode a value.

CHREST has been able to successfully simulate a large number of phenomena, not only in chess but also in other domains of expertise and even beyond expertise. In chess, it has simulated chess players' behaviour (from beginner to grandmasters) in perception, memory and problem-solving tasks. The memory simulations concern experiments where different kinds of positions (positions taken from actual masters' games, positions modified by mirror-image and various types of randomised positions) were briefly presented. The program was able to simulate not only the percentage of pieces correctly recalled as a function of skill level, but also the way players group pieces during the reconstruction of the position and the type of errors they make (Gobet, 1993a;

Gobet & Simon, 1996b, 2000a; Gobet & Waters, 2003). It also simulates the chunks and templates acquired by non-players trained to memorise chess positions (Gobet & Jackson, 2002). Finally, strong support for the theory was obtained by the simulations of an experiment where the presentation time was systematically varied from 1 second to 60 seconds (Gobet & Simon, 2000a). This was a strong test of the theory, since it directly tested the validity of some of the time parameters used by CHREST, such as the time to create a new chunk (8 seconds), the time to add information to an existing chunk (2 seconds) and the time to add information to the slot of a template (250 ms).

Another strong test was carried out by Waters and Gobet (2008), this time with respect to the mechanisms and parameters used to process information in the mind's eye. The interest centred on the mental-imagery parameters used to move the pieces mentally, and in particular on the two parameters the model uses for shifting chess pieces in its mind's eye. Based on relatively sparse experimental evidence, de Groot and Gobet (1996) had estimated that it took 100 ms to start the process of generating a move, and 50 ms to move a piece diagonally over one square in the mind's eye. The validity of these parameters was tested in a memory experiment that required players to recall briefly presented positions in which the pieces were placed on the intersections between squares, rather than on their centre. Position types ranged from game positions to positions where both the piece distribution and location were randomised (see Figure 3.9). Recall was impaired on the intersection positions compared to the standard positions, an impairment that

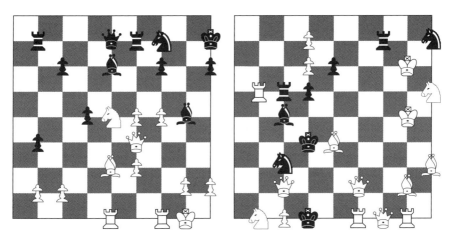

Figure 3.9 Examples of the type of *intersection positions* used by Waters and Gobet (2008). On the left a game position; on the right, a totally random position, where each piece has the same probability of being selected.

Source: From Waters, A. J., & Gobet, F. (2008). Mental imagery and chunks: Empirical and computational findings. *Memory & Cognition, 36*, 505–517. Adapted with kind permission from Springer Science + Business Media.

was especially pronounced on the positions taken from actual games. In the simulations, it was assumed that pieces must be centred back to the middle of the squares in the mind's eye before chunks can be recognised. The human data were simulated fairly well using, as a parameter for the time to shift pieces, the parameter used by the model to move pieces diagonally.

We have mentioned earlier, in Section 2.2, the striking differences between the eye movements of novices and masters when they look for 5 seconds at a novel position in a recall task (de Groot & Gobet, 1996). CHREST does a very good job of simulating these differences. It replicates the skill effect found with the average duration of eye fixations (272 ms for the simulated masters vs. 315 ms for the simulated novices) and also the difference in variability, as measured by the fixations' standard deviation (97 ms vs. 154 ms, respectively). The CHREST model of a master player covers approximately the same proportion of the important parts of the board as human masters, whereas the novice version of the model covers a much smaller area, just like human novices. CHREST also captures the skill differences in the percentage of the board covered, and in the percentage of critical squares covered. How does CHREST explain the speeding-up of the eye movements and the increase of the number of important squares fixated as expertise increases? The reason for this is that many more fixations are directed by the structure of the discrimination network with the master version of the model than with the novice version, since the discrimination network is larger with the former than with the latter. The novice version relies on simple heuristics or rules of thumb (e.g. fixate the centre), which take longer to perform.

A variant of CHREST implements the idea that moves are recognised by pattern recognition (Gobet & Jansen, 1994). Finally, another variation of CHREST simulates some of the key results in decision making in chess, such as how depth of search increases as a function of the skill level (Gobet, 1997b). Beyond chess, CHREST has also simulated the development of expertise in the African game of awele (Gobet, 2009), prediction of moves in Go (Bossomaier et al., 2012), and memory for computer programs (Gobet & Oliver, 2002). It has also successfully simulated phenomena in a variety of domains including problem solving in physics, explicit and implicit learning, concept formation and children's acquisition of first language (for reviews, see Gobet & Lane, 2010; Gobet et al., 2001). This last application suggests that first language learning may be considered as a type of skill development mediated by the acquisition of a large number of chunks.

3.11.4.3 Evaluations of EPAM-IV and template theory

The work with EPAM-IV and CHREST has several strengths. First, these two theories have simulated a number of different phenomena not only on expertise in particular, but also on learning in general. Second, as they are expressed as computer programs, both theories are very detailed and do not suffer from any vagueness in their description. Third, they incorporate the characteristics of the environment, as they use an input that is representative of the type of input that humans receive during practice. For example, with chess, CHREST uses positions taken from masters' games. Finally, EPAM-IV and CHREST account for the empirical data at different levels of analysis: percentage correct, type and number of errors, time course of behaviour and the way the material is chunked during the recall phase. This last result, obviously crucial for a theory based on chunking, has been simulated in chess (grouping of pieces), the digit span task (grouping of digits) and physics (the way diagrams are drawn), and incorporates differences between individuals of various skill levels.

A number of weaknesses have also been identified. A series of papers in the *British Journal of Psychology* (Ericsson & Kintsch, 2000; Gobet, 2000b, c) have discussed the merits and demerits of LTWM, on the one hand, and CHREST/EPAM-IV, on the other. This is a good place to start our discussion. Ericsson and Kintsch argue that these two computational theories suffer from four weaknesses.

First, Ericsson and Kintsch argue that EPAM-IV/CHREST carve the mechanisms underpinning expertise at the wrong level (elementary processes, such as time to encode information in STM). They argue that a general theory of expertise should be described at the more abstract level used by LTWM theory. In his reply, Gobet (2000b) suggests that these two levels are not inconsistent. For example, low-level processes can be used to explain the development of structures described at a higher level of abstraction, such as schemata. This is essentially what has been done with CHREST.

Second, Ericsson and Kintsch criticise the retrieval structures used by EPAM-IV and CHREST, which they call "slotted schemata". This is a rather weak criticism; when it comes to schemata and retrieval structures, LTWM is on shaky grounds, as these are never specified in any detail in Ericsson and Kintsch's theory. By contrast, EPAM-IV and CHREST offer detailed mechanisms not only about how these structures are used by experts, but also how they are acquired. Computer simulations provide convincing support for them, both in the digit-span task and in chess. In particular, they can reproduce experts' behaviour both qualitatively and quantitatively, something that is impossible for Ericsson and Kintsch's theory, which is only expressed verbally and lacks detailed mechanisms. Finally, it is worth noting that the kind of schemata criticised by Ericsson and Kintsch are often used in cognitive psychology, beyond the study of expertise, and have proven to have a powerful explanatory power (Alba & Hasher, 1983).

Third, Ericsson and Kintsch propose that other mechanisms than those proposed by EPAM and CHREST could account for the relevant empirical data. As stressed by philosophers of science, however, no scientific theory is ever proven, and it is thus always possible to come up with new and better theories. So Ericsson and Kintsch are correct on this point, in a rather obvious way. This being said, models such as CHREST and EPAM-IV raise the theoretical bar high, since they are sufficient to reproduce the data under study. To our knowledge, no theory has been proposed that can simulate the data in question with the same level of precision.

Fourth, Ericsson and Kintsch state that computer simulations cannot account for individual differences. Gobet (2000b) argues that this statement is incorrect. In fact, it is more feasible to study individual differences with a computer model than with an informal theory, as specific hypotheses can be tested in simulations. For example, assumptions can be made about the size of STM capacity or the time it takes to learn a new chunk. The value of these parameters can be systematically varied and their effect on the simulations studied. This is particularly valuable when learning is studied, as the long-term effects of individual differences can be estimated. The interaction of individual differences and the type of input received during learning can also be studied, something that is not possible with an informal theory.

Whereas Ericsson and Kintsch's analysis is problematic, other criticisms are valid. First, the number of phenomena simulated by EPAM/CHREST is still limited. Although a number of phenomena have been simulated with respect to perception and memory, there are relatively few simulations on decision making and problem solving. Second, few links have been made between these theories and neuroscience (for one of the few attempts, see Chassy & Gobet, 2011a). Given the growing importance of this field, this is clearly a weakness.

3.11.5 Constraint Attunement Theory

This theory, proposed by Vicente and Wang (1998), differs from the theories we have reviewed so far in this chapter in that it emphasises the input-output coupling rather than the cognitive processes in play, and thus put the emphasis on the environment rather on the psychology of the person. In this respect, it is not unlike Skinner's behaviourism.

Vicente and Wang (1998) use an *ecological* approach to explain the correlation between skill level and performance in memory recall tasks where domain-specific material is presented for a short duration. Ecological approaches (e.g. Gibson, 1969) study behaviours that occur in natural environments, as opposed to the laboratory, and emphasise the organism-environment relation and the link between perception and action. Vicente and Wang's *constraint attunement theory* states that experts enjoy an advantage only when they are sensitive to the constraints linked to the goal to realise in a given task. Experts' superiority is proportional to the number of constraints that are present, again with the qualification that experts must direct their attention to these constraints. With truly random material (i.e. material in which all constraints have been removed), a direct prediction of the theory is that experts should not have any advantage.

Vicente and Wang (1998) distinguish between product theories and process theories. *Product theories* predict the relation between the input and the output of a system, but do not make any hypothesis about the mechanisms intervening between both. *Process theories* make predictions both about how a system performs given an input, and about the mechanisms mediating this performance. Vicente and Wang argue that, in the study of expertise, a product theory should be proposed before a process theory, and this is what they do with the constraint attunement theory. They show that several phenomena linked to experts' memory can be explained by studying the environment together with the goals used by the experts. Thus, they argue, it is not necessary to postulate internal mechanisms. According to these authors, their theory explains the data better than previous theories (including skilled memory, LTWM theory and chunking theory).

In a reply to Vicente and Wang's (1998) article, Simon and Gobet (2000) note that process theories (e.g. chunking theory) have long incorporated information about the environment and emphasised the adaptive nature of human cognition. For example, Simon (1969) argued that the complexity of human behaviour is due more to the complexity of the environment than that of the cognitive system. Directly related to expertise, the environment of some task domains has been studied in detail. De Groot and Gobet (1996) analysed the environment of chess using the mathematical tools offered by Shannon's (1948) information theory, which makes it possible to quantify information and complexity. They used information measures of the environment to predict chess masters' memory performance in a recall task. The role of the environment is of course also implicitly captured by models such as EPAM and CHREST, which are all adaptive systems that learn from inputs representative of real-life environments.

According to Simon and Gobet (2000), a weakness of constraint attunement theory is that it does not specify the conditions under which experts' potential advantage will be present. For example, the duration of presentation time matters. With a short presentation, expertise effects are likely to be present. With a very long presentation, say one hour, it is likely that all participants will have time to memorise the information, and thus one should not expect any difference between skill levels. Another weakness of constraint attunement theory is that it does not make many quantitative predictions and its parameters change from task to task. Indeed, constraints must be constructed independently for each task in a rather *ad hoc* fashion. Simon and Gobet's key point is that theories that ignore internal mechanisms are much weaker than theories that take such mechanisms into consideration. As they put it: "If one ignores a system's internal limits of adaptation, psychology becomes an impoverished science. There are, first, the limits of knowledge and, second, the limits of memory capacity and speed of storing new information. Dealing with these limits requires a theory of the organism, not just of the environment – that is, a process theory" (Simon & Gobet, 2000, p. 599).

We have seen in Section 3.6 that an experiment by Gobet and Waters (2003) directly pitted one of the key predictions of constraint attunement theory against that of template theory. When chess players had to remember positions where all constraints had been removed (truly random positions), there still was a small expertise effect, as predicted by template theory and the simulations with CHREST, but at variance with the predictions of constraint attunement theory.

3.12 Chapter Summary

Chase and Simon's (1973a, b) research used a recall and a copy task to provide three ways of operationalising the notion of a chunk, with converging results. Their chunking theory has been highly influential in later research on expertise. However, it overemphasised the role of STM, underestimated the importance of rapid encoding in LTM and under estimated the importance of high-level knowledge (such as schemas), as shown by research on chess and mnemonics. These limits led to the development of several theories (skilled memory, long-term working-memory, template theory, constraint attunement theory and EPAM-IV). Template theory and EPAM-IV, which are both built on chunking theory and have the advantage of being expressed as computer programs, appear to provide the best account of the empirical data.

3.13 Further Reading

In addition to the books recommended in the previous chapter, the following works address various aspects of expert memory. Two edited books – Klahr and Kotovsky (1989) and Chi, Glaser and Farr – contain some fascinating chapters on expert memory. Simon's (1979, 1989) two volumes of *Models of Thought* contain the key papers he wrote on chess perception and memory, as well as other important papers on expertise. Gobet et al. (2004) provide an overview of the considerable literature on board games and discuss numerous memory experiments.

CHAPTER 4

Problem Solving

4.1 Preview of Chapter

Most people would consider that problem solving and decision making are both instances of thinking. Not psychologists! Rather surprisingly for outsiders, these two topics have evolved into two different and independent fields of psychological research.[1] This divide, which is the outcome of historical vagaries, seems artificial, as both fields study the way people make decisions. This being said, there are some interesting differences. Studies in the field of problem solving typically ask participants to solve problems without providing them with possible answers, are interested in the cognitive processes involved and mostly use computer modelling as a formal theoretical tool. By contrast, studies in the field of decision making typically provide both problems and possible answers, are interested in whether participants choose correct answers and not so much in the detail of the cognitive processes involved, and tend to use mathematical modelling. As we shall see, these differences have clear implications for the kind of questions that have been posed about expertise.

This chapter reviews the empirical evidence on expert problem solving, covering the important topics of search, pattern recognition, planning and representations. The next chapter will cover decision making. A considerable amount of research on problem solving has been undertaken with chess, since it is one of the very few domains in which expertise can be precisely and quantitatively measured. In addition, most of the key theories on expert problem solving were developed to explain chess expertise. Thus, this chapter will discuss the data on chess expertise in some depth. The first part of the chapter presents the empirical evidence, and the second part discusses some of the key theories.

---

[1] The state of affairs is actually worse than this. Other fields that one would intuitively consider as studying thinking have gone their own ways, such as reasoning, probabilistic thinking and causal reasoning. However, as these fields have not (yet) had much impact on expertise, we will not consider them separately in this book.

4.2 De Groot's Research

As with perception and memory, it is appropriate to start with de Groot's (1965) seminal study, since it anticipates many of the key questions that shaped later research. As we have seen in the previous chapter, de Groot asked his participants, who included a world champion and several former world champions, to think aloud while they were trying to find the best move in a novel position. The analysis of these verbal protocols enabled de Groot to extract several quantitative and qualitative measures that described players' thinking behaviour.

De Groot's key findings, which can be summarised in one paragraph, are still a good description of the way experts solve problems. First, at all skill levels, search was highly selective. Typically, fewer than one hundred different positions (and the moves leading to them) were investigated before a move was chosen. Thus, the search trees of all players were small. (In the context of psychological research, a *search tree* is a summary of the problem states that have been considered when an individual thinks about her next action. See Figures 4.1, 4.2 and 4.3.) Second, and related to the first point, the size of the search trees tended to be the same across skill levels, in spite of vast differences in the amount of time spent practising and studying chess. In particular, grandmasters did not search deeper or wider than candidate masters, although they tended to choose better solutions. Third, better players were faster at generating moves. Fourth, as we have seen in the previous two chapters, better players examined more promising moves earlier. In other words, the branches of the tree they visited tended to be more relevant for an understanding of the position than those examined by weaker players. Finally, players of all

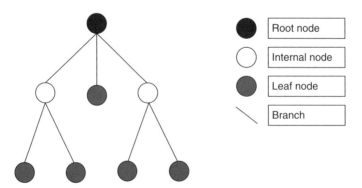

Figure 4.1 Illustration of the concept of a tree. With a game such as chess, the internal nodes represent positions, and the branches represent moves for white or black.

Source: From Gobet, F., de Voogt, A. J., & Retschitzki, J. (2004). *Moves in mind*. Hove: Psychology Press. Adapted with kind permission from Psychology Press.

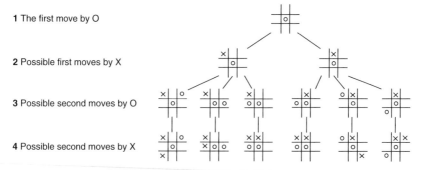

Figure 4.2 A full game tree for tic-tac-toe after the first player chooses to move in the central square. Note that some possible moves have been eliminated due to symmetries.

Source: From Gobet, F., de Voogt, A. J., & Retschitzki, J. (2004). *Moves in mind*. Hove: Psychology Press. Adapted with kind permission from Psychology Press.

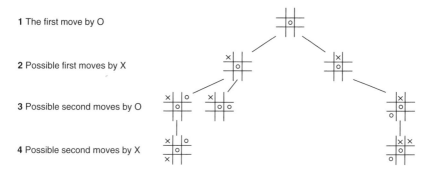

Figure 4.3 Example of a search tree. When thinking ahead, players normally consider only a small part of the game tree.

levels tended to examine the same branches of the search tree several times, a phenomenon that de Groot called *progressive deepening*.

Interestingly, as noted by Gobet et al. (2004), the impact on cognitive psychology was mostly made by de Groot's quantitative analyses, which cover only a handful of pages. His detailed qualitative analyses, running over several hundred pages, have been mostly ignored.

4.3 Phases of Problem Solving

According to de Groot (1965), decision making in chess consists of three phases: the first phase, the progressive deepening phase and the final phase. During the *first phase*, players familiarise themselves with the position and carry out a preliminary investigation. They note, in an unsystematic way, potential plans, strategic ideas, threats and possible moves. They also propose a quick and preliminary evaluation of the position. The characteristic feature of this phase is that no (or very little) search is carried out. In the *progressive deepening phase*, players elaborate on the information gathered in the first phase by carrying out search. Base moves[2] are analysed, and their number is progressively reduced to two, typically. Selected variations are iteratively examined more deeply. Note that it is not always easy to draw the boundaries between the first two phases; enumerating potential moves, which belongs to the first phase, overlaps somewhat with carrying out search, which is part of the progressive deepening phase. We will have more to say about progressive deepening in the next section. In the *final phase*, players summarise the conclusions of the second phase, select a move (usually one of the main moves previously considered) and double-check its correctness. De Groot's three phases were corroborated in chess by Tikhomirov and Poznyanskaya (1966), who used a combination of verbal protocols and eye-movement data. The presence of the first phase has also been documented in the game of Go (Yoshikawa et al., 1999).

Decision making is described as a two-stage process in Kahneman and Tversky's influential prospect theory (Kahneman & Tversky, 1979; Tversky & Kahneman, 1992). In the *framing phase*, the information is integrated to form a representation of the situation. During this phase, heuristics make it possible to perform a preliminary sorting of outcomes using the preferences attached to them. In the *valuation phase*, outcomes are assigned a value using a combination of weighted probabilities (i.e. subjective probabilities) and a value function (i.e. subjective expected utility). The framing phase roughly corresponds to de Groot's first phase, and the valuation phase to his last phase. It is important to note that, in the problems studied by Kahneman and Tversky, a list of solutions is already proposed, so there is no need to generate them. Also, contrary to chess, the type of problem chosen does not require extensive search in the problem space. This explains why the progressive deepening phase has apparently been eliminated.

4.4 Expertise Effects in Progressive Deepening

An interesting aspect of the progressive deepening phase is that players tend to investigate the same branches of the search tree several times (de Groot, 1965). This can be done either directly (*immediate reinvestigation*), or after having considered other branches (*non-immediate reinvestigation*). Each consideration of a specific branch enables the player to analyse it in more detail: the branch is analysed at a greater depth, or the evaluation of the final position is refined. De Groot notes that this behaviour is not particular to chess, but is actually common in decision-making situations. For example, when you decide where to go on holiday, you might first consider going to Rome, and imagine your first day there. You like the idea, and you then imagine yourself being in

---

[2]A *base move* is a move immediately playable in the stimulus position (at depth 1).

Rome for two days (immediate reinvestigation). However, after considering that eating too much pizza and pasta might not be good for your waist, you consider a sporting holiday in Lanzarote. But you do not enjoy the thought of sweating and puffing, so you revert back to imaging your holiday in Rome, this time with more healthy food (non-immediate reinvestigation).

At first sight, this search behaviour does not seem rational, since it appears to waste resources. However, at least two explanations support its use. First, it alleviates the constraints due to the limited capacity of human STM; second, it allows the information found in one branch of the search tree to be accessible in other branches (de Groot, 1965; de Groot & Gobet, 1996).

De Groot (1969) notes that this behaviour is not limited to chess and that it can be found in other tasks, most notably scientific research. A scientist goes back and forth between different hypotheses and ideas, and her problem conception develops following a spiral. The reasons for this behaviour seem to be the same as with chess. Beyond compensating for limits in memory capacity, it enables a good problem solver to use the feedback provided by the earlier steps of her search in later steps. Thus, there is nothing wrong in revisiting old plans and re-evaluating old conclusions – on the contrary.

In chess, there are some interesting skill differences with respect to progressive deepening (Gobet, 1998a). We have seen that there are two types of reinvestigations: with *immediate reinvestigations*, the same base move is considered in the next episode[3]; with *non-immediate reinvestigations*, at least one different move is considered between the analysis of a base move and its reinvestigation (see Figure 4.4). It turns out that the maximum number

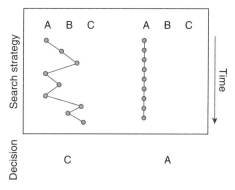

Figure 4.4 Illustration of the concepts of immediate and non-immediate reinvestigations. A, B and C denote possible solutions. In the left part of the figure, only non-immediate reinvestigations (*switch strategy*) are used. In the right part, only immediate reinvestigations are used (*stay strategy*). Of course, in practice, there is a continuum between the pure switch and stay strategies.

---

[3]An *episode* is a sequence of moves generated from a base move.

of immediate reinvestigations is proportional to players' skill level, while the maximum number of non-immediate reinvestigations is inversely proportional to it. Together with the fact that strong players tend to investigate better moves early on, these results can be explained by Newell and Simon's (1965, 1972) *win-stay* and *lose-shift* hypothesis. After positive evaluations, players would deepen their search by homing-in on favourable lines and reanalysing them; after negative evaluations, they would widen their search by investigating other moves. Reanalysing de Groot's (1965) data, Reynolds (1982) tested the hypothesis that skilled players are more likely to use this *homing heuristic* than weaker players. Consistent with this hypothesis, he found that grandmasters and masters tended to increase the number of base moves under investigation after a negative evaluation, to decrease this number after a positive evaluation, and to keep it constant after a neutral evaluation. By contrast, candidate masters and weaker players followed the homing heuristic only with negative evaluations.

So far, the results show that skill predicts search strategy. But does search strategy predict the quality of the decision? Gobet and Yousaf (submitted) showed that, in a chess problem-solving task, search strategy predicts the quality of a decision, even when the effect of expertise is statistically controlled for. In fact, in their data, search strategy accounted for slightly more of the variance than Elo rating. The conclusion drawn from this study is that search strategy affects the quality of the solution both with experts and non-experts.

4.5 Macrostructure of Search

The macrostructure of search concerns variables such as depth of search, the number of positions considered, the number of base moves and the rate of generating moves. De Groot (1965) did not find any skill differences with respect to the variables quantifying the amount of search. The only differences he found were that stronger players chose better moves, were quicker at generating moves, reached a decision faster, and tended to examine more promising branches in the search tree early on.

De Groot's conclusions of no skill difference with respect to these variables were somewhat misleading, since his key analyses compared grandmasters with candidate masters, who are relatively strong players. It is important to stress that he did not find an absence of difference between grandmasters and *beginners*, as is often incorrectly reported in the literature. There are actually vast differences between these two categories of players – e.g. beginners simply cannot anticipate several moves ahead. (For a discussion of this error and its theoretical and practical implications, see Bilalić et al., 2008a.)

Later recent research actually found some skill differences when weaker players are included (e.g. Charness, 1981b; Gobet, 1998a; Saariluoma, 1992), although these differences are rather small. The data suggest that average depth of search follows a power law of skill – it keeps increasing as expertise grows, but with diminishing returns (Gobet, 1997b, 1998a). For example, Charness's (1981b) class D players (seven standard deviations below world class players) searched 2.3 moves deep, de Groot's candidate masters (about three standard deviations in strength below the grandmasters) searched 4.8 moves deep, and his top-level grandmasters on average searched 5.3 moves deep. The presence of a power law would explain why skill differences are so difficult to identify with very skilled players, since changes are minimal.

The most recent data show that players at master level and above do not employ much search in simple, strategic or familiar positions. However, there can be large skill differences in complex, tactical or unfamiliar positions (Bilalić et al., 2009; Campitelli & Gobet, 2004).

Clearly, strong players are able to adapt their search strategy depending on the type of position they face and the thinking time available to them. This is good evidence that, as expertise develops, people become more flexible in the kind of problem-solving strategies they use.

4.6 Directionality of Search

In many domains, novices tend to carry out *backward search*, where one starts from the goal, and moves back to the current situation, while experts tend to carry out *forward search*, at least on simple problems. That is, they start from the givens of the problem and move to a goal state. When the problems are more complex, experts revert to searching backward from the goal. This is the case with domains such as physics (Larkin et al., 1980a; b), medicine (Patel & Groen, 1986) and geometry (Koedinger & Anderson, 1990). For example, a physician can propose a diagnosis by starting from the symptoms and moving to a diagnosis, while a medical student must first generate all plausible diagnoses, and then test them one-by-one by relating the underlying pathologies to the symptoms. These behaviours are of course consistent with our description in the previous chapter of the intermediate effect in medicine.

There are several exceptions to this rule. In computer programming, both experts and novices carry out backward search (Jeffries et al., 1981). In chess, players of all levels essentially use forward search (de Groot, 1965; Newell & Simon, 1972). While goals and plans are important in chess (see below), there is typically no single concrete goal at hand, but rather a combination of goals. This makes it hard to use backward search.

4.7 Planning

Planning can be defined as the long-term anticipation of the way events might unfold. It is more abstract than the kind of search we have described in the previous sections, and leaves out many details about the way the plan will be implemented. Given the importance of perception in chess, it is not surprising that chess masters often find the correct plan rapidly. As de Groot (1965) put it, masters literally "see" not only the next move, but also the appropriate plan, even before carrying out any look-ahead search or performing an explicit evaluation of the board position. Qualitative descriptions of planning in chess are offered by de Groot (1965) and Saariluoma (1984). In particular, Saariluoma shows how players construct schematic problem spaces initially when trying to find the best move in a position, and how they sometimes combine two simple problem spaces to construct a more complex one. He also presents data showing how insight can lead to the abrupt reorganisation of plans and problem spaces.

Interestingly, there is not much formal research documenting skill differences in planning. One possible reason for this is that much of the cognitive processing is undertaken by pattern recognition and is thus unconscious. There are two interesting exceptions. Koedinger and Anderson (1990) showed that, during initial planning, experts in geometry use inferences that skip less important steps. Hayes (1989b) reports data showing that successful writers plan more, and better, than less successful ones.

4.8 Evaluation

In most domains of expertise, it is important to be able to evaluate the situation one faces accurately and rapidly: Is it favourable? Should I take risks or play it safe? In chess, skill differences in the ability to evaluate a position were documented as early as the beginning of the twentieth century by Cleveland (1907), who based his conclusions on the responses to a questionnaire.

An interesting aspect of verbal evaluations in chess (de Groot, 1965) and in other domains (Shanteau, 1992b) is that they focus on only one, or at most a few, aspects at a time. For example: "Black has a weak pawn structure" or "The knight on square f4 is strong". In this respect, evaluations do not respect the canons of rationality, which would require all features being taken into account and weighted up. This is actually what chess-playing computers do, by mathematically combining a large number of features such as material balance, control of the centre and safety of the king.

Given that chess players look ahead, there are two sorts of evaluation, which vary in their difficulty. One can evaluate the situation currently present on the board, or one can evaluate positions that are imagined during look-ahead search. Using computer evaluations as an estimate of the correct evaluation, Holding (1979) and Holding and Pfau (1985) carried out several experiments investigating the way players evaluate positions at different depths of their search tree. They found that strong players evaluated positions better than weaker players, and that the quality of the evaluations was higher for the positions in reality than for imagined positions. Similar results were found by Charness (1981a), who found that, when endgame positions had to be evaluated rapidly (in less than 10 seconds), stronger players performed better. These results are not surprising, given that strong chess players can typically play speed chess at a high level and that they can play against 20 or 30 weaker opponents simultaneously, without much difficulty. As players improve in skill, they also show more discrimination in their evaluations (Holding, 1979): they tend to give high scores to advantageous positions, and low scores to disadvantageous positions. By contrast, weaker players tend to evaluate positions as close to equality. In chess, evaluations seem to be based on a number of factors: perceptual chunks, general principles, explicit memory for typical patterns on the board and episodic memory of previous games, played either by oneself or by other players (Gobet et al., 2004).

4.9 The Role of Pattern Recognition in Problem Solving

One of the great debates in cognitive science (and also in artificial intelligence) concerns the respective roles of pattern recognition and search in decision making. We have just seen that, whereas there are skill differences in search behaviour, all players are highly selective, rarely considering more than 100 positions before making their decision. De Groot (1965) and Simon (1969) consider that selective search, which is in part due to the limits in memory and processing capacity of the human cognitive system, is an essential feature of cognition.

Another important finding of de Groot's study was that expert players often honed into promising moves rapidly, and a fair amount of research has replicated this finding. Candidate masters are better than novices at predicting the moves of a novel game, needing fewer guesses to find the actual move – they often find it in their first try (Klein & Peio, 1989). Interestingly, limiting thinking time does not reduce the quality of masters' moves substantially, although of course it does lead to some reduction. Playing speed chess (about 5 seconds per move) leads to little loss of quality compared with normal chess (about 2 minutes per move; Calderwood et al., 1988). The most arresting example is perhaps chess grandmasters' ability to play simultaneous chess against strong players and still beat them. When former world champion Garry Kasparov played simultaneous games against national teams, consisting of 4–8 strong masters and grandmasters, his performance would still have ranked him within the best six players in the world (Gobet & Simon, 1996c). Why does this support the role of pattern recognition? Since Kasparov played against several opponents simultaneously, his thinking time was cut proportionally. If search plays the central role in chess expertise, a large cut in thinking time should lead to a heavy loss in performance, since search occurs serially and thus takes time. By contrast, if pattern recognition is more important, large cuts in thinking time should have much less impact, since better players can still rely on their ability to identify patterns and strong moves quickly. This interpretation of the data is discussed further in Lassiter (2000) and Gobet and Simon (2000b).

The role of pattern recognition has been established in nearly all domains of expertise, and is particularly clear with board games (Gobet et al., 2004), medicine (see Section 2.3) and sports (see Section 2.5). A key feature of expertise is that experts can quickly find the solution to routine problems, without much deliberation.

The importance of pattern recognition for problem solving has also been criticised, most notably by Holding (1985) and Holyoak (1991). The main line of their argument is that some experiments show that skill does not correlate with the recall of domain-specific material, but does correlate with the quality of decisions made (e.g., for chess, Holding & Reynolds, 1982). However, the weakness of this argument is its assumption that experts use pattern recognition only in the problem situation as presented to the participants, and not in the problem states that are anticipated during look-ahead search. Another issue is that experimenters may have misidentified the kinds of patterns experts pay attention to.

4.10 The Role of Perception in Problem Solving

In the previous chapter, we addressed the central role played by perception in expertise. Among other things, we examined a number of experiments that analysed eye movements. This methodology has also been used to study expert problem solving, and we discuss a few examples in this section. Tikhomirov and Poznyanskaya (1966) recorded the eye movements of a candidate chess master while he was selecting a move in a familiar position. The player focused his eyes on only a small number of squares, directing his attention on what Tikhomirov and Poznyanskaya called the *orientation zone*. Charness et al. (2001) collected eye movements of candidate masters and intermediate players choosing a move in an unknown position. As expected, better players were faster and selected better moves. They also made fewer fixations and the amplitude of their saccades was larger. During the first five fixations, candidate masters tended to look at empty squares more often. When considering only fixations on pieces, they were more likely to fixate upon relevant pieces more often than weaker players. According to Charness et al. (2001), strong players use perceptual chunks to encode chess patterns and use parafoveal or peripheral vision to find important pieces. This information is then used to guide the next fixation.

4.11 The Role of Schemata and Conceptual Knowledge in Problem Solving

The role of schemata in expertise in general, and in problem solving in particular, has been appreciated ever since de Groot's (1965) study. Their importance lies in the information that they provide for problem-solving. The fundamental contribution of de Groot's research was to establish a link between perception and schematic knowledge. According to him, expert chess players perceive a board position in "*large complexes*, each of which hangs together as a genetic, functional and/or dynamic nature"; each complex "is to be considered as a unit of perception *and* significance" (italics in original; de Groot, 1978, pp. 329–330). De Groot also noted that, when players describe a game, they tend to focus on the key positions in these games. Later research has amply corroborated the role of these complexes in expert knowledge (Cooke et al., 1993; Gobet, 1998b; Saariluoma, 1995). It is important to stress that the complexes identified by de Groot are larger than Chase and Simon's chunks.

According to de Groot (1965), much of chess masters' knowledge, what he calls their *system of playing methods*, is stereotypical. This knowledge consists of tactical (short-term) and strategic (long-term) methods, and techniques for handling typical positions in endgames. It also includes opening theory, a body of knowledge about how to handle the first moves of games, which has been incrementally constructed and refined over the centuries and is still in flux. "First moves" is a rather ambiguous concept since openings can include anything from 10 to 40 moves, and even more (Chassy & Gobet, 2011b). Depending on their style and preferences, masters acquire different systems of playing methods. Thus, rather than being innovative and discovering new methods, playing chess appears to be more about being able to apply well-known methods in the right situation efficiently. The importance and number of stereotypical and reproductive methods may come as a surprise to the uninitiated. However, these methods enable masters to play good chess without requiring much search or deliberation, simply by applying standard ideas and principles, undoubtedly complemented by the perceptual chunks we have described earlier.

There is direct experimental support for this hypothesis. Saariluoma (1990, 1992) as well as Bilalić et al. (2008b, c) showed positions to players in which there was a stereotypical solution. The results indicated that players tended to choose stereotypical solutions, even when shorter – but uncommon – solutions were available. Obviously, using stereotypical methods creates the risk of developing cognitive rigidity. We shall take this issue up when dealing with rigidity of thought (Section 4.13).

The role of schemas has been identified in other domains as well. For example, in physics, experts' competency relies on the complexity and completeness of their schemas (Chi & Glaser, 1985). The rules they contain not only allow problem-solving procedures to be mapped onto the superficial cues provided by the problem description but also to be understood in terms of basic physics principles.

The relationship between expertise, problem solving and conceptual knowledge is far from being straightforward, which might suggest limits in what can be inferred from verbal protocols. When chess masters provide commentaries for a game, they rarely provide a clear logical argument with neat and unambiguous concepts. What they do is to generate potential sequences of moves terminated by broad evaluations such as "White is better" and "White has counterplay". According to de Groot and Gobet (1996) this may be caused by the lack of suitable verbal terms for expressing chess concepts. It is also possible that we have here another example of encapsulation (see Section 3.8): a complex web of concepts linked by causal relationships summarised in just one term.

Specialisation effects in expertise

Physicians specialise in neurosurgery or paediatrics, and political scientists specialise in China's foreign policy or India's parliamentary system. While transfer is difficult between domains, as we shall see in a later chapter, is it easier between subspecialities within the same domain? Several studies have addressed this issue, typically comparing groups of individuals having the same level of expertise but specialising in different subfields. This approach has the advantage of controlling for the amount of experience and general level of expertise, while allowing one to study differences in types of knowledge. This *specialisation paradigm* has been used in medicine (Rikers et al., 2002), political science (Chiesi et al., 1979), and the design of experiments (Schunn & Anderson, 1999). The general conclusion of these studies is that experts employ general heuristics when they do not possess specific domain knowledge. While emphasising the role of general problem-solving methods, these studies also highlight the role of domain-specific patterns and methods, as some degree of expertise is clearly lost when domain-specific methods are replaced by domain-general ones.

Some of shortcomings of the studies used with the specialisation paradigm should be noted. Most studies used only one problem and not one problem from each field of specialisation, which would have made it possible to examine how experts solve a problem within and outside their subfield. Neutral problems were rarely used, although they would have been instrumental in teasing apart the specific effects of specialised knowledge. But perhaps the main weakness of these studies is that they could not measure the effect of expert specialisation, because expertise itself was not quantified.

Bilalić et al. (2009) rectified these weaknesses, and also compared individuals of different skill levels. They took advantage of several chess features: chess skill is precisely and quantitatively measured by the Elo rating; chess players enjoy trying to find the best move in a chess position; and chess players specialise in different openings (the first moves of a game), making it relatively easy to find players who have the same strength (as measured by their Elo points) but who have different, specialised, opening knowledge.

Bilalić et al. compared the performance of players who specialised in two different chess openings (half in the French Defence and the other half in the Sicilian Defence), in both a memory and problem-solving task. In addition to positions coming from these two types of defence, they also used neutral positions (positions difficult to classify with respect to the opening they came from). The players were candidate masters (with an average of 2,140 Elo), masters (2,300 Elo), and international masters/grandmasters (2,490 Elo). Both in the memory and problem-solving task, players outside their domain of specialisation performed about 200 Elo points (one standard deviation in skill) below their level with familiar positions. To put this in perspective, a grandmaster ($\approx$2,600 points) would perform at the level of an international master ($\approx$2,400 points) when dealing with positions outside his specialism. To put it another way, a player ranked #186 in the world would perform roughly like a player ranked #2,837 in the world – a considerable decrease in skill.

4.12 The Role of Representations

A correct representation can lead to substantial simplifications of a problem (Larkin & Simon, 1987), and experts' performance relies on their ability to represent problems adequately (Greeno & Simon, 1988). A crucial role of pattern recognition, beyond generating actions and suggesting strategies, is to enable the generation of suitable representations. Good representations offer at least four advantages (Simon, 1973): (a) they provide access to relevant knowledge while allowing flexibility in its use; (b) they enable the application of efficient search methods; (c) they make it possible to decompose problems into subproblems where specific solving techniques can be applied; finally, (d) they make it possible to coordinate several problem spaces that are *a priori* unconnected, something that is particularly important with ill-defined problems. The importance of correct representation is supported by data in a number of domains, including physics, medicine and economics (three topics we shall talk about in some detail in the next sections) and algebra (Paige & Simon, 1966). All these studies have used protocol analysis to identify the representations used by novices and experts.

4.12.1 Physics

In a previous section, we have already discussed one striking difference between novices and experts in physics. Novices tend to work backwards, starting from the goal, while experts tend to work forwards, starting from the data. Another important difference is that experts represent problems using fundamental principles in physics (e.g. the concept of force), whereas novices use superficial aspects (e.g. the kind of device involved, pulley vs. inclined plane) and can thus be easily fooled by irrelevant details in the way the problem is presented (e.g. Bhaskar & Simon, 1977; Chi et al., 1981; Larkin et al., 1980a, b; Simon & Simon, 1978). Unsurprisingly, these two results are linked: when fundamental principles are used, it is easier to generate unknown quantities from the givens as it is done in forward search. Expertise differences have also been documented with external representations. For example, physics experts are better at using diagrams to represent and solve problems (cf. Larkin & Simon, 1987) and at integrating their domain-specific knowledge with general reasoning methods (Greeno & Simon, 1988).

4.12.2 Economics

Economics is a particularly interesting domain for studying representations and especially diagrammatic representations, since diagrams play a central role in this field. Pick up any introductory textbook in economics, and you will find numerous diagrams of the sort shown in Figure 4.5 Studying economics in great part consists of learning how to interpret such diagrams and how they link to theories of classical economics.

Tabachnek-Schijf et al. (1997) argue for the importance of multiple representations in economics. For example, if we consider diagrammatic and verbal representations, these can both be used internally (diagrams are manipulated in the mind's eye and related to verbal information in the mind's ear) and externally (a diagram is drawn on the blackboard and its components are labelled with verbal terms). Altogether, this makes it possible for visual reasoning to be integrated with verbal reasoning.

Tabachnek-Schijf et al. (1997) provide empirical data supporting their claims. In one experiment, novice students in economics read an introduction to the theory of supply and demand. Thereafter, they must solve a problem related to this topic, such as finding the equilibrium point, and explain how the equilibrium is maintained when the supply curve is shifted to the right or the left. In addition to the verbal format used by the text, three different formats are used to present the data: graphics, such as in Figure 4.5, algebraic

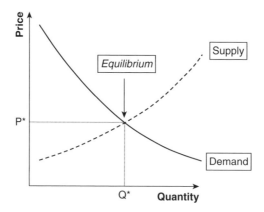

Figure 4.5   Example of the type of diagrams commonly found in economics textbooks to explain the concepts of supply, demand and equilibrium.

Source: Adapted from Cournot, A. A. (1838). *Recherches sur les principes mathématiques de la théorie des richesses.* Paris: Hachette.

equations and tables. In another experiment, students are asked to produce diagrams such as those used in the introductory text. Half of the students had seen the diagrams before, and the other half had not.

Verbal protocols recorded when participants attempt to solve the problems show that novices find it very difficult indeed to use diagrams as an aid to their reasoning. They find it even harder to generate such diagrams. By contrast, experts can integrate several representations smoothly and efficiently. As Tabachnek-Schijf et al. (1997, p. 335) put it, their economics expert "had, after long training and experience, distilled a model of supply and demand relations that exploits unique aspects of both graphical and verbal representations. Employing this model, he uses pictorial memory to draw relevant graph parts, to recognise significant graphical features and thereby drive forward the reasoning, and to reconstruct the record or summary of reasoning already accomplished that is embedded in the traces left on the blackboard. Verbal memory is used to supply causal reasoning, and verbal labels give semantic meaning to the various parts of the graph".

An interesting aspect of Tabachnek-Schijf et al.'s research is that they developed CaMeRa, a computational model that combines parallel mechanisms for handling low-level vision, a production system and a semantic network containing both verbal and pictorial information. The model also has a pictorial and a verbal STM. Just like a human expert, CaMeRa uses an external display in order to draw diagrams, reason about them, recognise features helping problem solving, and to refresh STM. While CaMeRa uses different kinds of representations for each modality, it is able to communicate efficiently between these representations. The presence of a running computer program shows that the theory developed by these authors contains detailed mechanisms and unambiguous concepts.

4.13 Automatisation and Rigidity of Thought

4.13.1 Automatisation

According to Fitts (1964), there are three stages in the acquisition of perceptual and motor behaviour. The *cognitive phase* is characterised by the learning of declarative rules through instruction, trial and error, and feedback; there is a conscious effort to acquire information and improve. In the *associative phase*, chains of responses are constructed by associating stimuli with responses, resulting in cognitive processes becoming more efficient; access to relevant information in the environment or in LTM is now quicker. In the *autonomous phase*, behaviour becomes autonomous and independent of cognitive control, that is, unconscious and automatic. Since little attention is required, it is possible to carry out several tasks in parallel. For example, an experienced driver can drive whilst conducting a conversation at the same time. The benefits yielded by this stage – behaviour is fluid and does not require attention – can also be accompanied by some cost: behaviour may be rigid and difficult to adjust when the demands of the environment change. Note that the fine-tuning observed during the second and third phase is in large part explained by practice and feedback.

4.13.2 Rigidity of Thought

Given that expertise relies on specialised knowledge, one consequence could be that, paradoxically, the more expert one is, the more rigid one's thoughts are. In this view, experts cannot adapt to novel types of problems, because their knowledge makes them unable to adopt new approaches. Thus, there should be cases where experts fail to solve problems that novices can solve. This view of experts' inflexibility is well summarised by Sternberg (1996): "…there are costs as well as benefits to expertise. One such cost is increased rigidity: The expert can become so entrenched in a point of view or a way of doing things that it becomes hard to see things differently" (p. 347). A similar view has been expressed with respect to the relationship between expertise and creativity, where there seems to exist a similar tension between possessing knowledge (expertise) and being able to generate novel ideas or methods (Csikszentmihalyi, 1996; Frensch & Sternberg, 1989; Sternberg, 1996). As creativity trainer de Bono (1968, p. 228) puts it: "Too much experience within a field may restrict creativity because you know so well how things *should be done* that you might be unable to escape to come up with new ideas". We shall see that these descriptions do not fit reality.

Let us start with some of the several studies that seem to illustrate experts' inflexibility. Frensch and Sternberg (1989, 1991) created a new card game by changing the rules of bridge. When the new game was played against a computer, bridge experts did better than novices. However, experts had more difficulties adapting to deep structural changes than novices, while the latter were more affected by perceptual changes. According to Frensch and Sternberg, the procedures that experts had automatised during their career hampered the acquisition of new ones.

In a classic study about what is now called the water-level task, Piaget and Inhelder (1956) demonstrated that surprisingly few people appreciate that the surface of a liquid should remain horizontal when the container holding it is tilted. Even more surprisingly, Hecht and Proffitt (1995) showed that waitresses and bartenders, despite their vast experience with serving drinks, were even less accurate than a comparison group in judging the angle of the surface of the drinks.

A final example of presumed inflexibility due to knowledge is offered by Wiley (1998), who used a version of Mednick's (1962) Remote Associates Test (RAT), a test of creativity (see Section 6.4.2). His participants were baseball experts and novices. When baseball knowledge suggested incorrect answers, experts performed worse than novices. Apparently, experts' knowledge of baseball created a mind-set that interfered with their search for suitable associations.

While these three studies show that experience can generate inflexibility, do they really show that experts are inflexible? Bilalić et al. (2008c) argue that they do not, because in these experiments the tested skill was taken from a different domain from the one in which experts excel. Modifying the rules of bridge generates a new card game: there is no reason why bridge experts should shine in the new game. Waitresses and bartenders are experts in serving drinks, not in Piaget and Inhelder's water-level task. They use a problem representation optimised for the skill they are paid for: not spilling the drinks they are bringing to customers. Individuals who have more baseball knowledge are not experts in Mednick's RAT. Thus, it is difficult to draw conclusions about the impact of experts' knowledge on their mental flexibility from these studies, as inflexibility was tested when experts moved to a domain different from that in which knowledge was acquired.

As noted above, Bilalić and colleagues (2008b, c; 2010) have studied this issue in a series of experiments where they tried to induce an *Einstellung* (mind-set) effect with chess players. Compared to the studies we have just discussed, the key difference is that inflexibility is tested within the original domain of expertise.

The Einstellung effect can be summarised as follows: the first idea that comes to the mind, cued by the known characteristics of the problem, blocks better ideas. The first study experimentally inducing the Einstellung effect was carried out by Luchins (1942) with the water-jug problem, a simple arithmetic task. Luchins trained participants to solve a sequence of problems that all had the same solution. When faced with a new type of problem that allowed both the old familiar method and a novel solution that was quicker, participants nearly always used the old method. When faced with critical problems that could be solved only with a novel method, participants failed to solve the problem, because they stuck to the old method. This failure cannot be explained by the difficulty of the problems, because a control group that was not exposed to the training problems could find the correct solution easily.

Bilalić and colleagues created chess positions that have two solutions: a familiar but non-optimal solution, and an unfamiliar but optimal solution. Just like in Luchins's experiment, they found that players tended to select the familiar but non-optimal solution. In fact, when asked to find another, better solution, players had great difficulty finding it. By contrast, players who saw positions that had only the unfamiliar solution did not show any difficulty in finding it. These authors also found that the Einstellung effect is present with strong, professional players, but that, importantly, the effect diminishes as the skill level increases. These results show that Sternberg (1996) was wrong: expertise does not make thinking more rigid, it makes it *less* rigid.

What is the mechanism behind the Einstellung effect? Bilalić and colleagues (2008c) used eye movement recordings to provide an answer. After having found the familiar solution, players – candidate masters – were requested to find a better one; all players said they did so. However, contrary to their statements, the eye movements showed that players kept fixating on the squares that were relevant for the familiar solution they had just found. It seems that the schema linked to the first, familiar solution, which was elicited by the familiar aspects of the board position, took control of attention so that players kept focusing on this first solution. Bilalić and colleagues argue that this mechanism is general and that it explains phenomena such as the confirmation bias shown in many experiments (e.g. Nickerson, 1998) and the tendency shown by scientists to ignore results that refute the predictions of their favourite theory. We leave it as an exercise to the reader to identify the passages of this book that fit the Einstellung effect!

4.14 Theories of Problem Solving

4.14.1 The Selz-de Groot Framework

It is now time to take stock and review some of the numerous theories developed to explain the data on expert problem solving. As before, we start with de Groot (1965). In his chess study, de Groot used the framework of productive thinking developed by Otto Selz (Frijda & de Groot, 1981; Selz, 1922), where thinking is considered as a linear chain of operations. Consistent with this framework, players often used a hierarchy of subsidiary methods. The framework turned out to be suitable to describe the structure of the verbal protocols he collected, and was also suitable to describe key aspects of these protocols, such as the problem-solving methods, the heuristics and strategies used, as well as the three phases of problem solving that he observed. Yet, contrary to the predictions of Selz's theory, there were no clear skill differences in the *structure* of thought. Rather, it was the *contents* of thought that mattered. Another limit of the framework used by de Groot is that it was essentially descriptive and that it did not provide mechanisms to account for players' behaviour, nor did it provide explanations for learning.

4.14.2 Newell and Simon's Problem-Space Theory

In Newell and Simon's (1972) theory, a *problem space* consists of the discrete states of a problem. One moves from one state to another using operators (e.g. rules of a game). The *external problem space* is obtained by an objective analysis of a problem (see Figure 4.2 at the beginning of the chapter), where all the possible states are listed. The *internal problem space* consists of the space that a particular individual has constructed (see Figure 4.3), which typically is only a small subset of the external problem space.

As we shall see in Chapter 6, the concept of a problem space elegantly links problem solving and creativity. The key idea is that the same mechanisms are used for creativity as for problem solving, although the problem spaces characterising creativity are larger and less defined than those used in problem-solving tasks.

Problem-space theory is very abstract, and can be seen more as a theoretical framework than as a specific theory able to make clear-cut predictions. In particular, whilst it says something about the structure of search, it does not say anything about the content of thought when search is carried out. However, as we have seen with de Groot's results, understanding the content of thought is essential to understand expert behaviour (see also Saariluoma, 1995). The theories discussed in the next section fill in this gap.

4.14.3 Chunking Theory and Template Theory

As we have seen, Simon and Chase's (1973) chunking theory, originally developed to explain perception and memory in chess, was also applied to problem solving. The key insight was to propose that chunks act as conditions of productions. Thus, recognising a chunk in the environment gives access to LTM information linked to possible actions, which vastly simplifies the selection of a move. In addition, the recursive recognition of patterns in the mind's eye, which elicits additional information, makes it possible to carry out searches mentally. These mechanisms account for several empirical results rather directly, including experts' tendency to follow stereotyped behaviour in routine problems (Bilalić et al., 2008b, c; Saariluoma, 1992), the importance of forward search and selective search, in particular with experts (de Groot, 1965; Larkin et al., 1980a), and the necessity even for experts to conduct progressive deepening, given humans' limited STM and their slow learning rates.

The chunking theory also accounts for the fact that experts rapidly find the solution to routine problems by recognising patterns, while novices do not have enough knowledge to do so and thus must carry out slower and more error-prone searches using heuristics. According to Chase and Simon, the rapid understanding shown by experts – intuition – can be fully explained by pattern recognition. When problems are more complex, it is unlikely, even for experts, that identical or even similar problems have been met in the past and have led to the learning of a solution; then, recognition of patterns is not sufficient and problem solvers fall back on the use of heuristic and search through the problem space. Finally, the recognition mechanisms proposed by chunking theory also account for the fact that experts use their knowledge to accurately and rapidly evaluate situations.

These comments on chunking theory also apply to template theory, but the presence of templates accounts for additional phenomena linked to problem solving. These include (a) the type of macro-search carried out in many domains, including chess, where individuals reason from one typical situation to another without explicit mention of the operators (sequence of moves, in chess; Charness, 1981b; Saariluoma & Hohlfeld, 1994); (b) the fact that experts often use larger knowledge structures than chunks (Cooke et al., 1993;

de Groot & Gobet, 1996); and (c) the holistic character of experts' intuition, an issue we shall return to in the chapter on intuition, insight and creativity.

4.14.4 Holding's Theory

The theory developed by Holding (1985, 1992) is worth mentioning, since it takes a position almost opposite to chunking theory. While Chase and Simon emphasised the role of pattern recognition and de-emphasised – without ignoring it – the role of look-ahead search, Holding argued that skill in chess is essentially search, made possible by knowledge and evaluation skills. The way humans search is then not dissimilar to what computers do: "the model simply postulates a tree of move judgments" (Holding, 1985, p. 247). The theory uses ideas from research into problem solving, but does not make clear-cut predictions since it is insufficiently specified. Incidentally, similar weaknesses affect long-term working-memory theory (Ericsson & Kintsch, 1995), which has also been used to account for expert problem solving.

4.14.5 Computer Models of Human Search

This section reviews several models of human search in chess that have been implemented as computer programs. Beyond chess, these models help us understand central aspects of skilled problem solving and decision making. We consider models without learning first and then models where some kind of learning has been implemented.

4.14.5.1 NSS and MATER

Using simulation programs, Simon explored several aspects of human problem-solving behaviour and in particular how heuristics are used during problem solving. Two programs capture the idea of selective search, an essential aspect of expert problem solving. With NSS (Newell et al., 1958a; Newell & Simon, 1972), one of the first chess programs, search is directed by a set of goals, such as controlling the centre and maintaining material balance. Using these goals, two move generators operate independently. The first generates base moves and the second generates moves that occur later in a branch; additional procedures evaluate the acceptability of a move. An important contribution of the program is to implement the mechanism of *satisficing* (Simon, 1955; 1956): the first moves that reach a value above a given threshold is selected. NSS showed that reasonable moves can be found with small search trees (around 100 nodes) and thus highly selective search, but it played only weak chess.

MATER, the program developed by Baylor and Simon (1966), also chose moves after limited search. It used a subclass of chess positions, where white can checkmate in a few moves. The key heuristic was to restrict search to forced moves and to variations where the opponent had only few responses. While MATER was successful with checkmate combinations, this heuristic is much less powerful with chess positions in general, and thus MATER's simulations were confined to that domain.

4.14.5.2 PERCEIVER

Based amongst other things on the initial (first 5 seconds) eye movements of a player trying to find a move[4], Tikhomirov and Poznyanskaya (1966) argued that chess players' early perception cannot be explained by the kind of information-processing theories used for example in NSS and MATER, since these cannot explain the holistic nature of human perception. To counter this argument, Simon and Barenfeld (1969) wrote a program called PERCEIVER that simulated eye movements and compared its behaviour to the data used by Tikhomirov and Poznyanskaya. The simulation program contained routines taken from MATER (see previous section) that stipulated chess relations between pieces (A is attacking B, A is defending B, A is attacked by B, and A is defended by B). PERCEIVER's simulated eye movements corresponded relatively well to the human data. Simon and Barenfeld argued that the simulations corroborated their two main assumptions: (a) the information that is gathered during the first few seconds of looking at the board concerns chess relations either between pieces (typically pairs of pieces) or between pieces and squares; and (b) when a piece A is fixated on and a chess relation is noticed in peripheral vision that connects piece A with another piece B, the next fixation may either remain on A or be directed to B. Note that the eye movements in a problem-solving situation differ from those in a recall task, in particular due to the large presence of relations of attack and defence in the former case. For Simon and Barenfeld, these results demonstrated that the same elementary information-processing mechanisms used for problem solving can account for perceptual processing, at least at the level of attention.

4.14.5.3 Connectionist models

In the 1980s and 1990s, there was a huge interest in connectionist models as a means to account for all sorts of phenomena in psychology. Authors such as Dreyfus and Dreyfus (1988), and Holyoak (1991) argued that connectionism offered a better formalism than the kind of models using symbolic processing (such as MATER and PERCEIVER) to account for expert behaviour, including the way they solve problems. However, the contribution of connectionism to the understanding of expert problem solving has been extremely disappointing, as very few models were actually developed. Two rare examples are the programs

---

[4] The position was taken from a game that the participant had just finished. So the position was not totally novel to him, which renders the interpretation of the data more difficult.

developed by Raufaste et al. (1998), who were interested in the way experts generate pertinent hypotheses in radiological diagnosis, and by Glöckner et al. (2012), who used eye-movement measures to predict what action was chosen by handball players. Thus, it seems that connectionism is better suited to account for perception and memory than for problem solving and decision making.

4.14.5.4 CHUMP and SEARCH

None of the simulation programs just discussed included the recognition-association mechanism central in chunking theory. This lacuna was corrected by CHUMP (CHUnks and Move Patterns; Gobet & Jansen, 1994), which implements Chase and Simon's idea that chunks acts as conditions of productions. The program extends CHREST (see previous chapter) and selects moves by pure pattern recognition, without carrying out search. The program acquires knowledge by scanning a large number of master-level games, learning chunks and templates, and associating moves or sequences of moves to chunks whenever possible.

When a pattern on the board is recognised as a chunk, a move or a sequence of moves is elicited. Conflict resolution rules deal with the cases where the same chunk is attached to several moves or where several chunks are recognised. While CHUMP shows that pattern recognition works in practice, the absence of a search mechanism had the consequence that its playing ability was rather limited. Interestingly, CHUMP seems to fare better in awele (Gobet, 2009) and in Go (Bossomaier et al., 2012), perhaps because the search space is much smaller than chess in the former case and the game has a strategic character in the latter.

The integration of pattern recognition and search was realised in SEARCH (Gobet, 1997b), an abstract and probabilistic model implementing template theory. The model does not play chess but computes, as a function of the number of chunks and templates, a number of behavioural measures (e.g. depth of search, rate of moves generated per minute and the level of fuzziness in the mind's eye). Moves are generated in two ways: either through heuristics or automatically because they are linked to chunks and templates. The first mechanism is assumed to be much slower than the second. The evaluation of a position at the end of an episode (a sequence of moves) is also done either through heuristics or automatically. Three conditions determine when an episode is ended: an evaluation has been proposed; the level of fuzziness in the mind's eye has reached its limit; or no move has been generated. See Figure 4.6 for a flowchart of SEARCH.

Every cognitive operation in SEARCH has a time cost. For example, it takes 2 seconds to carry out a move in the mind's eye and 10 seconds to compute an evaluation using a heuristic. The model also makes a few assumptions about how rapidly information in the mind's eye decays; the more the information decays, the harder it is to search. Templates facilitate search in three ways: they make it possible for information to be stored in LTM rapidly; they allow search to be carried out in the template space in addition to the move space; and they

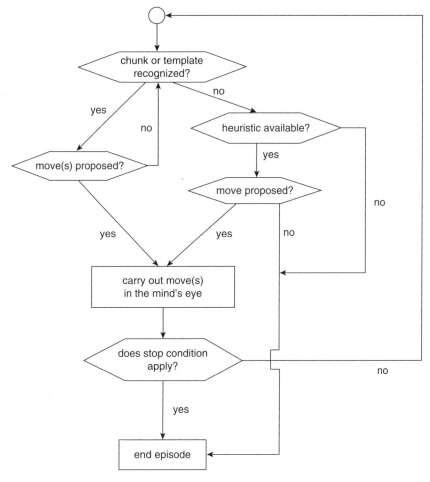

Figure 4.6   Flowchart of SEARCH.

Source: From Gobet, F. (1997b). A pattern-recognition theory of search in expert problem solving. *Thinking and Reasoning, 3*, 291–313. Adapted with kind permission from Routledge, www.tandfonline.com

compensate for the loss of information in the mind's eye that has occurred because of interference and decay.

The program makes a few interesting predictions. With skill level as an independent variable, depth of search should follow a power law. This was not an obvious prediction when it was made, because most researchers agreed with Charness's (1981a) proposal that, after a rapid increase, depth of search stays constant at high levels of skill. (With a power law, there is still some increase.) However, as we have seen in Section 4.5, SEARCH's prediction is correct. The program also predicts substantial variability in depth of search, in particular when simulations are carried out with a small number of runs.

As shown by Gobet (1997b), this is consistent with the empirical data; for example, Saariluoma (1990) found that weaker masters searched more than international masters and grandmasters.

4.15 Chapter Summary

Starting with the ground-breaking research by de Groot, this chapter has (partly) reviewed the considerable research on expert problem solving. Some key phenomena were identified. First, unless the problem is particularly complex or unfamiliar, the structure of search does not differentiate clearly between top experts and average experts. Second, progressive deepening is a ubiquitous method when solving problems, but there are skill differences. Experts tend to reinvestigate the same solution immediately more often than non-experts, who tend to consider different options before returning to a particular solution. Third, search is highly selective. With experts, this is made possible by the efficacy of pattern recognition and the presence of heuristics, while with non-experts heuristics dominate. Fourth, in many domains, experts tend to carry out forward search, while novices tend to carry out backward search. Fifth, experts are better at selecting useful representations, planning and evaluating outcomes than non-experts. Sixth, in most domains expertise is made possible by an interaction between pattern recognition and search, which is supplemented by high-level, schematic knowledge. Among the theories reviewed in this chapter, some emphasise search while others emphasise the role of perception and pattern recognition. A limit of several theories is that they lack specificity and are thus difficult to test empirically. By contrast, several simulation programs have been developed, which emphasise pattern recognition and search to various extents. Models based on chunking and template theory, such as SEARCH, have the advantage that they seamlessly link the literature on perception, memory and problem solving. Several of the concepts discussed in this chapter will be taken up in Chapter 6 on intuition, insight and creativity.

4.16 Further Reading

De Groot (1965) is of course the big classic in the field of expert problem solving, and an inexhaustible source of ideas. Holding (1985) argues that search plays the central role in (chess) expertise and that pattern recognition is of little importance; although Holding's case is too extreme, the book is an interesting read. Newell and Simon (1972) present their theory of problem solving in great detail, with many verbal protocols painstakingly analysed. Simon's (1979, 1989) two volumes of *Models of Thought* contain several papers linking expertise and problem solving.

CHAPTER 5

Decision Making

5.1 Preview of Chapter

A common assumption in the social sciences, in particular economics, is that humans are fully rational: they have unlimited access to information and unlimited computational resources. Against this assumption, Herbert Simon proposed the idea of bounded rationality: humans are rational within the stringent limits imposed by their cognitive system. Research into expertise throws important light on this issue: to what extent can experts assuage the constraints imposed by bounded rationality and reach full, or at least approximate, rationality? A variation of Simon's bounded rationality theory is Kahneman and Tversky's approach, which focuses on heuristics and biases. Again, expertise illuminates aspects of this approach. Heuristics also play an important role in two alternative theories, the fast and frugal heuristics theory and naturalistic decision making. The chapter will discuss these different views of rationality in turn. Anticipating some of the topics of Chapter 11 on the social aspects of expertise, the current chapter then discusses the conditions under which expertise in decision making fails. Finally, the chapter discusses decision making in sports.

5.2 Rationality and Bounded Rationality

A key assumption in economics and related fields is that individuals are perfectly rational agents who maximise utility. In other words, their decisions are consistent with the rules of logic, probability and mathematical optimisation and they have full access to the information required to make such decisions. Simon (1955, 1956) strongly criticised this hypothesis of perfect rationality and instead argued that humans' rationality is bounded. Maximisation is simply impossible in most decision-making situations encountered in real life, for two reasons. First, the environment is too complex to enable full access to information; second, as we have already seen in previous chapters, a number of limitations hamper the human cognitive system. Rather than maximising utility, people *satisfice*: they choose a good enough option, but not necessarily the best one. That is, they use an adequacy criterion to decide whether an option is satisfactory, and the first option that meets this criterion is chosen.

Thus, in human decision making, not all available options are evaluated and no full cost-benefit analysis of the possible alternatives is carried out – this is simply impossible in most situations. Rather, decisions are made with small amounts of computation and using only a small subset of the theoretically available information.

An important aspect of Simon's theory, which is in sharp contrast with mainstream economic theory, is that aspiration levels used to select a criterion are not fixed but vary according to a number of factors. These include the structure of the environment, the demands of the task being performed, the current state of search (Has search progressed rapidly or slowly? How much information has been gained so far?) and, most importantly for our discussion, the decision maker's level of expertise.

Bounded rationality has set the scene for two research traditions that include research on expertise. We have already discussed the first tradition at length in the previous chapters; its aim is to understand, through experiments and computer simulations, the detail of the cognitive processes used by humans when they make decisions. The second research tradition was inspired by Edwards (1954), who introduced decision theories to psychology. Its aim is to discover, through experiments in the laboratory and the field involving relatively simple decision-making situations, whether people behave as predicted by *expected utility* theory. According to this theory, people should consider all options, combine their value and probability, and choose the best one. Its best-known output is the work carried out by Tversky and Kahneman, which led to the now vibrant field of behavioural economics.

According to Campitelli and Gobet (2010), Simon made three key recommendations for the study of decision making. First, before imposing formalisms such as logic or statistics, actual decision making should be studied experimentally. Second, understanding decision making requires studying both the environment and the decision maker, including her knowledge or expertise. Third, formal computational models should be developed in tandem with the collection of empirical data, and close comparisons should be carried out between the predictions of these models and actual human behaviour. While the field of problem solving has taken up these recommendations, as has been illustrated in the previous chapter, they have been largely ignored in the field of decision making. This, in part, explains why there has been little interaction between these two fields.

5.3 The Heuristics and Biases Approach

Kahneman and Tversky's numerous experiments on decision making and judgement under uncertainty and risk were aimed at testing theories of perfect rationality (e.g. Kahneman et al., 1982; Tversky & Kahneman, 1974). They were able to show many ways in which people systematically diverge from what would be expected by these theories. An important finding in this respect is that changes to irrelevant features of the options or the outcomes of these options can affect preferences strongly. For example, the way in which information is presented affects the decisions made (McNeil et al., 1982; Tversky & Kahneman, 1981) – a phenomenon called the *framing effect*.

In line with Simon's views, Kahneman and Tversky suggested that people use a number of heuristics to reduce, or even avoid, the complex tasks of calculating probabilities and expected values. These heuristics are useful most of the time; however, in some circumstances, they can lead to critical and systematic errors or biases. This is consistent with results from other areas of research interested in rationality, in particular, research on logical reasoning and probabilistic reasoning. The solutions chosen by humans are not the optimal and rational solutions predicted by normative models.

A weakness of the kind of bounded rationality proposed by Tversky and Kahneman is that it seems to assume that human cognition is, to a large extent, fixed. There are few references, if any, to the large literature on expertise research showing that individuals have the capacity to massively improve their performance, up to the level of an expert, by acquiring better heuristics and other kinds of knowledge.

5.4 Biases in Experts

Biases can also be observed with experts. Tetlock (2005) showed that political science experts are prone to hindsight bias, overconfidence, illusion of consistency and belief perseverance. Consider the example of hindsight bias. In the 1980s, Tetlock asked experts in politics to make a number of predictions, including the likelihood that the Soviet Union would collapse. Several years later, they were asked to recall their predictions. The experts were systematically wrong in their recall and thought that they had rated the actual outcome much higher than they actually did. The differences in likelihood were large: between 0.10 and 0.15 on average, and always confirmed what actually happened. Thus, an expert having originally given a 0.40 chance to a collapse of the Soviet Union thought, years later, that he had given a 0.55 chance. We will take up Tetlock's research in more detail in Chapter 11.

Research into medicine has found that experts tend to suffer from the same biases as non-experts. For example, Dawson et al. (1988) have shown that both less experienced and more experienced physicians succumbed to the hindsight bias: knowing the correct diagnosis led to an overestimation of the probability that the correct diagnosis was made when the case was first shown. Interestingly, the more experienced physicians only fell prey to the bias with easy cases, whilst the bias was always present with less experienced physicians. Another example concerns the neglect of base rates. It is widely accepted in the clinical literature that head injuries are commonly followed by a number of subjective, cognitive, physical and psychological symptoms; however, this conclusion does not take into account base rates. In fact, when Gouvier et al. (1988) compared the rate of reporting such symptoms between head-injured individuals, relatives of head-injured individuals, uninjured individuals and relatives of uninjured individuals, they found no differences between the four groups. In order to interpret data on patients' symptoms, it is necessary to establish base rates for these symptoms in non-clinical populations, but this is not always done.

Another domain where experts suffer from biases is forensic identification (e.g. analysis of fingerprints from a crime scene). In many cases, the available evidence is noisy and incomplete, which makes the analysis difficult. Focusing on fingerprinting, Dror and colleagues (Dror & Rosenthal, 2008; Dror & Cole, 2010) found that, in particular with "hard-to-call" evidence, experts were not reliable, since they reached different conclusions with the same fingerprints but in different contexts (e.g. whether the conclusion reached by an international expert was provided or not). Decision making was affected by motivation, emotions and expectations, and different experts were affected to different degrees by these factors.

Scientists themselves are not immune to the deleterious effects of cognitive biases. Focusing on psychologists, MacCoun (1998) discusses how motivational and cognitive biases affect the way scientists interpret and use empirical data. MacCoun argues that while some of these biases are scientifically defensible (e.g. championing a theory with imperfect and limited evidence, taking an advocacy role), most biases (e.g. assuming that correlation implies causation, using incorrect deductive syllogisms or appealing to a researcher's reputation) affect the quality of the research being carried out.

In some cases, expertise does help to reduce bias. We have seen earlier that chess grandmasters were less prone to the Einstellung effect than weaker players. Similarly, research into auditing (Smith & Kida, 1991) has shown that experts succumb to biases (e.g. base-rate neglect, inattention to sample size and negligence of source reliability) less frequently than students. When present with experts, the biases tended to be different (e.g. anchoring heuristic). In some cases, biases found with the student population were absent with professional auditors (e.g. confirmatory bias in information search and recall).

5.5 Fast and Frugal Heuristics

Gigerenzer and Goldstein (1996) note that cognitive psychologists have mostly focused on decision makers' cognitive limitations but have not paid much attention to the extent to which individuals are adapted to the environment. In particular, they take exception with Tversky and

Kahneman's method for testing human rationality, which uses unrealistic and non-ecological stimuli that ignore the properties of the environment. But humans adapt very well to their environment. Thus, in order to study rationality, one should use real-world stimuli that are representative of those normally used by people. This approach has led to the emphasis on *fast and frugal heuristics*: strategies for decision making that do not involve much searching for information or computation (Gigerenzer et al., 1999). Fast and frugal heuristics include (a) a search rule that stipulates how information is searched for, (b) a stopping rule that specifies when search is stopped and (c) a decision rule that prescribes how the information that has been found is integrated and used to make a decision.

Some research on fast and frugal heuristics has been carried out with experts (Gigerenzer, 1996; Hoffrage et al., 2000). However, according to Campitelli and Gobet (2010), a limit of this approach is that, while ecological environments are used, they are not systematically varied. Therefore, the presumed importance of fast and frugal heuristics could be an artefact of the limited range of tasks that have been studied in this approach. People use more than fast and frugal heuristics when making decisions, in particular when they are experts. In fact, the considerable amount of data reviewed in the previous chapter points to two essential conclusions: (a) in addition to fast and frugal heuristics, people use more sophisticated heuristics and (b) in addition to heuristics, people use other mechanisms, most importantly pattern recognition and search. Thus, the fast and frugal heuristics hypothesis seems too simple an account of decision making and expert decision making in particular. The empirical evidence suggests that using fast and frugal heuristics is sometimes, but not always adaptive, and there are cases where slower search behaviour is more adaptive. A difference between novices and experts, however, is that the former rigidly use frugal heuristics, since they have no other choice, while the latter have a larger repertoire of methods, including slow and fast heuristics among others (Campitelli & Gobet, 2010).

5.6 Naturalistic Decision Making

The naturalistic decision-making approach (Klein et al., 1993; Klein, 1989; 1998) consists of studying real-world decision-making behaviour, in particular, decisions made by experts under time pressure. Domains include fire-fighters battling a blaze, soldiers in combat and chess players playing speed chess. In all these domains, experts make decisions that are good enough in a matter of seconds. Some of the evidence we will present when discussing intuition (Section 6.2) comes from this line of research. Klein (1998) argues that, in certain situations, experts consider just *one* course of action, which they then carry out. Obviously, this is inconsistent with expected utility theory.

When expertise falters

In some domains, experts do not perform well; a well-known example is diagnosis in clinical psychology and psychiatry. In his classic book *Clinical vs. Statistical Prediction*, Meehl (1954) shows that simple mathematical models provide better diagnoses than clinical psychologists and psychiatrists. More recent research confirms these findings. In a meta-analysis of 136 studies (Grove et al., 2000), the algorithmic predictions obtained better results than predictions based on clinical judgement in more than one third of the studies (between 33 per cent and 47 per cent of studies, depending on the type of analysis done). Similar results were found by Hammond (1955), in a study where clinical psychologists used responses in the Rorschach test to estimate the IQ (intelligence quotient) of a group of people. (IQ was independently measured by the Weschler-Bellevue test.) Again, the finding was that professionals' judgement could be predicted using a simple multiple-regression model.

Are these results surprising? Not necessarily. They simply indicate that, in these domains, it is difficult to combine in one's head a large number of variables, while this can be done easily with mathematical or computational methods. In addition, clinical diagnosis is a domain where it is difficult to learn the relationship between symptoms and other cues, since the data are noisy and feedback is both rare and delayed. Interestingly, Meehl's (1954) and Grove et al.'s (2000) work did not seem to have much impact on the kind of methods used in clinical diagnosis, as clinicians still prefer subjective methods to mathematical ones.

Other domains where it is difficult to learn predictive patterns and where experts do not perform well have been singled out in the literature. Just like clinical diagnosis, these domains tend to be unpredictable, or at least difficult to predict, and lack immediate feedback. They include prediction in the stock market (Cowles, 1944), judges' decisions (Ebbesen & Konecni, 1975), probation officers' recommendations (Carroll & Payne, 1976) and selection of future university students (Dawes, 1994).

Of course, in the same vein as Tversky and Kahneman's findings, the findings initiated by Meehl give a rather pessimistic view of humans: we are not rational. Even experts – who are expected to show high levels of rationality – cannot make reliable predictions.

Klein and colleagues (Klein, 1998; 2003; Zsambok & Klein, 1997) have developed a model of expertise that highlights the same features as Chase and Simon's (1973a) model: pattern recognition, selective search and the fact that experts, like non-experts, find satisfactory rather than optimal solutions.

In our opinion, Klein's (2003) view that experts do not make a choice but just execute the first option that comes to their mind is valid only for simple routine problems. Furthermore, this approach underestimates the amount of search that is being carried out with more difficult problems, in particular when decisions are high-stake and there is no time pressure.

5.7 The SOS Effect

In radiography and diagnostic imaging techniques such as MRI, many diagnosis errors are due to failures to detect an abnormality – "misses" account for around 50 per cent of radiologists' errors (Berbaum, 2012). A special case of expertise failure occurs when an abnormality is not identified because another abnormality has been previously reported. This phenomenon is called the satisfaction of search (SOS) effect, since search is assumed to stop because its goal has been satisfied by the discovery of the first anomaly. This effect cannot simply be explained by assuming that radiologists stop searching after finding an abnormality, as originally proposed by Tuddenham (1962). Berbaum et al. (1991, 1998) manipulated chest radiographs containing a native lesion by adding a simulated nodular lesion. They measured the total inspection time and the extent to which expert radiologists were able to detect the native lesion in both conditions (i.e. only native lesion or native plus added lesion). They found that, while the native lesion was more likely to be missed when another abnormality was added, the inspection time was the same in the two conditions, and that search behaviour (as revealed by eye movements) was similar in both cases. Thus, the SOS effect cannot be explained by search termination. It is worth noting that in a different type of diagnosis – radiographies of the abdomen – SOS is due to inefficient scanning behaviour (Berbaum et al., 1996).

What then produces the SOS effect? Berbaum (2012) proposes two explanations. First, the pool of perceptual resources that can be used for a given search is limited. Thus, when the image contains two abnormalities, there are fewer resources available for finding each compared to the case where only one abnormality is present. Second, finding the first abnormality creates a perceptual set: images are interpreted so that the diagnosis suggested by the first abnormality is supported. This has a twin effect: features consistent with the diagnosis are perceived and features that are consistent with different diagnoses are ignored. As you might recall, Bilalić et al. (2008b, c) proposed a similar mechanism in their chess study, which was supported by players' eye movements. Consistent with this explanation, providing the patient history, which presumably primes searching for several potential abnormalities and diagnoses, has been shown to increase the likelihood of detecting the native abnormality (Berbaum et al., 1993).

5.8 Shanteau's Framework

In an influential paper, Shanteau (1992a) notes that the literature on expertise offers two contradicting assessments. The research on judgement and decision making has emphasised the poor quality of experts' decisions. Their judgements have poor validity and reliability, are not well calibrated and do not use all relevant information. On the other hand, research in cognitive science emphasises that experts are not only competent but are vastly superior to novices in most aspects of cognitive functioning.

To explain these diverging conclusions, Shanteau argues that the two traditions have tended to look at different domains and tasks. Research in cognitive science has used tasks where experts outclass novices and that have the characteristics displayed in column 1 of Table 5.1. These domains concern experts such as weather forecasters, livestock judges, chess masters, physicists and accountants. By contrast, research in the tradition of judgement and decision making has focused on domains that have the characteristics of the second column of Table 5.1, domains in which experts perform poorly. Experts such as clinical psychologists, psychiatrists, court judges, behavioural researchers, parole officers, personnel selectors and astrologers belong to this category. Thus, the differences between the two traditions can be accounted for by the domains and tasks each has studied. Clearly, this indicates that the environment must be taken into consideration when trying to make sense of expertise.

Table 5.1   Quality of performance in experts as a function of task characteristics.

Good performance	Poor performance
Static stimuli	Dynamic (changeable) stimuli
Decisions about things	Decisions about behaviour
Experts agree on stimuli	Experts disagree on stimuli
More predictable problems	Less predictable problems
Some errors expected	Few errors expected
Repetitive tasks	Unique tasks
Feedback available	Feedback unavailable
Objective analysis available	Subjective analysis only
Problem decomposable	Problem not decomposable
Decision aids common	Decision aids rare

Source: From Shanteau, J. (1992a). Competence in experts: The role of task characteristics. *Organizational Behavior and Human Decision Processes*, 53, 252–266. Reproduced with kind permission from Elsevier.

5.9 Decision Making in Sports

In most sports, decisions are key to success: to whom should the ball be passed in football, when to attack in a Tour de France stage, or whether to use an offensive or defensive baseliner strategy in a tennis match. Decision making in sports has received a fair amount of attention in recent years, and interest has focused on two questions: the extent to which players use probabilities and how they select options.

5.9.1 Using Task-Specific Probabilities

In our discussion of perception, we have seen that athletes use perceptual cues and patterns (e.g. the position of the opponent's arm) to select actions. There is good evidence that the knowledge they have acquired about their sport also provides unconscious information about probabilities of different kinds: What are the chances of success for a difficult but unstoppable shot (e.g. a passing shot in tennis)? What are the chances that, in a team sport, the player directly facing you will run to the left rather than the right?

However, there is also clear evidence that players also use probabilities consciously and proactively, in particular when deciding what strategy to adopt. In doing so, they typically use past knowledge of how opponents played in previous games and their strengths and weaknesses. For example, in an experiment where baseball batters had to predict how the next pitch would be thrown, Paull and Glencross (1997) provided information about the progress of the game before half of the trials. Not only did both novice and expert batters improve their reaction time by 60 ms on average, but they also made better decisions than when no information was given beforehand. Similar results were obtained by McRobert et al. (2011) with cricket.

Alain and Proteau (1980) carried out a number of experiments where the role of probabilities was directly investigated, using decisions made by defending players in racket sports such as squash, tennis and badminton. In a real game situation, some rallies were filmed. Players were later shown the film and had to answer questions about their decisions, report the subjective probabilities they had about their opponent's shots, and estimate the probabilities of various possible actions. The results showed that players' anticipatory movements were informed by these probabilities. Based on this research, Alain and Sarrazin (1990) built a simulation model of decision making in squash. The key assumption of the model was that the defending player's strategy could be represented as a specific, preformed algorithm that is stored in LTM and activated depending on the information in STM. The model also suggested that the strategy of the player could be influenced by a number of factors, including the player's level of expertise, the presence of time pressure and the players' expectations. In related research, Ward and Williams (2003) showed film sequences of soccer where a player was about to pass the ball. The participants' task was to highlight the passing options that the player had, and their answers were compared to those of a group of expert coaches. The elite players were better than non-elite players at identifying players who were best located on the pitch and were more accurate in evaluating probabilities related to the level of threat posed by players.

5.9.2 Option Selection

We have seen in Sections 4.4 and 4.5 that a considerable amount of research has been devoted to the study of the structure of search in chess. Recently, researchers have studied this question in other domains as well, focusing on the issue of option generation – that is, how different possible courses of action are generated. Johnson and Raab (2003) studied handball players. Brief video clips of play were interrupted at a critical moment, when the player with the ball faced several possible actions (shooting, passing the ball to player A and so on). Participants were required to (a) highlight the first option that came to their mind; (b) report any other option they could think of; and (c) indicate their final choice. Johnson and Raab found a negative correlation between the quality of the final choice and the number of options generated: the players choosing better options generated fewer options. In addition, the option generated first by the better players, but not by the weaker players, tended to be the best. Johnson and Raab (2003, p. 218) proposed the *take-the-first* heuristic: "In familiar yet ill-defined tasks, choose one of the initial options generated once a goal (and strategy) has been defined, rather than exhaustively generating all possible options and subsequently processing them deliberatively".

Johnson and Raab's results, which were replicated and extended in a longitudinal study where eye movements were also recorded (Raab & Johnson, 2007), are in line with those found by Klein et al. (1995) in chess, and in general with the idea of selective search – a recurrent theme in this book. However, further research in sports has provided less support for the take-the-first heuristic. Ward and colleagues (2013) applied Johnson and Raab's paradigm to football. The participants' task was to predict what action the target player (a defender opposite to the team with the ball) would carry out next, with the three steps outlined earlier. As in previous studies, the better players selected better options than the weaker players and the better options tended to be highlighted first. However, contrary to the prediction made by the take-the-first heuristic, the number of high-quality options was correlated with the quality of the final selection. According to Ward and colleagues, better players are able to maintain a better representation of the situation in their mind, which allows them to generate more relevant options.

The take-the-first heuristic seems to suffer from the following artefact: if the best options are generated (perhaps through the pattern-recognition mechanisms discussed in the previous chapters), there is no need and no motivation to generate other options, hence the fewer number of options generated. To take an extreme example, once the answer "4" has been generated for the problem "2 + 2 = ?", no additional solution needs to be provided. In addition, under severe time pressure, there is simply no opportunity to generate options, so take-the-first becomes true by default. The reader is reminded of Gary Klein's proposal that experts under time pressure do not choose between options (even two options), they simply carry out the first satisfactory action.

How can we explain the differences between the results described by Johnson and Raab (2003) and Ward and colleagues (2013)? As noted by Ward et al. (2011), there are a number of methodological differences between the two studies: deciding upon actions for oneself or for another player; predicting an action or assessing the outcome of a play situation; different levels of complexity; and different presentation times. A sobering conclusion might be that option generation is not a diagnostic measure of expertise, since it is too sensitive to a variety of other factors.

5.10 Chapter Summary

This chapter on decision making has addressed one of the central questions in the social sciences: Are humans rational? The data clearly show that the assumption of full rationality – made, for example, by most theories in economics and by several theories in psychology – is simply untenable. Indeed, both novices and experts often display suboptimal behaviour, even when they are not under time pressure. In some domains, such as diagnosis in psychiatry and clinical psychology, even simple mathematical models perform better than experts. Several theories of bounded rationality were also discussed. Kahneman and Tversky's approach, which emphasises the role of heuristics and biases, is consistent with many empirical results. However, it is silent about the role of search and learning, which are essential for an understanding of expertise. Gigerenzer's framework, which emphasises fast and frugal heuristics, underestimates the role of pattern recognition and search in expertise and says little about the use of sophisticated heuristics. The best explanation is provided by Simon's theory of bounded rationality and Klein's theory of naturalistic decision making, although the latter underestimates the role of search with complex problems and no time pressure. According to Shanteau, why experts perform well in some domains but not in others can be accounted for by the task characteristics typical of each domain.

5.11 Further Reading

Klein (1998) presents an entertaining introduction to the naturalistic decision-making approach, and several edited books address more technical issues (e.g. Salas & Klein, 2001; Zsambok & Klein, 1997). Meehl (1954) is the classic critique of decision making in psychotherapy, and an updated discussion is provided by Dawes (1994). A friendly introduction to Kahneman and Tversky's research, with a discussion of expertise, is provided by Kahneman (2011). Gigerenzer and Gaissmaier (2011) present the fast-and-frugal-heuristic approach, with a discussion of its application to experts' decision making.

CHAPTER 6

Intuition, Insight and Creativity

6.1 Preview of Chapter

The unifying theme of this chapter can be summarised as follows: What *really* characterises experts' problem solving and decision making, when compared to non-experts? We will argue that at least three phenomena should be considered: intuition, insight and creativity. Intuition characterises the speed with which experts find solutions, with an ease that baffles the non-expert. Insight can be defined as the ingenious solution that a problem solver generates after having been stuck with a problem for a long time – be it minutes, days or months. Creativity concerns the production of novel and valuable ideas. Two themes that have dominated the previous chapters will also be central to this chapter: the role of pattern recognition and the description of problem solving as search through a problem space.

6.2 Expert Intuition

You know expert intuition when you see it: the uncanny speed with which experts find a solution to a problem, and the lack of introspection they have about the way they found it. A medical doctor diagnosing an illness, a mechanic spotting a fault in a car's engine or a philosopher having a deep, emotional certainty that a philosophical argument is wrong – all these are examples of intuition in action.

One of the first people to have investigated intuition scientifically is de Groot (1965) – the usual suspect. As we discussed earlier, de Groot found that strong grandmasters were able to understand a chess position and pick up its key features (e.g. strategic weakness suggesting a possible attack) *within seconds*. An early investigation into intuition was also provided by Polanyi (1958), whose term *connoisseurship* emphasised that skilled perception was a central component of expertise.

Since this early work, intuition has been scientifically documented in a number of domains. In physics, it has been argued that it is physical intuition that allows experts to construct a complex internal representation of a problem rapidly, combining several principles of physics (Larkin et al., 1980a; Simon & Simon, 1978). In nursing, intuition has been documented by substantial research

(Benner, 1984; Benner et al., 1996; McCormack, 1993; McCutcheon & Pincombe, 2001). For example, by picking up subtle differences in newborns' skin appearance, nurses can suspect metabolic complications that are missed by sophisticated medical equipment which does not indicate a problem (Klein, 2003). In business, executives typically make decisions rapidly, without a systematic evaluation of the different options available (Klein, 2003; Prietula & Simon, 1989). This behaviour actually contradicts what is taught in business schools, where the approach based on neoclassical economics is recommended: executives should evaluate all the possible options, compute their utilities and choose the option that maximises utility. Finally, intuition has been proposed as the experts' decision-making method of choice in situations characterised by time pressure, such as fire-fighters dealing with a blaze and soldiers reacting to an enemy's attack (Klein, 2003). Even expert burglars display features highly characteristic of intuition: automaticity, limited planning, selective search and reliance on perceptual cues (Nee & Meenaghan, 2006).

Current theories of expert intuition can be classified into two main headings: mechanistic (Chassy & Gobet, 2011a; Klein, 2003; Simon, 1995) and non-mechanistic theories (Benner, 1984; de Groot, 1986; Dreyfus & Dreyfus, 1988). We briefly describe three of them, using the list of five criteria proposed by Gobet and Chassy (2008b) for defining intuition: (a) rapid perception and understanding of the situation at hand, (b) lack of awareness of the processes involved, (c) holistic understanding of the problem situation, (d) the fact that experts' decisions are better than novices' and (e) concomitant presence of emotional "colouring".

6.2.1 Simon's Theory

Using ideas similar to those expressed in his chunking theory, Simon proposed that expert intuition can be accounted for by pattern recognition (Larkin et al., 1980a; Prietula & Simon, 1989; Simon, 1989; 1995). Over the long hours devoted to practice and study, experts acquire a large number of perceptual chunks, which encode the key features of the domain of expertise. For example, in medicine, chunks encode a constellation of symptoms, or, in chess, chunks encode groups of pieces. Additional information is also associated with some of the chunks, such as the general or particular action that should be carried out when a chunk is recognised. Thus, the acquisition of a large database of chunks associated with relevant knowledge explains the intuitive understanding and acting shown by experts. Experts access solutions automatically using their memory. In contrast, non-experts reach solutions, if they can at all, using slow and error-prone problem-solving methods. An important aspect of Simon's theory is that it assumes that experts suffer from the same cognitive limits as novices, such as narrow attention span and small STM capacity. Moreover, following de Groot (1965), the theory assumes that experts, for the most part, use the same problem-solving strategies as novices (e.g. means-end analysis or progressive deepening). These strategies aim to reduce the search space.

With respect to Gobet and Chassy's criteria, Simon's theory is successful with rapid perception and understanding, lack of awareness, and the fact that experts' decisions tend to be correct. The holistic nature of perception is not covered, and was in fact explicitly criticised in Simon's previous work (Simon & Barenfeld, 1969). The theory does not cover the link between emotions and intuition either.

6.2.2 Dreyfus and Dreyfus's Theory

Dreyfus and Dreyfus (1988; 2005) reject the sort of mechanistic explanations proposed by Simon and, instead, use phenomenology for explaining intuition. (Phenomenology is the part of philosophy that studies conscious experience using a first-person point of view.) Of human cognition, they stress its embodied, situated and experiential nature. Dreyfus and Dreyfus's approach is essentially descriptive, and there are few references to experimental evidence.

According to Dreyfus and Dreyfus (1988), there are five stages to becoming an expert. In the *novice stage*, information about domain-specific facts, features, rules and actions is acquired through instruction. The rules are context-free since they do not incorporate specific features of the environment. The second *advanced beginner stage* is reached only after substantial and concrete experience with the domain. The key difference with the previous stage consists in the use of context. *Situational elements* – elements that depend on the context – now become meaningful. In the third *competence stage*, behaviour becomes progressively more efficient: decision-making procedures are structured hierarchically but planning is still conscious and deliberate. It is only at the fourth *proficiency stage* that intuition appears. Now, individuals perceive some features as salient and ignore others. Decisions are still based on analytical thinking, but intuition starts to play an important role: problem situations are organised and understood intuitively. In the final *expertise stage*, both the understanding of a task and decision making is intuitive and fluid. To be precise, experts do not really solve problems or make decisions when they face typical situations: they simply execute the actions that normally work. Dreyfus and Dreyfus have speculated that the holistic nature of expert intuition could be simulated by connectionist models of associative memory (Hinton & Anderson, 1989), and that some aspects of the way experts learn could be accounted for by reinforcement learning (e.g. Tesauro, 1992).

Dreyfus and Dreyfus have also criticised standard explanations of expertise developed in cognitive psychology. Interestingly, however, their five-stage theory shares many features with these approaches, including Simon's theory that we have just presented. Specifically, the central tenet of their theory is that, as one becomes an expert, one progresses from conscious, analytic, and deliberate behaviour and reliance on instruction to behaviour that is intuitive, fluid and naturally aligned with the requirements of the environment; the parallel with Fitt's (1964) and Anderson's (1982) theory is obvious. Unique to Dreyfus and Dreyfus's approach, however, is its emphasis on the holistic nature of expert intuition.

The strength of Dreyfus and Dreyfus's theory is that it provides an account of experts' rapid perception and understanding, their lack of awareness of the processes involved, the superiority of experts' decisions to novices', and the holistic nature of intuition. However, the lack of detailed mechanisms is certainly a weakness of the theory. In addition, just like Simon's theory, Dreyfus and Dreyfus's theory does not say anything about the link between emotions and intuition. A particularly serious weakness concerns its neglect of the analytical aspects of expertise (e.g. search, planning), which we have documented at length in Chapter 4 and which play an important role in complex and novel problem situations. In sum, the theory is too simple to account for experts' intuition.

6.2.3 Template Theory of Intuition

Chassy and Gobet (2011a; Gobet & Chassy, 2008b; 2009) applied the template theory of expertise (see Section 3.11.4.2) to account for expert intuition. Since template theory is an extension of chunking theory, it inherits some of the ideas used in Simon's theory of intuition, namely: chunks, their links to suitable actions, the recognition of patterns and the hypothesis that experts suffer from the same cognitive limits as novices (limited attention span, slow learning rates and so on). Two additional strengths of this theory are that it links intuition to emotions by proposing that chunks and templates are associated to positive or negative emotions during learning, and that it makes a direct link with neuroscience.

In comparison to Simon's theory, the key addition is the idea that chunks which are used often in experts' practice develop into templates. Not only do templates enable rapid storage of new information in LTM, they also make it possible to "glue" together smaller chunks. Thus, one weakness of Simon's earlier account – the relatively small size of the chunks he hypothesised – is removed in the new theory. Since it combines relatively small chunks with large templates, Gobet and Chassy's theory shows that the holistic vs. non-holistic dichotomy is artificial. Holistic perception is incrementally constructed using smaller components, over years of interaction within a domain.

6.2.4 Too Much of a Good Thing?

There has recently been a lot of interest about intuition in general and expert intuition in particular. This is in part due to the popularity of *dual theories* in a number of fields including decision making, reasoning and social cognition, to cite just a few (Chaiken & Trope, 1999; Evans, 2003; Kahneman & Frederick,

2002). Dual theories postulate two systems: system 1 is rapid, unconscious, associative and intuitive, while system 2 is slow, conscious, sequential and deliberate. System 1 proposes intuitive answers, and system 2 decides to keep them or to override them using deliberate thinking. In dual theories, the two systems are independent and compete for controlling behaviour.

In our view, several authors have pushed the role of system 1 and intuition too far, to the detriment of system 2. We have already mentioned Dreyfus and Dreyfus (see Section 6.2.2), but there are numerous recent examples (e.g. Dijksterhuis et al., 2006; Gigerenzer, 2007). These authors propose, to different degrees, that system 1 is sufficient for producing good decisions or even that better decisions are produced when system 2 not engaged. The idea has also been taken up in the popular-science literature (Gladwell, 2007).

The aim of this short section is to remind the reader that the existence of intuition does not rule out look-ahead search, deliberation and other slower cognitive processes. The considerable evidence we have reviewed in Chapter 4 on search and other deliberate cognitive mechanisms clearly shows that these mechanisms are employed by experts. One of the characteristic features of experts is that they use strategies – either based on intuition or deliberation – adaptively and flexibly, while novices use them inflexibly. With simple problems or high time pressure, experts will rely on intuition. With complex problems and enough time to think, they will use a combination of intuition and deliberation.

On the other hand, a good case can be made that intuition pervades most thinking (de Groot, 1965). Perhaps the error of dual theories is to present the two systems as independent and competing. Another possibility is that they interact together closely. Such a proposal was made by Gobet (1997b), where the issue was phrased in terms of pattern recognition and search rather than system 1 and system 2. The central idea was that pattern recognition is applied recursively during search (i.e. after each new state is generated in the mind's eye, pattern recognition mechanisms are at work). In this case, intuition (pattern recognition) is essentially always at work, with or without look-ahead search.

6.3 Insight

Insight is related to intuition, with the important qualification that insight is preceded by an often lengthy and laborious search for a solution during which no solution comes to mind and few useful steps toward progress are taken. By contrast, intuition characterises a rapid solution immediately after the presentation of a problem. Both have in common the sudden realisation of a solution as well as the inability to explain how the solution came about. Insight emphasises the creative aspect of thought (De Groot & Gobet, 1996) and the need to generate the correct internal representation for a problem (Kaplan & Simon, 1990; Simon, 1995).

The problem solving associated with insight is infructuous and frustrating because a wrong representation has been used. This is actually the point of so-called insight puzzles: they provide cues that lead the problem solver to the wrong representation. As a simple example, consider the following puzzle (Knoblich et al., 1999). You are given an incorrect equation written in Roman numerals using matchsticks, and your task is to move only one matchstick to get a correct equation:

$$IV = III - I$$

Most people find this task hard, because they focus attention on the numbers in the equation. In fact, the solution requires using a different type of representation, where not only numbers can be changed by moving the matchsticks, but also the operators (minus, plus and equal signs). In our case, the solution is to move one matchstick from the equal sign (so it becomes a minus sign) to the minus sign (so it becomes an equal sign). The new equation is then $IV - III = I$. What makes this puzzle hard is that people normally attempt to solve it by tackling it in the wrong way. They create a problem space consisting only of numbers, which is the natural interpretation of the puzzle, while the solution requires using a problem space consisting of both numbers and operators. When this is done, the solution becomes simple, almost trivial.

Clearly, what is an insight problem to a novice might not be so for an expert, who can rely on his previous knowledge to retrieve the solution from memory. If you solve a few hundred matchstick problems, your new expertise in this (admittedly tiny) domain will allow you to solve these problems nearly instantaneously.

Scientific discovery has been characterised by Simon and others (e.g. Langley et al., 1987) as a heuristic search through a problem space. Routine problems can be solved by the use of previous knowledge, including heuristics. However, with some hard problems, the scientist might be "stuck" for several weeks, months or even years. Although the time frame is longer, this is the same as what happens to most people trying to solve insight puzzles: a laborious and unsuccessful search. The advantage available to experts is that they have acquired a number of heuristics that allow them to both search a problem space efficiently and change it to a new one. (They also have more patience, as creating a new problem space might take a few years.)

Numerous examples of insight can be found in the biographies of scientists and artists, as well as in books describing famous discoveries (e.g. Aczel, 1996; Gardner, 1993; Jacob, 1988; Watson, 1969). Insight can in part be explained by pattern recognition, and in part by search that is made more efficient by employing heuristics specialised in changing representations (Klahr & Simon, 1999; Richman et al., 1996; Simonton, 1999). These heuristics include: redefining the problem; exploring variations of partial solutions; relaxing the constraints of the problem; using symmetries; taking the contrary of some assumptions of well-known theories; using analogies; exploring one's knowledge in a playful way; brainstorming; and incorporating ideas from other domains. In addition, domain-specific heuristics are used.

6.4 Creativity

In many domains, being an expert requires being creative. This is the case, for example, in scientific research, where success is judged by the production of novel scientific theories and the discovery of new phenomena, and in the arts, where artists simply must be creative – or else, they are just critics or business people. Although the details have been subject to nourished discussion over the years, the main features of creativity are generally admitted: something must be produced that is novel, contains an element of surprise and has some value (Boden, 1990).

Creativity is notably difficult to study, for two main reasons. First, the criterion of "value" in the last paragraph's definition can be problematic; its meaning changes from place to place and from time to time. Andy Warhol was able to flourish in the democratic United States but probably would not have been able to do so in the communist Soviet Union. Albert Duchamp's iconoclastic approach to art worked perfectly at the beginning of the twentieth century but it is doubtful whether it would have had the same success during the Italian Renaissance when classicism was prevalent.

Second, highly creative acts are by definition very rare, and the likelihood of observing real creations in the laboratory is very small indeed. So researchers have used alternative ways to study this phenomenon: experiments with novices and experts, study of archival data (databases, biographies, historical records and so on), questionnaires with creative and less creative individuals, and mathematical and computer simulations. Overall, these studies have tried to infer or test general or *nomothetic* theories – that is, theories that apply to all humans. Contrasting with the approach, other studies have carried out an *idiographic* approach, where a creator is studied as a single case, without necessary generalising the findings to other individuals.

In the remainder of this chapter, we shall focus on the nomothetic approach, considering results based on the analysis of historical data, experimental results and computer simulations. This being said, we will also provide examples of creators, in the spirit of the idiographic approach. We first discuss the questions as to whether there is any agreement between experts about the quality of creative products and whether creativity can be measured by psychometric tests. We then consider factors predisposing the development of creativity. Finally, we discuss the main theories of human and artificial creativity.

6.4.1 Are Estimations of Creativity Reliable?

If there were wide disagreements in establishing who is a great creator and what has strong creative value, there would not be much point in studying creativity scientifically. Fortunately, empirical studies have found that there is at least reasonable agreement between experts. Most research has been interested in classical music composers, and we will thus focus on this domain. We consider four rankings of the best composers in history of classical music (see Table 6.1): Folgman (1933) asked members of four famous orchestras to rank 19 composers; Farnworth (1969) asked musicologists to rank 100 composers; and Moles (1968) ranked 250 composers as a function of performance frequency. To these formal sources, we have added an informal one. The site www.digitaldreamdoor.com/pages/best-classic-comp.html ranked 100 composers using as criteria: innovation, influence, aesthetic importance and historical significance. While there are differences between the four rankings, there is also considerable agreement. Beethoven was always ranked first or second, Mozart always appears in the first three places, Bach in the first five places, and Brahms, Wagner, Schubert and Haydn in the first ten places. Given that these rankings were made using different approaches and that more than 70 years separate the oldest and the newest, the agreement is actually quite impressive.

Table 6.1   Four rankings of classical composers. The brackets indicate that the rank was not among the top ten.

	Source			
	Folgman (1933)	Farnworth (1969)	Moles (1968)	digitaldreamdoor.com
Beethoven	1	2	2	1
Brahms	2	5	5	6
Mozart	3	3	1	2
Wagner	4	9	4	4
Bach	5	1	3	3
Schubert	6	8	6	7
Haydn	7	4	10	5
Debussy	8	7	(15)	(14)
Schumann	9	(14)	(11)	(11)
Mendelssohn	10	(20)	(14)	(13)
Handel		6	7	9
Chopin	(14)	10	(12)	(12)
Tchaikovsky	(11)	(21)	8	8
Verdi	(15)	(13)	9	(17)
Stravinsky	(12)	(44)	(21)	10

6.4.2 Tests of Creativity

There have been several attempts to develop psychometric tests using the idea that creativity consists of generating ideas in a fluid fashion. Among these attempts, we can mention four. Binet and Henri (1896) developed, with little success, a test for creativity consisting of generating the largest possible number of interpretations of an inkblot – a precursor of the Rorschach test. They also experimented with open-ended tasks such as producing words that rhyme with a given word.

Guilford's (1967, 1982) theory of intelligence has led to the development of several tests of creativity. Guilford proposed that intelligence is organised into three dimensions: operations, products and contents. Regarding operations, he distinguishes between convergent and divergent operations. Tasks measuring convergent operations accept only one answer – conventional intelligence tests are an obvious example. Tasks measuring divergent operations, by contrast, require participants to give as many answers as possible.

Based on the principle of divergent operations, Guilford has developed several tests of creativity; a few examples will suffice. Divergent production tests may involve divergent semantic units (e.g. "Name things that are green and edible"), may focus on relationships (e.g. "In what different ways are a father and daughter related?") and may also include production of systems (e.g. "Write as many sentences as you can in which you use the words 'desert', 'army', and 'food'").

Torrance has also developed several tests of creative thinking (Torrance, 1972). In the test "ask-and-guess", an intriguing image is presented and the participant has to say what happened before and what will happen after. In the test of "product improvement", the picture of a stuffed animal is presented and the participant is asked to make it more fun to play with. In the test of "unusual uses", a common object is given, such as a brick or a paper clip, and the participant is asked to provide as many unusual uses as possible. Both the number and uniqueness of answers are encoded.

Mednick (1962) proposed the theory that creativity concerns finding common links between different ideas. As a measure of creativity, he developed the RAT (Remote Associates Test), where three words are given and one has to find a term that is associated with these three words. For example, for the trio "blue - cottage - rat", the answer would be "cheese": blue cheese, cottage cheese and rat cheese.

All these tests measure the ability to generate words or ideas fluently and flexibly. Opinion about their validity is varied. Some authors (e.g. Wallach, 1970) argue that there is little empirical support that the capability of generating items, and therefore the tests we discussed, correlates with creativity. They take as evidence the fact that the correlations are stronger with verbal intelligence and general intelligence. In addition, it is not even certain that creative people are more fluent in their field. For example, a study of famous poets showed that there was considerable variability with respect to the rate of speech production (Perkins, 1988). Other authors (Eysenck, 1995) have a more positive evaluation, and argue that at least some of the tests correlate more with creativity than with (verbal) intelligence.

6.4.3 Factors Supporting the Development of Creativity

6.4.3.1 Family environment and socioeconomic conditions

It has been established that world-famous creators often come from families with a distinctive profile. Some belong to families whose pedigree is unusual, such as the Bachs (music), the Bernoullis (mathematics) and the Darwins (science). Much of the influence is of environmental origin, although some evidence suggests that there is also genetic origin – in particular, some high-level creators come from families who have had a history of psychiatric problems (Eysenck, 1995; Jamison, 1993).

The socioeconomic conditions also seem important. For example, there is a strong correlation between socioeconomic conditions, the probability of having a good education and IQ (Mackintosh, 1998), with the result that children of affluent parents are more likely to go to university and have a scientific career. In addition, it has been shown that birth order correlates with the probability of becoming famous (Goertzel et al., 1978).[1] Interestingly, this order varies with fields. In most fields, children born first are more likely to become prominent, followed by last-born children. Single children are underrepresented in the political elite, and first-born children rarely become great revolutionaries. Finally, the type of family environment is also important. More so than artists, scientists tend to have spent their childhood in a stable and conventional family and have parents with a high level of education.

6.4.3.2 Education and training

A second important, if not surprising, finding is that most creative minds have particularly good training. This training includes features such as the quality of schools in which the future creators are enrolled in as children and then adolescents, the access to private education, the advice of coaches or mentors, and also the presence of a rich library at home, which the future creators use abundantly. (Note that the number of books, newspapers and magazines at home is an excellent predictor of IQ; Chapin, 1928). The presence of role models is also important: Walberg et al. (1980) showed that in a sample of prominent individuals, 68 per cent grew up surrounded by people working in the field in which they later made a career, and 63 per cent met eminent persons very young. Zuckerman (1977) found that, among Nobel laureates in

---

[1]This is consistent with the result that there is a birth order effect with respect to intelligence: first-borns tend to be more intelligent than later born siblings (e.g. Bjerkedal et al., 2007).

science, more than half had worked during their studies or at the start of their career with scientists who were awarded the Nobel Prize themselves.

Some authors have argued that, while some knowledge is required for being creative, too much knowledge is detrimental (Amabile, 1996; Csikszentmihalyi, 1996; Frensch & Sternberg, 1989). Knowledge leads to stereotypical thinking, and the essence of creativity is to go beyond what is currently known and codified in experts' knowledge. Thus, the story goes, Einstein was lazy and never studied physics at school, Mozart composed outstanding music when he was a child, and the Beatles produced hit after hit unexpectedly. In none of these cases was there any need for the kind of substantial practice that other experts require.

While influential, this view is incorrect. To begin with, it does not square with the data we have reviewed earlier in this section, which highlighted the importance of training. In addition, the role of practice and knowledge is evident with Mozart, Einstein and the Beatles. Mozart's father was a music teacher who gave his son a considerable amount of guidance and training. In addition, it took Mozart 15 years of extensive training and experience with music to compose his first master work, Piano Concerto no. 9 (Hayes, 1989a). As a child Einstein excelled in mathematics and enjoyed building models and mechanical devices. He read avidly on science, philosophy and mathematics, including Euclid's *Elements* and Kant's *Critique of Pure Reason*. While it is true that 16-year-old Einstein failed the examinations to enter the Swiss Federal Polytechnic in Zurich because of poor grades in the general portion of the examination, his results in physics and mathematics were exceptional (Fölsing, 1997; Pais, 1982). Finally, the Beatles had been playing together for nearly 10 years when they released the albums *Revolver* and *Sgt. Pepper's Lonely Hearts Club Band*, which contained revolutionary music and are considered their masterpieces (Weisberg, 1999).

6.4.3.3 Sociocultural contexts

Finally, creativity tends to blossom in specific sociocultural contexts (Simonton, 1984). As could be expected, the number of creators in a given generation predicts the number of creators in the next generation. In addition, creators in a given field tend to be grouped either geographically or historically. Before the First World War, Vienna was an intellectual centre that produced a large number of revolutionary ideas, including, among many others: Sigmund Freud (psychoanalysis), Oskar Kokoschka (painting), Adolf Loos (architecture), Arnold Schoenberg (music) and Ludwig Wittgenstein (philosophy). In sport, Kenya has dominated long-distance running competitions, including the marathon, since the late 1960s onwards. Although a rather small country (just over 3 million), Armenia is one of the best performing chess nations in the world. In science, people of Jewish origin constitute less than 1 per cent of the world's population, but have won nearly one Nobel Prize in five (Berry, 1981). However, cultural background is not enough – the political environment is also important: according to Berry, a Jew living in Switzerland is 83 times more likely to win a Nobel Prize than a Jew living in Russia. More generally, the political situation is also a predictor of the rate of creativity. Creators are much less likely to develop during a period of political anarchy than during a period of political fragmentation, which is characterised by a civilisation being partitioned into several nations (Simonton, 2006). In addition, the culture and political system of a given period will constrain the areas where one can be creative: Picasso would not have the necessary freedom in contemporary Iran, and Einstein could not develop his theories in a country devastated by civil war and famine.

6.4.4 Theories of Creativity

In the following sections, we consider three broad approaches to creativity. Chapter 7 will consider more approaches related to personality and psychopathology.

6.4.4.1 Creativity as the product of unconscious mechanisms

Perhaps the most popular approach to creativity is that it is the product of unconscious mechanisms; this is essentially the content of Wallas's (1926) old but still influential theory. Wallas proposed that there are four stages in creativity. First, during the *preparation* stage, there is a conscious attempt to solve the problem. Assuming this fails, as it is likely the case with difficult problems in science or radically novel ideas in art, the problem is left aside. It is during this second phase, called *incubation,* that unconscious mechanisms start grasping with the problem, by trying a number of more or less random solutions in parallel. According to Wallas, not only is the unconscious more rapid than conscious thought but it is also able to relax the usual constraints between concepts. Thus, new and sometimes surprising combinations are possible. The solution comes unexpectedly to mind during the third phase, called the *illumination* phase. During the last phase, the *verification* phase, the solution is examined to assess its validity and to fill in the gaps. There are numerous examples of these four stages in the biographies and autobiographies of famous scientists and artists. A classic example is the French mathematician Henri Poincaré, who incidentally was the first to propose the incubation and illumination stages. Poincaré (1913) describes how he was working on a difficult mathematical problem but was making no progress; so he put it aside and worked on other problems. A few weeks later, he went with friends on a small trip and, upon stepping out of the train, the solution to the abandoned problem occurred to him suddenly. Another example tells us how Coleridge wrote his famous Kubla Khan poem after having slept and dreamed for several hours about the Kubla Khan palace. When he woke up, he wrote the poem in one go, without much deliberate effort. A final example is the reminiscence of the chemist

August Kekulé, who told how he found the structure of benzene while daydreaming about snakes.

While romantic, these examples suffer from being based on memories. Sometimes, these memories go back to events that occurred several decades back in time. It is well known that human memory is reconstructive and cannot be fully reliable for memories that are that old (e.g. Baddeley, 1990; Gobet et al., 2011), and there is no reason why famous creators should be an exception. Even if we accept these descriptions at face value, it should also be pointed out that other creators claim that their creativity does not rely on incubation and illumination, but simply on a conscious and sometimes systematic search for a solution. For example, Thomas Edison, who had more than one thousand patents to his name, told that the invention of the first commercial electric bulb was inevitable, since he was running out of bad options! Similarly, while Crick and Watson's discovery of the double helix structure of the DNA (Watson, 1969) was marked by many twists and turns, it does not fit the phases described by Wallas.

Despite this somewhat pessimistic picture, it should be noted that there is some empirical support for the phenomenon of incubation (Sio & Ormerod, 2009), although this support is related to problem solving rather than creativity itself. It is also interesting to note that Simon (1966) has shown that the idea of a problem space can be used to explain the phenomenon of incubation.

6.4.4.2 Creativity as search through a problem space

Simon's problem-space approach to problem solving (see Section 4.14.2) has been used by him and his colleagues to account for scientific discovery (Langley et al., 1987; Simon, 1966; 1977). In this view, creativity is considered simply as a kind of problem solving and does not fundamentally differ from tasks such as solving a puzzle and finding the shortest way to the airport. In all cases, problem solving consists of searching a problem space. Thus, creativity is simply the application of standard thinking methods, including pattern recognition, search and heuristics (both domain-specific and general) facilitating search. Obviously, the problems tackled by Joan Miró in art or Jean Piaget in science were much more complex than solving the Tower of Hanoi, but Simon's key claim is that the complexity of the task does not imply the use of different cognitive mechanisms.

Two sources of evidence support this hypothesis. First, it has been shown that naïve participants in experiments (e.g. university students) can re-enact famous scientific discoveries using fairly simple heuristics. It has also been shown that participants sometimes use processes that are not dissimilar to those presumably used by the creators themselves, as inferred by documents such as autobiographies or laboratory notebooks. A good example of this approach is offered by Qin and Simon (1990), who gave graduate students the data that Johannes Kepler used in 1619 when he discovered his third law describing the planets' movement around the sun. About one third of the students found the correct equation within one hour.

The second approach consists of showing that, with the right heuristics, even computer programs can replicate famous scientific discoveries. Langley et al. (1987) describe a number of production systems (see Section 3.2.2) that do just this. The discoveries that were simulated include Kepler's third law in astronomy and Snell's law in optics. These programs use heuristics that identify patterns in the data to find regularities, such as constancies and trends.

In some cases, exploring a search space is not sufficient. As we have seen when we talked about insight (Section 6.3), a new problem space must be generated, which normally requires radically changing the representation of the problem. Thus, search is no longer confined to just one problem space, but takes place between multiple problem spaces. According to Simon and colleagues, experts have an advantage here as well, since their more extensive knowledge includes a richer repertoire of representations. Therefore, it is easier for them to generate new problem spaces and to use them efficiently than for non-experts.

In many scientific and artistic fields, we can identify the heuristics used – consciously or unconsciously – by human designers. For example, in science, good scientists like finding new problems, exploring variations of a solution, and tend to change directions and redefine problems. They also believe in using symmetries and do not hesitate to use the negation of a hypothesis to advance the solution of a problem. Some heuristics are obviously much more specialised and their application is limited to a particular area.

6.4.4.3 Creativity and selection mechanisms

An influential view of creativity is that it is the product of two processes. First, potential solutions are generated and second, the best solutions are selected. Where specific theories disagree is about the way solutions are generated. Some theories argue that this is done without any constraint; in other words, generation is random (Campbell, 1960; Mednick, 1962; Simonton, 1997; 1999). In fact, Simonton (1999) proposes that the Darwinian mechanisms of variation and selection are at the core of creativity. Other theories argue that the generation of solutions is essentially a kind of selective search using heuristics (Newell et al., 1962; Newell & Simon, 1972). Generation can be decomposed into two sources: abilities (computational power) and knowledge (e.g. plans, schemas). For both types of theories, selection will be a function of the values used during the evaluation of possible solutions.

Both kinds of theories, but in particular the former, make the interesting prediction that famous scientists and artists generate more ideas and outputs than their less famous colleagues. They generate and let the field select. Although they generate more "hits", they also generate more "misses". By chance, producing a lot increases the chance of hitting a scientific or artistic jewel. This is one of the many predictions of Simonton's (1999) mathematical

Artificial creativity

How do you rate the painting shown in Figure 6.1? We have asked this question of more than 1,000 undergraduate students, and most of them found the painting creative, rating it between four and five on a scale ranging from 0 (not creative) to 5 (highly creative). This painting was actually produced by AARON, a computer program developed by Harold Cohen, an artist who became a researcher in artificial intelligence in order to understand the process behind his creativity. Although most people loathe the idea that computers can be creative, this is actually predicted by the problem-space theory (Newell & Simon, 1972), which describes problem solving as a search through a problem space and considers creativity as a special case of problem solving. Creators use a variety of general or domain-

Figure 6.1 AARON in action: "Meeting on Gauguin's Beach" (Original in colour). Reprinted with kind permission from Harold Cohen and Gordon Bell.

specific heuristics. These heuristics allow them to mentally generate and evaluate possible actions, and select the best one.

If creativity mostly depends on carrying out search with the help of heuristics, then it follows that computers should be creative: they are excellent at carrying out search, never becoming tired or bored. The heuristics can be given to them by humans. Newell and Simon's hypothesis has been confirmed, as there are many examples of artificial-intelligence programs that display creativity, to various degrees, in the arts and science (Boden, 1990; Langley et al., 1987). A good example is AARON (Cohen, 1981), the drawing program we have just mentioned. It consists of a production-system architecture and uses a variety of rules and constraints (e.g. "don't put too many people in the scene"). Its style is admittedly limited, but it is creative within it. In fact, when they do not know how the drawings and paintings were created, critics praise their aesthetic value. When they learn of the existence of AARON, they tend to change their mind!

The problem-space theory has also been applied to artificial scientific discovery. The task of the *Logic Theorist* (Newell et al., 1958b), one of the first artificial-intelligence programs, was to prove theorems in logic. Some of the proofs it found were more elegant than those proposed by Whitehead and Russell, two of the leading mathematicians of the beginning of the twentieth century. The production system KEKADA (Kulkarni & Simon, 1988) simulated, in detail, the discovery of the urea cycle, which earned Krebs the Nobel Prize in Physiology or Medicine. Using a number of heuristics, KEKADA was not only able to make theoretical inferences, but it could also evaluate the acceptability of its knowledge and propose novel experiments to test its hypotheses.

Artificial-intelligence systems currently play a valuable role in scientific research, either as true creators or as tools extending humans' cognitive capabilities. They are sometimes coupled with robots. For example, King and colleagues (2004) developed an autonomous "robot scientist" in genomics: not only does it generate hypotheses, but it also physically carries out experiments to test them – without any human help!

(See http://www.aber.ac.uk/compsci/Research/bio/robotsci/press/)

model of creativity, which incorporates the idea of random generation and predicts the evolution of creative careers over several decades. (Simonton's predictions about the way entire careers develop will be discussed in Chapter 9.)

The empirical data support Simonton's model: there seems to exist a strong link between creativity and the quantity of output; a few examples will suffice. Wolfgang Amadeus Mozart, who died at age 35, composed over 600 pieces. Johann Sebastian Bach composed over 1,000 works – that is an average of 20 pages of finished music per day. Rembrandt produced about 650 paintings,

300 etchings and 2,000 drawings. Pablo Picasso must have established some kind of record, since he produced more than 20,000 works. (Arguably, the generation of some of these works must have taken less than a few minutes.) On the scientific side, Thomas Edison held 1,093 patents, Albert Einstein produced 248 publications and Herbert Simon, whom we have met several times in this book, produced around 1,000 publications.

The fact that most world-class creators produce an amazing number of outputs is captured by several mathematical laws, of which Price's (1963) law is perhaps the simpler:

Half of all scientific contributions are made by the square root of the total number of scientific contributors

Let us consider an example. With 10,000 scientists in a given discipline, *just 100* of them will account for *50 per cent* of all publications. This law, which is of course rather brutal for the 9,900 scientists who are left to share the remaining 50 per cent of the publications between them, also applies to art.

6.5 Chapter Summary

While they play a central role in science and the arts, intuition, insight and creativity have always been surrounded by an aura of magic and mystery. Of all the topics addressed in this book, these phenomena are perhaps the most difficult to address scientifically and therefore the least understood. This is partly due to the fact that their definitions are themselves fuzzy.

Intuition and insight characterise a rapid and unconscious access to a solution. The difference between the two is that insight is preceded by several unsuccessful attempts to solve the problem. Both phenomena are supported by many anecdotal observations but much less so by experimental data; research into intuition has led to several theoretical debates.

The standard definition of a creative product is to require that it is novel, surprising and valuable (e.g. Boden, 1990). The last criterion is the most problematic. Determining whether something has value is typically difficult and open to discussion, especially within the arts where tastes and fashions change frequently. At the same time, this problem is not insuperable since there is reasonable agreement between experts about what are the most valued scientific discoveries and pieces of art.

Just like with phenomena discussed in previous chapters, pattern recognition and search seem to play an important role in explaining intuition, insight and creativity. One could say that, with intuition, pattern recognition takes preponderance over search, while the opposite is true with creativity. This asymmetry probably comes from the fact that knowledge is more easily used in problems that can be solved by intuition – these problems tend to be common in the area – whilst knowledge is less useful in problems of creativity, which by definition are at the limit of current knowledge.

Mechanisms of pattern recognition are obviously unconscious, but another role of the unconscious has been put forward to explain creativity: the linking of concepts that were previously unconnected and the idea is that these new relationships allow creative solutions. Despite its popularity, the empirical support for this explanation of creativity is rather meagre. More so than the role of the unconscious, which still remains somewhat "magical", we must emphasise the importance of motivation and personality traits (see next chapter) for acquiring knowledge and making it possible for one to explore – either systematically or non-systematically – large spaces of possible solutions.

Together, the chunking theory and problem-space theory offer a powerful theoretical framework that integrates the research not only on problem solving, intuition, and creativity, but also on perception and memory. This theoretical unity is not a surprise: it is a natural extension of Simon's concept of bounded rationality that we met in Chapter 5. Human rationality is limited due to the constraints imposed by the small capacity of STM, the bottleneck of attention and slow learning rates. To mitigate the effect of these limitations, humans use their knowledge, perform a highly selective search, and must settle for good enough solutions rather than optimal ones. The data on creativity clearly support this view of human rationality.

6.6 Further Reading

Runco (2014) offers a detailed account of research and theory on creativity. Klahr and Simon (1999) provide an overview of different approaches to the study of scientific discovery, and discuss artificial creativity. Weisberg's (2006) book gives a comprehensive description of research on human creativity, with a focus on how ordinary thinking processes can explain creativity. Numerous case studies of famous discoveries are used as evidence, which makes the book interesting from a historical point of view, too.

If you are interested in becoming a researcher in psychology, you can consult the interesting article by McGuire (1997), which lists 49 heuristics for making discoveries in psychology. Abbott (2004) provides a number of heuristics for sociology and the social sciences in general. Oliver (1991) discusses the process of discovery and provides practical advice on how to optimise it. While the focus is on geology, the heuristics that are offered are general and apply to most sciences.

CHAPTER 7

Talent, Individual Differences and Gender Differences

7.1 Preview of Chapter

This chapter will address the question of talent directly, starting with individual differences. After providing a brief history, it presents a number of studies and theories that have tried to link extraordinary performance with intelligence. Other explanations of talent are then addressed, focusing on chess, music and sports. When dealing with sports, we review recent data that provide strong support for a genetic basis of talent in sport. We then consider the role of personality, focusing on creativity, and of psychopathological disorders, which can be seen as extreme forms of personality. The chapter ends with a discussion of gender differences, with a particular emphasis on mathematics and science. Both cognitive and non-cognitive explanations are provided.

7.2 Talent Approaches Based on Intelligence

7.2.1 A Brief Overview of Early Intelligence Research

In his seminal book *Hereditary Genius* (1869), Francis Galton proposed a theory of genius combining two ideas that were then fashionable: Darwin's theory of natural evolution and Quetelet's application of statistical methods to the social sciences. In particular, Galton argued that genius is distributed normally and is transmitted genetically. This hypothesis was supported by an analysis of genealogical records of men with "high reputation", including scientists, artists and athletes. For example, he found that there were "far more than twenty *eminent* musicians among the Bachs..." (p. 240). Galton's line of research has been continued to this day by the research tradition known as *psychology of intelligence*. While the details differ considerably between different theories, the central idea is that intelligence is innate and that it correlates with performance in general and expert performance in particular.

Alfred Binet, who created the first widely-used test of intelligence (Binet & Simon, 1905), was actually an exception in that he thought that his test did not measure innate aptitudes, but rather practical intelligence: common sense and the ability to interact with the external world. The test included tasks such as pointing to the parts of one's body and defining words. Biological age was used as an external and independent criterion, making it possible to establish a *mental age*, and thus to compare children of the same biological age. The concept of *intelligence quotient* (IQ) was developed later by Stern (1912).[1] Modern tests of intelligence (e.g. Stanford-Binet test and Wechsler test) take their origin from the Binet-Simon test, but have also gone through substantial procedures of standardisation and validation.

The psychology of intelligence and the field of statistics share part of their early history. Two important statistical methods – correlation and factor analysis – were in fact created by individuals associated with intelligence research. Developed by Karl Pearson and Charles Spearman, correlation measures the linear relationship between two variables; it ranges from -1 (a perfect negative correlation) to $+1$ (a perfect positive correlation), where 0 indicates a lack of correlation. Using this measure to study intelligence, Spearman found that the correlations between several measures of sensorial discrimination, such as discriminating between two weights, are positive and they can be summarised by a single value. He also found that these aptitudes correlate positively with measures of intellectual aptitudes measured by grades at school.

Spearman was also one of the creators of factor analysis (Spearman, 1927). This technique aims to extract the factors common to a set of measures that correlate highly one to another, so that a large number of measures can be summarised by a small number of factors. He proposed that the variability of different measures of intelligence can be partitioned into two sources (see Figure 7.1, left panel): g (general intelligence) and s (specific sources of variability). Operations such as reasoning, perceiving relations, transferring relations from one situation to another, or even learning Latin, were seen as requiring g to a large extent. Jumping nearly one century ahead, there is now substantial evidence that intelligence, as measured by g, is in part heritable (Mackintosh, 1998; Plomin et al., 2012).

Louis Thurstone (1935) is the other main creator of factor analysis. Importantly, he used a slightly different method to decompose the test variance into independent factors. While Spearman reached the conclusion that general intelligence existed, Thurstone argued that there were seven primary mental abilities: verbal comprehension, word fluency, number facility, spatial visualisation, associative memory, perceptual speed and reasoning (see Figure 7.1, right panel). Thus, while Spearman and Thurstone essentially used the same mathematical technique to analyse test results, they reached an opposite conclusion with respect to the unity or multiplicity of intelligence. These diverging conclusions will define the main two approaches to intelligence and their application to talent for the rest of the century.

---

[1] The definition is: IQ $= 100 \times$ (mental age / biological age).

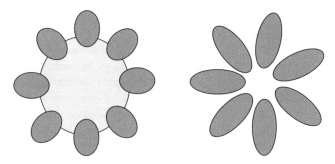

Figure 7.1 On the left, illustration of Spearman's theory of intelligence. The large circle in light grey represents the variability of different measures of intelligence explained by *g*, and the dark grey ellipses represent the variability explained by specific sources. On the right, illustration of Thurstone's theory of intelligence. The dark grey ellipses represent the variability explained by the primary mental abilities.

Source: From Gobet, F. (2011). *Psychologie du talent et de l'expertise*. Bruxelles: De Boeck. Adapted with kind permission from De Boeck.

7.2.2 Two Classic Studies on Intelligence and Talent

Two classic studies have used the idea of IQ to understand the basics of talent. The first study (Holohan & Sears, 1995; Terman, 1925–1959) is the longest ever carried out in psychology: this longitudinal study began in 1921 and is still ongoing. Approximately 1,500 Californian children with an IQ of at least 135 were selected, and followed during the development of their adult career. Most of the participants enjoyed prestigious professions, such as lawyers, business leaders and politicians, but few had particularly creative careers. In fact, there was a future Nobel Prize in physics in Terman's starting population – William Stockley, who co-invented the transistor – but he was not selected because his IQ was too low!

Catharine Cox (1926) used a different, weaker methodology. She tried to retrospectively estimate the IQ of 301 famous personalities in the history of Western civilisation, from 1450 to 1850: statesmen, composers, general scientists, to name a few. Two IQs were estimated: before 17 years old and from 17 to 26. To do this, she used information from biographies, such as the age when the child learned to read, early examples of creative activities and so on. Goethe obtained an IQ of 210, Pascal of 195, while Mozart obtained an IQ of 165. The inter-rater correlation was reasonable (around .70), and so was test-retest reliability. However, Cox's method and results have been criticised (Eysenck, 1995; Mackintosh, 1998): the data used are often not reliable and sometimes the argument is circular. For example, due to the lack of information, Mozart's IQ before 17 is in part based on his early musical achievements.

7.2.3 Gardner's Approach

Working in Thurstone's tradition, Howard Gardner explicitly argued that talent is directly related to the seven intelligences he had identified. In his book *Frames of Mind* (Gardner, 1983), he criticised the notion of intelligence as a single construct and defended the idea of multiple intelligences. In addition, he criticised the traditional use of intelligence tests. Using well-defined criteria, he identified seven types of intelligence: logical-mathematical, linguistic, musical, spatial, bodily-kinaesthetic, interpersonal and intrapersonal. Gardner employed a set of objective criteria to decide upon whether a given ability really counts as a type of intelligence. For example, this capability must be measurable by psychometric tests, be impaired by specific brain lesions, characterised by a developmental trajectory feature, and dependent on specific cognitive processes.

In his book *Creating Minds*, Gardner (1993) chose seven particularly creative personalities to illustrate the seven intelligences predicted by the theory. Einstein is considered as an archetype of logical-mathematical intelligence, the Anglo–American writer T. S. Elliot of linguistic intelligence, Stravinsky of musical intelligence, Picasso of spatial intelligence, the dancer Martha Graham of bodily-kinaesthetic intelligence, Gandhi of interpersonal intelligence, and Freud of intrapersonal intelligence. Clearly, each of these figures showed a very high level of functioning in the type of intelligence for which they were selected. However, contrary to the predictions of Gardner's theory, these individuals tended to have developed skills not only for the intelligence that they represented, but for two or three types of intelligence. In addition, other factors also played a key role, for example an unusual motivation, a nearly obsessive rage to master the field of election, a supportive environment, not to mention a bit of luck.

Although fascinating, Gardner's book is very qualitative and leaves many issues open to other interpretations. More generally, a problem with his approach is that the criteria that Gardner had selected to identify what constitutes an intelligence are not as restrictive as desired. Indeed, Gardner himself has added two other types of intelligence since the publication of his book on multiple intelligences. The first is *naturalist intelligence*, characterised by the ability to recognise animals, plants and other natural entities, for which Darwin is a typical example. The second is *existential intelligence* (or *spiritual intelligence*), which Gardner defines as the ability to reflect on philosophical questions about the meaning of life, death and the universe. An example of this type of intelligence is Winston Churchill.

In addition, some critics have argued, rightly in our view, that other skills meet Gardner's criteria, such as face recognition (Brody, 1992) or foreign language learning (Ellis, 1994). Finally, several authors, for example Waterhouse (2006), have noted that the empirical support for this theory is rather weak.

7.2.4 IQ as Predictor of Expert Performance

Most of the researchers within the talent tradition have used a general measure of intelligence, typically obtained through an IQ test. Although it has been shown that IQ correlates with measures such as academic success and wages (e.g. Mackintosh, 1998), the data are less clear regarding expertise. Both Sternberg et al. (1995), who studied business leaders' practical intelligence, and Ceci and Liker (1986), who were interested in horse-race handicappers, found no correlation between level of performance and IQ. By contrast, Hunter and Hunter's (1984) meta-analysis has shown that the best predictor of job performance is g, with an average correlation of .53, which is better than the correlation obtained between job performance and education level, work experience, interviews and reference letters.[2] These results have been confirmed more recently by Schmidt and Hunter (1998). Importantly for the conclusions that can be drawn on expertise, this correlation is higher with complex jobs than with simple jobs, and remains when considering only high levels of work experience (Schmidt et al., 1988).

There are some areas, such as mathematics or physics, where a minimum IQ is needed to acquire the necessary technical knowledge before being productive. It has been suggested that this minimum IQ is 120 (Barron, 1963), more than one standard deviation (15 points) above the mean (100 points). Do ability differences matter beyond this threshold? This was thought not to be the case (Torrance, 1974), but more recent data question this hypothesis. Lubinski (2009) and Lubinski and Benbow (2006) report the results of a longitudinal study of intellectually gifted children. In the framework of a youth talent search, the SAT was administered to a large number of children by age 13.[3] These authors found that there were large differences, two decades later, between the participants who scored in the top 1 per cent with regard to their success in science. When compared to individuals who were in the 99.1 percentile for the overall SAT score, those who had scored in the 99.9 percentile performed to a higher degree: they were three times more likely to have earned a PhD in a science, technology, engineering or mathematics (STEM) discipline, five times more likely to have a scientific publication, and three times more likely to have a scientific patent to their name. This is significant, given the very highly restricted range of abilities. Thus, even above the postulated threshold, higher general cognitive ability provides better chances of success. These results support Eysenck's (1995) view that general intelligence is a strong predictor of creativity.

A fair amount of research has been conducted on the relationship between chess skill and cognitive abilities, including intelligence. Three studies have

---

[2] Even so, g accounts for only 28 per cent of the variance, leaving 72 per cent unexplained.

[3] The SAT, which consists of three components (critical reading, mathematics and writing), is a standardised test that most universities in the United States use to admit students. SAT scores strongly correlate with measures of general intelligence (Frey & Detterman, 2004).

shown that children playing chess have higher intelligence than children who do not play chess, and that there is a positive correlation between chess skill and IQ (Bilalić et al., 2007; Frydman & Lynn, 1992; Horgan & Morgan, 1990). Interestingly, Bilalić et al. found a *negative* correlation when the analysis was restricted to the best players in their sample. The pattern of results is less clear with adults, with some studies finding no differences (Djakow et al., 1927; Unterrainer et al., 2006) and other studies (Doll & Mayr, 1987; Grabner et al., 2007) finding significant differences between chess players and control samples in intelligence measures. Grabner et al. also uncovered a significant correlation between chess skill and intelligence, even after the amount of deliberate practice was controlled for statistically. Since all masters had verbal IQ above 110 and numerical IQ above 115, a plausible conclusion is that a certain level of intelligence is necessary to reach a high level of chess expertise.

In music, Shuter-Dyson and Gabriel's (1982) extensive review found that most studies displayed a low positive correlation (.30) between musical ability and general intelligence. Typically, low intelligence goes with poor musical ability, but there are disagreements with high intelligence, which can occur along with a low score on a musical ability test.

7.2.5 Components of Intelligence

One might have expected that similar correlations would be found with components of intelligence, for example those identified by Thurstone or Gardner. According to these theories, musicians should achieve high scores in aptitude tests measuring hearing, and architects should perform well in tests of spatial manipulation. However, it seems that this is not the case. For example, the Seashore test of musical talent, which uses tasks requiring the discrimination of pitches, timbres and rhythms, barely correlates with the level of musical performance (Kline, 2000). Similarly, chess players do not have a better visual memory than non-players when the material has nothing to do with chess (Waters et al., 2002). A particularly striking study was carried out with Go players. Masunaga and Horn (2001) studied 263 Go players from beginner (30 kyu) to grandmasters (9 dan). They used a series of tests measuring STM capacity, fluid intelligence and processing speed (eight tests in total). Each test had two versions: one linked to the game of Go, and a version unrelated to this game. An expertise effect was found with all the tasks related to the game of Go, but with none of the neutral tasks.

7.2.6 Intelligence: Discussion

A difficulty with research on intelligence is that some techniques are impractical with experts. For example, monozygotic twins and dizygotic twins have often been compared to determine the inheritance of intelligence. However, this approach is not possible for the study of talent and expertise, because there are too few cases of twins having reached high levels of expertise. In addition, this approach assumes that talent is transmitted by simple genetic traits. However, several authors (e.g. Chassy & Gobet, 2010; Simonton, 1999) have suggested that factors facilitating access to high levels of expertise are not encoded by a single gene, but by a constellation of genes. For example, in their "expertise specific optimal pattern" (ESOP) theory, Chassy and Gobet propose that such constellations of genes, which differ from domain to domain, lead to an optimal cooperation between cognitive mechanisms, including mechanisms associated with learning. If this gene-constellation hypothesis is correct, the importance of heredity in the development of expertise would be much more complex than assumed by authors such as Eysenck (1995) and Plomin and Petrill (1997), and the probability that expertise runs in families would be very small. Therefore, the study of the genetic basis of talent and expertise should be done with more sophisticated techniques than the correlations between twins and should be interested in the details of the mechanisms of transmission, for example with the techniques developed in genomics.

In this regard, it is worth mentioning that there is no clear pattern regarding the transmission of expertise in families. Although there are several families with famous creators, such as the Bernoulli family who produced a number of leading mathematicians and the Bach family with several famous musicians, there are also famous creators who seem to come from nowhere, with no other creators in their family history. Simonton (1999) gives the example of the mathematician Carl Gauss, the mathematician-physicist Isaac Newton and the composer Ludwig van Beethoven – the very best in the history of creativity.

7.3 Talent Approaches Not Based on Intelligence

The advocates of talent argue that factors other than practice are important for becoming an expert. These factors can be classified in three broad categories. First, they can be genetic; second, they can be innate but not genetic; and third, they can occur after birth. This section presents data obtained with other measures than intelligence.

7.3.1 Talent in Chess

Given the presence of the Elo rating, chess is an ideal domain for studying the respective roles of talent and practice in the acquisition of expertise, and a fair amount of research has been carried out on this topic. In addition to the link between intelligence and chess, which we have just considered, several kinds of empirical data point to talent and factors unrelated to practice: handedness, season of birth and sensitive period.

According to Geschwind and Galaburda's (1987) theory of talent, high exposure to testosterone in the uterus causes the right hemisphere of the brain to develop more than normally, which increases the probability of being talented in visuospatial domains and being a non-right-hander (i.e., left-handed or ambidextrous). This hypothesis was tested by Cranberg and Albert (1988) and Gobet and Campitelli (2007), who gave a questionnaire about hand preference to chess players. In both studies, the proportion of non-right-handers was higher in the chess sample (around 18 per cent) than in the general population (around 12 per cent). However, handedness did not differentiate players of different levels of expertise.

A possible biological marker for superior performance is offered by season of birth. For example, viruses affect a foetus' brain development during pregnancy, and the presence of viruses varies depending on the season. In line with this hypothesis, expert chess players in the Northern Hemisphere tend to be born more often in the first half of the year (52.3 per cent of births) than in the second half (47.7 per cent; Gobet & Chassy, 2008a). Although a small difference, the large sample (nearly 42,000 players) makes it highly reliable statistically. The effect was even stronger with grandmasters (56.9 per cent of births in the first half of the year). Importantly, chess players' birth distribution differed from that in the overall population of European Union countries from 1973 to 2001.

Seasonality effects have often been documented in school education (Sharp & Benefield, 1995) and in sports such as football (Brewer et al., 1992), ice hockey (Addona & Yates, 2010) and tennis (Edgar & O'Donoghue, 2005). According to the standard explanation of these effects, children born earlier have a considerable advantage when they compete with younger children of the same year cohort, because they are stronger physically and display better coordination. Younger children find it hard to compete and tend to drop out. Significantly, this explanation is not valid with chess: in most countries, there is no age selection in chess and children play games both with younger and older children and even with adults. In addition, Gobet and Chassy's data are international in nature and cover countries with a variety of cut-off dates for school entry.

Elo (1978) postulated that there should be a sensitive period for starting to practice chess. The existence of a sensitive period has been established with language acquisition and the development of the visual system; a common explanation is based on the fact that the brain is more malleable at younger ages. Elo's hypothesis was supported by Gobet and Campitelli (2007), who found a reliable negative correlation between starting age and chess skill (-.37; similar correlations were observed in Charness et al., 2005, and Grabner et al., 2007). Twelve years of age seemed to be a turning point: for players who started to play seriously at 12 or before, the probability of becoming an international-level player was .24; for players who started after 12, this probability was only .02. In line with Ericsson et al. (1993), it is tempting to explain this result by proposing that children who start playing earlier accumulate more deliberate practice. However, this explanation does not work: controlling for deliberate practice still yields a partial correlation that is significant ($r = -.40$).

7.3.2 Talent in Music

In an influential paper on musical talent, Howe et al. (1998) proposed five properties to decide whether an ability counts as talent, rather than something that could be learnt simply by practice: (a) it is partly genetically transmissible and thus is, at least to some extent, innate; (b) there are early signs of its existence, although a full deployment might come only relatively late; (c) these early signs can be used for predicting later excellence in the domain; (d) it is rare; and (e) it tends to be domain-specific. They concluded that most abilities in music seem to be environmental: "differences in early experiences, preferences, opportunities, habits, training and practice are the real determinants of excellence" (p. 399). However, there is evidence that this conclusion might be too extreme. We have already discussed absolute pitch (see Chapter 2), which clearly counts as a kind of talent. In addition, it has been shown that musical ability moderately correlates with intelligence (Shuter-Dyson & Gabriel, 1982), STM (Huntsinger & Jose, 1991), reading ability (Barwick et al., 1989) and spatial ability (Hassler, 1989). Recently, Meinz and Hambrick (2010) studied pianists' performance in a sight-reading task. Deliberate practice accounted for about half the variance in performance, but, critically, working memory capacity explained a further 7.4 per cent of the variance. It is known that working memory correlates strongly with general intelligence (e.g. Kane et al., 2005). Another important result supporting the hypothesis of musical talent is that there was no interaction between deliberate practice and working-memory capacity: working-memory capacity predicted performance as much with individuals who had spent thousands of hours practising the piano as with beginners.

In a recent book, Kirnaskaya (2009) proposes that, in addition to factors common to most humans, what she calls "the musical ear, the sense of rhythm, and musical memory" (p. vii), three rare factors are present only with musically talented individuals: extreme motivation, the expressive ear and the architectonic ear. The *expressive ear* concerns the ability to extract the underlying emotions and feelings of music, while the *architectonic ear* concerns the capability to extract the structural unity and aesthetic coherence of a piece of music. Kirnaskaya also suggests that all people possess innate talents and that music can be seen as an instrument that facilitates the discovery of these talents. These ideas are interesting but await further testing.

7.3.3 Talent in Sports

Sport is probably the domain where the debate about nature and nurture has been the most publicised, perhaps because it is a domain with massive financial interests. On the whole, sport scientists and coaches tend to agree that talent exists and that a (good) part of skill in sport is genetic in nature.[4] In a recent review, Ahmetov and Fedotovskaya (2012) identified 79 genetic markers associated with superior performance in sport (59 endurance markers and 20 power/strength markers). In this section, we review some of the data that support a genetic source for sport talent. For extensive and detailed reviews of the extensive literature, see Lippi et al. (2010) or Puthucheary et al. (2011).

The first genetic influence, so obvious that it is often omitted, is sex – the presence of two X sex chromosomes or the presence of X and Y sex chromosomes. The sex differences are so vast in sports (e.g. strength, speed, endurance) that men and women almost never compete against each other. A good example is offered by the marathon (see Figure 7.2). The female world record set by Paula Radcliffe in 2003 when she won the London Marathon in 2:15:25, commonly considered as one of the greatest running feats in history, is similar to the male world record established in 1960 by Abebe Bikila (2:15:16) – a lag of more than 40 years.

Another obvious factor, which is partly genetically determined, is height. Smaller individuals tend to have better endurance, greater agility and a lower

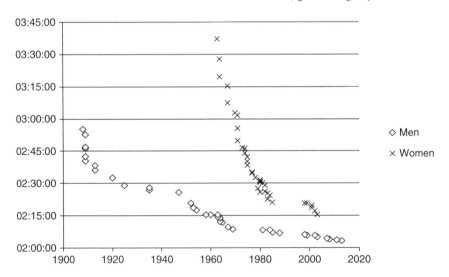

Figure 7.2 Progression of marathon times for males and females.

Source: Data from www.topendsports.com/sport/athletics/record-marathon.htm and https://en.wikipedia.org/wiki/Marathon_world_record_progression.

---

[4]The important exception concerns scientists and practitioners endorsing the framework of deliberate practice. More about this in Chapter 8.

centre of gravity, an advantage in sports such as gymnastics, long-distance running and weightlifting. Taller individuals tend to have longer reach, greater speed and greater strength, and tend to excel in sports such as sprinting, swimming and basketball.

Energy is obviously an essential ingredient for most sports and most of a cell's energy is generated by mitochondria. Therefore, mitochondria underpin the ability to perform endurance sports, and genes that code for mitochondria are candidates for factors affecting talent in such sports. In line with this hypothesis, Eynon et al. (2010) showed that carriers of a specific variant of the NRF2 gene show higher training response in endurance performance.

Except for short periods of time where anaerobic metabolism is possible, the body needs oxygen to generate energy (aerobic metabolism). Maximal oxygen consumption ($\dot{V}O_2$max) is the volume of oxygen that can be used by the heart, lungs and muscles whilst exercising at maximum capacity; it measures aerobic fitness and is one of the key factors behind endurance capacity during sustained exercise, such as long-distance running. Bouchard et al. (1999) studied the response of $\dot{V}O_2$max uptake to a standardised 20-week endurance training programme. The results showed that heritability accounts for 47 per cent of the variance in improvement of $\dot{V}O_2$max. Further studies failed to identify the putative gene coding for $\dot{V}O_2$max, but a genome-wide exploration has identified 21 single nucleotide polymorphisms that predict $\dot{V}O_2$max trainability (Bouchard, 2012; Bouchard et al., 2011). More specifically, an individual with 19 favourable alleles shows three times more improvement than an individual with less than ten.

Injuries and pain are the two oldest curses in sports. Injuries might mean the difference between being a superstar and a nobody. Some sports involve violent contacts with others (e.g. martial arts and rugby) or entail high speed, with an obvious risk of crashing (e.g. cycling and downhill skiing). Others requires gruelling training programmes that put heavy demands on muscles and tendons (e.g. some top marathoners run about 200 km or more a week during training; Noakes, 2003). Clearly, being less likely to suffer injuries is a big advantage for the competitive athlete.

The COL5A1 gene codes for a component of collagen, a protein supporting and strengthening tissues such as skin, cartilage, bone and tendon. Carriers of a specific variant have decreased risk of connective tissue injuries and also have Achilles tendons that are less elastic. This inflexibility is actually an advantage for endurance running, since it may improve running economy (Jones, 2002). Posthumus et al. (2011) addressed this question by studying 313 participants of the South African Ironman triathlon (3.8 km swimming, 180 km cycling, and 42.2 km running). In line with the hypothesis, they found that carriers of the "rigid" variant of COL5A1 completed the running component faster than non-carriers. Crucially, this was not the case for the swimming and cycling components.

Many sports involve pain, including combat sports such as boxing, team sports involving violent contact such as American football, and endurance sports such as the triathlon. Being less sensitive to pain provides a competitive advantage to an athlete, although it might also increase the risk of injuries. Several genes have been recently discovered that affect pain perception (Reimanna et al., 2010). For example the COMT gene has two forms, *val* and *met*, and codes for a chemical controlling brain response to pain. In an experiment where saltwater was injected into participants' jaw muscles, Zubieta et al. (2003) found that carriers of two copies of the *met* allele were extremely sensitive to pain, carriers of two copies of the *val* allele were less sensitive, and the participants with one copy of each gene were somewhere in-between. While the results are interesting, one should keep in mind that pain is a complex phenomenon, with multifarious causes. In particular, it should be mentioned that learning plays an important role in pain perception (Apkarian, 2008).

A considerable amount of research has been carried out on the genes predisposing sprint and distance running. About 16 per cent of the world population totally lacks the alpha-actinin-3 protein, which is found (when present) in fast-fibre skeletal muscles (Berman & North, 2010). This is due to the fact that they are carriers of the XX variant of the ACTN3 gene. The absence of this protein does not cause any disease or other obvious disadvantage but it means that the carriers of the XX variant (more than one billion people worldwide) have, essentially, zero-chance of winning the gold medal in a sprint competition! The XX variant tends to be absent in sprinters, and is nearly never found with top-level sprinters. This result was originally found with Australian sprinters and has been since replicated with sprinters from numerous countries, including Jamaica, Nigeria and Greece, to the point that Berman and North have called ACTN3 "a gene for speed". With the XX variant, there is a shift from an anaerobic towards an aerobic muscle metabolism. This means that carriers, whilst disadvantaged for power performance and sprint, are actually in theory advantaged for endurance performance (e.g. running a marathon). However, the empirical data have been inconsistent on this point and no firm conclusion can be reached (Ehlert et al., 2013).

Since the late 1960s, runners from East Africa (especially Kenya and Ethiopia) have dominated middle- and long-distance running disciplines, from 800 metres to the marathon. Even more surprisingly, a single Kenyan tribe, the Kalenjin, which accounts for 12.5 per cent of the Kenyan population and 0.06 per cent of the world's population, has produced 75 per cent of the top Kenya runners and has won nearly 50 Olympic medals in middle- and long-distance races (Epstein, 2013; Wilber & Pitsiladis, 2012). Several hypotheses have been proposed to explain this phenomenon, including: genetic predisposition, high-altitude training benefits, children's extensive running to go to school and high extrinsic motivation (Olympic medallists are national heroes in Kenya).

Physiological analyses do not support the hypothesis of a genetic advantage with respect to $\dot{V}O_2$max, the proportion of slow-twitch muscle fibres or response to endurance training: sedentary Kalenjin boys do not differ from sedentary Danish boys (Larsen, 2003). However, the comparison between Kalenjin and

Danish boys revealed significant anatomic differences: the Kalenjin boys not only have proportionally longer legs (i.e. a higher leg-to-torso ratio) but also thinner legs. These morphological characteristics, which are ideal for distance running since they improve running economy, are largely heritable (Clark, 1956).

A final important phenomenon is that some athletes have hereditary conditions that clearly put them at an advantage against their competitors. Finnish cross-country skier Eero Mäntyranta started winning races as young as 7 years old and became a national hero, winning 12 medals (five gold) in Winter Olympics and World Championships. He had primary familial and congenital polycythaemia, due to a very rare mutation in the erythropoietin (EPO) receptor gene (de la Chapelle et al., 1993). EPO is a hormone that stimulates red blood cell production.[5] Mäntyranta had remarkably high levels of haemoglobin, at times 65 per cent higher than normal. This increased capacity of the blood to carry oxygen gave him a considerable advantage in an endurance sport such as cross-country skiing. It should however be pointed out that Mäntyranta himself denied that this was the case. He attributed his success to his determination and his mental strength (Epstein, 2013). At least two other factors are of importance: his long training sessions at night and the fact that everybody used skiing as a standard mode of locomotion in his native Lapland.

Interestingly, two relatives of Mäntyranta with the same mutation together won one World Championship and two Olympic medals (gold and bronze). Epstein (2013) also notes that other athletes have benefitted from naturally high levels of haemoglobin, such as Italian cyclist Damiano Cunego and Norwegian cross-country skier Frode Estil.

When the human genome was completely sequenced in April 2003, there was an expectation that numerous physiological and psychological traits would be coded by a single gene or at least a few genes. This turned out to be vastly overoptimistic: it is now agreed that most traits are caused by a much larger number of genes. While there is now considerable support for the presence of genetic factors linked to talent in sport, one should remember that genomics is a young field, and that not all results have been replicated. In addition, many details about gene expression and their interaction with environmental and psychological factors are still poorly understood (Ehlert et al., 2013; Lippi et al., 2010). However, the fact that genes (partly) determine important aspects of sport performance is now unquestionable.

7.4 Personality

Personality is an important topic in the discussion of talent, since most personality traits are moderately heritable, with heritability explaining from 20 to 50 per cent of phenotypic variability (Maltby et al., 2010; Plomin et al.,

---

[5]Synthetic EPO is used in sport doping with the same purpose. For example, it was used by US cyclist Lance Armstrong.

2012). On general grounds, it is highly likely that at least some personality traits, such as competitiveness or the capacity to work during long hours, facilitate the acquisition of expertise (Eysenck, 1995; Mackintosh, 1998). While a reasonable amount of data has been collected about the role of personality traits in creativity, little is known about their role in most domains of expertise.

7.4.1 Creativity

It has been suggested that creative minds are characterised by a series of psychological traits and biographical features. Winner (1996) discusses this issue in relation to gifted children, and Eysenck (1995) focuses on adult creators.

Two essential components are energy and motivation (they seem to be even more important than IQ). As Winner notes, the creators show a "rage to master". For example, as mentioned earlier, an artist like Picasso has produced around 20,000 works and a scientist such as Herbert Simon has produced nearly 1,000 publications. At present, it is not clear whether this energy and motivation are of intrinsic or extrinsic origin, although the former seems more plausible. These individuals also devote a considerable amount of attention and interest to their field. They are capable of intense concentration in their work, which can lead to what Csikszentmihalyi (1990) calls the phenomenon of *flow* – a total disregard for everything except the object of their work, accompanied by a feeling of success and full participation.

According to Winner, the creators are also dominant, confident and able to face the competition. They are independent and introverted. Finally, they are willing to take risks and accept the consequences of failure, and have a deep need to change the established order. Winner also mentions some factors not related to personality. First, boys are more likely to have creative careers than girls. Second, certain family configurations seem to favour the emergence of creative individuals, including: poorly structured families, subject to tension and reluctant to show support for the child. Third, the luck factor is not to be overlooked.

Eysenck (1995) notes that people who score highly with psychoticism (one of the three personality traits he identified, the other two being extraversion and neuroticism) are more likely to be creative. These individuals are normal, but tend to be eccentric, egocentric, impulsive, aggressive and emotionally cold to the point of being antisocial. They are also characterised by a relaxation of the mind, which promotes creativity. From psychoticism (a personality trait) to psychosis (a mental illness), there is only one step that has been merrily crossed by some researchers, as we shall see later.

Eysenck further argues that creativity requires the making of new associations and that there are individual differences in the extent to which individuals are able to do so. Two factors are important. First, there is the speed of making associations, which is related to intelligence. Second, there is the range of associations, which is related both to personality (e.g. psychoticism) and the speed of learning. In addition, since many associations are irrelevant for a given problem, it is necessary to have an efficient "comparator" that will provide critical evaluations.

7.4.2 Other Domains of Expertise

There are relatively few studies on the personality of experts outside of creativity. Two domains, however, might provide useful information about the role of personality in expertise: academic success and job performance. While researchers have sometimes used the concept of *need for achievement* (McClelland et al., 1953) in these domains, they have recently focused on the Big Five model (Costa & McCrae, 1992), which includes five factors: openness, conscientiousness, extraversion, agreeableness and neuroticism.

In a study on Croatian students aged from 15 to 18 years, Bratko et al. (2006) found that conscientiousness was the best predictor of school grades, presumably because it helps students to be disciplined, organised and motivated to succeed. The importance of conscientiousness for academic success has been documented in numerous other studies (see Poropat, 2009, for a meta-analysis). To explain the lack of predictive value of neuroticism and extraversion, Maltby et al. (2010) note that, while neuroticism might help exam preparation because of its association with worry and perfectionism, it might actually be detrimental in actual exams, because it will increase anxiety. With respect to extraversion, they argue that extraverted individuals might be less worried, too optimistic and might also prefer spending their time engaged in other activities rather than studying.

Conscientiousness is also a good predictor of job performance, accounting for more of the variance than (low) neuroticism (e.g. Salgado, 2003). By contrast, openness, agreeableness and extraversion are only inconsistently related to job performance. As noted by Ackerman and Beier (2006), there is an important difference between intelligence and personality as predictors of job performance. Intelligence always correlates positively with performance, while the direction of personality traits depends on the occupational context. For example, being extravert is a useful trait in occupations such as marketing, sales and politics, but not in occupations such as mathematics and chess that ask for considerable solitary mental activity.

7.5 Psychopathology

We have seen that some researchers believe that the ability to build surprising associations between concepts was one of the most important characteristics of creativity. If this is the case, one would expect that certain mental disorders such as schizophrenia and bipolar disorder (manic-depressive disorder) promotes the emergence of creativity. This is the hypothesis of the *mad genius* theory. Schizophrenia should facilitate creativity because it generates strange ideas and incongruous connections. The manic phase of bipolar disorder, in which the individual has great energy and enthusiasm, a high speed of thinking, and is overly optimistic and self-confident, could also encourage productivity and thereby creativity. It seems that this assumption is at least partially correct (e.g. Jamison, 1993), and several major creators seem to have suffered from serious mental problems, among which we can mention Newton, Rimbaud and Rembrandt for schizophrenia, and Balzac, Schumann, Schopenhauer and Van Gogh for bipolar disorder (Simonton, 1999). Jamison (1989) conducted interviews with a sample of 47 English writers and artists. She found that over 38 per cent of them had received treatment for mental disorders while 30 per cent had severe and durable mood swings. Most individuals in this sample indicated the presence of highly productive creative episodes, and their descriptions of these episodes correspond well to the manic phase of bipolar disorder.

Post (1994) studied the biographies of 291 world-famous men, using the DSM-III (Diagnostic and Statistical Manual of Mental Disorders). The more creativity the fields required, the more likely the individuals were to suffer from severe psychopathology. In ascending order, the percentages were: politicians (17 per cent), scientists (18 per cent), thinkers (26 per cent), composers (31 per cent), artists (38 per cent) and writers (46 per cent). Post also found that, while there was a high incidence of psychopathology in their families, these individuals rarely suffered themselves from schizophrenia and affective disorders (1.7 per cent). This makes sense: such psychoses disrupt mental life massively so that the person afflicted simply cannot function in society.

While such results are interesting, one must remember that they provide only little information about the direction of causality. There are at least three possible models: (a) psychopathology causes creativity; (b) creativity causes psychopathology; and (c) a common factor, such as stress or psychoticism, causes both. There are obviously many other possible causal models; some might for example include feedback loops: psychopathology causes creativity, but creativity in turn reinforces psychopathology.

Creators have a strong ego and are driven by perseverance and the urge to create, as shown by several studies (e.g. Cox's (1926) study of 301 geniuses, Barron's (1969) study of writers and architects, and Post's (1994) study of 391 famous people). The role of ego strength in creativity is actually paradoxical, as ego strength in general correlates negatively with psychopathology. It is possible that high creativity requires a combination of psychopathology and ego strength.

A fair amount of the data that we have presented in this section consists of using current psychiatric classifications with biographical data and sometimes even historical data. There are several problems with this approach. First, biographical and historical data are unreliable. Second, times have changed – the prevalence and contributing factors of various psychiatric illnesses are likely to have varied over the years, making the use of current diagnostic methods fallible. Third, as we have seen in Chapter 5, psychiatric diagnoses suffer from poor reliability (e.g. Meehl, 1954). In this respect, it has been argued that the various versions of the DSM have not really improved matters (e.g. Kirk & Kutchins, 1992).

7.6 Gender Differences

In 1980, Abbie Conant took part in an audition for solo trombone of the Munich Philharmonic. She was invited as Herr (Mister) Conant and would have been unlikely to be in Munich at all if the jury had noticed she was a woman. All candidates played behind a screen, and Conant won ahead of 32 male players. One year after, she was demoted to second trombone, with the explanation: "You know the problem; we need a man for the solo trombone". After 6 years of hearings, appeals and expert evaluations, she was able to regain her position as first trombone in 1990. However, there was another battle ahead: her salary was lower than that of all her male soloist colleagues. Although this was a clear case of discrimination, support was refused by the administration of the Munich Philharmonic and other Munich authorities such as the Munich Equal Rights Office, the City personnel office and the City Mayor. When Conant won the trial against her employer (the City of Munich) in 1991, the latter appealed. Conant won the appeal.

Conant's story (Osborne, 1994) is a dramatic example of the large gender gap that has been endemic in the history of science and art. When Cox's (1926) review of 301 geniuses, Roe's (1951) study of 64 eminent scientists, Bell's (1965) biography of leading mathematicians and Simonton's (1991) analysis of 120 classical composers are put together, the grand total of women is zero. Nobel Prizes tell a similar story: there is only one female Nobel laureate for every 20 males. Only six Prizes were won by women in chemistry and physics, of which two went to Marie Curie.

Women are still underrepresented in science, in spite of many initiatives to correct this imbalance and nearly equal participation at undergraduate level. In the USA in 1999, females represented 24 per cent of the science and engineering workforce but 46 per cent of the overall workforce (National Science Foundation 2010). Women's underrepresentation is also reflected in academic positions in STEM (Ginther & Kahn, 2009), with only 29 per cent of women having a tenured academic position compared to 58 per cent of men. Similarly, among fulltime ranked faculty, only 23 per cent of women were full professors compared to 50 per cent of men. A similar distribution is found in the United Kingdom (University and College Union, 2013). Between 2000/2001 and 2010/2011, the proportion of professorial staff who are women has increased from 12.6 per cent to 19.8 per cent, but the underrepresentation is still substantial. In addition, during the same time period, the pay gap in favour of men has been between 6 and 7.5 per cent.

Gender differences in mathematics

Girls tend to do better in mathematics during the early years of school, in particular with respect to computational aspects and speed. Boys tend to do better later, mainly with inferential and spatial aspects, which are more important for advanced mathematics. At the end of high school, boys' superiority is especially clear at the top. For instance, in the Project Talent, the male-female ratio was 1.5 in the top 5 per cent and 7.0 in the top 1 per cent (Hedges & Nowell, 1995). Benbow and Stanley (1983) provides even more striking data. In a study on mathematical talent, gifted children aged 12 to 13 took the Scholastic Aptitude Test for Mathematics, which is normally administered later for university admission. The average score on the test is around 500 points. The ratio of boys to girls achieving more than 500 points was 2:1, more than 600 points 4:1 and more than 700 points 13:1. Thus, the gender gap dramatically increases as one progresses into very high levels of mathematical ability. The common wisdom was that gender differences in mathematics have remained stable over time (Benbow et al., 2000), but Hyde et al. (1990) found that they were decreasing, and a recent meta-analysis even concludes that these differences have disappeared (Lindberg et al., 2010). The resolution of these apparently contradictory data is that the difference between the average of the male and female distributions is now small, but there are still substantial differences in the top end.

7.6.1 General Explanations

A simple statistical explanation must be considered before using cultural or biological explanations: participation rates. With two groups of different sizes, the best individuals are more likely to come from the larger group, even if the two groups have the same average and variability. Chess is a domain where this explanation is plausible: there are many more male than female players and there is only one female in the best 100 chess players. Extending a statistical method developed by Charness and Gerchak (1996), Bilalić et al. (2009) tried to predict the rating of the best 100 German male and female chess players, using the size of the two populations as predictor. The much greater number of men who play chess could predict 96 per cent of the observed differences. Using different statistical assumptions, Knapp (2010) found that participation rates accounted for 66.9 per cent of the variance, which is still considerable.

So far, we have assumed that the means and standard deviations of the distributions are equal. But this is not the case with many IQ and mathematical tests. More specifically, the standard deviations are higher for male scores and the distribution of male scores is more platykurtic (i.e. flatter; Mackintosh, 1998). In addition, IQ scores do not follow a normal distribution: there are more scores at the extremes than predicted. Put together, these features imply that there will be more males at the two extremes of the distribution – both the low and high extreme. Thus, extraordinary performance and genius might be a statistical artefact.

Another explanation concerns sexism and the glass ceiling – "the unseen, yet unbreachable barrier that keeps minorities and women from rising to the upper rungs of the corporate ladder, regardless of their qualifications or achievements" (US Glass Ceiling Commission, 1995, p. 4). These biases are still present in spite of anti-discrimination laws. Family life is another likely factor: domestic chores are more often undertaken by females than males, and women will obviously be more affected by pregnancy and children's care. However, it should be pointed out that this explanation is not as simple as it appears: the publication output in academia is the same for married women with children as for childless single women (Cole & Zuckerman, 1987).

Attributions also play an important role. Talented girls are more likely than talented boys to attribute their success to luck (Heller & Ziegler, 1996), to underestimate their abilities (Reis & Callahan, 1989) and to see their ambitions inhibited by their parents, which will affect their self-confidence (Jacobs & Weisz, 1994). A related factor is fear of success. McClelland and Atkinson's (1953) theory of need achievement assumes two main dispositions: the motivation to succeed and the motivation to avoid failure. Extending this theory, Horner (1972) proposed the concept of *fear of success*. The idea is that there is a belief that success could have negative consequences, for example losing femininity; this belief acts against the two motivations highlighted by McClelland and Atkinson. Since women have a greater fear of success, which has been learnt together with sex-role identity, their actual success will be less than that of men. While Horner's theory is interesting, the empirical support for it has been inconsistent (Piedmont, 1988).

A recent influential explanation concerns the *stereotype threat*, defined as "the experience of being in a situation where one faces judgment based on societal stereotypes about one's group" (Spencer et al., 1999, p. 5). Osborne (2007) carried out an experiment on the role of stereotypes regarding females' ability in maths with two conditions. In the high stereotype group, participants were told at the beginning of the experiment that "when students take these tests, girls consistently do worse than boys". In the low stereotype group, they were told that "previous research has often noted that girls score lower on math tests than boys. However, there are many cases where girls score as well or better than boys". Girls performed significantly worse than boys in the high stereotype condition, while there was no difference in the low stereotype condition.

The presence of other people can be sufficient to induce stereotype threat and affect performance. In Inzlicht and Ben-Zeev's (2000) study, women taking a mathematics examination with two other women got 70 per cent correct, while they got only 55 per cent correct when they took the examination with two other men. Maass et al. (2008) carried out a similar experiment with chess players. There were three conditions: in the control group, participants were unaware of the gender of the opponent; in the high gender stereotype condition, they were told they would play against a man; in the low gender stereotype condition, they were told that they would play against a woman. In the last two conditions, the gender stereotype was explicitly made active by telling players that men outperform women in chess. While male and female players did not differ in the control and low stereotype conditions, the females performed more poorly than the males in the high stereotype condition.

Two theories have tried to explain gender differences in creativity and science using psychopathological mechanisms. Eysenck's (1995) theory is based on the link between psychoticism and creativity, which we have discussed earlier in this chapter. Since males score twice as high on measures of psychoticism and psychoticism has been linked to schizophrenia and manic depression, males are both more likely to be creative and to suffer from psychopathological troubles. Baron-Cohen's (2009) empathizing–systemizing theory emphasises two factors: empathizing (interest in others' thoughts and feelings) and systemizing (interest in rule-following systems). Females tend to score high on empathizing and low on systemizing, and vice versa for males. As scientists and mathematicians tend to score high on systemizing, they are more likely to be men. The link with psychopathology is that people with Asperger's score high on systemizing. In fact, people with Asperger's tend to have scientists and mathematicians among their relatives.

Another explanation based on social aspects is that males and females have different interests (Achter et al., 1996). These authors studied young men and women in the top 0.5 per cent of the population in mathematics. Males were interested in theoretical values and investigative areas, while females were interested in social values and investigative, artistic and social areas. In general, theoretical values correlate positively with interest in physical science, while social values correlate negatively. Thus, to put it bluntly, males are interested in things, females are interested in people. Another important aspect concerns differences in commitment. Lubinski and Benbow (2006) found that the commitment to fulltime work until retirement was 95 per cent for males but only 55 per cent for females.

7.6.2 Explanations Based on Intelligence

Several explanations of the gender differences present in science have been based on the concept of intelligence. General Intelligence (g) has been of little use for this purpose: there are no consistent and reliable male-female differences (Mackintosh, 1998), and in fact most tests are constructed so as to avoid such differences by balancing items favouring males and females. However, even without such balancing, overall gender differences are trivial (Terman, 1916). The only interesting difference is that boys tend to show greater variability than girls; this result is valid not only for g, but also for specific abilities.

Looking at the components of intelligence has been more fruitful. Males do better on tasks measuring spatial and mechanical abilities, with differences starting early (at kindergarten and primary school). The effect size varies substantially from one study to another (from 2 IQ points to more than 10 points) with the largest differences found in spatiotemporal tasks (e.g. tasks measuring time to collision). Males also obtain much higher scores on mental rotation items (13.5 points, nearly one standard deviation; Masters & Sanders, 1993). There is also a male superiority for 3-D virtual environments, way-finding tasks and reading maps. A review by Feingold (1988) found that the male advantage had diminished over the years but is still significant, in particular with mechanical tasks (see Figure 7.3).

By contrast, girls do better than boys with verbal tasks: they learn to talk sooner than boys and have a larger vocabulary by the age of 2 or 3 (Halpern, 2013). This verbal superiority remains with adults, for example with the fluent production of words within a category. In the USA, gender differences are small in elementary grades but become considerable towards the end of high school. This female advantage has been documented internationally, for example in all 75 countries participating in the Programme for International Student Assessment (Stoet & Geary, 2013).

Female superiority can be found in other domains as well, such as episodic memory tasks (Herlitz et al., 1997), and the ability to recognise faces (Lewin & Herlitz, 2002). In particular, females are better at recognising other females. This could explain why females are more "people oriented". Females also outperform males with measures of perceptual speed (Mackintosh, 1998). In his review,

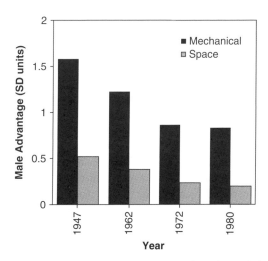

Figure 7.3 Male advantage in mechanical and spatial tests, as a function of year.

Source: Data from Feingold (1988).

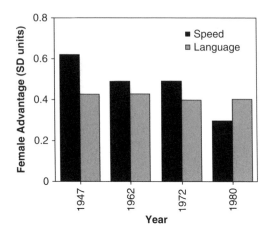

Figure 7.4   Female advantage in speed and language tests, as a function of year.

Source: Data from Feingold (1988).

Feingold (1988) found that female superiority with language and speed tasks has slightly diminished since the 1940s, but is still present (see Figure 7.4).

A few comments might be appropriate here. First, the abilities we have discussed consist of many components; for example, language consists of, amongst other things, spelling, grammar, reading and comprehension. Second, it should be pointed out that most of these abilities – both those favouring males and those favouring females – are required in science and mathematics, not only for learning the skills of the trade but also for performing as an expert. In particular, women's language and social abilities are useful in science: they allow one to communicate research clearly, to collaborate with people smoothly, to persuade funding agencies and to function efficiently in the bureaucratic environment of universities (Halpern et al., 2007). So the different pattern of abilities favouring men and women does not fully explain male superiority in STEM fields.

In summary, there are clear gender differences in art and science. While there are no consistent and reliable male-female differences for general intelligence, differences exist for specific factors. The reasons for this are not well understood (Halpern, 2013). In addition, men and women often use different strategies, in particular with novel problems, with men preferring spatial strategies and women favouring verbal strategies. Furthermore, women tend to be better in a school environment, and men better in a testing environment (Halpern et al., 2007). Thus, there are several factors underlying gender differences in expertise, with no single dominating explanation, but a complex interaction between these factors.

7.7 Chapter Summary

The chapter started with the discussion of different approaches to explaining talent. There is substantial empirical evidence that general intelligence, as measured by IQ tests, correlates with expertise in several domains. The evidence is weaker for components of intelligence, such as visual and verbal intelligence. Support also exists for approaches to talent not based on intelligence, particularly with sports, where specific genes and groups of genes have been shown to be related to superior performance. With respect to personality, most researchers believe that it plays an important role in expertise development; however, relatively little research has been carried out on this topic, where the best evidence concerns creativity. Psychopathology has been linked to creativity, although the research is limited by methodological issues. Genders do not differ with respect to general intelligence, but there are clear differences with respect to the components of intelligence. Several explanations have been proposed to explain these differences, although no agreement has yet been reached. The general conclusion of the chapter is that there is good empirical evidence that there are large individual differences in personality and intelligence between non-experts and experts, and that part of these differences are genetic in nature.

7.8 Further Reading

Gould (1981) presents an understandable but also critical introduction to the technical details of Spearman and Thurstone's methods of factor analysis. Eysenck (1995) argues passionately for the role of talent in expertise, with data supporting the importance of intelligence and personality; the book discusses his theory of psychoticism in detail. In an entertaining book supported by rigorous data, Epstein (2013) discusses the respective roles of practice and talent in extraordinary athletic performance, and provides compelling data for the importance of genetic influence. Halpern (2013) provides an extensive discussion of sex differences in cognition.

CHAPTER 8

Learning and Education

8.1 Preview of Chapter

Is learning important for becoming an expert? Different researchers have different views on this question. Those focusing on innate talent tend to downplay the role of learning. By contrast, those emphasising practice argue that, at the extreme, learning is the only path towards expertise. This is, of course, the age-old debate between nature and nurture. Depending on where one stands on this question, one will draw different conclusions for education. Not surprisingly, a large amount of the material discussed in this chapter is based on psychological research into practice. (The philosophy of expertise also has implications on education, including vocational education, and this will be discussed in Chapter 13.)

As a field, education is not particularly concerned with producing individuals excelling in some domain. Rather, the aims are to develop teaching methods and practices that favour the development of all individuals and that provide a balanced set of knowledge and skills. These aims are almost the opposite of those that are designed to develop experts.

This chapter first discusses the implications that theories giving precedence to talent have for education. Then, we focus on theories emphasising practice to varying extents. We revisit some of the theories we discussed in the previous chapters (chunking theory and template theory) and discuss other theories (ACT-R). We will spend a fair amount of time on the deliberate practice framework, which has been both influential and controversial in recent years. The chapter concludes with a discussion of transfer, expert teachers and expert learners.

8.2 Approaches Based on Talent

With respect to talent research, educational applications have focused on talent identification and finding a good fit between the abilities of an individual and the domain of study, as is illustrated, for example, by Gardner's (1983) framework of multiple intelligences. Talent identification can be highly efficient. Staff et al. (in preparation, a) found that athletes in the GB cycling Olympic team who were identified using physiological measures needed nearly four years fewer to reach elite level than athletes selected due to their performance results. To put it bluntly, the logic of this approach is that, while practice is important for fine-tuning existing skills, no coaching or instructional method will compensate for a lack of talent. However, softer conclusions exist. For example, Chassy and Gobet (2010) suggest that current technology in computer-based instruction can be used to develop curricula that closely dovetail into students' abilities and interests. Thus, the opportunity of learning is maximised for all students, even though the targeted levels may be different.

8.3 Approaches Based on Practice

Given their focus on learning, expertise approaches based on practice have more to say about education than those based on talent. However, some adaptation from basic research is necessary. To begin with, becoming an expert requires many years of intense practice and study, something that is not possible in educational settings. In addition, as we shall see in a later section, expert knowledge is difficult to transfer whereas it is hoped that knowledge acquired in school will be applicable to a variety of settings. As noted by Gobet and Wood (1999), the key contribution of this research is that it has led to an understanding of the *processes* involved in the acquisition of expertise. Thus, the central assumption is that these processes are the same for a child learning to add, a teenager learning high-school physics and an adult studying a foreign language.

8.3.1 Identifying Strategies

In some cases, identifying the strategies used by experts makes it possible to develop powerful instructional methods. An excellent example is provided by Staszewski's research on landmine detection (Davison et al., 2001; Staszewski, 2013b). Landmines are used in most conflicts and cause horrific injuries and deaths, often long after the conflict has ended. Although de-mining units try to destroy them once a conflict is over, their task is difficult given the increasing sophistication of landmines. A major development occurred in the 1990s: new-generation landmines started to contain minimal amounts of metal, making their detection considerably more difficult. To counter this development, the US Army developed new and highly complex equipment. However, despite this cutting-edge technology, most soldiers achieved very low positive detection rates in tests. Staszewski carried out a detailed cognitive analysis of an expert who was able to identify landmines with high reliability. This led to the development of training methods that allow, in a relatively short time (about 30 hours), soldiers to be trained so they reach near perfect detection rates.

8.3.2 Chunking Theory

Together with Chinese colleagues, Simon applied his research on expertise and chunking to education (Zhu & Simon, 1988; Zhu et al., 1996). In a project aimed at improving the teaching of mathematics and physics in China, they used the production-system formalism to analyse what is learned by students. As we have seen earlier, productions consist of two parts – *conditions* and *actions* – and ideally, when learning, students should acquire both. Zhu et al. found that this is not the case with traditional classroom and instruction manuals: students tend to learn the actions, but not the clues that indicate that these actions are appropriate for a given problem. Consequently, the authors developed teaching methods based on *learning by example*, and showed that these methods allow students to focus more on the conditions when solving problems, allowing them to learn productions where perceptual chunks and actions are well balanced. It is possible that one of the reasons behind the success of computer-assisted teaching methods is that, in addition to providing individual feedback, these methods force students to solve problems and thus encourage the creation of more sophisticated productions. According to Zhu et al., students using these methods have learned the material at least as well as a control group, and faster.

8.3.3 Template Theory

Gobet and Wood (1999) and Gobet (2005) drew the consequences of template theory for teaching and coaching. Several features were emphasised: the importance of training; the perceptual aspect of knowledge; the cost associated with the acquisition of new knowledge; the importance of finding a suitable order and segmentation in the curriculum; the importance of variability in educational materials (so that templates can be learnt); and finally the importance of taking individual differences in learning seriously.

More concretely, Gobet and Jansen (2006) used template theory to propose principles of education, which were then applied to teaching chess. They drew three basic principles from the theory. First, the acquisition of knowledge must proceed from the simple to the complex. Second, learning is enhanced if the learning elements are clearly identified. Third, learning is facilitated if it follows a *spiral of improvement*. That is to say, the teacher begins with the basic material to teach, and thereafter regularly returns to this material, gradually adding information, so that the students' knowledge will be enriched without exceeding their learning abilities.

Part of their advice is different to what is commonly found in the chess teaching literature. In several cases, common sense is challenged by principles based on scientific research. For example, some authors (most notably Kotov, 1971) recommend that, to increase one's level of chess skill, the ability to anticipate moves should be improved. Gobet and Jansen argued that depth of anticipation and problem-solving skills mainly depend on knowledge; thus, understanding positions by recognising patterns is more essential than anticipatory ability. As shown by de Groot (1965), this understanding can actually reduce the amount of search that is required for finding a good move.

A second example relates to the recommendation of playing blindfold (that is, without seeing the chessboard) as a method of improving chess. This method is often proposed as a means to enhance the powers of visualisation. For reasons similar to our first example, Gobet and Jansen suggest that this method is unnecessary and perhaps even detrimental. Rather, being able to play blindfold seems to be the consequence of a well-organised and easily accessible knowledge base. Playing blindfold games without thorough knowledge of the strategies and tactics of chess is like practising the visualisation of mathematical functions without the knowledge of geometry.

8.3.4 ACT-R and Intelligent Tutoring Systems

The development of skill acquisition theories has led to the construction of intelligent computer tutors. The main idea here is that production rules represent the proper level of knowledge for teaching. Of particular interest are the tutoring systems based on the cognitive architecture ACT-R (Adaptive Control of Thought – Rational; Anderson et al., 2004), because their operation is derived from a detailed theory of cognition and skill acquisition. This contrasts with most other computer tutors that either rely on general principles of psychology or whose development is based on technological considerations.

Building on Fitt's theory (1964), Anderson (1993) emphasises that the key to learning is to translate declarative knowledge into procedural knowledge (by proceduralisation), using weak methods to accomplish a goal. If it is not proceduralised, declarative knowledge is in danger of becoming what Whitehead (1929) called *inert knowledge*. According to Anderson, the advantage of computer tutors encouraging problem solving is that they promote the acquisition of productions and, therefore, they avoid Whitehead's danger. One important contribution of Anderson's theory is that it synthesised theoretical research on memory and learning, two fields that were mostly disjointed (Gobet & Wood, 1999).

An ACT-R tutor creates a model of a student, which it compares with the "ideal model" (i.e. a model of the knowledge that a student is supposed to master at the end of the course) in order to estimate the student's current knowledge state. Feedback is given when the output of the two models differs, for example when the student makes a mistake. These tutors have been used to teach subjects such as geometry, algebra and computer programming, and are used in thousands of schools in the United States. In general, they produce better results than conventional teaching methods, even allowing students to learn three times faster (Anderson et al., 1995; Koedinger et al., 2012).

Interestingly, although the concepts of chunks and schemas have played an important role in the study of expertise, they have not been used directly in the creation of tutorials, perhaps because they are difficult to operationalise. The consequence is that computer tutoring systems (including ACT-R) are often criticised for exaggerating the importance they give to procedural knowledge and the lack of attention they give to the conceptual understanding of a domain. Ideally, a new generation of computer tutors should be able to teach the material in a more conceptual manner while maintaining the ability of existing programs to teach procedural skills.

8.3.5 Deliberate Practice

It is well known that behaviourist John Watson put forward an extreme view of practice: "Give me a dozen healthy infants, well-formed, and my own specified world to bring them up in, and I'll guarantee to take any one at random and train him to become any type of specialist I might select – doctor, lawyer, artist, merchant-chief and, yes, even beggar-man and thief, regardless of his talents…" (1925, p. 82). Deliberate practice (DP; Ericsson & Charness, 1994; Ericsson et al., 1993) might be seen as a modern day version of Watson's view.

8.3.5.1 The theory

With deliberate practice, the role of practice takes centre stage. Proponents of this theory consider that the key to expertise is to engage in goal-directed activities for huge periods of time. These activities are highly structured and aim to improve performance by eliminating weaknesses through optimising opportunities for error correction. These activities, typically effortful and not enjoyable, not only must be at the appropriate level of difficulty but must also be monitored to provide regular and detailed feedback, usually by a coach. DP is not without risk, in particular with sports: individuals must practice intensively to progress, increasing the danger of injuries and burnout. Finding the right balance between practice and the possibility of physical damage is a constant challenge at high levels of performance; coaches play an important role in monitoring training and minimising risk of injury. Because of these risks, DP activities cannot be carried out more than a few hours a day in most domains.[1]

A strong claim of the proponents of the framework is that performance improves as a monotonic function of the amount of DP. Thus, individuals devoting more time to DP should progress faster. In addition, individual practice is preferred to group practice, because it maximises the efficiency of DP activities (e.g. feedback can be provided more precisely when practice is carried out individually than within a group). The framework also stresses the

---

[1]Deliberate practice can also have unexpected unfortunate consequences. In November 2013, a pianist went to trial in the Catalan city of Girona, after she was accused by her neighbour of "causing psychological harm and noise pollution". Her neighbour complained of the anxiety caused by having to hear piano practices eight hours a day, five days a week. Although the pianist faced seven years in jail, she was finally acquitted, the court finding "no evidence that the piano playing was the direct cause of [the neighbour's] problems". http://www.theguardian.com/world/2013/nov/27/spanish-pianist-acquitted-noise-pollution-psychological-damage

support of the environment and in particular of the family, as without them it would be difficult for an individual to carry out DP activities. A distinction is also made between activities that allow for the acquisition or improvement of skills, and activities that "merely" allow maintaining skills at a desired level. Building on Chase and Simon's work, a final assumption of DP is that "expert performance is not reached with less than 10 years of deliberate practice" (Ericsson et al., 1993, p. 372).

The DP framework makes it very clear that talent plays only a minimal role. According to Ericsson et al. (1993), individual differences do not impose constraints on levels of performance, with the exception of motivation, general activity levels and, in some sports, height. For example, Ericsson et al. state that "our theoretical framework can also provide a *sufficient* account of the major facts about the nature and scarcity of exceptional performance. Our account does not depend on scarcity of innate ability (talent)…" (p. 392, emphasis added). More recently, in an interview for *Fast Company*, Ericsson argued that "with the exception of some sports, no characteristic of the brain or body constrains an individual from reaching an expert level" (Collier, 2006).

In recent years, the DP framework has been very influential in the literature on expertise and skill acquisition, and has captured the attention of the popular press, as can be seen by the publication of several pop-science books, such as *Talent is Overrated* (Colvin, 2008), *The Talent Code* (Coyle, 2009), *Outliers* (Gladwell, 2008), *The Genius in All of Us* (Shenk, 2010) and *Bounce* (Syed, 2011).

8.3.5.2 Data supporting deliberate practice

One of the earliest, and in fact strongest, supports for DP was provided by Ericsson, Chase and Faloon's (1980) experiments on digit span memory, which were reviewed in Chapter 3. College students who had average STM for digits at the beginning of the experiment were trained to increase this memory. After substantial practice, these students could memorise surprisingly long sequences of digits: much longer than those memorised by individuals who were thought by some to enjoy innate talent. However, a result not in line with the theory is that the students practised much less than the 10,000 hours (or 10 years) estimated to be necessary by Ericsson et al. (1993).

Music has also provided strong support for the role of deliberate practice, and indeed was the focus of Ericsson et al.'s (1993) influential paper. In two studies, participants were asked to estimate, retrospectively, how many hours they had spent in practice activities since starting music and to rate how effortful, enjoyable and useful for improving performance these activities were. The first study focused on violinists at an elite music academy in Berlin. The results showed clear differences between groups of musicians. By age 20, the violinists nominated by the faculty as the "best" had accumulated over 10,000 hours of deliberate practice on average. The "good" violinists had accumulated about 7,500 hours and the "teacher" group, the least skilled group, about 5,000 hours. The second study replicated these results with pianists: by age 20, the "expert" pianists had practiced for over 10,000 hours, and the "amateur" pianists less than 2,000 hours. A study on piano sight-reading (Meinz & Hambrick, 2010) found similar results: deliberate practice explained almost half of the total variance in performance.

As noted earlier in this book, chess is nearly unique in having a reliable and quantitative measure of expertise (the Elo rating). It is thus possible to compute how much variance is accounted for by DP. Three studies with adult players found correlations of .42, .48 and .54 between DP and skill (Charness et al., 2005; Gobet & Campitelli, 2007). Thus, between 17.6 per cent and 29.2 per cent of variance in skill is accounted for by the amount of DP.

Considerable research has been carried out on DP in sports, but the results only partly support the DP framework. On the positive side, many studies have shown that better athletes have accumulated more deliberate practice. For example, Helsen et al. (2000) found that, over a career period of 18 years from 5 years of age, international soccer players had accumulated 9,332 hours of deliberate practice, national players 7,449 hours and provincial players 5,079 hours. Indirect support for DP also comes from the vast improvements observed in many sports and other domains in the last century or so. For example, Figure 7.2 shows the improvement in marathon world records since the beginning of the twentieth century. The world record in 1908 (2:55:18) is a time beaten by many serious amateurs today. Similarly, in swimming, committed amateurs perform better than Olympic gold medal winners at the beginning of the twentieth century. Although Ericsson et al. (1993) have argued that these and similar results offer strong support for the DP framework, one must acknowledge that the support is only indirect. In addition to improvements in training methods, which directly support DP, other factors are at play such as better nutrition, better equipment, and changes in practices and rules. Even with marathons, where everything would seem straightforward, such changes have occurred: until the early 1970s, runners were advised not to drink water during a race, since digestion was thought to interfere with running. Consequently, some marathons prohibited runners from drinking any fluid before 15 km (Noakes, 2003). Nowadays, proper hydration is seen as essential.

The link between DP and skill has received support from many other domains, including Scrabble (Halpern & Wai, 2007; Tuffiash et al., 2007), darts (Duffy et al., 2004) and spelling (Duckworth et al., 2011). In general, the results indicate that more skilled individuals engage in more DP.

8.3.5.3 Evidence against deliberate practice

While the evidence we have just reviewed supports the hypothesis that DP is necessary for reaching high levels of performance, there is also considerable evidence that is at variance with DP. This evidence concerns: the high variability in amount of DP between individuals; the assumption of monotonicity; the fact that many experts have reached top levels in less than 10 years; the assumption that DP is not enjoyable; team practice; the presence of other activities beyond DP; and finally logical and methodological issues with the DP framework.

1. Inter-individual variability.

Measures of variability (e.g. standard deviations, error bars) are rarely presented in the literature on DP. However, there are considerable individual differences: some individuals need much more deliberate practice than others to reach high levels of skill or, at lower levels, to progress from one skill level to the next. Reanalysing previously published data on chess, music and Scrabble, Hambrick et al. (2014b) found substantial evidence for such inter-individual variability. Perhaps the most striking evidence is provided by Gobet and Campitelli's (2007) study on chess. While it took, on average, 11,053 hours of DP to reach master level, variability was high: some players needed as few as 3,016 hours and others needed as many as 23,608 hours. This 1:8 ratio is hard to reconcile with the DP framework. Moreover, the skill levels overlapped considerably as shown by Figure 8.1.

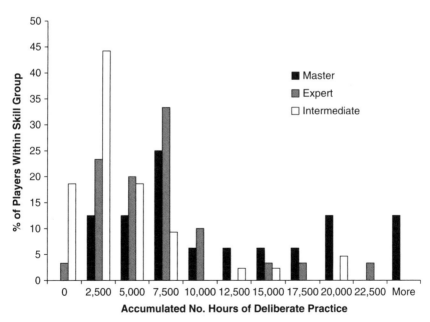

Figure 8.1   Overlap of number of hours of deliberate practice between chess masters, experts and intermediates.

Source: From Hambrick, D. Z. et al. (2014). Deliberate practice: Is that all it takes to become an expert? *Intelligence, 45*, 34–45. Reproduced with kind permission from Elsevier.

2. *Assumption of monotonicity.*

A key assumption in the DP framework is that expert performance is a monotonic function of practice – the higher the amount of practice, the higher the skill. Campitelli and Gobet (2008) present data on chess that contradict this assumption. First, after 3 years of playing chess seriously, masters' rating was higher than that of candidate masters, although both groups had accumulated the same amount of DP. Second, candidate masters improved little after 3 years, in spite of spending much time in DP.

3. *Violation of the 10-year and 10,000-hour rules.*

While biographies of top chess grandmasters confirm that intense practice is necessary to reach world-class levels, they also contain several exceptions to the 10-year rule (Gobet & Campitelli, 2007). Of particular importance in this context is the time needed to reach grandmaster level; several recent players did not respect the 10-year rule. For example, former world champion Ruslan Ponomariov attained the grandmaster title at the age of 14 years, 0 months and 17 days (14, 0, 17) and world champion challenger Peter Leko at 14, 4, 22.

Since both had started playing chess at the age of 7, they needed only 7 years to become a grandmaster. Current world champion Magnus Carlsen started playing chess seriously at the age of 8 and became a grandmaster at the age of 13, 3, 27 – only 5 years and 4 months of DP!

Business is another case in point, where very successful entrepreneurs did not need 10 years or 10,000 hours of practice to start what became multibillion-dollar companies (e.g. Mark Zuckerberg of Facebook). There are also many exceptions in sport. In Baker et al.'s (2003) study, the period to excellence was 5,908 hours for basketball players, 2,260 hours for netball players and 3,583 hours for field hockey players. In the 2012 Olympics, a number of UK athletes started practising their sport just a few years before the event (Staff et al., in preparation, b).

4. *Lack of enjoyment.*

Ericsson et al. (1993) considered that deliberate practice should be effortful and not inherently enjoyable. This assumption has been violated several times in studies on sports, where deliberate practice activities are often described as enjoyable. In addition, there is often a positive correlation between effort, relevance and enjoyment (Starkes et al., 1996). These results have been replicated several times, including soccer and field hockey players (Helsen et al., 1998) and karatekas (Hedge & Deakin, 1998). It is also important to mention that the idea of deliberate practice as effortful and unpleasant is inconsistent with Csikszentmihalyi's (1990) phenomenon of flow.

5. *Individual vs. team practice.*

A tenet of the DP framework is that practice activities are best performed individually, as this optimises feedback and error correction. However, there is ample evidence that in some domains such as soccer and field hockey, team or group practice is as efficient, or more efficient, than individual practice (Helsen et al., 1998; Ward et al., 2007). This is not really surprising in team sports, but still contradictory to DP's predictions. More counterintuitive is the fact that group practice was a better predictor of current performance than individual practice in chess, an activity that is considered individual par excellence (Campitelli & Gobet, 2008; Gobet & Campitelli, 2007).

6. *Presence of other activities beyond DP.*
Consideration of the training methods used in various domains indicates that they are not all related to DP as defined by Ericsson et al. (1993). For example, these authors state that DP in chess consists of trying to predict the best move in published games, which allows rapid feedback by comparing the predicted and the actual move. Chess players do use this method, but this is only one among several others. In particular, they take advantage of the new possibilities offered by recent computer technology, including the Internet (Gobet et al., 2002). Training games are also played against other players or against computer programs. A substantial amount of time (possibly 50 per cent of the time, according to Chassy & Gobet, 2011b) is spent studying "opening theory" (i.e. the first moves of the game). This includes memorising sequences of moves, studying tactical and strategic techniques that are typical to a specific opening, and devising new moves or strategies that are likely to upset future opponents. Often, these activities are performed with books and electronic databases (Campitelli & Gobet, 2008; Chassy & Gobet, 2011b).

As another example, take practice in scientific research. Budding researchers will carry out activities such as learning new techniques, reading to keep abreast of the literature in their field, carrying out experiments, analysing the results, and writing papers. They will not repeatedly write the same paper from scratch to improve their performance, and feedback on their submitted papers will take months. Similarly, a number of training activities in sport that are used more often by elite than intermediate athletes are different from the repetitive activities emphasised by DP. These include mental concentration, imagery to reduce anxiety and maintaining fitness levels (Nordin et al., 2006; Starkes et al., 1996). Finally, there are domains where it is difficult to pinpoint activities that would satisfy all or even some of the requirements of deliberate practice (Abernethy et al., 2003). In total, practice in many domains, such as chess and scientific research, is richer than the kind of repetitive activities proposed by DP. (See also the section below on "Early specialisation in sports".)

7. *Logical and methodological issues.*
According to several authors (Davids, 2000; Gobet, 2011; Hambrick et al., 2014a; Sternberg, 1996), DP also suffers from a number of logical and methodological weaknesses. Since the research on DP is mostly correlational,

it is not possible to draw causal conclusions about the respective roles of talent and deliberate practice. Moreover, it rarely uses control groups, such as individuals who unsuccessfully tried to become experts. Thus, it is not possible to rule out the possibility that DP is an effect of talent: more gifted individuals are more likely to remain in the domain because they are more successful, thus accumulating more DP. Finally, although mostly descriptive, DP suffers from internal contradictions. For example, Ericsson et al. (1993) consider 10 years of DP necessary to reach top levels of performance but also take experiments on the digit span task as support for their theory, despite the best participant devoting around 800 hours and less than 3 years to this task.

Deliberate practice, the assumption of monotonicity and Magnus Carlsen

As discussed in this chapter, the deliberate practice framework argues that superior performance is an increasing monotonic function of deliberate practice – the more goal-oriented practice, the higher the level of skill – and denies the role of talent in most domains. Chess grandmaster Magnus Carlsen (Norway), who beat Viswanathan Anand (India) for the title of world champion in 2013 and 2014 and outrageously dominates the world of chess, throws considerable doubt on this theory. In the December 2013 international rating list, 23-year-old Carlsen was ranked first with 2,872 points, the highest rating ever. There was a 69-point difference between him and the second player, grandmaster Levon Aronian from Armenia. This difference was *the same as that between the second and the twentieth player* in the list, Dutch grandmaster Anish Giri. In the world championship qualification tournament held in London in March 2013, Carlsen was the youngest participant (mean age of competitors = 35.1 years). We can assume that, at this level, all players practise with extreme dedication and with the best training methods. (If anything, Carlsen is known to be more interested in playing or watching football than studying chess.) We can also assume that age did not negatively affect Carlsen's competitors, since all were younger than 45 years. (At the time, world champion Anand was 43 years old.) If expertise was solely a monotonic function of practice, then it follows that Carlsen, who started playing chess seriously at the relatively old age of eight, should be much weaker than his older opponents, who had time to accrue substantially more deliberate practice (on average, at least 13 years more). The fact that Carlsen so clearly dominates the chess world, winning two world championships, refutes this central hypothesis of deliberate practice.

8.3.6 Discussion: Talent vs. Practice Revisited

For more than a century, the nature-nurture debate has raged in psychology and other social sciences, and the study of expertise is no exception. The pendulum has swung between the two extremes several times. Currently, the curious situation is that the extreme nature and nurture positions are both highly influential: nature with genetics and nurture with the framework of deliberate practice.

Progress in the genetics of talent was hampered with the difficulty of using genetics' best tool – the study of monozygotic and dizygotic twins reared apart – with expert individuals, due to the rarity of such people. However, with the remarkable progress in genetics and genomics over the last few decades, it is now possible to test hypotheses about the role of specific genes on superior performance. As we have seen with sports, several genes or groups of genes have been identified as playing a likely role in sports such as running and cross-country skiing. Progress has been slower with cognitive abilities, though it is likely that genetic differences exist here as well, for example with respect to the rate with which information is acquired (Chassy & Gobet, 2010).

Deliberate practice has enjoyed considerable success, but has also been controversial – not surprisingly, given its strong claim that practice is both a necessary and sufficient condition for reaching high levels of expertise. Nobody except an extreme nativist would argue with the statement that practice is necessary; indeed, study after study has documented the considerable amount of practice that experts have to undertake. The sticking point is the assumption that deliberate practice is *sufficient*. First, as we have seen, there is now substantial evidence showing that other factors play an important role. Second, research in the DP tradition has rarely measured factors related to talent, meaning that many conclusions drawn by DP proponents about talent are illegitimate. Third, the extensive regimen of practice required for reaching high levels of expertise is likely to call for strong intrinsic motivation and special personality traits, such as introversion, which are in part determined genetically, as we have seen in Chapter 7. Finally, it is likely that future experts are self-selected early on: an individual with a discordant voice and a bad sense of rhythm will not insist on becoming a singer and will try out other activities.

These limits of the DP framework are important and should not be underestimated. On the other hand, it is also appropriate to highlight an important contribution of DP. Western society tends to underestimate how far goal-directed and sustained practice can aid committed individuals. They might not earn a Nobel Prize or a gold medal at the Olympics, but they will reach a level of performance that most would have thought impossible. Another important contribution of DP is that it has directed attention to the detail of the training methods used in different domains.

8.4 The Question of Transfer

8.4.1 Differential Predictions of the Talent and Practice Approaches

Transfer – the generalisability of skills – is an important question theoretically and practically. The talent and practice approaches make different predictions on this issue. The talent approach predicts at least some transfer, because the innate abilities that allow somebody to shine in a domain will also allow him to excel in another. The extent of transfer depends on the exact kind of theory one subscribes to: it will be largest if one assumes general intelligence but more limited if different kinds of intelligence or specific talents are taken for granted. In the latter case, transfer should happen only within the domains where the specific intelligence or talent applies; for example, an individual scoring high on Gardner's linguistic intelligence should excel not only in writing poetry, but also in telling stories and learning new languages.

The approach based on practice makes much more pessimistic predictions about transfer. If expertise relies largely on perceptual information, then it should be difficult to transfer expertise from one domain to another. As much as perceptual knowledge enables fluid behaviour in the domain where it has been acquired, as much it is of no avail in other domains. For example, being good at geometry does not mean that one will be good at English.

More than a century ago, Thorndike and Woodworth (1901) showed that transfer between domains was very difficult indeed, and more recent data support this view. Chess players' planning capabilities do not transfer to the Tower of London, a standardised test of executive function and planning (Unterrainer et al., 2011) and their domain-specific perceptual skills do not extend to visual memory for shapes (Waters et al., 2002). In addition, a systematic review of the literature found no clear evidence that playing chess improves scholastic abilities (Gobet & Campitelli, 2006). Another example comes from Voss and Post's (1988) study: when expert chemists were confronted with a real-world problem dealing with improving the productivity of Soviet agriculture, they behaved more like novice political scientists than like political scientists expert in the Soviet Union. As we have seen in the box on specialisation in Chapter 4, transfer is difficult even between subdisciplines of the same field.

One of the rare domains in which transfer has been found is playing violent action video games (Green et al., 2009). This kind of game seems to improve perceptual and attentional processes and reduce reaction times in other tasks where one must be both fast and accurate. A possible explanation is that these kinds of video games improve probabilistic inference (Green et al., 2010). Note that this research is controversial due to the presence of possible confounds and replication failures (Boot et al., 2011; Gobet et al., 2014).

Expertise research may underestimate the extent to which skills can be generalised. In line with Thorndike and Woodworth's (1901) theory of *identical elements*, where transfer between two domains is possible only to the extent that there is an overlap between the components of the skills required by each domain, it is clear that some aspects of expertise do transfer. For example, a basketball player with strong cardiovascular capacity will benefit from this when playing football, a violinist can use his knowledge of music theory to understand a piano concerto, and a mathematician will understand the mathematics of Einstein's general theory of relativity better than a non-mathematician. But even in these cases, transfer is not perfect; for example, the kind of fitness optimised by playing basketball is different to that obtained by playing football.

More dramatically, some individuals have excelled in different domains in their career. Eric Heiden, widely considered as the best speed skater of all time – he won all five races in the 1980 Olympics games in Lake Placid – became a professional road-racing cyclist in his second career and an orthopaedic surgeon in his third career. Simen Agdestein concomitantly was a strong chess grandmaster and played for the Norwegian football national team, and later became a successful chess coach. Arnold Schwarzenegger had at least four careers: one of the most titled bodybuilders ever; then a successful businessman; then one of the most famous actors in the world; and finally a prominent politician. What is behind these successes is subject to debate. Is it a transfer in the strict sense of the term, where knowledge from the first domain was applied to the second domain? Is it the successful application of powerful heuristics in different domains? Is it a tactical and clever use of the aura gained in the first domain? Or, finally, as proposed by the proponents of talent, is it simply the realisation of innate aptitudes in different domains?

8.4.2 Early Specialisation vs. Diversification in Sports

The issue of transfer has spurred much debate and research in sports, with a focus on the question of whether it is better for young individuals to specialise in a sport from a young age or rather to participate in different sports. With early specialisation, little scope is given to transfer whereas with late specialisation, one expects that at least some of the skills acquired in early sports will transfer to the sport of choice.

The support for early specialisation comes from the numerous cases where individuals focused on their target discipline at a very young age. Examples abound in sports such as swimming, gymnastics and tennis. In the section on DP, we have seen that Ericsson et al. (1993) argued for the importance of goal-directed practice aimed at improving performance in the target domain. Thus, from the very start, the emphasis is on the specific skill one wants to excel in. We have also seen that, in most domains, the amount of practice correlates with skill level. Good examples are offered in sport by Helsen et al.'s (2000) study of footballers, Starkes et al.'s (1996) study of wrestlers and figure skaters, and Law et al.'s (2007) research on rhythmic gymnasts.

Early specialisation has been criticised on several grounds (Baker et al., 2009; Gould, 2010; Wiersma, 2000), although critics acknowledge that surprisingly little is known about this topic given its importance. First, it has not been established beyond doubt that early specialisation is a good predictor of later performance. In particular, the presence of puberty and the physical changes it involves makes such a prediction difficult. Second, early specialisation limits the range of possible motor skills, which might negatively impact the target discipline. Third, intensive training limits socialisation, integration with family and community, educational opportunities and the development of the self. Consequently, it may lead athletes to feel like that they have lost their childhood. Fourth, early specialisation increases the risk of injuries, for example overuse injuries (Dalton, 1992), and might lead to health problems, for example eating disorders (Beals & Manore, 1994). Fifth, it increases stress and the risk of burnout. In a study on elite swimmers in the former Soviet Union, Barynina and Vaitsekhovskii (1992) found that individuals who specialised early had shorter careers and thus spent less time on the national team than those who started to specialise later.

Some researchers have expressed preference for early diversification and late specialisation: youngsters participate in a number of sport activities before they decide to focus on a single discipline. For example, in his study of exceptional individuals in sports, arts and science, Bloom (1985) identified three phases in the development of expertise: (a) the introductory phase, where an individual explores a domain but also starts practising seriously; (b) the preparation phase, where an individual works on mastering the techniques, strategies and skills of the domain, and (c) the specialisation phase, where an individual becomes fully engaged toward mastery, with the aim of becoming a professional. Bloom emphasised that specialisation was not necessary in the first and second stages.

In what Cote et al. (2003) call *deliberate play*, children sample different sports and their performance is loosely monitored, with no weight on immediate correction of errors. Rather, the emphasis is on excitement and enjoyment, the basis for later intrinsic motivation. Another advantage of deliberate play is that it enables children to develop a wide range of basic motor skills. As the child gets older, the number of sports they engage with is progressively decreased until the phase of specialisation, where most of the energy is devoted to only one sport. In line with this analysis, a study on field hockey, netball and basketball (Baker et al., 2003) found a reliable negative correlation between the number of sporting activities and the number of hours invested in deliberate practice to reach international-level performance in the target sport. That is, if the individuals were engaged with a greater variety of sports early on, the fewer hours of sport-specific training they needed later. Thus, there was some form of transfer from non-specific sport activities to the sport of choice.

8.5 Expert Teachers and Learners

8.5.1 Expert Teachers

There has been considerable research on what makes expert teachers. In an overview of the last 50 years of this research, Bromme (2001) identifies three main phases. In the first phase, researchers were interested in identifying the personality traits that characterise expert teachers. This research was not fruitful, since the identified traits were either trivial or too complex, and they could not be related to differences in classroom situations, teaching topics and children's age. In the second phase, researchers tried to identify the skills possessed by good teachers. However, this approach was not successful either, as too many important factors were ignored (e.g. students' actions and interpretations, and timing and sequence of the teachers' actions). In addition, teachers' skills were analysed in isolation so that it was not possible to generate a picture of the expert teacher as a whole. The last phase, which Bromme (p. 15460) calls "the expert approach in teacher research", aimed to correct this weakness by analysing successful teachers in all their complexity.

In line with what has been found in other domains of expertise, several important differences have been identified between novice and expert teachers. The first important difference concerns categorical perception: compared to novice teachers, expert teachers simply see a classroom situation differently. In an experiment by Sabers et al. (1991), expert and novice teachers simultaneously watched three television screens, each focusing on a different group of students attending a science class. As they viewed this intricate visual and auditory environment, participants talked aloud and answered questions about instruction and the way the classroom was managed. Novices were unable to make sense of the information they received from television screens, and made many contradictory statements, in particular with respect to classroom management. By contrasts, experts' comments and answers were fluid and effortless. They made more comments, which contained not only descriptions but also interpretations of what they saw. Their more developed knowledge base also allowed them to identify typical situations and events, and to take appropriate action, if necessary. These differences mean that experts are much more selective in how they perceive and interpret a situation. For example, Carter et al. (1988) showed slides with classroom scenes very briefly (1 second) and asked participants to report what they saw. While novices' responses were descriptive (e.g. the hair colour of a student), experts' responses tended to focus on aspects that were important from an instructional point of view (e.g. students' age or their learning activity).

Another advantage provided by experts' superior perception and categorisation is that they can predict potential problems and events more precisely. For example, as expert teachers have stored a large knowledge base about students' patterns of thought and typical errors, they can predict what kinds of error students are likely to make. This ability is critical for diagnosing and rectifying errors (Berliner, 1988).

Another important difference between expert and novice teachers is that the former use many more automatisms than the latter (Leinhardt & Greeno, 1986). They often use routines (or scripts), which are domain-specific and depend on experience. These routines allow expert teachers to free their working memory and attention, and thus focus on important aspects of the classroom situation at hand, such as discipline management. Given that expert teachers have many such routines, they can be more flexible when a problem arises or with students of different skills. The importance of this flexibility cannot be overstated. For example, consider the *expertise reversal effect* (Kalyuga, 2007). Two crucial factors affect a learner's performance: prior knowledge and processing limitations such as working memory. The consequence is that teaching methods that are effective with low-knowledge students become ineffective with high-knowledge students, and vice versa. The same applies to students with low and high working-memory capacity. It is thus crucial that teachers can dynamically adapt to these different circumstances.

Two expert–novice comparisons yielded surprising results. The first concerns emotions. Expert teachers show stronger negative emotions than novice teachers (Berliner, 1988): while novices did not show much affect when reflecting on their performance, experts were often disappointed, stressed and angry about theirs. Berliner links these emotional responses to experts' sense of responsibility – as with other experts, expert teachers care deeply about their successes and failures, in particular when other persons are involved. The second surprise concerns subject-matter knowledge. While it is necessary to master the subject matter, beyond some threshold there is little connection between such knowledge and pedagogical outcomes (Berliner, 1988). For example, Druva and Anderson (1983) found that only about 10 per cent of student achievement was accounted for by teachers' subject-matter knowledge.

Based on a synthesis of over 500 meta-analyses comprising over 180,000 studies and several millions of students, Hattie (2003; see also Hattie, 2009) shows that teachers' characteristics account for 30 per cent of the variance in students' achievement. (Students' characteristics account for 50 per cent of the variance, home for 5–10 per cent, schools for 5–10 per cent and peers for 5–10 per cent.) According to him, the key qualities of expert teachers comprise 16 attributes, which can be summarised in five major dimensions (Hattie, 2003, p. 5): (a) an ability to identify essential representations of their subject; (b) an ability to guide learning through classroom interactions; (c) an ability to monitor learning and provide feedback; (d) an ability to attend to affective attributes; and (e) an ability to influence student outcomes.

How do expert teachers develop? There is agreement amongst authors that the acquisition of expertise requires time and practice in real classroom settings. In addition, expertise is topic and age specific: somebody successful in teaching algebra will not necessary be competent in teaching English literature, and a teacher excellent with 6-year-olds will not necessary successfully cope with 12-year-olds. Berliner (2004, p. 13) estimates that it takes 5–7 years "to acquire high levels of skill as a teacher". While performance keeps improving for a few more years, it then tends to peak due to stress, burnout and decrease in enthusiasm (Barnes, 1985; Bromme, 2001). These negative factors are not fully compensated for by increasing experience. Thus, overall, performance with expert teachers forms an inverted U-curve, not unlike creators' (see Chapter 6).

Berliner (1988) warns against providing novice teachers with too much knowledge about complex and subtle aspects of teaching, as is commonly the case in Western countries. He argues that teachers would be in a much better position to assimilate this knowledge after having acquired substantial experience in teaching in the classroom. While emphasising the importance of feedback, he warns against encouraging novice teachers to be creative in their teaching methods, since this directly negates the practical importance of the routines that skilled teachers use.

8.5.2 Expert Learners

Some children or students learn better than others. There is a fair agreement in the small literature on *expert learners*, dominated by researchers in the self-regulation tradition (Pintrich et al., 2001), that these individuals use strategies consciously and that they reflect on the process of learning (Ertmer & Newby, 1996; Lindner & Harris, 1993). This awareness and self-regulation allow them to improve their learning strategies and also to understand how they can be used in other learning situations. Strategies are used in a goal-oriented fashion and are purposely selected, controlled and monitored. This means that expert students continuously adjust their strategies when they feel that they are not learning or that they are meeting difficulties. Strategies contain cognitive, motivational and environmental aspects, and are used to plan learning; feedback is used efficiently. One key difference between expert and novice learners is that the former, but not the latter, are aware when skills are missing from their repertoire of learning strategies and take the necessary action to learn these skills. As Ertmer and Newby (1996, p. 5) put it, "expert learners are strategic strategy users." Most students do not possess these learning strategies and are clueless about the process underpinning their learning, be it in lectures, seminars or work placements (Candy et al., 1985). More specifically, they rarely test and question their knowledge, meaning that they also rarely use feedback to rectify misconceptions (Brown et al., 1983).

Beyer (1987) notes that expert learners are more evaluative and they direct their attention to several dimensions of learning at the same time: whether the goal of learning has been achieved; whether they were effective in their learning; the extent to which they foresaw obstacles and dealt with them; and whether the overall plan was efficient and effective. Consistent with the deliberate nature of expert learning, self-regulation researchers argue that only few students are able to develop learning strategies themselves, and that the majority must be explicitly taught them by teachers. Just like any other skills, metacognitive and self-regulatory skills require extensive practice and feedback (Derry & Murphy, 1986). Thus, to really become an expert learner, several years of practice across a variety of topics are necessary.

What is striking in this brief review is the emphasis on deliberate, conscious self-regulation. However, as you will remember from previous chapters, such conscious behaviour characterises novices more than experts. Thus, to use Dreyfus and Dreyfus's (1988) stages, we are not dealing with the expert stage, but rather with the competent or even advanced beginner stage. Rather than "expert learners", the label "good learners" seems more appropriate. Another striking aspect of this research is that not much is said about intelligence. Now, the link between IQ and achievement in school has been well established (e.g. Mackintosh, 1998). Thus, intelligence may be a possible confound in expert learner research: more intelligent students may be more likely to use efficient strategies. A slight variation of this argument is that more intelligent students learn the basics of a domain quicker, which in turn allows them to use self-regulation and strategies in a more efficient way.

8.6 Chapter Summary

The talent approach does not say much about learning but focuses on identifying individuals with extraordinary potential and adapting instruction level and methods to students' abilities. Approaches based on practice provide more detail about learning processes and the methods that should be used to exploit them profitably. Teaching the use of correct strategies can have spectacular results in some domains, such as landmine detection. Chunking and template theories have direct implications for instruction. One of them – a direct consequence of the idea of chunking and the hierarchical organisation of knowledge – is that teaching should progress from simple to complex, with frequent visits to less advanced concepts in order to strengthen this knowledge. Another is that teachers should make sure that learners acquire productions that are well balanced with respect to the condition and action parts. ACT-R is based on a detailed theory of production acquisition and has led to intelligent tutoring systems that have been successful and widely used in US schools.

According to the deliberate practice framework, talent plays a minor role, if any, and performance level is directly related to the amount of goal-directed practice, which is repetitive, effortful, not enjoyable and based on feedback. While deliberate practice is important in reaching superior performance, the framework suffers from serious weaknesses. Two of them are that it underestimates inter-individual variability and ignores the presence of other practice activities.

The question of transfer provides support both for the talent and practice approaches. While it is not easy to transfer skills from one domain to another (as predicted by theories based on practice), it is also the case that transfer exists (as predicted by theories based on talent). In spite of clear successes and of being recommended by the deliberate practice framework, early specialisation in sports has attracted much criticism. Rather, it is suggested that children should diversify their sporting activities, so that a broader repertoire of skills can transfer to the main sport that is later selected.

Expert teachers show similar characteristics to those identified with experts in other domains. The concept of an expert learner, based on the ideas of self-regulation and metacognition, is less convincing: it ignores the role of inter-individual differences in intelligence and seems to deal more with "good" learners than with "expert" learners.

8.7 Further Reading

Ericsson et al.'s (2006) handbook contains many papers devoted to learning and practice, with an emphasis on deliberate practice. Starkes and Ericsson (2003) discuss various aspects of expertise in sport, including training methods. An interesting feature of the book is that each chapter is followed by the comments of a coach or an athlete. The July–August 2014 issue of the journal *Intelligence* is entirely devoted to deliberate practice. A number of leading intelligence and expertise researchers discuss the concept, and Anders Ericsson replies to his critics. Finally, the authors of the first wave of papers write a rebuttal. Bereiter and Scardamalia (1993) discuss various aspects of learning and expertise, with a focus on education and writing expertise.

CHAPTER 9

Development and Ageing

9.1 Preview of Chapter

So far, this book has essentially focused on adults. But expertise is a lifelong phenomenon. What happens at the two extremities of the life span – at young and old ages? This is the question that this chapter will try to answer. Beyond the obvious result that age matters (e.g. the tennis abilities of a 7-year-old child differ from those of a young adult, which in turn differ from a 70-year-old competitor), we will discuss several aspects of expertise: at young ages, the presence of gifted children and "savants"; at old ages, how experts attempt to maintain their skills and how expertise changes during life. A recurring theme in this chapter will be the role of knowledge and strategies in acquiring and maintaining expertise.

9.2 Expertise and Development

A standard question in developmental psychology concerns the mechanisms underlying cognitive development. Several contenders have been proposed (e.g. Siegler, 1986): reorganisation of cognitive structures, increase in metacognitive skills, increase in processing power, acquisition of knowledge and acquisition of strategies. The first three mechanisms are supposed to occur in all cognitive domains, while the last two are assumed to apply to specific domains, for example mathematics or tennis.

9.2.1 Domain-General Mechanisms

The reorganisation of cognitive structures is, of course, at the core of Piaget's theory of development (Flavell, 1963), which was dominant in the second half of the twentieth century. Put simply, the theory proposes that a child goes through a number of stages, each characterised by a particular organisation of cognitive functions. These functions are assumed to cut across cognitive domains: for example, when a child moves from the stage of concrete operations to the stage of formal operations, this is supposed to affect thinking as much in mathematics as in causal reasoning. However, a number of empirical

158

results are inconsistent with the theory. The main problem is the presence of developmental asymmetries within a given stage, which Piaget called *horizontal décalages* (lags). That is, some problems are solved earlier than others by a child, although they should be of equivalent difficulty according to Piaget's theory and so should be solved at the same time.

Partly as a function of the difficulties met by Piaget's theory, the second mechanism – increase in metacognitive skills – was very fashionable at the end of the twentieth century. Here, metacognition refers to the knowledge one has about one's own cognitive processes and how it helps regulate them (Flavell, 1976). While still playing an important role in psychology in general and in education, the notion of metacognition has now lost popularity as a central explanatory mechanism for cognitive development.

Perhaps the dominant mechanism in recent decades has been that cognitive development is underpinned by changes at the "hardware" level. These include changes in memory capacity, rate of information processing and executive functions (Case, 1985; Casey et al., 2005; Pascual-Leone, 1970). This paradigm has enjoyed a resurgence in popularity with recent developments in neuroscience. For example, the development of executive functions (e.g. planning, error correction, inhibition) is essentially seen as being mediated by the development of the prefrontal cortex, including increased myelinisation and increase in the number of synapses (Blakemore & Choudhury, 2006). As with the previous two theories, the effect of these changes should be ubiquitous: improvements in executive functions should be reflected in mathematics, social decision making and playing chess, for example.

9.2.2 Domain-Specific Mechanisms

Research into expertise – which focuses on increase in knowledge and improvement of strategies – shows that a general mechanism is only part of the story. Indeed, before conclusions can be reached about such a general mechanism, one ought to be able to reject the (simple) explanation that development is the product of learning. In many cases, the empirical data available just do not allow such a rejection.

Perhaps the most striking evidence for the role of knowledge in cognitive development was the study carried out by Chi (1978) on the recall of chess positions and digits in adults and children. It is well known that the capacity of STM is severely limited (see Chapter 3) and that, in general, adults have a higher STM capacity than children. This is clearly the case with the digit span task, the most popular measure of STM. In this task, participants are presented with increasingly longer sequences of digits and must recall them in the correct order; when they fail to recall two sequences of a given length correctly, the task finishes. Results show that adults can memorise around seven items on average, while children at age 4 memorise around 3.5 items and children at age 6 around 4.5 items. The dominating assumption was that

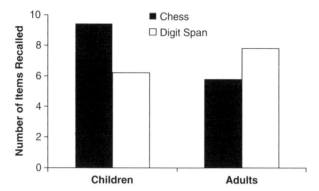

Figure 9.1   Number of items recalled as a function of age and domain.

Source: Data from Chi (1978).

the increase in memory capacity is a function of brain maturation, and Chi (1978) was interested in showing that this explanation was oversimplified. She measured the digit span of both adults and children of 10 years of age using the standard procedure. As expected, adults performed much better (see Figure 9.1). However, Chi also submitted the participants to de Groot's chess recall task. The children in her sample were good chess players while adults were only novices. In line with previous results in expertise research (Chase & Simon, 1973a; de Groot, 1965), but against the prediction of a general increase in memory capacity, children were much better than adults with the recall of chess positions. This interaction between age and domain clearly indicates that brain maturation is not the only mechanism underpinning the capacity of STM, and that knowledge also plays a crucial role in memory development.

You could argue that Chi's experimental design was incomplete: a group with adult chess experts and a group with child novices were missing. Schneider et al. (1993) replicated Chi's study with a complete design, with all factors fully crossed. They also included two control tasks: random positions and boards where both the squares and pieces were a variety of shapes. The children's average age was just below 12 years. Again, the adults did better than the children with the digit span task. With chess material, the results were similar for adults and children: experts' advantage was the largest for meaningful chess positions, was reduced with the random positions and was insignificant for the control task with shapes. As in Chi's study, the chess expert children performed better than the novice adults. Interestingly, when considering only the chess experts, the children performed better than the adults.

The role of knowledge was also documented in a study by Chi and Koeske (1983), who described a 5-year-old child with considerable knowledge about dinosaurs. This child had developed a fairly sophisticated representation of diverse types of dinosaurs, and had an excellent memory for this type of material – better than novice adults.

The case of the digit span

The conclusion of the studies reviewed in Section 9.2.2 is that knowledge plays an important role, perhaps as large as brain maturation in the development of memory. Thus, the idea of chunking can be used to explain not only data with adults, but also with children. Explicitly (by studying chess) or implicitly (by playing or watching games), children in these studies had learned a large number of chunks, allowing them to perceive chess positions as groups of pieces rather than individual pieces and thus to reconstruct the positions relatively well. In these experiments (as in most of the psychological literature), the digit span is considered as a pure measure of STM (or working memory). However, if the chunking idea is correct with chess, it should also apply to the digit span task! Just like adults, children are exposed to many sequences of digits every day, such as times, dates and prices. Thus, some of these sequences should be learned as chunks. Children who have been exposed to an environment rich in digit sequences should have chunked a large number of them. If they are tested by the digit span task – by far the most common means to measure STM capacity – their score should show a larger STM capacity than children who have chunked fewer digit sequences. Similarly, if memory for digits is compared to memory for words that appear infrequently as sequences in the environment, the span for digits should be larger than the span for the less-encountered words. Thus, a difference in LTM knowledge will lead to a difference in STM capacity!

Jones et al. (submitted) established that sequences of digits are more frequent than sequences of words and names by carrying out computer simulations using the mechanism of chunking. As input, they used child-directed speech and story books such as Snow White, which is representative of the kind of speech heard by children. They then asked 8 and 10-year-old children to memorise sequences of digits, words and child names. As predicted by the simulations, older children were better than younger children across all verbal span tests, and children had a higher span for digits than for nouns and names. These results, which support Jones et al.'s explanation based on stimuli frequency in the environment, throw a shadow of doubt on the previous studies that had used the digit span task as a pure measure of STM capacity. If STM capacity for digits is inextricably linked to long-term knowledge, as shown by Jones et al.'s results, then the digit span task is actually both a measure of STM capacity and knowledge of digit sequences stored in LTM.

9.2.3 The Role of Strategies

In line with the studies reviewed in the previous sections, some authors have considered development essentially as the acquisition of knowledge and expertise in several domains (Chi, 1978; Keil, 1989; Siegler, 1986; Wood, 1998). This approach has to some extent replaced the Piagetian theoretical framework in developmental psychology. Note that, with this approach, horizontal décalages, which were problematic for Piaget's theory as we have seen at the beginning of the chapter, are fairly easy to explain: they are due to different levels of expertise in different cognitive domains, which in turn reflect differences in the amount of (learning) time devoted to them. As noted by Siegler (1986), the acquisition of knowledge in a domain makes it easier to acquire strategies as well as self-regulatory competences (e.g. meta-memory).

Strategies can have profound consequences, as the following two examples illustrate. When presented with lists of words or pictures, children of different ages use different strategies. In particular, a rehearsal strategy was used by only 10 per cent of the 5-year-olds in an experiment by Flavell et al. (1966), while 60 per cent of the 7-year-olds and 85 per cent of the 10-year-olds used such a strategy, with massive improvement in performance. In addition, while young children rehearse information with only shallow processing, older children tend to rehearse information more actively, for example by grouping information using meaning (Ornstein et al., 1975). Similarly, the use of strategies for retrieving information from LTM varies as a function of age. Adults and older children, but not younger children, can use categories as a means to help retrieve the items that had been previously presented (Kobasigawa, 1974). Thus, as they grow up, children become experts at using strategies, a process that continues until adolescence and beyond.

9.2.4 Gifted Children

There is a considerable literature on gifted children: children who demonstrate abilities significantly higher than the average. In her detailed analysis of the topic, Winner (1996) reaches several conclusions. First, the talent of most gifted children is usually limited to a single domain (e.g. music, mathematics). Second, there is no clear relationship between gifted children's talent and their general IQ. For example, a child might show excellent aptitudes in music but might not do well in school in general. These two results are more in line with a pluralist view of intelligence, such as Gardner's (1983) theory of multiple intelligences, than with a monist view such as Spearman's (1927).

According to Winner, although the environment plays an important role, the role of talent is at least as important. "No matter how early they begin and how hard they work, most children will never learn as rapidly, nor make as much progress, as those born with exceptional abilities" (Winner, 1996,

p. 308). Winner also notes that neither talent without parental support nor parental support without talent will lead to a gifted child.

It is not always easy to be a gifted child, and these children often suffer from integration problems, especially if they do not benefit from an education adapted to their level of competency. It should also be pointed out that many gifted children do not become exceptional and creative adults, whereas some "normal" children will. Winner emphasises that, rather than a specific talent, the presence of traits such as high motivation and the *rage to master* seems to be of critical import. (See also the section on personality in Chapter 7.)

9.2.5 Savants

Savants are individuals who perform vastly below average in most domains with the exception of a very small number (sometimes a single domain) that are spared. About two thirds suffer from profound mental retardation and one third are autistic (these proportions are approximate as both pathologies often co-exist). Their IQ is low (between 40 and 70) and they tend to be male. There are two types of savants: *ordinary savants* show severe deficits in nearly all domains, but have normal abilities in some spared domains; *prodigious savants*, while also suffering from deficits in most domains, demonstrate exceptional performance in the domains that are spared. The second type is very rare – fewer than one hundred in the entire literature. According to Winner (1996), prodigious savants' exceptional aptitudes are limited to four domains: graphical arts, music (piano, most often), mental calculation and calendar calculation. The following examples will help the reader to understand this phenomenon.

Tom Wiggins (nicknamed Blind Tom) was born in 1849 in the state of Georgia (USA), to slave parents. He was blind and retarded, perhaps autistic. Early on, he showed remarkable aptitude for music and could play a tune he had heard only once on the piano: at the age of four, he played a Mozart sonata. During his musical career he had memorised about 7,000 pieces of music, from classical to popular songs and could play these pieces in any key. He was also capable of imitating human voices and natural sounds remarkably well. However, his talent went far beyond the simple reproduction of sound and pieces of music by rote memory. He was one of the most famous pianists in the United States in the nineteenth century, had composed numerous piece and was the first black artist to perform at the White House.

At the age of six, Nadia, who was both retarded and autistic, began producing a huge number of drawings depicting horses and knights, with a perspective reminiscent of the Renaissance. She drew quickly, usually from memory, and her strokes were confident and direct: she did not need to sketch anything. She had a good command of two advanced drawing techniques: perspective and foreshortening (a drawing method for rendering an object or body in three dimensions). Interestingly, this "gift" for drawing disappeared at 8 years of age, when she developed better verbal communication skills. Her drawing then returned to the level typical of her mental age. It is therefore possible that there was a conflict between verbal communication and drawing (Selfe, 1977). Another explanation for this change could be that the death of her mother had deprived Nadia of motivation and encouragement.

Stephen Wiltshire is another autistic person with a highly developed ability for drawing (e.g. Wiltshire, 1989). He specialises in drawing buildings, preferably with many details. Once he has seen a scene, it seems etched in his memory and he can draw it with surprising precision. He has drawn panoramic views of several city centres – including London, Tokyo, Rome and Hong Kong – after having flown over them by helicopter for a few dozen of minutes. In the case of Tokyo, he drew, within 7 days after his helicopter tour, the panorama of the city on a 10-meter canvas. Despite the accuracy of the drawings, this is not a photographic copy, because there are differences between the drawing and the model. Stephen Wiltshire also has a remarkable talent for the piano, a talent that was discovered long after his talent for drawing.

Some researchers have used the example given by savants to corroborate the hypothesis that extraordinary memories have innate components, not necessarily related to IQ. Various neurological mechanisms have been proposed to support this (Fein & Obler, 1988; Winner, 1996). However, as noted by Ericsson and Faivre (1988), it is not possible in most cases to rule out the hypothesis that such individuals have developed their skill(s) by acquiring considerable amounts of knowledge through practice. In addition, most of the cases, including that of the famous mnemonist investigated by Luria (1968), have not been studied with sufficiently sophisticated techniques to determine whether the nature of their talent is really different from normal memory.

9.3 Expertise and Ageing

The potential loss of expertise due to ageing poses a serious economic threat in industrialised and non-industrialised countries. Finding means to maintain workers' expertise and thus productivity is an important and urgent issue (Willis & Dubin, 1990). This explains the considerable recent interest directed towards research concerning the effects of ageing on expertise.

Understanding the relationship between ageing and cognition has thus become a major challenge for scientific psychology. To age successfully, one has to find the means to compensate declines in physical and mental abilities. The objective of much current research is to understand the detail of the compensatory mechanisms that make it possible to counteract age-related ineffectiveness in cognitive processing (Baltes, 1993). One way to address this issue is to study the pattern of ageing in experts and non-experts, and to use the insights gained to develop efficient methods of training and retraining (Krampe & Charness, 2006). Several strategies have been identified, including prioritization of maintaining a high level of performance in certain areas, while reducing such maintenance in other areas.

9.3.1 Effects of Age

The effects of age on general cognitive abilities are well known (e.g. Schulz & Salthouse, 1999). Although there is great variability between individuals, the trend is clearly for faculties such as eyesight, hearing, memory and learning to decline. With respect to intelligence, fluid intelligence (ability to solve new and unfamiliar problems, real-time processing) is particularly affected, while decline is lower for crystallised intelligence (information and knowledge accumulated during life). A general rule is that reaction times are slower by a factor of 1.6 to 2 when 70-year-olds are compared to 20-year-olds (Cerella, 1985; Charness, 1988). Another general rule is that age effects are more pronounced with complex rather than simple tasks.

9.3.2 A Paradox

Putting together the data on ageing and expertise leads to a paradox: in spite of considerable cognitive and perceptual declines, there appears to be no relationship between age and job performance (McEvoy & Cascio, 1989). In general, experts seem to be, at least to some extent, spared these declines (Didierjean & Gobet, 2008). In a seminal paper, Charness (1981b) found that, despite carrying out a less extensive search in a problem-solving task, older chess players chose moves that were as good as those chosen by younger players of the same skill level. Older players were also faster to make a decision. In an unexpected recall task, Charness (1981b) found that more skilled players used fewer but larger chunks than less skilled players, while older players used more but smaller chunks than younger players. In a standard memory task where recall was expected, Charness (1981c) found a positive correlation between chess expertise and recall performance, and a negative correlation between age and performance. Importantly, the difference between young and old players increased as the presentation time became longer, with young players improving more quickly than old players. Unlike the previous experiment, no variable linked to chunk use (including chunk size and number of chunks) discriminated between younger and older players.

   The results are difficult to analyse in terms of compensatory mechanisms, for methodological reasons. The problem is that older players are probably weaker than they were a few years or decades ago. If so, the knowledge they possess corresponds to the knowledge of stronger players and not to the knowledge of young players of equal level. The ideal solution to clarify these issues would be to conduct a longitudinal study incorporating a larger sample.

9.3.3 Expertise as a Moderating Variable

It has been proposed that expertise is a moderating variable against the negative effects of ageing (e.g. Charness & Campbell, 1988); as Blum and Jarvik (1974, p. 372) put it in the conclusion of their study: "age [is] kinder to the initially more able". Whether this hypothesis is correct is unknown at the moment, since there have been only a handful of studies on how ageing affects experts and non-experts. Research on typing (Salthouse, 1991) has shown that, despite motor slowdown (measured by the rate of repetitively typing a letter), older typists perform at a level similar to that of young people in measures reflecting typing expertise. They are able to do so by planning their movements better and recording more information before typing, as confirmed by their larger eye-hand span. Masunaga and Horn (2001) gave Go players a dozen domain-specific and domain-general tasks. Age-related decline in reasoning, STM, and cognitive speed were found both for Go-specific and general measures. In Go measures, the age-related decline in reasoning appeared to be mediated predominantly by the decline in domain-specific memory. An important result was that the decline with the Go-specific measures of reasoning and STM was milder with higher skill levels. The results support the hypothesis that substantial practice in a domain of expertise mitigates age-related decline. The hypothesis was also supported by research with pianists of different skill levels (Krampe & Ericsson, 1996). However, Blum and Jarvik's hypothesis was not supported in other domains such as chess (Charness, 1981a; Jastrzembski et al., 2006), architecture (Salthouse et al., 1990) and music (Meinz, 2000), where age had a similar effect on skilled and less skilled individuals.

9.3.4 Theories

Several theories have been developed to explain the link between age and expertise. Proponents of the deliberate practice framework argue that older experts must implement training strategies to specifically maintain the mechanisms central to their expertise that are in danger of being affected by ageing (Charness et al., 1996). In their selection, optimisation and compensation model, Baltes and Baltes (1990) propose that compensation consists of the development and use of new strategies to mitigate the negative effects of ageing. Inspired by chunking theory, Charness (1988) developed a computational model of ageing. He was particularly interested in investigating the hypothesis that less information is correctly encoded per unit of time by older chess players, due to the general slowing down of their cognitive system. The model operationalised expertise by varying the probability of detecting salient pieces on the chess board and accessing chunks in LTM. Ageing was modelled by assuming that older players' cognitive processes are slower by a factor of 1.6. The model was able to simulate how the difference between young and old players' memory for chess positions increases as a function of presentation time (Charness, 1981c). A similar model, based on template theory and developed by Smith et al. (2008), also simulated the data well. Finally, focusing on the learning of chess opening positions, Mireles and Charness (2002) used artificial neural network simulations to investigate the extent to which knowledge might offset age-related declines. Manipulations of neural noise indicated that knowledge played a protective role against the negative effects of ageing. The models also simulated the fact that variability of performance increases in older groups.

9.3.5 The Careers of Great Creators as a Function of Age

Historiometry consists of studying human behaviour through the analysis of historical documents relating to famous individuals. Although this is a non-standard approach, it has informed several major issues related to talent and expertise. Nowadays, it has primarily been defended by Dean Keith Simonton (e.g. 1984, 1999, 2006). Importantly, this approach uses quantitative and statistical analysis, although the origin of the data would suggest rather a qualitative analysis. It is primarily interested in finding scientific laws in human behaviour, applicable to a wide subpopulation if not the entire population, rather than understanding the behaviour of one person in particular (see Section 6.4).

Historiometry has shed important light on how performance, in particular with creativity, changes during one's career. Attention has focused on the study of performance based on *career age*, where age "0" corresponds to an individual starting in a particular area. The seminal results of Lehman (1953) have been refined by later research (Simonton, 1996, 1997), and can be summarised as follows. First, the profile differs from one area to another, sometimes significantly. Second, the relationship between creative production and age can be described by a quadratic function (see Figure 9.2). Typically, production increases rapidly at the beginning, reaching a maximum in the thirties and forties, and then gradually decreases. In the last years of a career, the production is only half of what it was in the best years.

Third, the location of the peak and the rate of decline after the peak differ from one area to another. For most activities, the peak is around 40 years (e.g. artists, musicians, inventors; Schulz & Salthouse, 1999). In chess, Elo (1965) found that the peak for top players was around 35 years, and performance at 20 years was about the same as performance at 65 years, although recent trends suggest that the peak has moved towards the early thirties (Gobet et al., 2004). The peak is present very early on in disciplines such as mathematics, theoretical physics and poetry, and the decline is rapid. By contrast, in disciplines such as history, philosophy and psychology, the peak occurs later and decline is slow. Fourth, there are obviously important differences regarding when early career starts: for example, some individuals obtain a PhD in their mid-twenties, while others obtain it much later. In the latter case, the peak of career will occur later but the shapes of the curves are the same (see Figure 9.3).

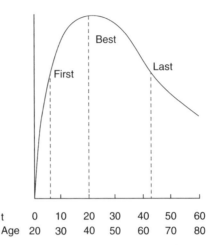

Figure 9.2   Production of creative ideas as a function of career age and chronological age. Dotted lines show the first, best and last creative production.

Source: From Simonton, D. K. (1997). Creative productivity. *Psychological Review, 104,* 66–89. Copyright © 1997 by the American Psychological Association. Adapted with kind permission.

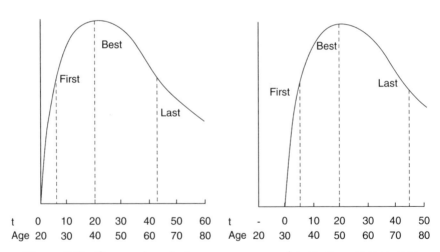

Figure 9.3   Comparison between a person who starts a career very young (left) and a person who starts later (right). The curve shows the production of creative ideas in terms of career age (t) and chronological age. The dotted lines indicate the first, best and final creative production.

Source: From Simonton, D. K. (1997). Creative productivity. *Psychological Review, 104*, 66–89. Copyright © 1997 by the American Psychological Association. Adapted with kind permission.

Fifth, the performance curves are not affected by whether the quantity or the quality of the output are taken as measures. Thus, the best productions of a creative individual will be generated when the person produces the largest number of productions. Finally, in areas where physiological factors are important, such as the vast majority of sports, careers curves are similar to curves defined by chronological age. It is interesting to note that all these results have been summarised by a sophisticated mathematical model (Simonton, 1997).

9.4 Chapter Summary

Theories of development have tended to use general mechanisms that could be either cognitive or biological. However, research on expertise has shown that many phenomena linked to development can be explained by domain-specific learning. Thus, a child becomes an expert in a particular domain by spending many hours playing or otherwise dealing with this domain, allowing her to acquire considerable knowledge, including suitable strategies. The data on gifted children and savants tend to support the view that talent is underpinned by specific types of intelligence, although the role of practice should not be neglected.

While cognitive functions tend to decline with age, some individuals retain very high levels of expertise. Whether expertise acts as a moderating variable against ageing has led to much debate, but no resolution has been reached yet. The careers of creators follow an inverted U-shape, with a peak typically at 40 years of age, although there is considerable variation between domains.

9.5 Further Reading

Radford (1990) investigates child prodigies in a variety of domains, including Boris Becker, Wolfgang Amadeus Mozart and Bobby Fischer. In her book on gifted children, Winner (1996) addresses many issues of giftedness but focuses on educational implications. A systematic and extensive discussion of giftedness is provided in the volume edited by Shavinina (2009). Simonton (1999) discusses genius using evolutionary theory and presents the development of creativity throughout careers.

CHAPTER 10

Neuro-Expertise

10.1 Preview of Chapter

Speculations about the biological basis of expertise date back to the end of the nineteenth century, with the work of the French psychologist Alfred Binet on mental calculators and chess players. While always present in the last century, this type of research has increased exponentially in the last two decades or so with the recent technical developments in neuroscience and, in particular, brain imaging.

There is now a considerable literature in neuroscience about expert behaviour in many different fields, and a complete discussion would require several volumes. Therefore, we will limit ourselves to providing snapshots of some key results, which will mostly cover the domains we have discussed at great length in this book (chess, music and sport). Before addressing domains of expertise requiring extensive practice, we present some important results from research into skill acquisition, where the training duration is relatively short. We then discuss some of the main neural mechanisms that have been proposed. A central question in this chapter concerns the brain markers of skill acquisition: does the activation in a given area increase, does it decrease, or is there a change in the location of the activation? The latter would indicate a functional reorganisation of the brain. The chapter ends with a discussion of gender differences and smart drugs.

10.2 Skill Acquisition in Novices

Learning and novice training are obviously key topics in psychology and neuroscience. A substantial amount of data has been collected on these topics, and we limit ourselves to two illustrative examples: one with short training duration and one with medium training duration. More extensive discussions are provided by Gauthier et al. (2009), Hill and Schneider (2006) and Guida et al. (2012).

Garavan and collaborators (2000) used a visuospatial delayed-match-to-sample task. Three dots were displayed for only 200 ms. After a 3-s delay, a probe circle was displayed and participants had to decide whether the circle was surrounding one of the initial three dots. In the first experiment, participants

---

Brain-imaging techniques

Since this chapter mentions several brain-imaging techniques, it may be useful to present a brief explanation of them. With electroencephalography (EEG), electrodes placed on the scalp record the electrical activity of the skull. Since this activity reflects the electrical activity of a large number of neurons, EEG does not provide high spatial resolution, although it does provide high temporal resolution (Luck, 2005). Thus, researchers using EEG are more interested in the time course of cognitive processes than their location in the brain. In a variant of EEG, called event-related potentials (ERP), the electrical activity is measured while similar stimuli are presented several times, making it possible to produce more reliable data than those obtained by EEG since some noise can be removed.

Functional Magnetic Resonance Imaging (fMRI) is a technique that measures changes in blood oxygenation in response to neural activity (e.g. Huettel et al., 2004). Neurons need energy to function, and this energy is supplied by the glucose and oxygen present in blood. Thus, an increase of activity in a brain region is accompanied by an increase in the blood flow to that region. By using fMRI, it is possible to produce activation maps that show which brain regions carry out specific mental tasks. fMRI is the most commonly used brain-imaging technique in psychology and cognitive neurosciences.

Positron emission tomography (PET) detects a radioactive substance (called a *tracer*) that has been injected into the bloodstream. Tracers bind to compounds such as glucose, which is used extensively by the brain (see the discussion of fMRI above). The PET scanner detects the level of radioactivity in different regions of the brain, making it possible to construct a three-dimensional image of the distribution of the tracer. PET and in particular fMRI have an excellent spatial resolution, but a poor temporal resolution.

With transcranial magnetic simulation (TMS), small brain regions are stimulated via electromagnetic induction. This is done by placing a *coil* (a magnetic field generator) over the scalp. The coil generates short magnetic pulses and thus creates small electric currents that go painlessly through the skull and affect brain function.

---

completed 80 trials, which took about 20 minutes. In the second experiment, they completed 880 trials (over 8 hours). In both experiments, response times decreased but accuracy did not improve. There was no functional reorganisation in the brain. The decrease in response time was matched by a decrease in activation in the occipital cortex and in the prefrontal and parietal areas thought to be involved in working memory (WM).

In Hempel et al.'s (2004) study, participants were scanned three times: before training, after 2 weeks of training and after 4 weeks of training. The n-back task, a common measure of WM, was used. In this task, a sequence of stimuli is presented to the participants, who have to decide whether the current stimulus is the same as the stimulus n steps earlier. The variable n makes it possible to vary the load factor: the larger n, the more difficult the task. Hempel et al. used three n values: 0-back, 1-back and 2-back. The results indicated a non-linear pattern: WM areas showed an initial increase in activation of fMRI signals, followed by a decrease. The regions involved were the right inferior frontal gyrus and the right intraparietal sulcus. As the load factor increased, activation increased in these areas.

10.3 Typical Data in Neuro-Expertise

10.3.1 Mental Calculation

In a PET study on mental calculation, Pesenti et al. (2001) compared an expert prodigy with a group of non-experts. The experiment contrasted the calculation of complex results to the retrieval of arithmetic results by memory look up. The expert and the non-experts used some of the same brain areas, which corresponded to posterior areas involved with working memory and visual imagery (e.g. supramarginal gyrus and intraparietal sulcus). Most of the areas that were activated only by the expert concerned episodic memory (right prefrontal and medial temporal areas). Only the mental calculation expert was able to switch between strategies involving working-memory storage and strategies using episodic memory to efficiently encode and retrieve information. Overall, the results with this expert support the hypothesis of a cerebral functional reorganisation implicating LTM areas.

10.3.2 Memory Champions

Maguire et al. (2003) compared memory experts to control participants using fMRI. The expert group, which included participants in the World Memory Championship, had been using mnemonic techniques (mostly the method of loci; see Chapter 3) for 11 years on average. The participants were required to memorise sequences of six items presented visually and individually for 4 seconds each. Three types of stimuli were used: three-digit numbers, faces and snowflakes. While participants in both groups showed activation in WM frontal areas, three brain regions were active only for the mnemonists: the left medial superior parietal cortex, the bilateral retrosplenial cortex and the right posterior hippocampus. These LTM regions play an important role in spatial memory and navigation (e.g. Burgess et al., 2002). Their activation is consistent with the fact that the mnemonists used the method of loci, a learning strategy that uses spatial locations as retrieval cues.

10.3.3 Chess

In Campitelli et al.'s (2007) study, chess players performed a task in which a visual display had to be maintained in memory. The stimuli were related or unrelated to chess. In addition, there was a control task in which chess stimuli were used, but with no requirement of memory. When the activation in the control task was subtracted from that in the memory task with chess stimuli, there was activity in frontal and parietal areas. These areas are related to working-memory processes. In the contrast between chess and non-chess stimuli, chess players displayed a pattern of activation in medial temporal areas (including the fusiform gyrus, the parahippocampal gyrus, and inferior temporal gyrus), which are thought to be involved in LTM storage. However, some unexpected activations were also found in the precunei, the posterior cingulated and the supramarginal gyrus.

Wright et al. (2013) were interested in the neural events that take place when novice and expert chess players make simple judgements. With chess positions presented for 0.5 seconds, the four experimental conditions were to indicate whether the white king was in check, whether it was not in check, whether the black knight was present and whether it was not present. Experts were able to identify check configurations with near perfect accuracy within about 500 ms. The analysis of the event-related potential responses indicated that there were differences between experts and novices as early as the onset of N2 (second negativity peak). This suggests that, 240 ms after a chess configuration is presented, a strong player's brain already carries out a functional analysis of it by accessing complex neural structures.

10.3.4 Music

Several studies have shown that playing musical instruments leads, compared to non-musicians, to increased cortical representations in the motor cortex of the relevant hand. These representations are specific to the muscles used. For example, Elbert et al. (1995) found that playing string instruments leads, with right-handed musicians, to increased representations of the fingers on the left hand, which must make fine movements for fingering the strings, but not on the right hand. Interestingly, the cortical reorganisation was more prominent in musicians who started playing music early in their lives. Bengtsson et al. (2005) demonstrated an increased myelination in white matter tracts in professional pianists. The effect was mostly present in areas that were engaged with practice at age 16 or younger.

Jancke et al. (2000) found that extensive practice led to greater efficiency and less processing, as shown by the fact that the primary and secondary motor areas were less active in professional musicians than in a control group.

Comparing professional musicians to non-musicians, Schneider et al. (2002) found that, as rapidly as 19 ms after the presentation of pure tones, the activity in the primary auditory cortex was twice as large in musicians. In addition, the grey matter volume of a specific portion of the Heschl's gyrus (a region in the primary auditory cortex) was 130 per cent larger with musicians. Both measures correlated strongly with musical aptitude.

10.3.5 Taxi Drivers

To obtain their licence, taxi drivers in London have to learn *the Knowledge*: the location of thousands of tourist attractions and about 25,000 streets that lie within 10 kilometres of Charing Cross train station. Acquiring this takes between 3 and 4 years on average and is challenging: 50 per cent of the candidates fail the exam. Maguire et al. (2000) were interested in how acquiring this knowledge affects the brain. The interest focused on the hippocampus, a brain structure known to process spatial information. They found that, compared to matched controls, there was more grey matter in taxi drivers' posterior hippocampi, but less grey matter in the anterior part.

10.3.6 Sports

In badminton, the index finger and the thumb play an essential role in holding the racket, changing grips depending on the kind of shots used (e.g. serve, forehand or backhand) and shifting between power and precision play. Pearce et al. (2000) were interested in the way the acquisition of badminton skill affected the parts of the brain controlling these fingers. Using transcranial magnetic stimulation (TMS), they contrasted a group of five right-handed elite badminton players with a group of amateurs and a control group consisting of individuals who did not play badminton. Compared to the amateurs and the non-players, the elite players showed increased motor-evoked-potential amplitudes. There was evidence for structural differences between novices and experts: experts showed changes in their cortical motor maps, but only for the playing hand and not for the non-playing hand. This asymmetry in motor maps suggests that the changes are task specific. According to Pearce et al., these results suggest that the experts' corticomotor system undergoes a process of long-term functional reorganisation as they acquire motor skills.

Draganski et al. (2004) studied how novices acquire a simple juggling routine (a standard three-ball cascade). There were two groups of participants, equally inexperienced in juggling at the beginning of the experiment. The first group learned juggling during 3 months. The second group served as a control and did not practise juggling. Three brain scans were performed: before training, at the end of training (defined as being able to juggle for at least 60 seconds) and 3 months after the end of training. The participants in the juggling group did not practise between the second and the third scan, with the consequence that most of them were not able to carry out the three-ball cascade fluently any more when the final scan was taken.

A comparison between the first and second scans showed that there was, for the juggling group but not for the non-juggling group, a bilateral increase in grey matter in the mid-temporal area and in the left posterior intraparietal sulcus. Interestingly, these brain areas are devoted to the processing and storage of visual motion rather than motor processing. There was also a strong correlation between the expansion of grey matter and level of performance. At the third scan, when participants in the juggling group had stopped practising, grey matter in these brain areas tended to revert back to the baseline. These results show that changes due to learning lead to transient structural changes in the brain. Thus, as noted by Draganski et al. (p. 311), this research "contradicts the traditionally held view that cortical plasticity is associated with functional rather than anatomical changes".

Using voxel-based morphometry, Bezzola et al. (2011) studied brain plasticity in participants between 40 and 60 years of age. Compared to a control group, a group of golf novices showed grey matter increases after a period of 40 hours of golf practice that was undertaken as a leisure activity. The brain areas implicated included sensorimotor regions and parts of the dorsal stream. There was also a correlation between the intensity of the training (the number of days needed to finish the 40-hour training; thus, the fewer days needed, the more intensive the training) and the increase of grey matter in the parieto-occipital junction.

In sports such as archery, rifle shooting and golf, the preparatory period before initiating any movement (the so-called "pre-shot routine") plays a crucial role, and experts can display more consistent behaviour during this period (Hatfield & Hillman, 2001). Milton et al. (2007) aimed to find brain differences between novice and expert golfers during this phase of motor planning. Participants were placed in a scanner and had to perform their pre-shot routine when viewing golf scenes. Some brain regions were activated with novices only (the posterior cingulated cortex, the basal ganglia and the amygdala-forebrain complex), while others were activated with experts only (the superior parietal lobule, the occipital cortex and the dorso-lateral premotor area). The authors propose that these differences indicate a more efficient organisation of networks with experts. In addition, the fact that the novices displayed a higher overall brain activity suggests that they found it difficult to filter information.

We have seen in Chapter 2 on perception and categorisation that expert athletes excel at predicting their opponent's behaviour using kinematic cues from their body. Aglioti et al. (2008) investigated the neural correlates of this ability with professional basketball players using transcranial magnetic stimulation. They used two control groups: novices and *expert watchers* (sport journalists and coaches), that is individuals with similar visual experience as expert players. The task consisted in predicting the outcome of free throws shown on a video. Expert players predicted the outcome of free throws earlier and were more accurate. In addition, in comparison with the two other groups, experts were better at predicting the outcome of the shot before the ball had left the shooter's hands. Watching throws led to an increase of motor-evoked potentials with both expert players and expert watchers, but missed shots led to a time-specific activation only with players.

In the same line of research on sport anticipation tasks, Wright and Jackson (2007) (with tennis) and Wright et al. (2010) (with badminton) have identified specific brain areas where greater activation occurs in experts than novices. The relevant areas of what they call the "Expert Mirror Neuron System" comprise a core mirror neuron system (Rizzolatti & Craighero, 2004) and various extensions including areas underpinning visual attention.

In Wright et al.'s study (2011), expert and novice football players were shown video clips in point-light format, from the point of view of the defender. There were two tasks, which used the same stimuli: to determine whether the attacker used a deceptive move (step-over) or not, and to predict the ball direction. A subset of the mirror neuron system displayed greater activation for experts than for novices. Compared to direction identification, deception identification led to greater activation in the dorsolateral prefrontal cortex, the medial frontal cortex, the anterior insula, the cingulate gyrus and the premotor cortex. In contrast, activation was larger for direction than for deception in the anterior cingulate cortex and the caudate nucleus. The authors conclude that explicit detection of deceptive moves requires cognitive effort and recruits brain regions linked to emotions and social cognition.

10.4 Proposed Mechanisms

10.4.1 The Fixed Localisation vs. Perceptual Expertise Debate

A hallmark in many domains of expertise concerns the ability to carry out fine object discriminations between members of a category. Often, the members look very similar, making discrimination challenging; for example, an ornithologist will discriminate between birds that differ only by subtle variations in colour, or a car expert will recognise car models that look alike to a novice.

Face recognition is a paradigmatic example of expertise in object discrimination, where most of us can easily recognise faces in spite of the fact that they all consist of the same subparts (eyes, nose, mouth) arranged in a similar way spatially.[1] Among the many theories that have been developed in neuroscience to explain face recognition, two are worth mentioning since they create incompatible views and have generated a long-lasting debate. Both theories use bottom-up approaches, meaning that they assume that face recognition is automatic and stimulus driven. Both also assume that cognitive functions are modular and localised in specific parts of the brain. The difference concerns the specificity of the brain region concerned.

Kanwisher et al. argue that a specific region of the brain (the fusiform face area, FFA, which is located at the bottom of the temporal lobe) responds preferentially to faces (Kanwisher et al., 1997). The evidence is based not only on fMRI, but also on single-neuron recordings in monkeys, which suggest that specific neurons preferentially respond to faces. An additional source of evidence is behavioural and relates to a number of experimental results that seem to apply to faces only and not to other objects. For example, it is more difficult to recognise photographs of faces when they are presented upside down or as negatives.

The second view is that the FFA is a visual area that carries out the visual processing of objects we are highly familiar with (Gauthier et al., 1999). Since we perceive a large number of faces every day and thus have become experts in face perception, it logically follows that the FFA is activated when recognising faces. Therefore, rather than being a part of the cortex innately and uniquely specialised with face processing, the FFA is engaged in any domain where one acquires expertise in object recognition. The line of research known as *perceptual expertise* has actually taken face recognition as a model domain to explain expertise in other domains.

Recently, Harel et al. (2013) have systematically criticised these two theories and called the debate between them fruitless. While the debate has generated many experiments, not much progress has been made in resolving it, since many results have been inconsistent and non-replicable. Specifically, Harel et al. argue three main points. First, expertise differences in the neural processing of face perception and, more generally, perceptual expertise are present not only in the FFA but throughout the visual cortex, including the early stages of visual processing. Second, perceptual expertise engages parts of the cortex (e.g. parietal cortex and prefrontal cortex) that lie outside the visual cortex. Third, perceptual expertise is modulated by top-down processes such as attention, and thus is not fully automatic and stimulus driven. Harel et al. (2013) propose an alternative approach where information processing in expert cognition is not localised but distributed in areas that interact (see Uttal, 2011, for the same argument about cognitive processing in general). In general, Harel et al. argue that the focus on the FFA to explain perceptual expertise is misguided, since expertise in most domains relies not only on object recognition, but also on conceptual knowledge, memory and decision making. Arguing for a similar

---

[1]Note that face recognition does not fit our definition of expertise (see Chapter 1), which limits the term to top-level performers in a field. However, we address face recognition expertise in some detail, because of the large literature it has generated.

point, Gobet et al. (2004) note that an understanding of perceptual expertise requires computational theories covering all these cognitive functions.

10.4.2 Mechanisms Linked to Intelligence

In Chapter 7, we have noted that intelligence correlates with expertise in several domains. Thus, an obvious hypothesis is that intelligence plays a causal role in the acquisition and maintenance of expertise. Spearman (1927) argued that differences in general intelligence (g) are due to differences in *mental energy*, but beyond this metaphorical proposal did not propose concrete biological mechanisms. The next step is obviously to postulate the presence of such mechanisms and to speculate on them. Several explanations have been proposed, many of which are still being explored. We briefly review some of the most important explanations and the extent to which they have been supported by the data.

A first possibility is that individual differences in nerve conduction velocity (the speed at which nerve fibres transmit electrical impulses) set a limit on the rate of information processing and thus on intelligence (Reed, 1984). A similar idea was proposed by Eysenck (1986), who viewed information processing as the transmission of signals and argued that intelligence is a function of both the fidelity and the speed with which a message is transmitted. Errors of transmission add noise, which can be reduced through additional sampling, but this requires time. Biologically, a possible mechanism is offered by myelin (the fatty substance that insulates the electrical conductivity of axons): as myelin affects neural transmission rates, individual differences in myelinisation should affect intelligence. The prediction is then that intelligence should correlate with speed of transmission. Several studies have measured the speed of peripheral nerve conduction velocity, for example from elbow to wrist, and correlated it with IQ. Overall, the results have been inconsistent, so this hypothesis has received only weak support, if any at all (Vernon et al., 2000).

A second possibility is that, because they contain more neurones and synapses, larger brains have more computational power and are more efficient, and thus lead to more intelligence. The strong form of the argument (larger brains imply more intelligence) is clearly empirically wrong: females have about 4 billion (about 16 per cent) neurons less than males, but there are no differences in IQ. However, evolutionary considerations and empirical data suggest that a weaker version of the argument (brain size is one of the factors underpinning intelligence) might have some truth. There have been important changes in brain capacity in the last 3 million years: while the brain of the Australopithecus weighed 450 g, that of Homo Sapiens weighs 1,200–1,500 g. In addition, the brain is an "expensive" organ; while it represents only 2 per cent of body weight, it uses 20 per cent of metabolic energy of the body, so any increase in brain size should have led to some evolutionary advantage worth the energetic cost.

In addition, the correlation between the size of the head (and, consequently, the volume of the brain) and IQ seems to be genuine, as shown by an analysis of more than 54 experiments (Vernon et al., 2000), where it ranged from .15 to .40. This correlation holds when considering only the most sophisticated measures such as those obtained with brain-imaging techniques. The size effects are manifest throughout the brain, and not limited to particular areas. Brain volume correlates mainly with *g*, fluid ability and memory, and does not correlate with crystallised ability. Interestingly, the correlation is equally strong in males and in females. However, the meaning of these results is unclear. There were methodological problems with some of the early studies (e.g. age, body size or the presence of neurological troubles were not always controlled for) but these were corrected in later studies. But more importantly, the correlations can be accounted for both by genetic and environmental factors, or an interaction of both. Two environmental factors might be mentioned here: nutrition and the presence of an intellectually stimulating environment (Mackintosh, 1998).[2]

A third possibility is that brain efficiency correlates with intelligence. If this is the case, then intelligent people should perform better even with very simple tasks such as discriminating, as quickly as possible, between two vertical lines (one long and one short) that appear on a computer screen. While early experiments found a strong negative correlation (−.70) between IQ and detection time in this task (Nettelbeck & Lalley, 1976), subsequent experiments found much weaker correlations or failed to find any correlation at all (Mackintosh, 1998).

A different way to explore the hypothesis of brain efficiency is to measure the ongoing bioelectrical activity of the brain using electroencephalography (EEG) or event-related potentials (ERPs, aka evoked potentials), which are computed by averaging EEG activity over a series of repeated stimulus presentations. As ERPs are waves, a number of variables can be computed: amplitude, location of negative and positive peaks, and measure of waveform complexity. Generally, in spite of considerable research efforts in this direction using a variety of tasks, the results have been highly inconsistent, in part because a number of confounded variables (e.g. participants' strategies) are difficult to control for (Mackintosh, 1998).

In spite of a substantial amount of experimental and theoretical research, the search for the biological basis of intelligence has not yielded convincing results (Mackintosh, 1998). This lack of success has not abated enthusiasm for this line of research. On the contrary, recent developments in brain imaging and genomics have given it renewed vigour. Our view is that *g*, albeit a measure that has great practical advantages, loses too much information by pooling together different kinds of intelligences into a single variable. A more promising way to study the link between expertise and intelligence and to

---

[2]This line of research is obviously very controversial and has generated multiple debates. For a critique, see Gould (1981); for a sympathetic view, see Hunt (2011).

understand its biological basis is to use more refined measures of intelligence, such as verbal and visuospatial intelligence.

10.4.3 Functional Reorganisation of the Brain: The Role of Retrieval Structures and Templates

Guida et al. (2012) reviewed the neuroimaging literature about the acquisition of expertise in tasks involving working memory (e.g. mental calculation, abacus calculation, chess and n-back tasks). As the examples given in this chapter have made clear, this literature is confusing, since two apparently contradictory patterns of results co-exist. On the one hand, when experts are included, activations are found in brain regions that are typically activated when LTM tasks are performed. Thus, experts seem to use part of long-term memory as a virtual working memory; this kind of activation is not observed with novices. This pattern of results is consistent with functional reorganisation of the brain.

On the other hand, studies involving novices progressing through a training program show a decrease in brain activation, with no functional reorganisation. Guida et al. argue that the practice periods used in these studies (typically several hours and at most dozens of hours) are too short to allow the full acquisition of LTM knowledge structures such as retrieval structures (Ericsson & Kintsch, 1995) and templates (Gobet & Simon, 1996d), which allow parts of LTM to be used as working memory. They propose that the two patterns of brain activation described in the literature are not contradictory, but involve two stages of the same process of expertise acquisition: first a decreased activation relying mostly on chunk acquisition, and second a functional reorganisation of the brain when retrieval structures and/or templates are fully acquired, which enable a rapid encoding into LTM. This two-process model uses both the principle of brain localisation and that of brain plasticity.

10.4.4 Geschwind and Galaburda's (1987) Theory

Geschwind and Galaburda's (1987) theory aims to explain a complex pattern of results linking brain lateralisation, autism, dyslexia and proneness to allergies, among other things. They argue that talent in visuospatial domains (e.g. chess, mathematics) is linked to handedness, with experts in these domains being more likely than the population to be left-handed or ambidextrous. Since visuospatial abilities are mostly underpinned in the right hemisphere of the brain, a more developed right hemisphere should allow better performance in visuospatial tasks. The proposed mechanism is that great exposure or high sensitivity to intrauterine testosterone in the developing male foetus results in a less developed left hemisphere than normal and, by compensation, a more developed right hemisphere. Differences in testosterone levels will also impact the immune system.

The theory is partly supported by empirical data. For example, non-right-handers tend to be more represented in visuospatial domains such as chess (see Chapter 7), and there is a correlation between aptitudes in mathematics and spatial skills. Some developmental data are particularly striking: children with mathematical talent are twice as likely to be left-handers, twice as likely to suffer from allergies and tend to have language difficulties such as stuttering and dyslexia (Winner, 1996). In addition, most savants with mathematical talent are autistic, and autism is four times more likely to affect boys than girls. The gender differences in mathematical ability that we have discussed in Chapter 7 are also in line with the theory.

However, not all the predictions of the theory have been supported by the data. Brain-imaging data with board game players shows that bilateral activation is typical, and not just activation in the right hemisphere as predicted (Gobet et al., 2004). Finally, the links with allergies have been disputed (e.g. Dellatolas et al., 1990).

10.5 Gender Differences

We have seen in Chapter 7 that there are no gender differences at the level of general intelligence. However, there are differences with respect to brain volume. Females have a smaller brain than males on average, and the difference remains when corrections are made for body size. On average, females have about 4 billion (about 16 per cent) neurons less than males. The difference in brain size is almost certainly due to genetic differences, since the difference exists at birth, with the brain being about 12 per cent heavier and head circumference about 2 per cent greater in males than in females (Janowsky, 1989). However, making sense of these differences is challenging. There is no difference in general IQ and the correlation between brain size and IQ is equally strong in males and in females. When put together, these results are puzzling and raise questions about the utility of measures such as brain size.

By contrast, clear gender differences have been found with respect to different aspects of intelligence (e.g. verbal, spatial and mechanical intelligence), with a fair amount of research devoted to understanding the brain substrates of these differences (see Halpern, 2013, for a review). Females have a higher ratio of grey matter (the body of neurones) to white matter (axons connecting neurons together), and males show the inverse proportion (i.e. more white matter than grey matter). Note that this difference in proportion nearly disappears when the overall size of the brain is controlled for. Amongst other differences, the corpus callosum is larger in females, and female brains show higher left-right symmetry.

The reasons for these differences are not well understood. A classic explanation for differences in brain organisation is that they are shaped by evolutionary pressures. In prehistoric times, men hunted (which relied on spatial ability) and women gathered (where verbal abilities were useful in communication).

However, the validity of this explanation is debatable: communication was surely useful in hunting as well, for example in coordinating efforts, and spatial intelligence would similarly have helped women to remember the way to places rich in berries and other fruits.

Given the high plasticity of the brain, a simple environmental explanation seems at least as plausible as the evolutionary explanation just mentioned. Given social pressure, in our culture children receive different toys and games depending on their gender: boys tend to play with small cars, toy weapons and construction sets, while girls tend to play with dolls and kitchen sets. Different socialisation and expectations may also be significant factors in explaining differences in the types of intelligences in which girls and boys excel. In any case, there is substantial evidence showing that intelligence is the product of a complex interaction between biological and environmental factors (Halpern, 2013).

10.6 Smart Drugs

Acquiring expertise is hard work. Could novel technologies make this process quicker and smoother? In Chapter 8, we have already seen that this has been achieved to some extent by better training methods, and in Chapter 11 we will discuss doping in sports. Recently, there has been much excitement in using *smart drugs* in cognitive domains. Smart drugs, also known as nootropics, memory enhancers and cognitive enhancers, cover a large number of drugs and food supplements that are supposed to improve learning, memory, intelligence, problem solving, decision making, planning, concentration and other mental abilities. Amongst many others, they include products such as amphetamines, methylphenidates and modafinil. To some extent, they can be considered as the cognitive equivalent of doping substances in sports.

While such substances have been used for a long time in our society, as is witnessed by the widespread use of caffeine and nicotine, there has been an increase in the use of more powerful substances in recent years. Although estimates vary considerably, surveys "suggest that the practice is commonplace" (Smith & Farah, 2011, p. 717). A large nationwide survey in the United States (10,904 students at 119 colleges and universities, both public and private) found that 2.1 per cent (past-month), 4.1 per cent (past-year) and 6.9 per cent (lifetime) had used smart drugs (McCabe et al., 2005). Prevalence seems to be higher in leading and competitive universities, where estimates are as high as 25 per cent. There is little information about smart-pill use outside of university students.

In their review of literature, Smith and Farah (2011) conclude that stimulants seem to improve declarative memory, but that the effects on cognitive control and working memory are weaker and less reliable. In some cases (e.g. modafinil, a substance used for treating individuals with narcolepsy or attention deficit disorders), the positive effects seem limited to "lower-performing" individuals

(Müller et al., 2004). While the benefits of smart drugs are still limited, it is likely that they will be more efficient in the future as our understanding of the brain improves.

The use of artificial substances for improving cognition raises important ethical issues. For example, several smart drugs are known to have side effects (e.g. psychotic symptoms); their long-term effects are, as of yet, unknown; and they offer an unfair advantage, akin to doping in sport. Cakic (2009) refutes the last issue by arguing that commonly accepted educational practices, such as private tutoring, can also be considered as providing an unfair advantage that can be enjoyed only by students whose parents are wealthy. He also notes that it is likely to be impossible to enforce a prohibition of smart drugs. In a similar line of argument, Sententia (2004) promotes the notion of *cognitive liberty* and argues that, as long as cognition enhancing substances do not harm other people, they should be tolerated. In addition, it is crucial that individuals possess the necessary information for deciding what constitutes an acceptable risk for themselves.

10.7 Chapter Summary

In this chapter, we have met the nature vs. nurture debate yet again, this time in a slightly different guise. Proponents of talent tend to defend modularity and brain localisation of cognitive functions, while champions of practice emphasise the role of brain plasticity. The available data support both sides: there is evidence for localisation (e.g. data on music or chess) while there is also evidence for brain plasticity (e.g. fMRI changes picked up after one hour of practice in a skill acquisition task or brain functional reorganisation as a function of expertise, with LTM areas acting as virtual working memory). If anything, the evidence seems to more strongly support the hypothesis of plasticity.

A weakness of the research in neuro-expertise and of brain-imaging research in general is that participants' strategies are ignored in most of the studies. Now, it is clear that brain activity is a direct function of the strategy used (e.g. a strategy favouring verbal information processing will lead to different brain activation than a strategy based on visuospatial processing) and it is known that strategies play a role even in simple tasks such as categorisation (Gobet et al., 1997; Medin & Smith, 1981). If anything, the role of strategies is likely to become more important as tasks become more complex. Thus, at least some part of the noise in the data can be accounted for by the different strategies used.

Interestingly, this chapter has provided support for two theories discussed in Chapter 3 that were developed to account for psychological data and did not discuss neuroscientific data: template theory (Gobet & Simon, 1996d) and long-term working memory (Ericsson & Kintsch, 1995). Guida et al. (2012) show how the apparently confusing pattern of data in the expertise and skill acquisition literature could be explained by the central assumption of these two theories, that LTM structures can be recruited to expand working memory so long as experts have the requisite knowledge structures. Thus, decreased activation and brain functional reorganisation are two stages of a same process of expertise acquisition.

In spite of considerable amounts of research and some interesting data, it is unclear whether neuroscience has really taught us anything surprising and critical regarding the understanding of expertise. For example, the data about the neuroscience of music relate to brain regions (e.g. auditory cortex and motor areas) that were already known to be essential for music perception and motor action. The fact that extensive practice affects the brain is not surprising either: when knowledge – be it implicit or explicit – is acquired, it has to be stored in the brain, which must cause changes at the biological level. The data on brain functional reorganisation in working-memory tasks are interesting and useful in evaluating psychological theories, but they did not lead to new theories or mechanisms. Some authors (e.g. Uttal, 2011) have argued that studying the brain at the level of brain regions, as is commonly done in cognitive neuroscience, is the wrong level of analysis. This discussion is relevant here, and it could be argued that studying the nervous system at lower levels, such as the level of neurons, neurotransmitters or even DNA, may be more fruitful. Examples of this approach include Eysenck (1995) and Chassy and Gobet (2011a). Another limit of current research in neuro-expertise is that little is said about the role of the environment and how it interacts with the brain.

10.8 Further Reading

Levitin's (2006) *This is Your Brain on Music* provides an entertaining introduction to the psychology and neuroscience of music. More technical material is presented in the collection of papers edited by Peretz and Zatorre (2003). Geschwind and Galaburda (1987) describe their theory of laterality in exquisite detail, and Winner (1996) provides a more accessible description. Halpern (2013) reviews the biological mechanisms underpinning gender differences in cognition.

CHAPTER 11

Experts and Society

11.1 Preview of Chapter

In the introductory chapter, we have considered a number of definitions of expertise. The definition we proposed stated that an expert is someone performing better than the majority of individuals in a field. Other definitions stressed the importance of diplomas and reputation, and more generally the fact that experts are defined by social constituencies. Such definitions are common in social psychology and sociology, which have broadly focused either on the failings and limits of expertise and experts, or on experts' fight for power. Exactly why these fields provide a rather negative picture of experts is not clear, but the fact is that social psychologists and sociologists have rarely emphasised the great achievements obtained by experts in various domains. Thus, the contrast between the previous chapters and this (and the following) chapter is stark. For example, while previous chapters emphasised the problem-solving ability of Einstein, these two chapters will highlight his failed predictions. Lest the reader reach wrong conclusions, we emphasise that the studies discussed in these two chapters present an analysis of expertise that is too negative in our view: it is true that Einstein made dreadful errors in some of his predictions and indeed failed to fulfil his dream of a unified theory of fundamental physical forces, but his positive contributions changed humankind's understanding of the universe for ever.

This chapter addresses various aspects of the link between experts and society. It considers several fields where experts perform poorly and tries to understand why it is so. It then addresses the role of the media and the Internet, and the way expertise is affected by group phenomena. After dealing with another failure of expertise (fraud and cheating in science), it tries to understand why people tend to believe experts in spite of all these shortcomings. The following chapter will focus on the sociology of the professions and on the way sociology has addressed the identification and classification of experts. It will also cover the issues of trust, expert testimony and how experts communicate their expertise.

11.2 The Difficulty of Making Correct Predictions

The failures of experts can have serious consequences. For example, there is currently a large debate as to whether global warming is a threat or not, with most scientists arguing that it is but some dissenting. Obviously, global warming cannot be both a threat and not a threat at the same time, and some experts must be wrong. Either way, to err is costly: on the one hand, unnecessary environmental measures can be implemented and money wasted if the threat is illusory; on the other hand, lack of action could have catastrophic ecological consequences if the threat is real. Here we can see experts' importance, social responsibility and the difficulty of their task. With most of the serious problems facing humanity – global warming, starvation, economic crisis, terrorism, international conflicts – there is no easy solution because these problems are extremely complex.

The bad news is that experts do not have a particularly good track record with these crucial issues. You will remember that few experts predicted the financial crisis that crippled the world markets in 2008 and in the following years. Cerf and Navasky (1998) have compiled a large number of experts' predictions that turned out horribly wrong. A few examples will suffice. Less than 2 weeks before Wall Street crashed in 1929, Irving Fisher, a renowned economist at Yale University, stated that the stocks would remain high for ever. In 1932, Albert Einstein predicted that it would never be possible to release nuclear energy. In 1962, Decca Records rejected the Beatles, arguing that guitar bands were becoming out of fashion and that the Beatles had no future.

11.3 A Miscarriage of Justice

A tragic example of the consequences of an expert's error was provided by the case of solicitor Sally Clark. In 1998, Clark was arrested and put to trial for the murder of her two young sons. Both had died suddenly a few weeks after their birth. The defence argued for cot bed death, formally known as sudden infant death syndrome (SIDS). However, paediatrician Professor Sir Roy Meadow, speaking for the prosecution, argued that the likelihood of having two children dying from SIDS was minimal, given that Clark's family was well off. According to him, the chances of one SIDS death in such circumstances were 1 in 8,500, and the likelihood of two deaths were 1 in 73 million (8,500 × 8,500). As Meadow put it in his book on child abuse (Meadow, 1997, p. 29): "one sudden infant death is a tragedy, two is suspicious and three is murder, until proved otherwise". Rather, he argued that Clark suffered from the Munchausen syndrome by proxy. This syndrome is a rare type of child abuse in which a caregiver induces, exaggerates or fabricates physical or psychological illnesses or symptoms in a child, with the goal of receiving attention. Meadow's testimony had considerable weight, given that he was a top expert in this topic, having himself coined the term in a seminal paper (Meadow, 1977).

Clark was convicted. She appealed. The convictions were first upheld but then overturned on second appeal, on two main grounds. First, microbiological evidence suggesting natural causes for the death of Clark's second son was not disclosed by the prosecution to the defence. Second, as discussed in detail by Hill (2004), the statistical argument that Meadow presented to the jury contained several important errors. Essentially, Meadow incorrectly argued that the likelihoods of each child dying from SIDS were independent, while in fact they should be considered as dependent (e.g. due to the presence of genetic factors). Thus, the estimate of 1 chance out of 8,500 for the second death was exaggeratedly small: the probability of a second SIDS death given a first one is closer to 1 chance out of 100. Finally, the risk estimate of Clark being guilty should have included the (low) a priori probability that somebody with a socioeconomic background similar to Clark's would commit a murder.

As a result of this case, the General Medical Council struck Meadow off the medical register. (He was later reinstated.) This case also brought about a review of several hundred other cases and led to the acquittal of two other women that had been jailed for murdering their children. As for Clark, she had spent more than three years in jail when her name was cleared and never fully recovered from this traumatic experience. She died four years later from alcohol poisoning, after having suffered from alcoholism and other psychiatric problems.

11.4 When Experts Fail

So, are experts really expert? This question has been recently tackled in several books focusing on experts' failed predictions, such as Freedman (2010) and Gardner (2011). Their answer is a scathing "No!". Some, as investor Jim Rogers does, go as far as to argue that most experts are wrong most of the time. What is the evidence supporting this damning verdict on experts' incompetence?

Financial crises, global famine and management are three domains where experts fare particularly badly, to the point that Freedman (2010) and Gardner (2011) have argued that their predictions have been consistently worthless. In economics, a string of authors have incorrectly predicted depressions. But, ironically, hardly any economists predicted the 2007–2008 financial crisis and even months into it, many experts considered it to be minor. The situation is no better in academic research. Based on a statistical analysis of 276 empirical papers in the top economic journals, Delong and Lang (1992) concluded that essentially all economic null hypotheses in published articles are false, meaning that not much can be learnt from these articles. (If the research fails to reject the null hypothesis, this is due to lack of statistical power, and if the research rejects the null hypothesis, nothing is learnt, as nearly all null hypotheses are false.) Delong and Lang pointed to the publication bias as a likely explanation for this sorry state of affairs (more about the publication bias below).

A second topic where predictions have turned consistently wrong concerns the imminence of catastrophic world famine. Famed biologist Paul Ehrlich, starting with his book *The Population Bomb* (Ehrlich, 1968), has repeatedly predicted that, due to the exponential increase in world population and limited capacity resources of Earth, hundreds of millions will starve to death in the near future. Ehrlich claims that, unavoidably, this world famine would lead to a Mad Max type of anarchy and unrest. Similar predictions can be found in academic papers and other books on the topic, which has become a profitable cottage industry (see Gardner, 2011, for details). While, sadly, too many people still die of starvation, this is not due to lack of food on Earth, but to political and economic reasons. Considerable progress in agricultural science and technology – what is often called the Green Revolution – has actually led to a surplus of food (Jain, 2010).

A third field where the presence of expertise has been debated is management science. An endemic problem of the field concerns the paucity of empirical research and, when such research exists, the lack of replication (Stewart, 2009). In spite of this, there are thousands of books advising how to manage a business, from the *Search for Excellence* (Peters & Waterman, 1982) to *The Future of Management* (Hamel & Breen, 2007). Most of these books, as well as much of the literature on management, concerns fads that are not backed by proper scientific research, do not yield the expected results and are thus of short duration. Miller and Hartwick (2002) argue that such fads share a number of characteristics that make them fairly easy to spot. Fads offer simplistic advice and ignore the complexity of the real world. They are prescriptive, make false promises and propose one-size-fits-all practices, in spite of the fact that businesses come in multiple shapes and forms. They can be implemented only partially, to limited aspects of a business. They are novel, but not radically so, and resonate with current ideas and themes. Finally, they are typically endorsed by "gurus" who may have a number of followers.

Regrettably, these examples are not exceptions. In many domains, including science, experts obtain relatively poor performance or make incorrect predictions. In art, experts can be fooled surprisingly easily, as can be seen by the number of fakes acquired by museums and art galleries (Hoving, 1997). Secret intelligence services can be horribly wrong, as was witnessed by the failure to find Saddam Hussein's weapons of mass destruction, although Western intelligence agencies were convinced of their existence. And according to Groopman (2007), doctors' diagnoses are wrong one-sixth of the time.

11.4.1 Difficulties with Scientific Research

We have mentioned earlier the failure to replicate results in scientific economic papers. The problem is actually endemic throughout science. In an influential article, Ioannidis (2005) offers telling evidence from medicine. He combed the three top medical journals (*New England Journal of Medicine*, *JAMA* and the *Lancet*) and a number of specialised journals with a high impact factor. He then selected all the studies reporting original clinical-research that were published between 1990 and 2003 and that were cited at least 1,000 times in the scientific literature. From the articles satisfying these criteria, 45 found that the intervention discussed was effective. These studies were compared with replication studies that had equal or larger sample sizes and that used an experimental design at least as good as that used in the original study. Ioannidis found that 16 per cent of the findings were contradicted in the replications and 16 per cent of the effects were weaker in the subsequent studies. These findings have considerable practical implications: about one-third of the medical treatments originally found effective in highly cited publications are not supported by further research. The consequences can be tragic: from the early 1980s to the early 1990s, antiarrhythmic drugs based on clinical trials were routinely used to treat heart-attack patients. A large study then established that these drugs, while correcting irregular beats, actually increased the mortality rate by a factor of three. It is estimated that, in the USA alone, about 40,000 people a year died because of these drugs (Freedman, 2010).

Why are scientific publications so likely to be wrong? By definition, scientific research is at the boundary of knowledge and explores new ideas, and thus is characterised by much uncertainty. In addition, our world is complex, non-linear and contains a huge number of variables that interact in intricate ways. Prediction is especially difficult, since there is good evidence that many aspects of our world are chaotic in the technical sense that minute differences in the value of initial conditions can have massive consequences later in the future (Ruelle, 1991) – as the example goes, a butterfly flapping its wings in South America could lead to the formation of a hurricane in Texas. As Yogi Berra put it, "It's tough to make predictions, especially about the future".

Another important factor is that, as can be seen in any textbook on research methodology, the perfect experiment does not exist. Numerous are the confounding variables and other infelicities (e.g. lack of statistical power, errors in measurements) that can make interpretation of the results difficult. In addition, in biomedical domains, there is the added difficulty of extrapolating the results of animal experiments to humans. The availability of powerful statistical packages and data-mining methods also makes it easy for researchers to fish for statistically significant results, even though these might not reflect the original goals of the study. In spite of the cliché that correlation does not imply causation, many incorrect conclusions are still drawn due to this confusion. The presence of complex statistical methods makes this and related issues even more insidious.

But perhaps the most important source of wrong conclusions is the twin problem of publication bias and lack of replications, which essentially affects all sciences. Journal editors are likely to reject articles showing null results (e.g. that there is no difference between the treatment group and the control group), arguing that they do not contribute to knowledge. There is also a strong tendency, particularly in top journals, to publish research yielding surprising and counter-intuitive results. Such results are actually likely to be incorrect – that is why their degree of surprise is high (Howson & Urbach, 1989). Another aspect of the publication bias is that studies that support current theories and frameworks have a higher chance of being selected.

The difficulty of publishing null results gives raise to the notable *file-drawer problem* (Rosenthal, 1979). For any published study finding a statistically significant difference in an experiment, there exists an unknown but sometimes large number of studies that were not published, since no difference was found. The difficulty of publishing negative results has also the consequence that researchers are not keen to replicate studies, which in turn leads to the problem that there are too few replications in science. In fact, while replication is, in theory, at the core of scientific research, most empirical results are never replicated (e.g. Bornstein, 1990).

The pressure for researchers to publish has dramatically increased in the last decades, in part due to national evaluations of the quality of research (e.g. the Research Excellence Framework in the United Kingdom). This pressure has exacerbated the issues we have just discussed, leading in some cases to sloppiness, haste and even fraud (see below).

Another issue is that the scientific literature, even the technical, is replete with errors in reporting results. Within the subject matter of this book, Bilalić et al. (2008a) report how de Groot's classic study on chess problem solving has been consistently misreported. Some of the errors concern details and are unlikely to have consequences, but others concern crucial aspects of the experimental design or the results. Once present in the literature, it is hard to eradicate an error or an incorrect result. Interestingly, the publication of errata, where a significant error in a previously published paper is corrected, has only limited effect. Thomsen and Resnik (1995) found that, with papers corrected with an erratum in *Physical Review Letters*, the erratum was mentioned less than 40 per cent of the time along with the original. The rate was even lower with *Physical Review B*: errata were mentioned less than 5 per cent of the time. The situation is similar with retractions, where scientific articles are withdrawn either due to fraud or honest errors. In a study on retractions in the biomedical literature, Budd et al. (1998) found that only 19 out of 299 citations to retracted articles mentioned the retraction; in the 280 other citations, the original research was considered valid. Without better means to prevent this kind of error propagation, the self-correcting nature of science, and therefore its integrity, are at risk.

11.4.2 Predictions in Political Science

The most detailed empirical study of when experts get it wrong is the multi-year experiment carried out by Tetlock (2005) on predictions in political science. In an experiment that started in the mid-1980s at the height of the Cold War and that lasted 20 years, Tetlock asked 284 experts, consisting of political scientists, journalists, economists and historians, to make predictions about various aspects of politics both within and outside their domain of expertise. The questions he used were precise, such as "Would the United States go to war in the Persian Gulf?" and "Will Quebec secede from Canada within the next 5 years?" For each question, respondents were required to state the likelihood of (usually) three logically exclusive predictions. Altogether, Tetlock collected 82,361 subjective probability estimates from 27,450 predictions questions.

The data were submitted to a number of statistical analyses. Two measures were of particular interest. *Calibration* measures the extent to which experts' confidence matches their rate of successful predictions. For example, if an expert is on average 80 per cent confident about his predictions, and if 80 per cent of the predictions were correct, he would be perfectly calibrated. By contrast, an expert with an average confidence of 80 per cent but correct 40 per cent (or 100 per cent) of the time would be poorly calibrated. *Discrimination* measures the extent to which an expert adopts extreme positions, the two extremes being 0 per cent (the event will not happen) and 100 per cent (the event will happen). Predictions for which the odds are 50/50 are obviously not particularly predictive.

The results were stunning. On average, the experts' predictions were no better than chance. Calibration was particularly poor. As Tetlock (2005) put it, the human experts were barely better than a dart-throwing chimpanzee. One simple heuristic consistently beat the experts: "Predict no change". But note that this heuristic was not much better than chance.[1] Discrimination was somewhat better, although it was still very poor. Even more humbling is the result that experts were clearly beaten by sophisticated statistical forecasting techniques, such as generalised autoregressive distributed lag models.

Another important result was that there was a great variability between experts. In particular, two groups stood apart. Using the terminology of Berlin (1953), itself based on a poem by Greek poet Archilochos (680 BC), Tetlock (2005) differentiated between foxes and hedgehogs: "The fox knows many things, but the hedgehog knows one big thing". In his study, hedgehogs were uncomfortable with complexity and tried to simplify complex issues into one single and simple theoretical theme. They had one Big Idea, which they used repeatedly, and they tended to be confident about the accuracy of their predictions. When confronted with their incorrect predictions, the hedgehogs did not admit their mistakes but tried to explain them away, using a variety of ingenious tactics. They would insist that they made the right mistake: the details were wrong, but the prediction was in the right direction – better to be safe than sorry. They would challenge whether the conditions behind the question were logically consistent. They would invoke exogenous, unpredictable factors. For example, Gore's unexpected defeat against Bush was due Clinton's sexual affair with Monica Lewinsky and the following cover-up attempts and impeachment, which redefined the battle ground of the election as moral rather than economic. They would argue that they were correct, but

---

[1] Interestingly, the same heuristic of predicting no change does better than more sophisticated algorithms in predicting the price of oil, although the actual accuracy is poor (Alquist & Kilian, 2010).

that the time frame was wrong – they will yet be proved right in the future. They would argue that sometimes even the very improbable things happen. And they would point out that politics is hopelessly indeterminate.

By contrast, the foxes were comfortable with the complexity of the world and were in fact fascinated by it. They did not rely on a single idea but pursued several objectives. They tended to be opportunistic, drawing information from various sources. They were self-critical: they admitted their mistakes and tried to correct them. When compared to the hedgehogs, the foxes made better predictions, were better calibrated, and showed better discrimination.

The mode of thinking, as exemplified by the different cognitive styles of the foxes and hedgehogs, was the main predictor of performance. Other factors did not matter, such as political views, the level of optimism/pessimism, the field of specialism and whether experts had access or not to classified information. In general, more ideologically extreme hedgehogs made worse predictions. Surprisingly, the hedgehogs' predictions were poorer in their field of specialism – indeed they were even inferior to those of informed laypeople. In addition, while all experts' predictions deteriorated the farther in the future they were, as could have been expected, the effect was stronger with the hedgehogs.

Based on his results, Tetlock (2005) provides a few pieces of practical advice about how to critically listen to pundits and other experts on TV, be they politicians, economists, health experts or authors of popular science books. There exists an inverse correlation between experts' media profile and the accuracy of their predictions: the more articulated, confident, one-sided, assertive and complexity-simplifying the experts, the more likely they are to be wrong.

Editors of radio and TV programmes are not interested in experts stating that the world is complex and the future uncertain – this might be true, but this is rather boring. Rather, they prefer experts that make surprising predictions, even though these are likely to be wrong. Hedgehogs do not need to worry about the consequences of their incorrect predictions: these are rapidly forgotten. Of course, the rare correct predictions will be duly celebrated and advertised.

One criticism of Tetlock's (2005) research is that, in many domains including political science, the aim is not to make predictions, but rather to make good decisions given many different possibilities and a complex and uncertain world. Thus, chess grandmasters are not particularly good at predicting the exact move that the opponent will make, but play moves that are good given all the possible responses from the part of the opponent. Thus, some of Tetlock's conclusions may be too harsh. At the same time, being able to make correct predictions certainly helps, and there are domains where predictions are the name of the game (e.g. weather forecasting and astrology). In these cases, whether predictions are correct or incorrect is certainly a fitting way to evaluate the quality of expertise.

Expertocracy

An important aspect of the role of experts in society concerns *technocracy* (a type of government where decisions are made by individuals who are experts on technology) and *meritocracy* (a type of government where decisions are made by the best qualified individuals). These kinds of government imply the presence of an elite – the (technical) experts – who enjoy power and the privileges that come with it. Such forms of government are obviously problematic in democratic societies, since the requirement of equality is not met and democratic control is difficult (Turner, 2001). However, given the complexities faced by modern societies, it is inevitable that some institutional control will be in the hands of experts (Evetts et al., 2006).

11.5 The Role of Media

The media contribute to the non-reliability of experts' views in several ways (e.g. Freedman, 2010; Kitzinger & Reilly, 1997; Moynihan et al., 2000). First, they are selective in the studies they present, for obvious reasons preferring the sensational (but probably non-replicable) findings to the more common-sense (and probably replicable) findings. Second, the media generally focus on a single study, and do not provide a cumulative view of the research in a given field. In some cases, for example whether drinking alcohol or being slightly obese has health benefits, media reports consist of a random sequence of "yes" and "no" assertions. A more prudent answer would state that the results are contradictory and thus it is not possible to reach a definite position. This focus on one-shot studies sharply contrasts with the incremental nature of science. Third, whether a study will be discussed in the media depends more on the reputation of the institution where it was carried out and the efficiency of its public relations service than on the intrinsic quality of the research. Fourth, there is a tendency in the media to idealise scientists, with the consequence that media stories are rarely critical on the quality of the research.

Fifth, there is sometimes a halo effect, so to speak. For example, experts in physics are asked to provide their views about the economy, with the implicit assumption that expertise somehow generalises from physics to the economy. As we have seen in Chapter 4 when discussing the importance of specialisation, this is not the case, and relying on an expert's aura in one domain to receive advice in another is therefore misleading. Finally, as is well known by any scientist whose research has been reported in newspapers or on TV, journalists will add a variety of errors, due to misunderstandings, oversimplification, narrow focus on a particular point at the expense of the big picture, and premature conclusions. For example, a report on the possible benefits of drinking red wine will result in general advice to drink one glass of wine every day, conveniently ignoring other findings showing that even a single glass of wine every day might have negative health consequences.

11.6 Fraud and Cheating in Science

Another reason why scientific research can be unreliable is scientific fraud. Unfortunately, fraud and cheating are more common in science than normally thought (Fanelli, 2009). Misbehaviours include tampering with existing data, creating new data and plagiarism. Scientists face strong competitive pressure, and it is all too easy to fiddle with or even invent data. To some extent, fraud can be seen as a heuristic for scientific creativity – obviously one that is not recommended. Some of the most famous scientists are known to have misbehaved (Broad & Wade, 1983). Newton is thought to have tampered with his data in his *Principia*, lest imperfect data would invalidate a theory he was convinced was true. Mendel's experimental results on the heredity of peas show a near perfect ratio 3:1, which is highly improbable given the noise typically present in experimental data. Both with Newton and Mendel, the fit between the data and theory was too good to be true. More recently, the German physicist Jan Hendrik Schön published a series of apparently ground-breaking papers on semiconductors in top journals, including *Science* and *Nature*. He won several scientific prizes for his research. Alas, the data in at least 16 of his publications had been tampered with or fabricated, and Schön was found guilty of scientific misconduct (Beasley et al., 2002).

Psychology does not fare better with respect to misconduct and fraud. Cyril Burt, one of the fathers of the psychology of intelligence, is thought to have tampered with the twin data he collected to show that intelligence is mostly heritable (Gould, 1981; Mackintosh, 1995). In recent years, Marc Hauser, an evolutionary psychologist at Harvard, was found guilty of fabricating data and manipulating findings by the National Institute of Health's Office of Research Integrity, most notably when reporting on tamarin monkeys' ability to learn abstract rules when listening to spoken syllables (NIH, 2012). The Dutch social psychologist Diederik Stapel, a superstar in his field and Dean of the Social and Behavioural Sciences faculty at Tilburg University, had to admit that he fabricated and manipulated data over several years. The extent of his scientific misconduct was stunning, with at least 55 publications affected (Levelt Committee et al., 2013). The affair caused considerable damage to social psychology and science generally, not the least because several young researchers had used Stapel's data for their PhD or postdoctoral research, unaware that they had been tainted.

These cases all concern top scientists belonging to top universities having published in top journals. Are they exceptions or rather the tip of the iceberg? Sadly, recent surveys tend to give support to the latter. For example, Martinson et al. (2005), in a survey of 3,247 scientists having received funding from the US National Institute of Health, found that one-third had engaged in at least one of the ten behaviours considered as threatening the integrity of science within the previous three years. While only 0.3 per cent answered yes to "Falsifying or 'cooking' research data", the percentage was 6 per cent for

"Failing to present data that contradict one's own previous research", 12.5 per cent for "Overlooking others' use of flawed data or questionable interpretation of data", and 15.5 per cent to "Changing the design, methodology or results of a study in response to pressure from a funding source". Given the nature of the survey, it is possible that the percentages actually underestimate the amount of malpractice in scientific research.

The existence of fraudulent practices in scientific research is obviously highly problematic, for at least three reasons. First, it undermines the knowledge of a specific field of research. Second, it throws a shadow of doubt on researchers' scientific integrity, which is the bedrock of the reciprocal trust that is normally implicitly assumed in scientific research. Third, it damages the reputation of science generally in society.

Cheating in sports

In sports, where the financial incentives are vastly superior to science, cheating is an even more common phenomenon. Examples abound: in football, Diego Maradona scored a goal against England with the "hand of God"; in boxing, Mike Tyson bit off Evander Holyfield's left ear; and in figure skating, members of Tonya Harding's team attempted to break the right leg of arch-rival Nancy Kerrigan with a metal baton. But in sports, cheating is almost synonymous with doping.

A bizarre case of double cheating happened in 1904 during the marathon of the Olympic Games, held in St. Louis, Missouri (Chambaz, 2011; Rosen, 2008). The conditions were dreadful: a dirt track where the support cars kicked up dust, high humidity and hot temperature. An exhausted Frederick Lorz stopped running after 9 miles and found an easier mode of transportation: he travelled in his manager's car for the next 11 miles, after which he went back to running. Only when he was about to receive the gold medal was he disqualified. The final winner, Thomas Hicks, also bent the rules. When he showed signs of exhaustion about 10 miles before the end, his trainers gave him brandy and an injection of strychnine, a toxic substance used as pesticide but that acts as a stimulant at low doses. As Hicks again showed signs of weakness shortly after, he received a second dose of strychnine. It is thought that Hicks would have died if he had not received immediate medical attention at the finish line – it took 1 hour to revive him.

Doping was a national industry in former East Germany from the late 1960s until the reunification of Germany in 1990, and it was done with the blessing of the government (Rosen, 2008; Ungerleider, 2001). In most cases, athletes were not aware that they were taking illegal substances, believing that they were just taking vitamin pills. As many as 10,000 athletes were secretly drugged, sometimes as young as 12 years old. The drugs of choice consisted of high doses of testosterone, especially with women.

This programme led to incredible successes for a country as small as East Germany (17 million people): it finished third in the 1972 Munich Summer Games, behind the Soviet Union and the USA, and second in the 1976 Montreal Summer Games, again behind the Soviet Union but ahead of the USA. Some of the world records established during this period by East German athletes still stand. But doping also led to considerable suffering for the athletes involved, both psychologically (depression, confusion about sexual identity) and physically (infertility, birth defects, breast cancer, heart problems, testicular cancer).

Recent cases have shown that doping is still endemic in sport. In road bicycle racing, Lance Armstrong had won the Tour de France seven consecutive times after having defeated testicular cancer at the age of 25. For several years, he denied allegations of doping, including those made by the United States Anti-Doping Agency, but he finally admitted to cheating in January 2013. In athletics, sprinter superstars Tyson Gay (USA), Asafa Powell (Jamaica) and Sherone Simpson (Jamaica) tested positive for banned performance-enhancing drugs in July 2013.

What to do against doping in sports? New methods of doping, more difficult to detect, are continuously developed. Thus, doping is an arms race, with cheaters almost always ahead of the testers. Given these difficulties, one solution would be to allow doping, assuming that the doses are not dangerous. According to Savulescu et al. (2004), this would have the advantage of increasing transparency while minimising the number of cases where medical problems are developed. Whether it would eliminate all practical problems is doubtful. In addition, Savulescu et al.'s proposal has been criticised for ethical reasons – essentially, allowing doping would violate the essence of sports.

11.7 The Internet

Nowadays, anybody with a smart phone or a computer and a link to the Internet can access ridiculously vast amounts of information. This has changed both the definition of an expert and the relationship between non-experts and experts. With sufficient dedication and a minimal background in science, one can essentially become an expert in any scientific, technical or professional field. Searching for the relevant information and assimilating this information is certainly challenging, especially if the target domain is quantum mechanics or ancient Greek, but the information, including online tutorials and university courses, is available in a matter of seconds. Access to online knowledge is thus more efficient than using a public library, by several orders of magnitude. In addition, self-made experts can have an impact on a large readership – larger than through any academic channel. This requires some savvy and time (e.g. by playing Google's search algorithm to one's advantage). Ironically, self-made experts can influence standard experts, as these will use the Internet to carry out research or find relevant information.

An important consequence of these technological developments is that novices are not as clueless as they were in the past. Insurers, mortgage advisors and travel agents, for example, used to have the monopoly on information; nowadays, this information and much more can be obtained by a few searches on the Internet, with comparisons between different options available and even feedback from previous customers. The consequences can be astonishing. In a study of the prices of life insurance in the 1990s that controlled for individual and policy characteristics, Brown and Goolsbee (2002) showed that the appearance of comparison shopping sites on the Internet reduced the price of term-life insurances by 8–15 per cent. In health, *expert patients* can challenge the diagnosis proposed by their doctors, but also prepare useful questions in the way a treatment should be followed (Fox et al., 2005; Groopman, 2007; Ziebland, 2004).

However, information is not knowledge, and would-be experts are likely to suffer from severe information overload. If you have ever tried to find information about some ailment, you will testify to the difficulty of such a quest: there is a considerable amount of "garbage" on the Internet about any topic, contradictory views abound, and the most recent official information – e.g. in the United Kingdom, the recommendations of the National Health Service (NHS) – might be hard to find. Finding suitable information requires an expertise in itself – search expertise. Not even Wikipedia provides useful and reliable information, since it tends, with respect to health, to provide factual information rather the kind of advice typically searched for. Some authors have argued that, paradoxically, the necessity to acquire this kind of expertise can actually increase the knowledge gap between highly educated and less educated individuals – just like wealth, knowledge is not evenly distributed in society (Bonfadelli, 2002; Hargittai & Hinnant, 2008). Another shortcoming of the Internet is that it encourages superficial rather than careful reading (Coiro, 2003; Zhang & Duke, 2008). This of course makes sense, given the huge amount of information at one's fingertips and the limited time available, not to mention limited cognitive resources.

11.8 Group Phenomena

Is it better to make decisions individually or as a group? This is a standard question in psychology, which takes a special flavour when put together with the notion of expertise. In his book *The Wisdom of Crowds*, Surowiecki (2005) defended the power of collective intelligence and argued that, when four criteria are met, better decisions are made by large groups than by smaller and more select groups. These criteria are (a) there should be a variety of opinions; (b) each person should be able to express their view independently; (c) knowledge should be local and decentralised; and (d) there must be a mechanism for aggregating personal judgements into a collective one. The wisdom-of-crowd hypothesis might be true in domains that are highly dynamic, non-scientific and affected by political considerations, such as the stock market, but it is clearly incorrect in domains where true expertise exists. For example, while an expert will readily provide the correct solution to a physics problem, aggregating the views of a large group of individuals with no knowledge of physics will clearly not do the trick. In fact, a natural experiment has established this. In 1999, chess world champion Garry Kasparov played a game "against the world" over the Internet (Marko & Haworth, 1999). Each move played by the world team was decided by simple majority. Voting on average included 5,000 individuals from more than 75 countries. Kasparov won the game after 62 moves.

While Surowiecki's proposal seems too naïve, it is true that experts in many fields work in groups. The best example is perhaps science, where the lone scientist is becoming an increasingly rare species and where large collaborative projects put together thousands of individuals (e.g. in particle physics, the construction of the Large Hadron Collider, to which more than 10,000 scientists and engineers collaborated). Clearly, such large groups are necessary for large-scale research projects, where a single individual does not have the required knowledge and physical resources to complete the job. Moreover, working in groups also has additional benefits, such as increasing the number of publications and citations. However, a more subtle question is whether it really leads to better research – or is it the case, as argued by sociologists Latour and Woolgar (1979) and other sociologists in the field of *science and technology studies*, that science is constructed socially as culture rather than as a set of principles and procedures and that collaboration, rather than the construction of new knowledge, is in itself the aim of science?

The evidence is mixed. There are clearly examples where scientific discoveries could have been done only by large groups. Think for example of the mapping of the human genome in biology or the verification of the existence of the Higgs boson particle in physics. There are also empirical data showing that collaboration leads to better decisions. For example, Okada and Simon (1997) carried out a study where the task was to discover scientific laws using experiments, and where pairs of subjects were compared with single subjects. Pairs found more laws and also were more active in taking part in explanatory activities, such as developing hypotheses and proposing different explanations. However, these explanatory activities led to better performance only when participants also carried out critical experiments and when one participant explicitly asked for explanation and the other obliged. More generally, Okada et al. (1995) showed that collaboration was most likely to succeed when the collaborators were deeply interested in the research questions, met frequently, had intense discussions that used an egalitarian and open-ended style, and brought various types of skill and knowledge.

But there are also clear examples where collaboration not only does not increase the quality of decision making, but actually decreases it. The classic examples are Janis's research on groupthink (Janis, 1982; Turner & Pratkanis, 1998) and the research on brainstorming (Osborn, 1963). In the case of groupthink, the group's desire for conformity leads to incorrect decisions. Groupthink is likely to occur in groups that are very cohesive, insulated from external experts, under stress and time pressure and under the direction of a leader. There are two broad classes of consequences of groupthink. The first class includes the illusion of invulnerability and the tendency to rationalise, self-censor and stereotype individuals not members of the group. The second class concerns a lack of information search, consideration of alternatives and critical evaluation. A classic example of groupthink is President Kennedy's decision to implement the Bay of Pigs Invasion in 1961, with catastrophic consequences.

In the case of brainstorming, a group attempts to solve a problem or make a decision by letting its members contribute freely to as many ideas as possible, without any self-censoring and by encouraging unusual ideas (Osborn, 1963). The claim was that this method would enhance creativity and lead to better decisions. However, research has shown that brainstorming actually leads to fewer and less optimal ideas than individuals working alone (Diehl & Stroebe, 1987, 1991).

Another related effect is herding (e.g. Strevens, 2013). When a new technology is developed, a new experimental paradigm proposed or a new theory advanced, there is a tendency for researchers to follow this new niche of research as a herd. The new subfield of research might turn out to be durable (e.g. artificial intelligence in computer science or cognitive neuroscience in psychology and neuroscience) or might just be a temporary fashion that disappears after a while (e.g. LOGO programming in education or cold fusion in physics). In the study of expertise, the deliberate practice paradigm offers a crystal-clear example of herding.

This phenomenon possesses a number of characteristics. First, the newly-formed group defines a scientific credo, both on what counts as acceptable scientific assumptions and what are considered suitable methods of investigation. Second, there are strong in-group behaviours (e.g. groupthink, adoption of a common style of research and even writing, and mutual support of the members, for example reciprocal citations). Third, there also exist strong out-group behaviours (exclusion of non-members, for example by making it difficult for outsiders to publish on the topic). Indeed, a good heuristic for publishing an influential paper in science is to write it so that it precisely invites herding. An effective way to do so is to come up with a new type of experiment that is elegant, relatively simple and leads to counter-intuitive results. The original experiment should be easily replicable, expandable, criticisable and applicable to different domains and populations.

It can be argued that, while beneficial at the beginning because it directs many resources on the study of an interesting scientific question, herding runs the risk of rapidly stifling originality. In addition, when the returns are diminishing, resources could be allocated to better research questions. In general, herding in science includes both the best (presence of a critical mass, pooling of resources and solidarity) and the worst (group thinking, rigidity of thought and narrow scope of interests) of group behaviour.

11.9 Why Do We Believe Experts?

As we have seen, the wisdom of the pundits and other mediatised experts seems rather limited. Why, then, do most people feel the need to listen to experts' opinion about matters related to finance, health, science, among many others? There are at least five explanations. First, people amalgamate different types of expertise in a single category, and fail to distinguish reliable and non-reliable experts. Second, we have an inherent need for order and certainty. There is substantial empirical evidence showing that we search for patterns and regularities, even in domains that are essentially random. A striking example is provided by gamblers who believe that there is a structure behind the random sequence of numbers in a roulette game or the position of the reels in a slot machine (e.g. Gobet & Schiller, 2014). This innate search for patterns is not limited to humans: even pigeons act as if they find regularities in random sequences of reinforcements (Skinner, 1948).

Third, and related to the previous point, we show an aversion for uncertainty and a need for control, but at the same time live in a mostly unpredictable world. Experts' knowledge and confidence can assuage our fears. Both experiments and field studies have confirmed what Langer (1975) called the *illusion of control* – people's tendency to overestimate the extent to which they control events, even random events. Gambling again is a good illustration of this phenomenon. The illusion of control might well be adaptive overall, however, by protecting people against the other extreme: the belief that we do not have any control at all over events, which might lead to severe depression, as shown by the research into learned helplessness (Gobet, 1992; Seligman, 1975).

Fourth, we listen to what experts say because they tell us what we want to hear. This is a form of confirmation bias, a pernicious but omnipresent bias in human cognition (Bilalić et al., 2010; Nickerson, 1998). This bias is reinforced by the fact that experts in the media tend to behave like Tetlock's (2005) hedgehogs: they tell straightforward stories that satisfy our tendency to prefer simpler answers to complex ones – as for example the kind of answer that could be found by analysing extensive statistical data. There is actually good evidence that stories are the most preferred mode of communication in humans, in particular simple stories (Bruner & Seymour, 2003; Herman, 2013). And some experts are great simplifiers.

Finally, one should not underestimate the importance of status. A PhD, laboratory coat and indeed the label "expert" will impress many people. Perhaps the most forceful evidence for this is Milgram's (1974) classic experiment, where participants were encouraged by a researcher wearing a laboratory coat to administer increasingly high electric shocks when another person (a confederate, in fact) made mistakes when trying to memorise verbal material. Status (e.g. whether the experiment was carried out by a prestigious university or not) was one of the manipulated variables that was shown to lead to larger shocks.

11.10 Situated Action

The approach called *situated action* (also known as *situated cognition*) aims to study the individual and society simultaneously. The focus has been on education, but there are also implications for the study of expertise. Situated actions theorists (e.g. Lave, 1988) chide theories in cognitive psychology for neglecting interactions with the environment, and in particular interactions with society. With respect to expertise, the claim is two-fold: experts play a role in society, and society plays a role in the way experts are defined. In addition, expertise does not reside "in the head" of the experts, but is distributed between individuals and even artefacts (Hutchins, 1983). As they neglect interactions with the environment, theories of expertise such as chunking theory fail.

While situated action is correct in stressing the bidirectional links between experts and society, it suffers from a number of shortcomings (Vera & Simon, 1993). From the point of view of expertise, perhaps the main weakness of situated action is its rejection of representations in human cognition. As we have seen several times in this book, most notably in Section 4.12, representations play an essential role in expert cognition. Indeed, in some cases, differences in representations can readily explain differences between experts and novices. In addition, referring to Gibson (1979), situated action theorists argue that perception is based on *affordances*: the environment offers invariants that can be simply "picked up", and information is perceived directly without any need for processing. One problem with this argument is that experts can make good decisions in the absence of any external perceptual cues. A good example is offered by blindfold chess: a strong player can play one or several games without seeing the board, and this ability tends not to be affected by being situated in totally different environments (posh café, sunny beach or ski slope). This is difficult to explain by theories based on situated action, but easy to explain by theories assuming internal representations (e.g. chunking and template theories).

11.11 Chapter Summary

So, are experts really expert? Several studies reviewed in this chapter have argued that they are not. However, it is almost certainly the case that the sample of experts reviewed in these studies is biased, and that other kinds of experts are really experts – even using the strict definition proposed in this book. The success of scientific research and technology bears witness to this. After all, experts made it possible, among uncountable other examples, to land on the moon successfully, to eradicate smallpox through vaccination and to overcome geographical barriers with computers and the Internet.

But the fact remains that experts are often bad at predicting the future. We have seen that some, perhaps most, events are inherently unpredictable, due to their complexity (many variables are involved), their chaotic nature (sensitivity to small differences in the initial conditions) and the presence of random factors. In this respect, the presence of humans makes it even harder to predict the future course of events, since their behaviour is somewhat unpredictable and thus the complexity of the task environment is increased. In addition, much of experts' behaviour is based on automatisms. These are fine when the problem at hand is routine, but they can backfire when the problems become more complex.

The most systematic study of experts' limitations and biases was carried out in political science by Tetlock (2005). In this domain, experts' predictions are essentially not better than random guesses. Science, seen by many as a paragon of expertise, also shows failings. These are due to the intrinsic complexity of the physical and social world, the difficulty of conducting perfect experiments, and the lack of replications. Just like the rest of us, experts can be victims of group phenomena and suffer from a number of biases, which might in extreme cases lead to fraud. The media and the Internet have changed what experts are and do too, with the information required to become an expert available within mere minutes.

11.12 Further Reading

Cerf and Navasky (1998) catalogue experts' statements and predictions that turned out incorrect. Depending on your mood, the book is either entertaining or depressing. Gardner (2011) provides a critical evaluation of expertise and experts, focusing on failed predictions. Tetlock (2005) reports the predictions made by 284 experts in political science. Although the book is rather technical, it is a fascinating read. Freedman (2010) discusses the problems faced by scientists, how they affect their expertise and how this might lead them to fraud. Cheating in sports is covered in Syed (2011) and Rosen (2008). Collaborative research in science is discussed in the book edited by Derry et al. (2005). The documentary at http://topdocumentaryfilms.com/the-trouble-with-experts/ provides a good overview of the fields in which experts perform below par.

CHAPTER 12

Sociology

12.1 Preview of Chapter

Professions are a topic of considerable interest in sociology. We start this chapter by considering a number of sociological approaches to them, focusing on the notion of expertise. We then consider three related issues: communication and expertise, expert witnesses in court and the notion of trust. The chapter ends with a discussion of two classifications of expertise and experts.

12.2 The Sociology of Professions

While psychology focuses on individuals, sociology studies individuals as parts of social contexts. A central idea in the sociological analysis of expertise is that of *social closure* (Murphy, 1988; Weber, 1922/1979): expertise is considered as a kind of exclusion, which discriminates experts from non-experts.

Sociology has mostly studied expertise through the topic of *professions*. Classical examples of professions include doctors, lawyers, scientists and engineers. Defining the term "profession" has been subject to much debate, as we shall see. For the time being, we will use the type of definitions proposed by functionalist sociologists, most notably Parsons (1939). Professions can be defined as occupations requiring specialised and often vocational training to acquire the necessary knowledge and expertise. They supply objective advice and service to others, for a direct compensation. Professions tend to enjoy autonomy, benefit from high status and prestige and have power. They play an important role in defining and monitoring quality standards with which expert performance is assessed. Another way of characterising professions is to see them "as the structural, occupational, and institutional arrangements for dealing with work associated with the uncertainties of modern lives in risk societies" (Evetts et al., 2006, p. 108).

12.2.1 Early Work

A good place to start our discussion is Max Weber's (1922/1979) *Economy and Society* – voted in 1998 as the most important book in sociology in the twentieth century by the International Sociological Association. Weber noted the superiority of bureaucracies (hierarchical organisations with vertical lines of authorities) as forms of rational organisations and emphasised the role of labour divisions in such structures. Bureaucracies make the most efficient use of specialised expertise and experts, by optimising the way they are connected. Professions do not fit well within this framework emphasising bureaucracies, and Weber said relatively little about them (Champy, 2009). Some of his analyses, for example on the concept of closure, where professions exclude rival groups by collective action from competing for economic opportunities such as markets and profits, do relate to professions but also apply to other occupations. Of particular interest are Weber's lectures on *Science as a Vocation* and *Politics as a Vocation*, which combine descriptive and normative descriptions of these professions.

Durkheim (1922/1992) examined the evolution of occupations (e.g. Roman collegia and medieval guilds) over time. He noted that the development of professional associations had political implications, both nationally and internationally. Typically, he considered labour division more as a social than an economic phenomenon. Professions, while they have played an essential role for solidarity in society through occupational membership, still need to provide more moral control and support. In particular, professions linked to economy lack moral authority. Professional bodies should in the future provide additional moral authority to maintain society's moral force and avoid social anarchy. Thus, for Durkheim, professions offer an important type of decentralised control for providing moral authority to the community.

Writing in the tradition of American functionalism, Parsons (1939, 1951) argued that society increases its complexity by what he called structural differentiation – increased specialisation and division of labour. Professions are a paradigmatic example of this process. They actually play an essential role in transmitting rational values. As producers and users of technological knowledge, they are also important in stimulating the economy. More so than capitalism or business economy – the two mechanisms usually proposed in sociology – professions form the most significant characteristic of modern society. They offer an efficient alternative to hierarchical bureaucratic organisations as bearers of moral values.

According to Parsons, professions have several characteristic features: affective neutrality (a solicitor has no emotional links with her clients); universalism (a doctor treats everybody with the same care); collectivity (shared interest is more important than self-interest); specificity (professionals focus only on the aspect of the problem for which they have expertise); and achievement (status is based on performance and not on inborn characteristics such as ethnicity and gender).

Hughes's (1958) approach to professions contrasts with that of previous scholars in three ways. First, he did not differentiate between occupations and professions, arguing that all occupations require some kind of knowledge and expertise. Thus, the difference is more of degree than kind (Evetts et al., 2006). Second, Hughes argued that professions define not only what is good and bad within their sphere of influence, but also the proper way to think about problems (Dingwall & Lewis, 1983). Third, while previous approaches underscored the benefits of professions for society and community, Hughes emphasised that professions draw direct benefits for themselves. For example, having the benefit of specialised knowledge ensures that only professionals within the discipline can evaluate the work of practitioners.

A series of sociological studies have tried to identify the characteristic features of professional work as compared to occupational work. Among others, these include lengthy education and institutionalised training, autonomy, orientation toward public service, presence of a professional code of ethics and/or conduct, special power and prestige, relation of trust with clients and presence of self-regulation (Wilensky, 1964). This *trait approach* has been criticised on various grounds. For example, Evetts (2006) notes that it did not contribute to an understanding of the power relations between professions; in addition, the division between professions and occupations is rather fuzzy.

12.2.2 Abbott's Seminal Work

Abbott (1988) criticised previous work on professional life as focusing on form rather than content, structure rather than work. In stark contrast, Abbott emphasised that the professions belong to a system. The professions define their *jurisdiction* – that is, "the link between a profession and its work" (p. 20). This being done, the professions compete with one another to establish and maintain their jurisdiction, essentially legitimising the monopoly of their practice. Abbott gives two telling illustrations of this process. First, how medicine competed with homeopathy in America in the first part of the nineteenth century as the healing profession of choice; second, in America again, how psychiatry competed during its entire existence with medicine as provider of mental health. In their respective cases, medicine and psychiatry followed a process of professionalisation, through multiple and complex episodes that differed considerably between the two (see Abbott, 1988, for details).

Knowledge, in particular abstract academic knowledge, is at the basis of the professions. Taking an economic stance, knowledge is the currency used in the competition between professions. The point of academic knowledge is not so much to back up practice with theoretical knowledge – Abbott argues that there is often a disconnect between practical professional knowledge and academic knowledge – as to legitimise the professional work by showing how it links with rational and scientific knowledge. According to Abbott (1988, p. 323), "professionalism has been the main way of institutionalising expertise in industrialised countries".

Professional practice has three parts, which often but not always occur in sequence: diagnosis, inference and treatment. Diagnosis and treatment are at the interface between a profession and systems external to it: diagnosis inputs information to the professional knowledge system, and treatment outputs information from it. By contrast, inferences stay within the professional system and thus are at the core of the professions. For example, while physicians can delegate diagnosis and treatment (e.g. to blood analysts and physiotherapists, respectively), they cannot normally delegate the inference linking the diagnosis and the treatment. In the rare cases where this is done, the delegation is made to somebody with status equal to or higher than the physician (e.g. a specialist in internal medicine).

Reviewing recent evidence about the sociology of work and occupations, Abbott (1993) stated that his 1988 book had three central arguments: first, an understanding of professions requires that one approaches them as interacting systems and not individually; second, a theory of professions requires the study of forces within, between and across professions; and third, theorising professions requires complex hypotheses. In a candid statement, Abbott noted that the impact of these arguments on sociology had been very limited. Non-systemic studies of professions taken individually are still the norm; few studies have used a multilevel analysis; and many studies still use simplistic hypotheses, such as identifying determining variables, rather than complex hypotheses.

12.2.3 Experts as Heuristics

In line with Abbott, Mieg (2001, 2006) emphasised a social/systemic conception of expertise. According to him, an expert is "the connection between a person and a function" (Mieg, 2006, p. 743), where a function is defined as the social context in which the expert performance takes place. Another way of defining a function is to use the amount of money that one would pay for receiving expert knowledge. Mieg emphasises that the terms "expert" and "expertise" are relational: these terms gain meaning only in reference to non-experts, that is, laypeople. The term "expert" is construed very broadly; for example, somebody being asked the way to the station and able to provide directions would be considered as an expert. In line with previous theories, Mieg argues that gradients of expertise are accompanied by gradients in prestige, power and other social benefits.

Since expert roles are defined in relation to context, including clients and laypeople, expertise is relative. This means that the amount of knowledge and skill that an expert shows varies from context to context. An example is provided by politics, where an individual might become a transport minister for political reasons without having undergone any formal training about this topic.

In general, experts enable a time-efficient way of using knowledge: rather than investing one's time for each new domain where expertise is required, one accesses this knowledge by paying for the time that the expert has invested through training and experience. More generally, expertise can be seen as human capital. In economics, Becker (1993) defines human capital as the sum of abilities, knowledge and attributes (e.g. intelligence and creativity) that have been created by investing in a given individual (e.g. by education and training). Since human capital can produce economic value, expertise has a market and monetary value, which is used when selecting or replacing an expert.

Mieg proposes the interesting notion that experts can be used as *heuristics*, particularly in domains characterised by a high level of uncertainty, such as management and financial markets. As we have seen in Chapter 5 when discussing Shanteau's (1992a) work, experts perform poorly in these domains. According to Mieg, one keeps consulting experts as long as they are successful; when the environment changes, one adopts new heuristics by switching to new experts.

12.3 Communication and Expertise

Different issues arise depending on whether we consider communication between experts or communication of expertise. These two issues will be taken up in turn.

A common problem in large organisations (both public and private) is the difficulty that specialists in one area have in communicating with specialists in another. There are several factors behind this difficulty. For example, when discussing management and public administration, Simon et al. emphasise the presence of specialised languages, loyalties and mental sets due to training (Simon, 1976; Simon et al., 1950). Together, and in line with what we have said in Chapters 2 and 3, these factors have the consequence that specialists with different backgrounds perceive and categorise the environment differently. Thus, different schemas will be accessed and used, and the situation will be construed differently. For example, a manager from an accounting department will discuss a business case in terms of financial issues, while a human resource manager will discuss it in terms of human relations. An obvious but unfortunate consequence of this is that communication between experts in different domains will be imperfect at best and seriously flawed at worst. Compounding this difficulty is the fact that the same terms often have different meanings in different fields, leading to an illusion of communication while in reality individuals talk about totally different things.

Discussing communications between societal systems rather than between individuals, Luhmann (1995) essentially reaches the same conclusion: systems code inputs from the environments in ways that are specific to each system. There is thus no possibility of communication and the consequences are serious. For example, expert witnesses in a court of law will speak the language of science, while the judge will speak the language of law; both systems encode messages from the environment in different ways, and thus communication will mostly be an illusion.

Communicating expert knowledge to laypeople raises different challenges. Due to its specialisation, expert knowledge tends to be abstruse and couched in technical language. How knowledge is communicated, including the level of explanation, will depend on the target users and on whether the aim is to increase public understanding of science or to train practitioners. The process is typically difficult, and made easier, at least apparently, by a hierarchy of formal experts (e.g. world expert in cardiology, professor of cardiology, cardiologist resident and general practitioner) and a number of informal experts (journalists, popular science writers) who act as an interface, as it were. Informal expertise is discussed at length by Collins and Evans (2007) in what they call interactional expertise. These various types of experts play different roles, rely on diverse kinds of knowledge and indeed provide different and sometimes contradictory pieces of advice. As vividly illustrated by Freedman (2010), this can be highly confusing for laypeople and actually lead them to doubt whether genuine expertise exists.

12.4 Experts in Court

The difficulty of communication is just only one of the many interesting questions related to the role of experts and expertise in law. Here, we briefly discuss two related questions: the different ways experts are used in common and statutory law and the selection of expert witnesses.

Common law, used for example in the United States and the United Kingdom, is based on court precedents (cases) and there is no regulatory or statutory system of laws. When expert witnesses testify, they are selected independently by the prosecution and defence so that they will argue in favour of their client. No system of selection based on official qualifications is used, and each party selects experts to the extent that they will defend their cause. Thus, while expert witnesses in general have a scientific background, it is not unheard of to have experts with bizarre credentials, so long as their testimony will be useful for one party in the trial (Rossi, 1991). For example, an expert was chosen in *United States vs. Johnson* (1978) to identify the Columbian origin of the marijuana involved in the case. Expertise was granted based on the fact that the expert had smoked marijuana over one thousand times.

Testimonies are given in a highly adversarial setting, with the lawyers of each party trying to discredit the argument and the expert witness of the other party. Although the expert witnesses receive training for dealing with cross-examination, where both the credentials and the specific line of argument of the expert are tested, the experience is typically difficult and unpleasant. As noted by Shepherd (1973, p. 21): "I have never met an expert of any kind who has any liking for lawyers". This confrontational approach has the advantage that the experts do not receive excessive credibility due to their credentials and reputation. However, it has drawbacks as well. First, as noted by Mieg (2001), the aim in this kind of proceedings is not to use expertise to reach the truth of the matter, but to vindicate the case made by the prosecution or the defence. Second, and related to the first point, experts are partial. This means that, more often than not, experts will contradict each other. Third, more than mastering the subject matter of their field, expert witnesses' expertise consists in explaining their viewpoint to laypeople in a clear, simple and convincing manner.

In countries with a statutory system (all countries in Europe except the British Islands), laws are made by legislative bodies and no reference is made to specific cases. When necessary, the judge selects the expert witness, who is considered as a helper of the court, for example to explain technical details of software engineering in a case related to software copyright violation. Typically, the selection of the experts does not depend on official accreditation but is left to the discretion of the judge. Expert witnesses may come from rather exotic occupations. Dippel (1986) notes a case in Germany where an astrologer was appointed as an expert witness, with the goal of establishing whether the procedure followed by another astrologer in preparing a horoscope was "correct". The fact that astrology has no scientific basis was not considered relevant in selecting this expert witness.

Trust and expertise

The theme of expert trust has been widely addressed in the academic socio-logical literature (see also Section 11.9). Luhmann (1979) notes that the function of trust is to reduce uncertainty in society; thus, trust plays the same role as power. Giddens (1990) emphasises that what he calls *expert systems* are a key consequence of modernity. Expert systems are "systems of technical accomplishment or professional expertise that organise large areas of the material and social environments in which we live today" (1990, p. 27). These systems are ubiquitous: for example, although most people have little to no knowledge of architecture or mechanical engineering, they must trust that the room in which they are standing will not collapse and that the boiler providing the heating to the house will not explode. Given the complexity of current societies, Giddens (1990) argues that we have no choice but to trust expert systems. At the same time, an important role played by societies is to make sure that there is some control mechanism to check them.

Mieg (2006) discusses two examples of misled trust in experts. The first concerns the scandals in the financial sector in the early 2000s (the Enron case, the failure of accounting firms to properly monitor it and the promo-tion of "toxic" products in the subprime mortgage crisis by financial ana-lysts). The second relates to the way experts are used in advertisement and public relations as a means to legitimise products or services. Such practices are common not only in business but also in national and international politics.

12.5 Classification of Experts

Sociology has a long history of classifying human activities, starting with Auguste Comte's hierarchical and systematic classification of sciences (Comte, 1830–1842). Several schemes have recently been proposed to classify experts. We focus on Mieg's (2006) and Collins and Evans's (2007) classifications.

12.5.1 Mieg's Classification

Taking Abbott's three-part analysis of professional work (diagnosis, inference and treatment) as a starting point, Mieg (2006) proposes a typology that distinguishes between four different types of expert roles (see Table 12.1). On the right hand side of the table, we find *relative experts*, who provide useful information in a given context; these do not need to be scientists or professionals. As examples, Mieg identifies people who know everyone in and everything about an organisation, members of a team assigned to specific tasks and people who know their local human environment well. The function of relative experts is to provide limited diagnosis. With respect to accountability, relative experts are responsible solely for the information they supply.

The second category concerns *expert researchers* or *analysts*. They provide full diagnoses, and the criterion for their performance is (supposed) validity; a good example is offered by scientists' public appearances. These experts focus on the aspects of a problem that are amenable, at least to some extent, to analysis, and do not agree to speculate on the aspects where little objective evidence is present from research; they also provide knowledge (e.g. understanding of principles and evidence). Expert researchers are only accountable for the correctness of the analyses they provide.

Table 12.1 Mieg's (2006) typology of expert roles

	Professionals	Formal experts/ Decision experts	Researchers/ Analysts	Relative experts/ Local "system experts"
Function	complete professional task	inference/formal decision support	diagnosis/ analysis	local information
Performance criterion	effectiveness & efficiency	effectiveness	validity	validity

Source: From Mieg, H. A. (2006). Social and sociological factors in the development of expertise. In K. A. Ericsson, N. Charness, P. J. Feltovich & R. R. Hoffman (eds.), *The Cambridge handbook of expertise and expert performance* (pp. 743–760). Cambridge: Cambridge University Press. Reproduced with kind permission from Cambridge University Press.

The third category, *formal experts* or *decision experts* (Otway & von Winterfeldt, 1992), do not carry out actual diagnosis, inference or treatment. Instead, they specialise on developing methods of inferences using techniques from mathematics and decision theory. Thus, they supply formal knowledge. Their success is evaluated by the extent to which they have developed an effective methodology for reaching decisions. When these experts want to be consulted for making actual decisions, they must professionalise themselves, for example by advertising themselves as risk consultants.

The final category concerns *professionals*. As you may remember, Abbott (1988) argues that inference represents the essence of the work carried out by the professionals. Thus, while professionals every so often delegate diagnosis and treatment, they normally deal with the inferences leading from diagnosis to treatment. When they delegate inference, it is either to individuals with the same status (e.g. colleagues) or to individuals with more specialised expertise (e.g. a generalist referring a patient to a cardiologist). Professionals are therefore accountable for the complete professional task – diagnosis, inference and treatment.

12.5.2 Collins and Evans's (2007) Periodic Table of Expertises

An influential classification of expertise is offered by Collins and Evans's (2007) periodic table of expertises (see Figure 12.1). The main aim of these

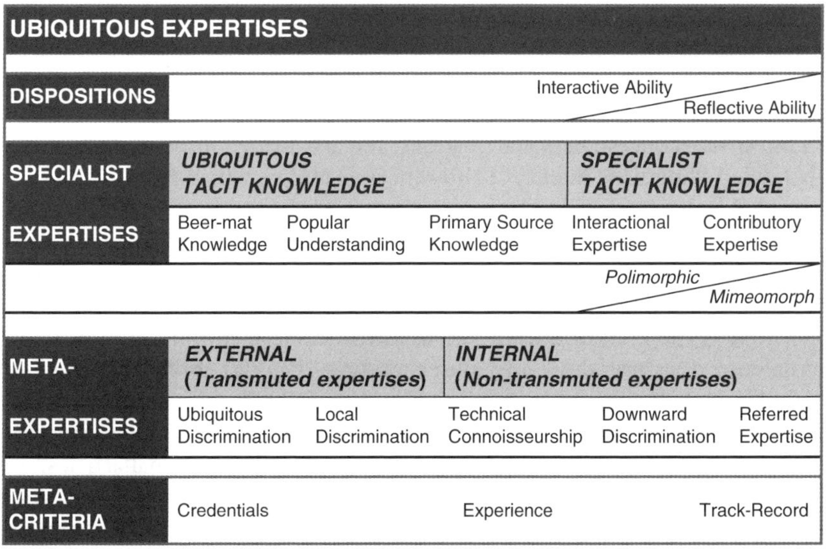

Figure 12.1 Collins and Evans's (2007) periodic table of expertises.

Source: From Collins, H. M., & Evans, R. (2007). *Rethinking expertise.* Chicago: University of Chicago Press. Reproduced with kind permission from University of Chicago Press.

two sociologists was to understand what they call "interactional expertise": the kind of expertise displayed by individuals who are able to interact with experts in a given domain without being able to contribute themselves to this domain. Examples include journalists, art critics and peer reviewers of grant proposals in science. As a paradigmatic example, Collins and Evans mention a sociologist participating in a given scientific group in order to study it. Drawing on his own experience of carrying out sociological research at the Laser Interferometer Gravitational-Wave Observatory (LIGO), a $365 million physics experiment whose aim is to directly detect the presence of (so-far elusive) gravitational waves, Collins argues that he was able to "pass as" an expert on the topic even though his own background was in sociology and he had never formally studied astronomy or physics. In fact, when nine real LIGO experts were asked to identify the sociologist amidst the gravitational wave physicists on the basis of answers to technical (but not mathematical) questions, they were unable to do so.

Beyond clarifying the role of interactional expertise, the general aim of the periodic table displayed in Figure 12.1 is to classify how individuals make a judgment. As one goes down the table, one meets different types of expertise. As one move from the left to the right, one encounters more specialised and more procedural types of expertise.

The first row in the table, *ubiquitous expertises*, refers to the kinds of abilities that everybody in a society possesses. (Note that such expertises are not consistent with our definition of expertise, which limits expertise to a top percentage of the population; see Section 1.3.) These abilities typically include a large amount of tacit knowledge (e.g. the ability to speak one's native language or the ability to make political judgements). Collins and Evans note that, below this first category, the table deals solely with scientific and technological knowledge.

Dispositions concern personal qualities, and are divided into interactive ability (also called "linguistic fluency") and reflective ability, which Collins and Evans also call "analytical flair"). The next category, *specialist expertise*, is subdivided into *ubiquitous tacit knowledge* and *specialist knowledge*, and includes a wide range of expertises, from superficial knowledge to deep understanding. Ubiquitous tacit knowledge consists of three kinds of expertise. *Beer-mat knowledge* is the kind of knowledge used to be successful in a pub quiz. It is factual and does not show any understanding. *Popular understanding* is the kind of knowledge gained by reading popular science books and magazines. It shows some understanding, but it is still very basic. *Primary source knowledge* goes one step further, and requires one to read technical journal articles.

Specialist tacit knowledge is divided into two subcategories. The first is *interactional expertise*, which we have already described above. To summarise, it refers to "the ability to master the language of a specialist domain in the absence of practical competence" (Collins & Evans, 2007, p. 14). Collins and Evans argue that this kind of expertise can be acquired only by closely interacting with individuals who directly contribute to their domain (e.g. physicists actually carrying out experiments). The kind of expertise displayed by the latter individuals is called *contributory expertise*. With these two types of expertise, Collins and Evans differentiate between polymorphic actions, which rely on social understanding, and mimeomorphic actions, which do not depend on social understanding and can be carried out by mere reproduction of fixed behaviours.

The next row of the table concerns *meta-expertises*. These can be either *external* (or "transmuted") in that they "use social discrimination to produce technical discrimination" (p. 15), or *internal* (or "non-transmuted"), as they rely only on technical knowledge. The first external meta-expertise is *ubiquitous discrimination*. This is the kind of knowledge that is normally acquired in Western societies (e.g. judgements about friends, neighbours, politicians) and that can be applied to make judgements about science and technology. For example, ubiquitous discrimination allows most people to realise that astrology is not a scientific discipline. As another example, Collins and Evans discuss the case of cold fusion. In 1989, two renowned chemists, Martin Fleischmann and Stanley Pons, claimed that nuclear reaction could occur at, or relatively near, room temperature, while nuclear fusion is normally thought to require extremely high temperatures, in the region of millions of degrees (Close, 1990). Because newspapers reported on the numerous failures to replicate Pons and Fleischman's original experiments, most laypeople who had read about cold fusion, but did not understand the technical details, would have assumed that this research line was fruitless. It is important to note that this judgement was made on social rather than technical grounds.

The second external meta-expertise concerns *local discrimination*, which uses local knowledge about people. Two studies by Brian Wynne offer good examples of this kind of discrimination. In a classic paper, Wynne (1989) studied how sheep farmers in Cumbria responded to restrictions imposed by radioactive contamination, supposedly caused by Chernobyl's nuclear accident in 1986. (The contamination turned out to be caused by the nearby Sellafield nuclear fuels reprocessing plant.) Not only did the sheep farmers show extensive (albeit informal) knowledge of sheep ecology – what Wynne called *lay expertise* – but they also displayed insight about local discrimination. Having had extensive experience with the statements made by the nuclear industry about radioactive contamination, they had learnt to doubt them. The second example is provided by Wynne's study of apprentices at the Sellafield nuclear plant and their surprising lack of scientific knowledge about radioactivity. Wynne argued that the apprentices used their social knowledge to decide whether to trust their employers. As Wynne (1993, p. 328) put it: "technical ignorance was a function of social intelligence".

Contrary to external meta-expertise, the following three types of expertise rely on possessing, to some extent, the expertise that is being evaluated. As such, they are called *internal meta-expertises*. *Technical connoisseurship* characterises the kind of declarative expertise that some individuals have about a domain without being able to use this knowledge procedurally (e.g. an art critic). *Downward discrimination* is the idea that, where specialists evaluate other specialists, only specialists with more expertise can do so. The other cases of evaluation (upward discrimination or same-level discrimination) lack reliability. *Referred expertise* concerns the application, to another domain, of expertise that has been acquired in a given domain.

Finally, the table list three *meta-criteria*, which are used by outsiders to a scientific or technological field to evaluate experts and discriminate between them: *credentials*, *experience* and *track record*. These are fairly similar to the criteria identified in Chapter 1. Interestingly, Collins and Evans argue that experience is the best meta-criterion, while we provided examples showing that experience can be unreliable.

12.5.3 Classifications of Expertise: Evaluation

These two classifications of expertise offer useful insights. Mieg's (2006) classification, while fairly simple, has the advantage of using Abbott's (1988) notion of diagnosis, inference and treatment; it also provides a link between different kinds of expertise and criteria to evaluate them. Collins and Evans's (2007) table offers a more fine-grained classification, whose strength is to clarify the notion of interactional expertise. Interestingly, both classification schemes explicitly address only a small subset of expertise – those linked to science and technology. It is also interesting that both include weak notions of expertise as part of the classification (relative experts for Mieg and ubiquitous expertises for Collins and Evans).

Both schemes suffer from a number of weaknesses. Mieg's classification seems too simple to discriminate between the numerous forms of expertise that exist. In addition, some specific claims are disputable. For example, Mieg argues that, when speaking publicly, expert researchers focus on issues that can be, at least partly, answered by analysis and empirical data, and that they avoid speculation. However, the previous chapter has provided – as does any quick look at news TV channels – several examples of technical experts going well beyond what is solidly established empirically.

Collins and Evans's classificatory scheme is more ambitious, and because of this can be subjected to stronger criticisms. Addis (2013) assails Collins and Evans's use of ordinary linguistic competence to draw inferences about the epistemology of expertise. Based on Wittgenstein's (1984) philosophy, Addis proposes that the term "expertise" should be used only with specialised and high-level expertise (what Collins and Evans call esoteric expertise), and not with every performance (what they call with ubiquitous expertise). We note five additional weaknesses. First, Collins and Evans make it clear that dispositions (linguistic and analytical abilities) are limited to scientific and technological expertises; this seems over-restrictive. Second, the table seems lopsided, since it contains logically distinct classes of information. While most of the entries concern types of expertise, the second row refers to traits or dispositions, and the last row to criteria to evaluate others' expertise. This baroque composition is handy as a rapid summary of ideas, but hinders theorising.

Third, the term "ubiquitous tacit knowledge" (third row) is disputable. Why *tacit*? As we shall discuss in detail in the next chapter on philosophy, tacit normally characterises knowledge that cannot be communicated verbally. It is often opposed to explicit, propositional knowledge. But beer-mat knowledge, popular understanding and primary source knowledge seem to refer to knowledge that is eminently declarative. Clearly, individuals with these kinds of knowledge cannot carry out the kinds of procedures in science and technology that are typical of tacit knowledge. Even if we use one definition proposed by Collins and Evans ("Tacit knowledge is the deep understanding one can only gain through social immersion in groups who possess it", 2007, p. 6), the "tacit" in "ubiquitous tacit knowledge" seems wrong.

Fourth, the periodical table is supposed to present a new explanation of expertise (hence the title of the book: *Rethinking Expertise*), but the book never makes it clear what the old notions of expertise are that it is expected to replace. Fifth, and related to the previous point, the literature on expertise is largely ignored, which results in exaggerated claims of novelty. In particular, interactional expertise has been discussed, admittedly under other names, in the sociology literature on journalism and art criticism, for example (e.g. Bauer & Bucchi, 2007; Harrington, 2004).

In spite of their limitations, these two classifications are important since they show how difficult it is to categorise different forms of expertise, even when only expertise pertaining to science and technology are considered. This is a sobering conclusion.

12.6 Chapter Summary

Expertise has been studied by sociologists through the concept of professions – occupations involving specialist training, and characterised by autonomy, high status, prestige and power. Durkheim emphasised the political role of professions; Parsons noted that professions dovetail with the increased specialisation and division of labour, and transmit rational values; and Abbott proposed that professions define their jurisdiction, which are used to justify monopoly of their trade. According to Mieg, experts allow time-efficient use of knowledge.

Communicating expertise is difficult, both between experts in different fields and between experts and laypeople. In the latter case, a hierarchy of formal experts and informal experts to some extent facilitates the process. There are vast differences in the way experts are selected and used in common law and statutory law. Several classifications of expertise have been proposed. Mieg's classification is based on a three-part analysis of professional work (diagnosis, inference and treatment). Collins and Evans's classification is motivated by the goal of capturing the concept of interactional expertise. However, both classifications focus on science and technology, and highlight the difficulties of categorising different kinds of expertise.

12.7 Further Reading

The works suggested in the previous chapter are also useful for several topics addressed in the current chapter. Abbott's (1988) book *The System of Professions* is the standard sociological work on the professions. Mieg (2001) covers various aspects of expertise from the point of view of social psychology, sociology and economics. In *Rethinking Expertise*, Collins and Evans (2007) discuss the periodical table of expertises and the notion of interactional expertise, as well as other aspects of expertise related to sociology and philosophy. Dwyer (2008) analyses expert evidence from the points of view of law and epistemology. Cohen (2008) provides advice for experts about how to present scientific testimony in court.

CHAPTER **13**

Philosophy

13.1 Preview of Chapter

As discussed in many of the previous chapters, the concept of knowledge is crucial for an understanding of expertise in psychology, neuroscience and sociology. Knowledge also plays a central role in other fields interested in expertise, most notably philosophy and artificial intelligence. This chapter deals with philosophical issues linked to the study of expertise and the next discusses artificial intelligence.

Given its close affinity to knowledge – a central issue in philosophy – expertise has been of interest to philosophers since time immemorial. This is particularly the case with epistemology, the branch of philosophy concerned with the nature of knowledge. One of the key issues that we have touched upon when dealing with psychology (and that we will address again when discussing artificial intelligence) is the distinction between declarative knowledge and procedural knowledge. This distinction has also been of central concern in philosophy, although it is known under different names: knowing-that vs. knowing-how, or explicit vs. tacit knowledge.

We first present some of Plato's and Aristotle's important views on knowledge and expertise, setting the stage for a discussion of knowing-how and tacit knowledge. We then deal with Feyerabend's full-blown criticism of science and in particular scientific expertise. Feyerabend obviously disagrees with most philosophers, which is a good example of epistemic peer disagreement, and this topic is examined at some length. Another knotty question concerns whether, and if so how, experts can be identified. Anticipating some of the issues that will be addressed in the next chapter, we discuss Dreyfus's philosophical criticism against artificial intelligence and knowledge systems. We also consider whether experts can be seen as rational. Finally, we present some practical implications of philosophical research on expertise.

13.2 Ancient Greek Philosophy

In *The Republic*, written in the fourth century BC, Plato reflected on the role of experts in society. He argued against democracy – at least against the kind of democracy that prevailed then in Athens – since this political system makes it possible for less intelligent citizens to impose their choices over more intelligent citizens. Plato argued for a better political system, which would be ruled by *philosopher kings*. Ruling a state is a craft, just like steering a ship, therefore individuals with expertise in ruling should be suitably selected and receive proper training. According to Plato, philosophers are the best choice: they have been trained in differentiating between true and false beliefs; they love knowledge and strive for the common good. These attributes give them not only theoretical knowledge but also the practical knowledge necessary to act as leaders and to educate other citizens. Importantly, philosopher kings gain their authority not only from their knowledge and expertise in philosophy, but also from moral attributes such as impartiality and love for the state. In addition, unlike other citizens, philosopher kings know themselves.

In the *Nicomachean Ethics* – perhaps the most significant treatise on ethics ever – Aristotle distinguishes between three kinds of knowledge: episteme, techne and phronesis. *Episteme* ("knowledge" in Greek) concerns theoretical knowledge or what logicians call propositional knowledge. It is universal, invariable and context-independent. In line with Plato, who defined episteme as "justified true belief", Aristotle thought that a critical characteristic of episteme is that it "cannot be otherwise" and is "eternal". It is derived by deduction from universals. One has to be careful not to equate episteme with scientific knowledge in the modern sense, since the concept of an experiment – essential in modern science – did not exist for the ancient Greeks (it was only systematically used by Alhazen in the eleventh century and in particular Galileo in the seventeenth century).

Techne can be translated as craft, technical know-how or, as Aristotle put it, "bringing something into being". Unlike episteme, techne is not aimed at understanding, but at carrying out useful actions. As such, techne refers to pragmatic knowledge, which is variable and context dependent. For Aristotle, techne can be seen as a representation of nature that is not perfect, because this representation is made by humans.

Phronesis can be translated as prudence, practical wisdom or practical thought, with a focus on practical ethics. "As for what concerns prudence, we might grasp it by contemplating whom we say to be prudent. It seems to belong to a prudent person to be able to deliberate nobly about things good and advantageous for himself, not in a partial way – for example, the sorts of things conducive to health or to strength – but about the sorts of things conducive to living well in general" (Aristotle, 2011, p. 120).

This brief review of ancient Greek philosophy is not only of historical interest: Plato and Aristotle posed key questions about the nature of expertise. Although the specific answers they proposed are often disputable – and have been disputed by philosophers for more than two millennia – they clearly set the tone for most modern philosophical debate about knowledge and expertise.

13.3 Knowing-How and Tacit Knowledge: Ryle and Polanyi

The dominant perspective in philosophy has been that explicit knowledge (or propositional knowledge) is the main kind of knowledge, and that tacit knowledge can be explained only with reference to explicit knowledge. A minority of philosophers adopted the opposite view and argued that implicit knowledge comes first and that explicit knowledge is a derivative of implicit knowledge. (In that respect, they were following the view of most psychologists.) The most significant of them were Gilbert Ryle and Michael Polanyi.

Much of the discussion in philosophy about knowing-how is motivated by Ryle's (1946) paper titled *Knowing How and Knowing That*, which was expanded in a chapter in his classic book *The Concept of Mind* (Ryle, 1949). Ryle's two central claims are that (a) knowing-how and knowing-that are different kinds of knowledge and (b) knowing-how cannot be reduced to knowing-that. Ryle called this view – that knowledge-how and knowledge-that are independent kinds of knowledge – anti-intellectualism. Intellectualism views the two types of knowledge as dependent: knowledge-how can be derived from knowing-that, in that whatever is covered by knowledge-how can be translated into propositions, i.e. into knowledge-that. Ryle opposed intellectualism; importantly, he does not speak in terms of skills, but in terms of dispositions. A *disposition* to behave in a given way means that a person will carry out a specific action if some condition is realised. Consistent with his emphasis on behaviour and actions, Ryle was opposed to concepts such as "mind". The main goal of his 1949 book was to refute Cartesian dualism, and Ryle's approach is sometimes known as philosophical behaviourism.

Part of Ryle's argument is that one can have much knowledge-that but not have any knowledge-how. Ryle used the example of chess: "We can imagine a clever player generously imparting to his stupid opponent so many rules, tactical maxims, 'wrinkles,' etc., that he could think of no more to tell him; his opponent might accept and memorise all of them, and be able and ready to recite them correctly on demand. Yet he might still play chess stupidly, that is, be unable intelligently to apply the maxims, etc." (Ryle, 1946, p. 5).

Ryle's proposal has raised much debate and criticism in philosophy, with much of the criticism aimed at the epistemological value of the distinction between knowledge-how and knowledge-that (Stanley & Williamson, 2001; White, 1982). Some authors (e.g. Snowdon, 2004) argue that the know-how concept is poorly defined, and that Ryle exaggerated the difference between know-how and know-that. Entering into the detail of this debate is beyond the scope of this book, but the interested reader is referred to Fantl (2008), Gascoigne and Thornton (2013) or Winch (2010) for an in-depth discussion.

Polanyi argued against the positivist view that science is value-free. Rather, he argued in his book *Personal Knowledge* (1958) for *tacit knowing* or *tacit knowledge*: creativity and discovery in science are coloured by personal feelings and intellectual commitments. These include informed guesses, intuitions, perceptual images and intellectual passion. Contrary to explicit knowledge, which can be easily communicated to somebody else, it is hard to codify and communicate tacit knowledge. The strong claim of the book is that *all* knowledge, including explicit and formalised knowledge, relies on personal and tacit knowledge. As Polanyi put it in a later book, *The Tacit Dimension*, "we can know more than we can tell" (Polanyi, 1966, p. 4). Interestingly, Polanyi focuses on scientific *discovery* while most philosophers of science, spurred by Popper (1959), have focused on theory refutation or validation (see the box on **Expertise and philosophy of science**).

Expertise and philosophy of science

Most philosophy of science is concerned with an epistemological analysis of science and aims to determine whether, and if so how, scientific knowledge advances. Early work, for example by positivists, aimed to identify the methods by which scientific theories can be verified. In his influential *Logic of Scientific Discovery*, Popper (1959) argued that theories cannot be proved correct; they can only be falsified. Later work (Kuhn, 1970; Lakatos, 1970) argued that even this is not possible because, amongst other reasons, not all scientific knowledge can be expressed explicitly and unambiguously, and experimental results are rarely unequivocal.

An extreme position against the possibility of testability of knowledge was taken by Feyerabend (1993). In *Against Method*, he carried out a full-scale attack against standard philosophy of science and science in general. Using case studies from the history of science, he argued that it is not possible to identify any methodological rules that are used by all scientists. As a consequence, it is not possible to create methods that can differentiate the products from science from the products of non-scientific fields (e.g. astrology). Thus, science should not have any privileged status in our society and the role of scientific experts is thus relegated to that of public servants. Making a comparison with religion, Feyerabend also argued that science has become gradually dogmatic – scientists avoid having their theories properly tested – and therefore oppressive. At the same time, experts play an increasing role in politics and thus are accruing greater power. For all these reasons, experts represent a threat to democracy.

Espousing what he called an epistemological anarchism, he advocated a pluralistic methodology. In his typical colourful language, Feyerabend put it this way: "Experts and laymen, professionals and dilettanti, truth-freaks and liars – they all are invited to participate in the contest and to make their contribution to the enrichment of our culture" (1993, p. 21).

Critical in his argument is the assumption that "non-experts often know more than experts and should therefore be consulted" (Feyerabend, 1993, p. xiii). The role of laypeople as overseers of experts is two-fold: to protect democracy and to make it clear to experts that their view of the world is limited.

Critics of Feyerabend have argued that he has carried out a wrong analysis of (scientific) experts and caricatured them (Laudan, 1990; Stove, 2000; Worrall, 1991). For example, the historical and technical exactitude of his case studies has been disputed. In addition, his comparison of science with religion seems flawed: while inconsistent empirical evidence forces individuals to change their mind in science, this is not the case with religion. Finally, Selinger (2011) argues that Feyerabend draws an idealised picture of laypeople to whom he gives super-powers. By assuming that they all share the same knowledge, skills and aptitudes, Feyerabend ignores the considerable individual differences they share.

13.4 Disagreement between Experts

Experts disagree all the time. History of science reveals profound conflicts of opinion about the foundations of all sciences: the notion of number, the nature of life or the building blocks of matter. In politics, experts from different parties disagree on nearly all topics. In arts, whether an author deservedly earned the Nobel or the Booker prize is hotly debated. As documented in this book, the research on expertise has highlighted deep schisms, for example in the debate on the respective roles of practice and talent, the disputes on the memory structures acquired by experts, and the heated discussions about the reality of artificial intelligence (to be discussed in the following chapter). Different experts: different views. Indeed, often not only different views, but total disagreement in some cases!

This state of affairs raises important questions about expertise and more generally knowledge. If, as argued by Einhorn (1974), consensus between experts is a requirement for expertise, then the fact that experts disagree in real life and in experiments (e.g. Shanteau, 2001) questions the existence of expertise. There are of course many possible sources of disagreement between two (or more) experts: different evidence or information about a specific question; different motivation; different knowledge of the field or the subfield of interest (expert vs. sub-expert); different cognitive abilities (e.g. difference in IQ); and differences in values (e.g. a mechanistic view of the world vs. a non-mechanistic view). While real and practically important, these differences are not interesting philosophically. The really interesting question, studied in a field sometimes called social epistemology, concerns *epistemic peer disagreement*, where *epistemic peers* are defined as individuals equal as regards "intelligence, perspicacity, honesty, thoroughness, and other relevant epistemic virtues" (Gutting, 1982, p. 83).

A first question is whether rational individuals who are epistemic peers can in fact disagree. Some philosophers have argued that this is not possible (e.g. Feldman, 2007). Disagreement implies that one of the peers has made an error of reasoning or that some of the evidence was not fully shared. Other philosophers accept the possibility of epistemic peer disagreement, even after the peers have considered each other's (inconsistent) opinions with an open mind. There is however divergence about what is the rational way forward in this case. Elga (2007) mentions three possibilities. First, there is the *equal-weight view*; in case of disagreement, judgement should be suspended, and the assessment of each epistemic peer should receive equal weight. Despite some "unwelcome consequences", such as spinelessness and lack of self-trust, this is the view favoured by Elga. Second, there is the *extra-weight view* or *egocentric epistemic bias*: more weight should be given to one's assessment than to the epistemic peers' assessment (e.g. Wedgwood, 2007). Third, there is the *right-reasons view* (e.g. Kelly, 2005). Essentially, this view says that peer disagreement is not relevant. Whether there is disagreement or not, the answer depends on how well the available evidence was assessed in the first place. If the evidence supports one's view, then one should stick to it. As can be seen from this brief discussion, there is, in a self-referential way, a very strong epistemic peer disagreement about epistemic peer disagreement!

13.5 Identification of Experts

In Plato's *Charmides*, Socrates notes that even a wise man will not "be able to distinguish the pretender in medicine from the true physician, nor between any other true and false professor of knowledge". Collins and Evans (2007) go further: even experts cannot distinguish experts from non-experts if the non-experts possess sufficient interactional expertise (see Chapter 12). Whether it is possible to identify experts has been a recurring theme in philosophy and sociology. This question has obvious practical implications, in particular with respect to trust: can we trust physicists about the theory of relativity, biologists about the theory of evolution, astrologers about their predictions, or scientologists about their analysis of our mental life? Traditional science says "yes" in the first two cases but "no" in the last two (Gardner, 1957). But is it a correct conclusion?

There is an astonishingly large number of examples of *fake experts* – individuals who manage to pass as experts while they do not have the requisite qualifications. A well-respected dean of admissions at MIT, who had co-authored a book about stress and education, resigned in 2007 after 28 years of good service. She turned out to have misrepresented her academic credentials (Freedman, 2010). In Germany, Defence Minister Karl-Theodor zu Guttenberg and Education Minister Annette Schavan lost both their jobs and their PhDs after allegations of plagiarism were substantiated. Perhaps the most astonishing case is that of James McCormick, a conman who duped military experts and security officers by selling them fake weapon detectors for more than £55 million. The devices, sold for £10,000 each, were totally useless for detecting weapons: they were gadgets for finding golf balls, worth only £15 each. McCormick was jailed for 10 years in 2013. Tragically, it was estimated that thousands of people died in Iraq because of the device.

While not condoning fraud and plagiarism, it is worth noting that it is sometimes possible to perform at an expert level without having formal credentials, as noted in Chapter 12. A striking example is offered by bogus doctors (Collins & Pinch, 2005). Apparently, it is surprisingly easy to fake medical skills: in 1985, a Select Committee on Aging in the US House of Representatives investigated fraudulent credentials and estimated that there were about 10,000 bogus doctors – one in 50 doctors – in the United States. Interestingly, bogus doctors are rarely uncovered through medical malpractice; rather, they tend to behave unprofessionally in non-medical matters (e.g. making false insurance claims). In addition, many of them had been praised by their employers and patients for their medical skills. As Collins and Pinch (2005, p. 56) put it, "indeed, an experienced bogus doctor is almost certain to be a better doctor than a novice straight from medical school".

Identifying experts is also critical for law, in particular in countries with an adversarial law system. The easy case involves separating genuine experts from fake experts, for which Coady (1992) proposes to use credentials (e.g. membership in highly regarded universities). More specifically with respect to bogus science, Coady (p. 287) proposes that "the courts should give initial credence to the verdicts of such bodies as universities on the issue of bogus science, though they should be prepared to hear argument about the matter if it can be produced". Trickier is the case in which experts have similar credentials but arrive at a different conclusion, without there being a rational way to tease them apart (e.g. one expert self-contradicts herself). This is the epistemic peer disagreement situation we discussed earlier. Brewer (1998) argues that, when dealing with scientific expert testimony, non-expert judges or juries must follow a "structured reasoning process" (p. 1679). Unfortunately, this process contains critical steps in which non-experts cannot make "epistemically nonarbitrary" decisions (i.e. decisions showing an understanding of the goals, methods and results of a given expert discipline). These decisions are necessary for legitimacy, as reflected by the "norm of intellectual due process" (p. 1680). The solution proposed by Brewer is to encourage judges and jurors to have both legal training and scientific training in a relevant discipline.

Identifying experts is not a problem for all domains of expertise. As noted in Chapter 1, there are domains where experts clearly outperform non-experts (e.g. tennis, chess) and the existence of bogus experts is nearly impossible. These domains tend to be in science, sports and games, where objective measures of expertise are available. Ericsson (e.g. 1996a; Ericsson & Smith, 1991a) has emphasised the necessity for expertise research to bring experts into the laboratory, so that their performance can be replicated under controlled conditions. However, this is not always possible. When one moves into "real-life" domains, discrimination becomes difficult. In particular, the problem of demarcation between expertise and non-expertise is acute in domains not based on scientific knowledge, although the boundary is not strict (think of medicine and bogus doctors, for example).

13.6 Dreyfus's Critique of Expert Systems

In the next chapter, we will discuss research into expert systems. This research, and more generally artificial-intelligence (AI) research, has raised many objections from philosophers. Here, we focus on the criticism levelled by Hubert Dreyfus, since it directly relates to the question of knowledge.

In the 1950s and 1960s, several proposals were made to develop computer programs able to exhibit intelligence. Most of these proposals assumed that intelligence can be explained by rules. One of the most influential was Newell and Simon's approach based on the manipulation of symbols, which started with a program able to prove new theorems in logic (Newell et al., 1958b) and led to the *General Problem Solver* (GPS, Newell & Simon, 1972), a program able to solve problems in any domain in principle, although it mostly was applied to games and puzzles. There was high optimism in the field, as witnessed by Herbert Simon's 1957 prediction that a computer would beat the world chess champion within 10 years.

It is against this framework that Hubert Dreyfus (1965) published a RAND technical report called *Alchemy and Artificial Intelligence*, which contained a blistering criticism of AI. In the report, which was later expanded in the book *What Computers Can't Do: The Limits of Artificial Intelligence*, Dreyfus (1972) systematically criticised four key assumptions of AI: first, the biological assumption that the brain is analogous to computer hardware and the mind is analogous to computer software; second, the psychological assumption that the mind works by performing discrete computations on symbols; third, the epistemological assumption that all behaviour (both that of animate and inanimate objects) can be formalised (e.g. using mathematics) using predictive rules or laws; and fourth, the ontological assumption that reality entirely consists of a set of mutually independent, atomic facts.

Dreyfus's criticism is based on phenomenology, that part of philosophy developed by Husserl (1900/1973) and Heidegger (1927/1962) and studying first-person subjective experience. According to phenomenology, we cannot understand ourselves the same way we understand objects, because we have a body and live in a world made of other things (Heidegger's notion of *Dasein*, which can be translated as *being-in-the-world*). Thus, while scientific laws are context-free, humans are context-bound. Dreyfus propounds that, because unconscious thoughts and intuition are critical for human behaviour, efforts in AI are doomed to failure.

In *Mind over Machine* (Dreyfus & Dreyfus, 1988), Hubert Dreyfus teamed with his brother Stuart to present the five-stage theory of expertise we have described in Chapter 6. Expert systems were very fashionable in the 1980s, and embodied a key assumption already criticised by Dreyfus in his 1972 book: knowledge can be formalised declaratively using rules. The book directly targets expert systems and the assumption that such systems should be able to perform at the level of a human or better. The book does not report empirical data, but rather uses anecdotal evidence and the reader's intuitions about the way human experts behave. The conclusion is that expert systems cannot go beyond the level of human novices, who manipulate rules consciously. In particular, they cannot behave like human experts, who use intuition, context-bound knowledge, and their body. In general, expert systems are good at knowing-that, but not at not knowing-how – a fatal weakness, since knowing-how is a necessary requirement for expertise.

Dreyfus's books and articles were (are) written in an abrasive style, which did not help communication and productive interactions. As detailed by McCorduck (1979) and Papert (1968), they contain many technical errors and incorrect predictions (e.g. that computers will never be good at playing chess because they only count out alternative moves while, for reaching expert level, any system must "use cues which remain on the fringe of consciousness"; Dreyfus, 1972, p. 40).[1] In addition, the five-stage model suffers from a number of weaknesses, as discussed in Chapter 6. But some of the criticisms levelled by Dreyfus were correct: artificial intelligence did suffer from some exaggerated optimism in its early days; while capturing declarative knowledge well, experts systems struggle with procedural knowledge; and finally, while not the only defining feature of expertise, as argued by Dreyfus, intuition does play an important role in expert behaviour, as documented in Chapter 6. Some of his ideas on the role of body in the study of cognition have also gained popularity in recent years, in particular in the field of robotics and embodied cognition.

13.7 Rationality and Expertise

As we have just seen, according to Hubert Dreyfus, experts rarely deliberate but rather act intuitively. By contrast, individuals who are only at the competent stage use analytic and deliberative thought. Dreyfus proposed that experts are *arational*: they cannot justify their actions rationally. Montero and Evans (2011), referring to McDowell's (1994) theory of rationality, argue for the exact opposite: intuitive aspects of expertise are grounded in reason, and experts can justify their actions rationally.

---

[1] This prediction was clearly refuted by the victory of Deep Blue against then chess world champion Garry Kasparov in 1997. Nowadays, chess programs running on a personal computer are so strong that even top grandmasters have stopped playing matches against them. The successes of Macsyma, to be discussed in the next chapter, are also inconsistent with Dreyfus's analysis.

Montero and Evans adduce some sensible criticisms against Dreyfus's theory, which are actually in line with the criticisms that were offered in Chapter 6 when we dealt with intuition (see also Gobet & Chassy, 2008b, 2009). For example, Dreyfus's statement that experts rarely use attention and deliberation is refuted by the substantial amount of data on search behaviour (see Chapter 4). Similarly, Montero and Evans convincingly argue that Dreyfus's contention that experts do not use rules to carry out decisions or justify them – they just act – is refuted by the fact that experts do use both basic and advanced heuristic rules explicitly and consciously. However, Montero and Evans seem to go too far in their rejection of unconscious processes, as they deny the possibility that advanced heuristics can be proceduralised with sufficient practice or that some heuristics are never stated explicitly and thus never conscious (Gobet, 2012).

In our view, while Dreyfus over-emphasises non-rational or arational thought, Montero and Evans do the same with conscious and rational thought. It is true that rational thought is an important component of expertise, as can be seen by experts' use of concepts and deliberation. However, rational thought is only one part of expertise. As documented at length in Chapters 2 and 3, perceptual knowledge together with pattern recognition represent a crucial component, in particular with respect to intuition. Thus, expertise appears to depend on a combination of intuition and conscious search, which are both mediated by perceptual processes. As for rationality, it seems that humans are just not rational: not in the sense of optimising behaviour (Simon, 1982), and not in Montero, Evans and McDowell's sense of always being able to describe conceptually what they do and why they do it.

13.8 Philosophy and Expertise: Applications

Philosophy is usually considered a theoretical discipline, with little connection to practical reality. However, a branch of philosophy called *applied philosophy* precisely tries to address practical questions, with the assumption that a better philosophical understanding enables better practice. Here, we briefly consider three applications of philosophy to everyday expertise: nursing, construction and education.

Benner (1984; Benner et al., 1996) applied Dreyfus and Dreyfus's (1988) phenomenological five-stage theory of skill to nursing. Benner's specific contribution was to emphasise the importance, during the development of nursing intuition, of knowing patients and being emotionally involved with them. Unlike beginners, whose emotions are limited to anxiety, experienced nurses deploy a wider repertoire of emotional behaviours, which magnify their perceptual awareness and also shape their clinical know-how, including ethical behaviour and emotional participation with patients and their families. Benner emphasises learning in context and criticises theoretical instruction in later stages of nursing education, when the focus should be on developing intuitive skills by directly interacting with patients. The notion of holistic understanding is essential in the theory, with the implication that it is not possible to decompose understanding into smaller parts. Her research has had considerable impact on nursing education, in particular in the US. Critiques of her theory note its weak philosophical foundations, difficulties with her definition of intuition and lack of empirical support (Cash, 1995; English, 1993; Gobet & Chassy, 2008b).

Referring to the work of philosophers such as Aristotle, Dreyfus, Heidegger and Wittgenstein, Boyd and Addis (2010, 2011) used methods from philosophy to solve practical issues in the field of construction. In particular, meeting individuals from bricklayers to senior managers, they were interested in the "why" behind these individuals' practice, covering both questions of knowing and doing. Boyd and Addis uncovered important differences between the sort of knowledge that was needed, according to the industry, and the kind of knowledge used in practice. For example, the industry emphasised factual and technical knowledge. However, interviews revealed that working practice relies to a considerable extent on non-factual knowledge (e.g. how to deal with people suitably). Similarly, the divergence between theoretical representations and actual activities has led to a number of misrepresentations with knowledge management, in particular with a computerised format.

A number of authors have used philosophical methods and theories to shed light on issues related to education. Winch (2010) has carried out a philosophical analysis of expertise within the context of vocational and professional education and curriculum design; for example, he has studied the professional qualifications for bricklaying in eight European Union countries. In Winch's view, it is not possible to develop a general theory of expertise, because of the diverse kinds of expertise and skill involved. At most there is a family resemblance, in Wittgenstein's (1984) sense, between them. Building on Rumfitt (2003), Winch also stresses an important linguistic ambiguity in English with *know-how*. The sentence "A knows how to F" means both that (a) A can carry out F and (b) A can provide an account of how F is carried out. Note that this ambiguity is not present in all languages. For example, in French the distinction is indicated by *savoir faire* and *savoir comment faire*, respectively, and in German it is signalled by *können* and *wissen wie*, respectively. Finally, while Winch (2009) agrees with Ryle's distinction between knowing-how and knowing-that, he argues that Ryle underestimates the role of knowing-that in many forms of knowing-how, for example for making judgements or carrying out inferences. Understanding how instruction using propositional knowledge (know-that) is provided before practice is important for professional and vocational education.

Lum (2012, 2014) focuses on the assessment of professional knowledge. He notes that there has been a considerable change in the field of assessment the last two decades or so. Assessments have shifted away from an emphasis on testing, prediction and selection towards an emphasis on assessing learners' achievements, skills, competences and knowledge. With this new emphasis in mind, two kinds of assessment are possible. In the first, *prescriptive mode*, the focus is on stipulated evidence; judgements compare the answers to what was taught, and the outcomes are binary (correct or incorrect). One issue with this mode of assessment is that it might fail to evaluate the learner's *understanding*. As Lum notes, a learner might answer a question correctly without understanding the topic, while another learner might fail to answer a question correctly (e.g. because of distraction), while understanding the topic well. In the second, *expansive mode*, any relevant evidence can be taken into account; judgement is made on significance, and the outcomes tend to be graded. According to Lum, the expansive mode has the advantage of providing a better assessment of knowledge and competences, but suffers from providing outcomes that can be ambiguous and from requiring considerable financial and temporal resources, although this might be assuaged by practical testing. Despite these shortcomings, Lum argues that the expansive mode should be used in professional practice.

13.9 Chapter Summary

A considerable proportion of this chapter has dealt with the opposition between knowing-how and knowing-that. The importance of implicit and procedural knowledge was already captured by Aristotle's concepts of techne and phronesis, and Plato's view that ruling is a craft. However, it is Ryle who framed the issue in modern philosophy. Although Ryle's views on knowing-how have been criticised and the majority of philosophers give more importance to knowing-that (propositional knowledge), his impact has been considerable. Polanyi framed the question in slightly different terms, focusing on scientific discovery and stressing that all knowledge is personal and tacit. Similarly, Dreyfus's critique of artificial intelligence and his emphasis on experts' intuition is a critique of explicit knowledge and a manifesto for tacit knowledge. Conversely, Montero and Evans's conception of rationality, which highlights explicit justification of decisions, is a critique of tacit knowledge. Finally, the applications from philosophy to a large extent relate to know-how, as they concentrate on practical knowledge.

The three remaining topics addressed different issues. Feyerabend's criticism of science and scientific expertise, with a negation that a universal scientific method can be identified, has raised fierce opposition. The literature on expert disagreement is interesting but also confusing, since totally opposite positions have been defended. As for the discussion of whether it is possible to identify experts, it overlaps with themes that were tackled in Chapter 1 (definitions of expertise) and Chapter 12 (expert testimony).

In contrast with psychology, and even more so than sociology, philosophy pays little attention to empirical data. Arguments are based on first-person evidence such as introspection, thought experiments, logical arguments and reference to classic books or articles. There is also much effort to provide suitable definitions. So, whilst philosophers have highlighted significant questions with respect to expertise, they have failed to provide convincing answers, in our opinion, since they appear to have largely ignored developments in other fields, including empirical evidence. We have provided an example of this state of affairs when discussing Dreyfus and Dreyfus's (philosophical) theory of intuition in Chapter 6. Another example where using empirical data would clarify conceptual issues is offered, we believe, by the discussion around knowing-how and knowing-that.

13.10 Further Reading

The collection of papers in Selinger and Crease (2006) addresses expertise mostly from the point of view of philosophy, although some contributions also cover sociology, history, literary theory and law. Gascoigne and Thornton (2013) provide a detailed discussion of the concept of tacit knowledge in philosophy. The June 2013 issue of *Phenomenology and the Cognitive Sciences* is fully devoted to tacit knowledge, with many articles discussing expertise.

CHAPTER 14

Artificial Intelligence and Expert Systems

14.1 Preview of Chapter

This chapter addresses the links between artificial intelligence (AI) and expertise, focusing on the role of knowledge in intelligent computer systems and on the subfield known as expert systems. The aim of AI is to build computers that make decisions and carry out actions that would be considered intelligent if they were carried out by humans (e.g. Cohen & Feigenbaum, 1982; Russell & Norvig, 2009). This aim, which includes building artificial experts, obviously raises deep philosophical questions; thus, some of the themes discussed in the previous chapter will crop up in this chapter again. Following a classic distinction, the large number of methods developed in AI can be divided into methods based on search and methods based on knowledge. The first class of methods rely on computers' ability to search vast problem spaces rapidly. The second rely on their ability to store and rapidly access large amounts of knowledge. In many domains, it can be shown that there exists a trade-off between knowledge and search: an agent able to carry out substantial amounts of search does not need much knowledge, while an agent having much knowledge does not need to search much (Berliner, 1984; Berliner & Ebeling, 1989; Newell, 1990).

There is obviously a parallel between the use of knowledge in AI systems and the way human experts use knowledge to solve problems (see Chapter 4). This parallel has been exploited most fully in the research on expert systems, where the aim is to build computer systems that make high-quality decisions based on human-like knowledge and reasoning. We first review different ways of representing knowledge and then focus on expert systems.

14.2 Knowledge Representation

Knowledge representation has attracted considerable attention in AI (and in other fields such as mathematics and philosophy), because the way a problem is represented often will considerably affect the ease and way in which it is solved, and indeed whether it can be solved at all (Larkin & Simon, 1987). Pertinent questions include: Are there more efficient representations? What different kinds of knowledge are necessary for developing intelligent computer systems? Is one type of representation sufficient, or are many necessary? Are some representations easier to understand and use for humans who have to interact with artificial systems?

To represent knowledge, AI has borrowed a number of formalisms from other fields and has developed new ones as well, as can be easily seen by skimming any introductory textbook to AI (e.g. Nilsson, 1998; Russell & Norvig, 2009). Among the many formalisms originating from mathematics, one can mention sets, vectors, matrices and graphs (Crowdis et al., 1978; Kemeny et al., 1960). Representation of uncertainty is critical in many domains, and ample use has been made of probability theory and statistics, and in particular Bayesian statistics (Howson & Urbach, 1989; Winkler, 2003). A number of logic formalisms have been used, from standard predicate calculus to more exotic kinds of logic (Stefik, 1995). Examples include fuzzy logic (where, unlike predicate calculus in which a statement is either true or false, statements have a truth value that ranges between 0 and 1) and non-monotonic logic (where adding new information to a database might invalidate previous conclusions). Some formalisms are inspired by biology, such as neural networks, where nodes are the equivalents of neurones and represent knowledge elements; the weight of the links between two nodes represent the strength of the association between those nodes (Bechtel & Abrahamsen, 1991). Several formalisms – some of them already discussed in the previous chapters – were inspired from theories in cognitive psychology or from intuitions that AI researchers had about the functioning of the human mind. The box **Knowledge representations inspired by psychology** describes the most important of these formalisms.

14.3 Expert Systems

Expert systems form a subfield of AI where knowledge is particularly important. They can be defined as computer systems encoding the knowledge used by human experts and solving problems (e.g. diagnosis, troubleshooting) at the same level as those experts. Expert systems started to be developed in the mid-1960s as a reaction to the (presumed) weakness of programs that tried to solve problems by general methods and/or brute search. The rationale behind expert systems can be summarised by philosopher Francis Bacon's dictum that "knowledge is power". Major successes include DENDRAL, MYCIN and XCON.

DENDRAL (Feigenbaum et al., 1971; Lindsay et al., 1993) is considered the first expert system in history. It used its knowledge of chemistry to infer the structure of unknown organic molecules, using data from nuclear magnetic spectrometry, amongst other empirical sources. Its considerable influence on AI was due to several innovative features: it was the first program to use heuristic search for the analysis of experimental data, the first AI application to deal with an important practical problem, the first large-scale computer system to use a large amount of task-specific knowledge, and the first program to separate its knowledge

---

Knowledge representations inspired by psychology

Some influential ways to represent knowledge in AI are based on psychology. *Semantic networks* represent concepts as nodes and relations between concepts as links between those nodes. *Schemas* encapsulate typical information about a particular situation or topic and include the kind of useful actions that could be carried out in that situation. They typically consist of a *core*, encoding fixed information, and of *slots*, where variable information can be encoded. Note that the exact meaning of the term "schema" changes considerably from one author to the next (Lane et al., 2000). Schemas can be organised in a strict hierarchy or in a loose or tangled hierarchy (also called heterarchy), where a given schema can belong to several hierarchies at the same time (Jackson, 1999). In the artificial-intelligence literature, schemas are often called *frames*. *Scripts* are schemas where the emphasis is on the sequence of events that typically occur in a given situation and on the actions that should be carried out given those events.

Production rules (or IF-THEN rules) are a popular way to represent knowledge in psychological theories (Anderson, 1993; Newell, 1990). They offer a very efficient way to represent knowledge, and have been used in many AI programs (e.g. Soar, MYCIN). They consist of conditions, which represent features of the problem, and actions, which indicate what actions should be carried out when the conditions are met. Some computer languages, such as OPS-5 (Cooper & Wogrin, 1988), are entirely based on production rules to optimise the efficiency of running production systems.

---

base from its inference engine. Not only was DENDRAL used by chemists to solve "real-world" problems, it was also the vehicle for theoretical and empirical investigations on automatic hypothesis formation, leading to (minor) scientific discoveries. While DENDRAL wholly relied on human experts to code new rules, a later version, known as Meta-DENDRAL, was able to infer new rules by itself.

MYCIN (Buchanan & Shortliffe, 1984), which stemmed from DENDRAL, was a medical diagnosis system. It diagnosed blood diseases caused by severe bacterial infections such as meningitis, and also recommended antibiotic treatment. Its knowledge base contained about 600 rules. One important innovation of MYCIN was to have introduced (informal) probabilistic reasoning methods to expert systems and thus a means to deal with uncertainty. In experiments, MYCIN came up with a suitable diagnosis in about 70 per cent of cases – a better performance than human experts. However, MYCIN was never used in actual diagnoses, not only for legal concerns about liability in case of incorrect diagnosis, but also because entering the necessary medical data was a linear and slow process, requiring doctors to type in answers to MYCIN's long list of questions.

XCON was an expert system developed by Digital Equipment Corporation (DEC) to configure VAX computer systems according to customers' specifications

(Barker & O'Connor, 1989). It contained more than 17,000 rules. Given the frequent changes in the products sold by DEC, 40 per cent of the rules changed every year. XCON processed more than 80,000 orders, with an accuracy of over 95 per cent. Barker and O'Connor estimate that DEC was able to save more than $40 million a year by using XCON.

14.4 Knowledge Elicitation Techniques

A major question in expert systems research concerns the elicitation and coding of the knowledge used by human experts. In some domains, this can be done by consulting textbooks, manuals and other teaching or technical material. However, in many cases, experts' knowledge is encoded nowhere but in their heads. Thus, this knowledge has to be extracted from them in some way. Knowledge elicitation has raised some interesting questions, some of which lie at the core of the nature of expertise: What is the best way to represent expert knowledge? Are some computer languages more suited than others to represent expert knowledge? What is the best way to extract and encode procedural and implicit knowledge?

To answer these questions, and others, a number of techniques have been developed in a field sometimes called knowledge engineering (Gordon, 1992; Hoffman et al., 1995; Reitman Olson & Biolsi, 1991). A first technique consists of asking experts to solve a problem and to record them while they work on it. The concurrent verbal protocols, as well as any other material produced by the experts during problem solving, are then analysed in order to extract both declarative and procedural knowledge. A variation of this technique, called retrospective protocol analysis, consists of asking experts for explanations and comments after the problem has been solved. A second class of techniques uses interviews, either structured (where questions about specific aspects of experts' knowledge are asked) or unstructured (where the experts simply talk about whatever aspects of their knowledge seem to them relevant). Interviews mostly tap experts' declarative knowledge.

Several methods have been developed to capture implicit and procedural knowledge more specifically. A first technique simply consists of asking an expert to solve many problems, without the necessity to speak aloud. The observations are then used to draw inferences between the characteristics of the problems and the solutions found. These inferences can be drawn either by humans (e.g. the knowledge engineer with the help of the expert) or by computer-based techniques such as those developed in the machine-learning literature. A variant of this technique is to let experts proceed as usual, but to interrupt them when there is a particularly interesting situation and to ask them to clarify the methods used.

A number of techniques used in experimental psychology (see Chapters 2 and 3) have also been used to infer experts' implicit and procedural knowledge. These include de Groot's (1965) recall task, tasks where experts are requested to draw lines grouping objects in a diagram that they think belong together, either perceptually or conceptually, and tasks where experts are asked to sort problems into different categories. A further method asks experts to produce a large number of similarity judgements between objects and concepts taken from their domain of expertise. Then, mathematical techniques such as multidimensional scaling or hierarchical clustering are used to infer the deep structure of experts' knowledge. When used with several experts, an advantage of these techniques is that they can highlight inter-individual differences in knowledge structures.

Eliciting knowledge turned out to be more problematic than originally thought, and raised a number of interesting problems about expertise and expert knowledge, as we shall see in the next section. Difficulties in knowledge elicitation represent one of the reasons why expert systems research has not been as popular recently as it used to be.

14.5 Decline of Expert Systems Research

Research into expert systems reached its climax in the late 1980s and early 1990s, but the field has declined since. There are several reasons for this, both positive and negative. On the positive side, some problems that were considered to be challenging and requiring an understanding of how human experts solved them led to spectacular successes. A classic example is the Macsyma program (and now other programs such as Mathematica and Maple), which can solve complex problems in many subfields of mathematics such as calculus and matrix algebra. Macsyma, developed at MIT from 1968 to 1982, was a considerable success and was used by hundreds of researchers to help them solve mathematical problems (Moses, 2012). Thus, as the research question had been mostly solved, there was no need for further efforts on this topic. To some extent, Macsyma became the victim of its own success.

There are negative reasons as well. First, there is the problem that expert systems, just like all AI programs, have knowledge only in a limited domain and lack common sense, a problem noted amongst others by Dreyfus (1972; Dreyfus & Dreyfus, 1988; see also Chapter 13). As a consequence of their brittle and narrow expertise, expert systems sometimes make errors that no human would make. For example, a medical doctor could not make the inference that an antibiotics treatment should be given to a person who died one hour ago, but MYCIN would, since the notion of dead patient is not explicitly encoded in its database. In spite of large-scale attempts to create systems replicating human everyday knowledge – for example the Cyc research programme (Foxvog, 2010; Lenat & Guha, 1990), which started in 1984 and is still ongoing – this twin problem of narrow knowledge and lack of common sense has clearly thwarted progress in this field.

Second, and perhaps more importantly, there is the problem of procedural knowledge. In psychology, research into implicit learning and implicit memory has highlighted the role of unconscious processing in many, if not most, aspects of cognition (Reber, 1993; Schacter et al., 1993). As we saw in Chapter 13, the importance of implicit knowledge in experts has also been emphasised by some philosophers. The common factor in all these approaches is a de-emphasis of the role of conscious, verbalisable and declarative knowledge – the foundation of research into expert systems and knowledge engineering. But if experts' knowledge is predominantly implicit and procedural, then it is less justifiable to develop techniques for extracting explicit and declarative knowledge.

Third, there is the surprising power of brute force in at least some domains of expertise, such as chess and chemistry. In chess, Deep Blue beat Kasparov with a great deal of search abilities but little knowledge (Campbell et al., 2002); in chemistry, programs based on search techniques led to the design of new molecules and the elucidation of reaction pathways (Cohen & Shatzmiller, 1993; Valdés-Pérez, 1995). But if brute search alone leads to such powerful results, without the need of painstakingly eliciting knowledge from experts, then why should researchers spend time on knowledge engineering? In a similar vein, progress made first in machine learning (Mitchell, 1997) and then in data mining (Witten et al., 2011) meant that knowledge could be more rapidly extracted, and more rapidly updated, from large databases than by interrogating experts.

Finally, several expert systems researchers have migrated to what they considered more exciting and promising fields. In addition to machine learning and data mining, which we have just mentioned, these fields include connectionism, robotics and evolutionary computation. These fields aim to develop intelligent systems by techniques that are wholly different to those used in expert systems – there is little or no emphasis on human knowledge and expertise.

14.6 Contributions of Expert Systems Research

In addition to the development of representational languages, knowledge elicitation techniques and the building of specific expert systems, two important contributions of the field might be noted. First, expert systems and AI more generally have led to changes in software engineering that have been widely accepted in computer science. A good example is offered by a software development technique known as rapid application development (RAD; Kerr & Hunter, 1993). In the 1970s and 1980s, the standard approach to software development was the Waterfall Model (Royce, 1970), a linear approach to programming with emphasis on specification and planning. By contrast, RAD approaches emphasised the need to flexibly adapt and react to the knowledge acquired during the development of the project. Rather than analysis and design, RAD thus emphasises creating and modifying prototypes that include only a subset of the specifications but that are operational. This approach was necessary with expert systems given the complexity of the domains for which such systems were developed. Another example concerns the fashionable field of the semantic web (Davies, 2006; Yu, 2011). Many of the techniques and representations developed in the research into expert systems are being reused in developing ontologies for the semantic web. (An *ontology* represents, in an unambiguous and formally agreed upon form usable by a computer, a specific area of knowledge, including its key concepts and the relationships they share.)

Second, some of the techniques motivated by the development of expert systems led to a better understanding of how to encode knowledge not only with experts, but with non-experts too, with impact for psychology in general (Gobet, 1997a; Shadbolt & O'Hara, 1997). However, given the way knowledge is defined in this field, this benefit has been limited to declarative and explicit knowledge.

Much work remains to be done on the development of artificial-intelligence systems behaving at high levels of expertise. One possible avenue consists in using formal theories of expert behaviour as springboards for developing expert systems, thus not necessarily using the techniques we have reviewed in this chapter. For example, programs could acquire knowledge by themselves, using the kind of theories reviewed in Chapters 2 and 3, rather than being fed knowledge by the programmers.

14.7 Chapter Summary

Artificial intelligence (AI) aims to build computer systems that act in an intelligent way. Expert systems are AI programs whose goal is to emulate the thinking and decision-making abilities of human experts. Several formalisms have been developed to represent knowledge, including formalisms based on research in psychology, such as schemas and production rules. The acme of expert systems research was in the late 1980s and early 1990s. Successful applications include DENDRAL (identification of unknown organic molecules), MYCIN (treatment of blood infections) and XCON (configuration of computer systems). Considerable research has been devoted to the development of techniques allowing knowledge to be elicited from experts. While successful with declarative knowledge, these techniques have difficulties with procedural knowledge. Research into expert systems has decreased in recent years, both because key problems have been solved (e.g. solving mathematical equations, with Macsyma) and because some issues did not find a satisfactory answer (e.g. common sense knowledge and procedural knowledge).

14.8 Further Reading

Russell and Norvig's textbook (2009) provides a broad introduction to artificial intelligence but contains much information about knowledge representation and expert systems. Jackson (1999) and Stefik (1995) are more focused introductions to expert systems and knowledge systems. The book edited by Hoffman (1992) looks at expertise from the point of view of artificial intelligence and experimental, applied and theoretical psychology. Written during the heyday of expert systems, it contains interesting contributions regarding knowledge engineering.

CHAPTER 15

Putting It All Together

15.1 Preview of Chapter

A lot of ground has been covered in our quest to understand expertise, and it is time to end our journey. We have visited many precincts of the social and human sciences, although we had to skip a few. For example, we only took a glimpse at anthropology, ethnography, history and law in passing, and we did not say much about how experts are depicted in the arts, for instance in literature and in the movies. Nor did we provide an analysis of experts from an economic point of view.

This chapter first reviews the good and bad news from expertise research. We then examine expertise using eight themes that cut across standard academic disciplines. This leads us to a consideration of the methods and kinds of theories that have been used to understand expertise. We then show how four of the theoretical tensions that recurred in this book can be at least partly resolved when they are cast in a different light. We end by discussing ethical issues and implications for practice, including advice on how to become an expert.

15.2 Good and Bad News

In this book, we have heard both good and bad news. On the positive side, there exists considerable scientific knowledge about expertise and how it is acquired, and much is known about perception and memory mechanisms in particular, allowing us to devise efficient methods of teaching and coaching. There is also the obvious fact that, in some domains such as sports and the arts, the level of human performance is simply awe-inspiring. Finally, in many domains, experts are reliable and can be trusted.

On the negative side, expertise is a complex phenomenon that cannot be reduced to a single mechanism or factor, as (implicitly) hoped for by many researchers. Thus, it is likely that a successful theory of expertise will be complex, with mechanisms interacting at different levels. Also disappointing, to some extent, is the fact that expertise is hard to acquire and requires lengthy practice and training. One book advertises "how to become an expert on anything in 2 hours" (Hartley & Karinch, 2008) – a bogus expert, perhaps, but nothing more. We can, of course, quibble about whether the figures of 10,000 hours or 10 years of deliberate practice often proposed in the literature are correct, but the fact remains that a substantial investment of time is necessary to reach high levels of expertise. Another disappointing result is the difficulty of transferring expertise from one domain to another, unless they both share common elements. A final piece of bad news is that, in some domains, "experts" are simply not experts when the definition proposed in the first chapter of this book is used: an expert is an individual who vastly outperforms the majority of the population. On a related note, it is not always easy to identify experts, particularly in domains that are important in our lives, such as health and finance.

15.3 Transversal Themes

The bulk of this book is organised around standard topics in psychology, and the last chapters cover other disciplines having contributed to our knowledge of expertise. It is also important to look at the material in a different way, so that we can see how key themes cut across disciplines. By showing how these themes apply or do not apply in the various disciplines, we can provide an integrated view of expertise. Eight themes have been identified, admittedly with some subjectivity (see Table 15.1). Given the level of analysis, the discussion will be somewhat broad-brush. Note that researchers' contributions sometimes overlap between fields. For example, Dreyfus and Dreyfus's (1988) five-stage model has been influential in several fields, including philosophy and psychology, and Collins and Evans's (2007) analysis of expertise has had an impact in both sociology and philosophy.

Table 15.1 Transversal themes. Themes can be present: ✓, partly present: (✓) or absent: ✗ in a field.

	Psychology	Education	Neuroscience	Sociology	Philosophy	Artificial Intelligence
Definition/ Identification	✓	✗	✗	✓	✓	✗
Rationality	✓	✗	✗	✗	✓	✗
Knowledge	✓	✓	✓	✓	✓	✓
Search	✓	✗	✗	✗	✗	✓
Generativity	✓	✓	✗	✗	✗	✓
Diachronicity	✓	✓	✓	✓	✓	✗
Nature vs. Nurture	✓	✓	✓	✗	✗	✗
Environment/ Society	(✓)	(✓)	✗	✓	✗	✗

15.3.1 Definition and Identification

Defining expertise has been an important task in psychology and sociology, and to a lesser extent in philosophy. In contrast, education, neuroscience and AI have not invested much effort in definitions. As noted in Chapter 1, psychology has focused on performance and processes, while sociology has been interested in the way society defines experts. The kind of definition used in a field will have an impact on the way experts are studied. In particular, experts investigated in psychology tend to have reliable levels of performance, while this is not the case in sociology. Put another way, some individuals considered as experts in sociology would not be so in psychology, since they do not meet the requirements of achieving levels of performance superior to non-experts.

Definitions will also affect how easy it is to identify an expert, if this is possible at all. With definitions typically used in psychology, including that used in this book, identifying experts is not an issue in domains where expertise can be consistently expressed and on request (e.g. sports, science). Most individuals would be decimated when playing chess against Kasparov or tennis against Federer. The exception, as discussed in Chapter 6, concerns creativity, which is harder to observe. Such clear-cut definitions can have consequences that are unwelcome for some classes of expertise. For example, considering the empirical evidence (Cowles, 1944; Meehl, 1954; Tracey et al., 2014), the definition used in this book would deny the label "expert" to stock market advisors and psychotherapists carrying out a diagnosis. Thus, this definition based on objective performance implies that there are domains of knowledge where expertise is difficult or even impossible to attain. With the second class of definitions, those typically used in sociology (e.g. those based on diplomas or reputation), individuals who do not have the knowledge or skill they advertise might be identified as experts. In general, the fuzzier the credentials, the easier it becomes to fake a type of expertise (e.g. astrology).

The contrast between these two kinds of definition warrants creating two concepts: performance-based expertise (p-expertise) and reputation-based expertise (r-expertise). This distinction, while in line with Shanteau's (1992a) analysis, is also different in that the emphasis centres on the way experts are defined rather than on the way they perform. Note also that expertise does not need to come in pure form in one of these two types, and often these two forms are mixed in varying proportions.

15.3.2 Rationality

Do humans make the best possible decisions to achieve their goals, given their knowledge? This is the assumption of *rationality*, which is at the heart of neoclassical economics, where it is accepted unreservedly. This assumption has also been increasingly present in psychology and philosophy, in particular due to the growing influence of the idea that humans behave as Bayesian agents (i.e. they update probabilities related to hypotheses in an optimal way). For example, it is central in the study of decision making and reasoning.

The field of expertise, which studies the very best individuals in a domain, seems an ideal place to test the hypothesis of rationality. The verdict is loud and clear: humans are *not* fully rational. In domains such as chess, medicine, radiology and sports, experts make minor and occasionally even major mistakes (see Chapter 5). These mistakes can sometimes be explained by stress and time pressure, but not always. In general, therefore, the literature on expertise supports Simon's hypothesis of bounded rationality (Simon, 1956; 1982). The same conclusion applies to a slightly different view of rationality, defined as the ability to always justify one's decisions rationally (McDowell, 1994; Montero & Evans, 2011). As noted in Chapter 13, this hypothesis is refuted by the fact that experts make many decisions intuitively, based on perceptual cues that may be unconscious or difficult to describe verbally. Experts are not irrational; they just display a kind of rationality that is bounded but adaptive.

How can experts reach such high levels of performance despite their bounded rationality? As noted in Chapters 2 and 3, they rely on their considerable knowledge, expressed both as perceptual skills and domain-specific heuristics. This knowledge, acquired through extensive practice and training, allows them to be highly selective when making decisions, rapidly focusing on promising solutions and not even considering irrelevant options.

An interesting question is why Simon's views on rationality and expertise have had only limited impact on mainstream economics,[1] in spite of the fact that Simon won the Nobel Prize in economics specifically for his work on bounded rationality. A first reason is that, by assuming that humans are perfect rational agents with unlimited access to information and unlimited computational powers, economists can develop elegant mathematical models. As soon as one makes the assumption that human rationality is limited, one has to use less elegant and more cumbersome mathematics. In fact, when additional assumptions are made, such as limited STM and use of heuristics, it becomes increasingly impractical to use mathematical models, and the use of computational models becomes necessary. However, economics is a field defined by its use of elegant mathematical models and has rarely accepted computational models as an alternative. A second reason, which also applies to most research on decision making in psychology, is that little attention is devoted to learning in economics (Campitelli & Gobet, 2010). Learning – changes in knowledge – is inconsistent with economics' assumptions concerning perfect rationality. If one assumes that there is unlimited access to information and that there are no restrictions on computation, then there is nothing to learn and the distinction between novice and expert is simply meaningless.

---

[1] The exception concerns the recent field of behavioural economics.

The issue of rationality has rarely been addressed in education, neuroscience and sociology. However, it is of some importance in artificial intelligence. Dreyfus (1972) famously entitled his book *What Computers Can't Do*; however, we can also ask *What can't humans do?* Humans' bounded rationality has the consequence that they do not perform that well with many complex issues, including global warming, economic disparities and epidemics (see also Chapter 11). There is, then, the real possibility that expert systems and other AI techniques can be used as tools, or even prostheses, to extend human intelligence to address these and other issues (Gobet, 1997a).

15.3.3 Knowledge

Knowledge is a central theme in all fields, although the key debates have tended to be different from field to field. Psychology has invested considerable effort in trying to understand the way experts represent knowledge and what memory structures they use. As noted in Chapter 3, the notion of a chunk has been supported by a substantial amount of research. Tacit knowledge has been studied in different ways, for example with respect to automatisation of skills and intuition. A lot of work has been devoted to understanding how knowledge, in its diverse guises, informs problem solving and decision making. Neuroscience has investigated the neural substrates of expert knowledge.

Knowledge obviously plays an important role in education, which is concerned with its transmission through teaching. Several key questions tackled by education are similar to those addressed in psychology, notably knowledge representation. A specific issue in education is that of transfer, or rather the difficulty of transfer. In sociology, the debate has mostly been about the kind of knowledge that is used in professions, and how it defines them. Knowledge has also played an important role in efforts to classify types of expertise. In philosophy, there has been a lot of discussion and argument about the respective roles of knowing-how and knowing-that. Finally, AI has focused on knowledge representations and knowledge elicitation.

15.3.4 Search

This theme has been the province of psychology and AI only. There are two main questions: How is search carried out, and what is the balance between search and knowledge? The answer to the first question is that experts' search is highly selective. They use their knowledge to cut down the search space and focus on the most promising avenues. Put forward in stark opposition, the second question becomes: Do experts make suitable decisions and solve problems by using their knowledge or by carrying out extensive search? The correct answer is certainly somewhere in the middle, with experts carrying out selective search informed by their knowledge (see Chapters 4 and 5). The theme has implications for education – depending on the importance of knowledge and search, different teaching and training methods should be used – but has not attracted much interest in that field.

In AI, search is a standard topic of research and much research has been devoted to the trade-off between knowledge and search. In particular, expert systems were the first programs to use heuristic search in knowledge-rich domains. While the central questions are essentially the same as those investigated in psychology, the answers differ: compared to humans, expert systems use less knowledge but search spaces larger by several orders of magnitude.

15.3.5 Generativity

Generativity is related to the issue of search, addressed in the previous theme. The question here is whether, to be called an expert, one needs to produce new ideas or products, or whether it is sufficient to perform at a high level, even though the performance itself might be only a repetition of what other people have done. For example, psychologists Hatano and Inagaki (1986) distinguish between adaptive expertise, which involves conceptual understanding so that new solutions can be discovered, and routine expertise, which only consists of mastering procedures to display proficient and correct behaviour. As made clear by research on the automatisation of skills, in many activities routine expertise is sufficient for reaching the highest levels of expertise. However, there are obviously other domains that require adaptive and creative expertise, such as the arts.

Generativity is also an issue of interest in education and AI. In education, is it better to focus on teaching knowledge and specific skills, or to teach general thinking methods that allow one to generate new knowledge? As it turns out, the latter is very difficult indeed. One reason is the difficulty of transfer; another reason is that generating interesting ideas within a domain requires a substantial amount of knowledge. In addition, emphasising knowledge discovery at the expense of knowledge transmission raises the possibility that learners might generate new and exciting knowledge – but also mistaken knowledge. Correcting erroneous knowledge might then be a long and arduous process.

In AI, expert systems and discovery systems often go together. Even though they start with human knowledge, expert systems often generate new solutions, which are often more cumbersome than those found by human experts, but in some cases are more elegant. The DENDRAL project (Lindsay et al., 1993) was actually aimed at both developing an expert system and understanding discovery processes in science. Even chess-playing computers, which favour brute search, sometimes produce moves that humans find highly creative.

15.3.6 Diachronicity

The time dimension is central to the understanding of expertise, in all fields except AI. Different levels of granularity can be employed when studying how expertise develops as a function of time. First, there is learning, where changes cover a wide time span, from seconds to days. Second, there is development – both child development and ageing – where change is studied in months and years. Note that learning and child development overlap with education both within and outside schools. Learning and development have been studied mostly by psychologists, although neuroscience too has studied the effects of the acquisition of expertise on the brain at different temporal scales: from minutes or hours to decades. Third, there is also development of expertise in society, across decades or even centuries. This is the province of sociology (e.g. Abbott, 1988).

15.3.7 Nature vs. Nurture

This theme is central in psychology, education and neuroscience, but absent in sociology, philosophy and AI. As noted in Chapters 7 and 8, research into superior performance is highly polarised, with most researchers supporting either an extreme view of talent or an extreme view of practice. No side denies the existence of the other factor, but only lip service is paid to them in reality.

Several authors have taken a more balanced, less dichotomous view, recognising the role of both nature and nurture (e.g. Bronfenbrenner & Ceci, 1994; Simonton, 1984; Sternberg & Grigorenko, 1997). When this is done, the complexity of the issue becomes apparent. Gobet (2013b) presents an integrative model including several variables and their interactions (Figure 15.1). While this model is vastly simplified and ignores many variables, it clearly shows how interactions occur at several levels and is more complicated than most of the current models of the development of expertise.

15.3.8 Environment and Society

There is no surprise here. Most of psychology, education, philosophy and neuroscience focuses on the individual, while sociology (e.g. sociology of professions) concentrates on society. Social psychology and, to some extent, education address group behaviour. There is some discussion of the role of the environment in psychology, and some theories have been developed to formalise it (see Chapter 3). Some approaches in psychology, such as situated action, have given more emphasis to the environment than the individual, but these approaches have had only limited impact in the study of expertise. Neuroscience also takes into consideration the environment, through its effect on learning and plasticity, but does not theorise the role of the environment per se.

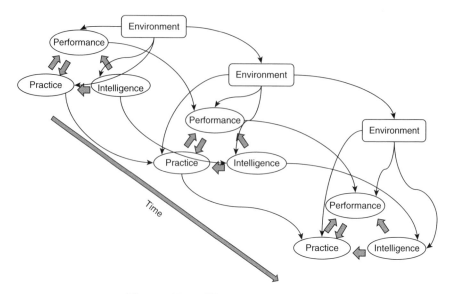

Figure 15.1   The spaghetti model.

Source: From Gobet, F. (2013). Expertise vs. talent. *Talent Development and Excellence, 5,*
75–86. Adapted with kind permission from The International Research Association for Talent
Development and Excellence.

15.4 Methods and Theories

Not surprisingly, each discipline has tended to study expertise with its own
methods. This first means that a staggering number of different methods have
been used to study expertise, from phenomenology to reaction times, from
knowledge elicitation to brain imaging. Putting together the results from
different fields is therefore difficult and thus rarely attempted.

Theories of expertise differ with respect to their scope and level of detail,
although these properties do not seem to correlate with disciplines. With
respect to scope, some theories address only one aspect of expertise (e.g.
cognitive decline in experts' ageing or epistemic peer disagreement), while
others aim to cover expertise in general (e.g. Ericsson et al.'s 1993 deliberate
practice framework or Dreyfus and Dreyfus's 1988 five-stage model of
expertise). With respect to level of detail, some theories are very detailed (e.g.
computer models such as CHREST or expert systems), while most other
theories provide very little detail indeed. This makes comparison between
theories difficult – especially when one tries to compare a general theory with
little detail to a specific theory with a lot of detail – as has been noted in several
debates in the literature (Ericsson & Kintsch, 2000; Gobet, 2000c; Simon &
Gobet, 2000; Vicente & Wang, 1998).

Readers consulting papers or books from the various disciplines – which we strongly recommend – will be struck by the different scientific languages and epistemologies used when addressing what is seemingly the same topic. Psychology has a heavy emphasis on experiments and descriptions of behaviour. Sociology favours descriptions and historical analyses. Philosophy draws on introspection, logical analysis, definitions and detailed analysis of key texts. Neuroscience employs experiments with measures of brain activation; more than the other disciplines, the focus is on its subject matter (how the brain functions) rather than on expertise per se. Finally, AI emphasises not only the building of programs but also the analysis, classification and description of knowledge.

In fact, there is no doubt that each of the disciplines would benefit from listening to at least one of the others. For example, psychology would gain from using philosophy's sharp analysis and sociology's broader outlook, and philosophy would profit from being informed by the kind of empirical data used in psychology and neuroscience. In an ideal world, a theory of expertise would sit in the middle of these five disciplines (and presumably others), drawing data and explaining phenomena acquired and observed by each of them. To our knowledge, no theory has even attempted to do this.

15.5 Four Tensions (Almost) Resolved

Social scientists love binary oppositions, and we have met many of them in this book. These oppositions are typically represented as the two poles of a continuum, as shown in the top of Figure 15.2 for the opposition of talent vs. practice. Thus, an individual whose expertise is explained entirely by

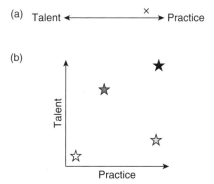

Figure 15.2   Talent and practice as the two poles of a continuum (top) or as the two dimensions of a plane (bottom).

Source: From Gobet, F. (2013). Expertise vs. talent. *Talent Development and Excellence, 5,* 75–86. Adapted with kind permission from The International Research Association for Talent Development and Excellence.

talent with no input from practice would be located at the extreme labelled "talent", an individual whose expertise is accounted for entirely by practice with no input from talent would be located at the extreme "practice", and an individual whose expertise is explained by (say) 20 per cent talent and 80 per cent practice, would be located on the point indicated by the cross. Similar representations have been used, conceptually if not graphically, with the debates about knowing-how vs. knowing-that, intuition vs. deliberation (roughly equivalent to pattern recognition vs. search in psychology) and expertise defined as objective performance vs. expertise defined as reputation. Obviously, there are more examples, but our discussion will limit itself to these four cases.

In all cases, most authors assume that being close to one of the extremes implies that one should be far from the other, just like in our example with talent vs. practice. However, this representation is incorrect, since the two dimensions are independent. For example, referring to the bottom of Figure 15.2, a football player may lack talent and practise little (white star) or be highly talented and practise extensively (black star); intermediate levels of practice are possible as well, as indicated by the grey stars. The same reasoning applies to the three other cases; thus, in all cases, the two factors are better represented as the two dimensions of a plane rather than as the two extremes of a continuum.

This change of representation has important theoretical implications. When these issues are seen not as false dichotomies but as orthogonal dimensions, their impact on expertise can be analysed more constructively. In particular, considering performance as a function of two variables and not a single one affords the possibility of studying the interaction between these two variables (see Figure 15.1). There is a cost, however. While the four tensions are resolved by showing that the opposition is illusory, the complexity of the questions studied becomes more apparent.

15.6 Practical Implications

As has been made apparent at several places in this book, research into expertise has important practical implications. Some of them are touched upon in the box **Some ethical issues**. Here we consider three important ones: becoming an expert, identifying and using experts, and the impact of experts on social policies.

While there are still unknowns, the mechanisms allowing somebody to become an expert are sufficiently well understood that practical suggestions can be made (see also Chapter 8). The factors in play are by and large unsurprising: early start, existence of role models, presence of feedback during practice and expertise development in general, family and community support, and presence of talent. While all these factors may not be present in every expert, they tend to accompany the development of expertise generally, in different proportions.

Some ethical issues

Ethics is a topic that this book has barely covered. Clearly, at least in Western cultures, the notion of expertise is associated with an emphasis on performance and excellence. This has several consequences. Distributions of rewards are highly skewed (e.g. money earned in tennis or number of CDs sold in music), with few individuals reaping a large share of the benefits. This can be seen as unfair and as a violation of egalitarian ideals. Another example concerns education. Some individuals receive better instruction, mostly for socioeconomic reasons, increasing, in what can be seen as an unfair way, their chances of becoming top experts. Similarly, talent selection raises interesting ethical issues: selecting the most talented might be seen as inequitable for the less talented, but conversely, submitting individuals that have little talent and thus are unlikely to succeed to large amounts of practice might cause unhappiness and be wasteful of resources. More generally, research into expertise reminds us – if this is still necessary – that life is unfair. Not only are there initial individual differences that increase some individuals' chances of success, but these differences are amplified over time. For example, in science, Merton (1968) describes the *Matthew effect* – named after the parable of the talents in the Gospel of Matthew – where famous scientists are apportioned more credit than lesser known ones for similar work.

It could be argued that focusing on performance and excellence misses more important and subtle points in life and ultimately leads to a superficial understanding of human nature. For example, happiness and the enjoyment of life may be considered as more important than success. Some contemplative philosophies might even suggest that true expertise consists in not being an expert. This might be true, but expertise is mostly defined by performance and reputation in our society, so it was surely appropriate to take this approach in this book.

Importantly, attainment of expertise in a given field entails a choice, both individual and societal. At the individual level, there is the question of whether one wants to spend several thousand hours practising one's skill, undergoing sometimes boring and repetitive training while more exciting activities may be available. At the societal and political level, there is the question of how to use limited resources for education: is it preferable to favour excellence, with the risk of not providing sufficient support for less talented individuals, or is it preferable to make sure that everybody reaches a minimum level, with the risk of failing to make the most of individuals with extraordinary potential? From sports, we know that talent identification and initiatives aimed at cultivating talent can have remarkable results, as was shown recently by the success of UK Sports' talent identification programme that led to several Olympic medals.

The second application concerns the identification and use of experts. In many cases, recognizing an expert is pretty straightforward. However, as discussed in Chapter 12, some cases are trickier. Often, there is no better option than using one's intuition and trust. Should society protect citizens against claims that are "obviously" (i.e. scientifically) wrong, such as those made by astrologers and practitioners of black magic? How about more borderline domains of expertise such as investing in the stock market? Or should citizens be considered as responsible enough to make their own decisions – the approach used in most Western societies?

Research into expertise has implications for social policy as well. Let us look at an example from science, where it is customary to employ panels of experts to make decisions on whether an article is accepted for publication in a scientific journal or whether a research project should be allocated funding. In some countries, panels of experts also evaluate the quality of research carried out nationally. This is the case, for example, in the United Kingdom with the Research Excellence Framework (REF). The outcome of the evaluation is used by the UK government to allocate billions of pounds for research.

Bilalić et al. (2009) carried out experiments on chess specialisation that directly relate to the reliability of expert panels. As we have seen in Chapter 4, it was found that there was a substantial decrease in skill as experts moved away from their subfield of specialisation. Gobet (2013a) argues that, since experts on grant panels, editorial boards or national research evaluations almost always have to evaluate documents that fall outside their subspeciality (e.g. a psychologist expert in memory might have to review a grant application on perception), they perform like average experts. While they still perform at expert level, their level will be reliably below the level of expertise within their subfield of specialisation. Other experiments by Bilalić et al. (2008b; 2008c), also reviewed in Chapter 4, do not provide better news. It was found that, as expertise diminishes, the likelihood of being victim to biases in thinking increases.

15.7 How to Become an Expert

How to become an expert depends on whether one deals with performance-based expertise or reputation-based expertise. As noted above, any mixture of these two types of expertise is possible as well, and thus the advice will need to be blended accordingly.

15.7.1 Performance-based Expertise

In most, if not all, domains of performance-based expertise, there is no doubt that a considerable amount of goal-directed practice is necessary, which is likely to extend over several years. As noted by the deliberate practice framework, rapid and veridical feedback is important and made easier by the presence of a coach or a teacher, since motivation, in particular intrinsic motivation, will have to be kept high. Having a bit of luck is necessary as well. This includes an ideal combination of factors, the details of which will depend on the specific domain of expertise but are likely to include genes, family characteristics, where and when one was born, and gender. Luck also consists in not being unlucky and avoiding accidents, illnesses and, of course, death.

The choice of the right domain is important too; it is beneficial to select a domain for which one is likely to be talented. Most often the choice will be the outcome of a number of factors (personal interests, parents' wishes, local opportunities and so on). The choice can be more strategic, since there is often a trade-off between the expected fame and the difficulty of a domain, which will be a function of the number and level of competitors present. Tennis offers the prospect of higher rewards than darts, but also a more arduous path to success. Choosing a smaller or somewhat more obscure domain, or even creating a new one, might be a wise move. There is also a trade-off between throwing all one's eggs in the same basket early on and keeping fall-back options open. In spite of all this, it must be accepted that the "choice" of a domain might be sometimes purely fortuitous, without any pre-determined notion of becoming an expert in it. Finally, the importance of being situated in a suitable environment during the development of expertise cannot be overstated. For example, as noted in Chapter 6, Nobel Prize winners often worked or studied, during their formative years, with mentors who had won a Nobel Prize themselves.

15.7.2 Reputation-based Expertise

Tetlock (2005) offers several pieces of advice with respect to pundits, but these are valid more generally with reputation-based expertise: one should simplify complexity, send simple messages, and be articulate, confident, one-sided and assertive. Whether one is right or not is almost irrelevant. Social connections are important, and time should be devoted to developing and nurturing one's social network; this includes attracting followers. In more ambitious cases, creating a complex hierarchy of followers will ensure that one can keep exercising control. In domains where expertise uses beliefs, such as religion, one should develop a balance between intuitively correct beliefs, on the one hand, and more surprising and counter-intuitive beliefs, on the other (Boyer, 2002; Russell & Gobet, 2013). As with performance-based expertise, the luck factor is also important.

15.8 Conclusion: Toward an Integration of Research on Expertise?

While a lot of progress has been made in understanding expertise, as illustrated by the many topics covered in this book, research on expertise suffers from a number of weaknesses. First, there is a tendency to focus heavily on a few issues at the expense of providing a more balanced coverage. For example, extensive attention has been devoted to deliberate practice in psychology and the question of knowing-how vs. knowing-that in philosophy, while other interesting issues have been ignored. Second, most theories about expertise are formulated in rather vague terms, making it impossible to make precise predictions, and indeed to provide coherent explanations. Third, research into expertise as a whole suffers from fragmentation, each discipline essentially ignoring research carried out in other disciplines, and integration across disciplines is an urgent necessity.

What would be the desirable directions for future research into expertise? The answer to such a question is bound to be subjective, but in our opinion the following directions, some of which address the weaknesses just mentioned, would be particularly fruitful. First, it is likely that a more balanced coverage would uncover important results. Second, expertise addresses complex phenomena, and better specified theories, ideally expressed as computer or mathematical models, would help provide a better understanding of these phenomena. A good example of how a well-specified model can help clarify theoretical issues is offered by CHREST, which led to an empirical and theoretical re-evaluation of experts' memory for unstructured material taken from their domain of expertise (see Chapter 3). Third, greater integration across disciplines could have important benefits, such as the avoidance of duplicating work in several fields, a better understanding of expertise and thus better ways to identify experts, and more data to resolve theoretical disagreements.

Fourth, the century-old question of nature vs. nurture (aka talent vs. practice) is likely to stay with us for many years, and it is likely that new developments in genomics and formal modelling will clarify the murky issues that are raised by this question. This is perhaps the topic for which integration between disciplines is the most needed. Fifth, and another topic for which cross-disciplinary efforts would be productive, is the question of expert knowledge. In particular, joint work by psychologists, philosophers, sociologists, computer scientists and legal experts could shed light on the kind of knowledge used by experts and perhaps suggest ways in which it could be improved or more efficiently acquired by non-experts. It would also provide guidance about how communication between experts and laypeople should occur, and might help answer deep-seated questions regarding epistemology and the philosophy of science. Sixth, the question of transfer raises a paradox, as discussed in Chapter 8. While transfer has been very limited indeed in controlled experiments, there is no doubt that some individuals are highly successful in different domains. Resolving this paradox would have tremendous implications for education and training.

Seventh, little is known about team expertise, a topic with obvious applications, for example in science. Eighth, many domains of expertise have received scant attention, such as religious expertise, philosophers' expertise and the role of emotions in expertise. Ninth, there is the tantalising concept of the development of super-experts. This book has provided examples of how individuals blessed with talent and extreme grit perform much better than even top-level experts. Can the occurrence of super-experts be increased by artificial means such as brain-computer interfaces, genetic manipulations and smart drugs? As noted in Chapter 10, some of these methods are currently being investigated and their successful application might be closer than many expect. Obviously, cyborgs and other mutants raise profound ethical issues. (See also Gobet et al., 2014, for a discussion of the notion of "better brains".)

Research into expertise thus far has been a fascinating journey of discovery, with setbacks and hopes, rapid progress and stagnation. This research is likely to be even more exciting in the decades to come and to lead to unexpected discoveries, which will have impact well beyond the narrow study of expertise, talent and genius. After all, understanding the nature of expertise will help us to understand our human nature.

15.9 Chapter Summary

The final chapter of this book takes stock of what has been learnt in the previous chapters. After considering the good and bad news from expertise research, transversal themes cutting across chapters are identified, covering fundamental topics such as rationality, knowledge and generativity.

The state of the art with respect to methods and theories is discussed, and it is suggested that an ideal theory should address expertise from different disciplines. Current theories tend to be simplistic, and this is illustrated by four well-known theoretical oppositions (including the nature vs. nurture debate), which are often presented as two poles of a single dimension. Instead of these false dichotomies, it is more likely that these apparently diametrically opposed concepts constitute two independent dimensions.

Expertise research raises ethical issues, most notably whether the focus should be on supporting highly talented individuals or ensuring that most individuals obtain satisfactory results. Expertise research also has practical implications, for example for education and policymaking. The chapter concludes by providing advice on how to become an expert (both with respect to performance-based expertise and reputation-based expertise), and by suggesting future directions of research that are likely to be fruitful.

15.10 Further Reading

In spite of an abundant literature on expertise, very few authors have addressed this topic from multiple disciplines, as this chapter (and indeed this book) has. Nevertheless, the following sources attempt some integration and are worth reading. Mieg (2001) looks at expertise from the points of view of social and organisational psychology and examines case studies about financial markets and climate change. The first three chapters of Ericsson et al. (2006) provide a broad description of expertise research, with a focus on psychology. Bereiter and Scardamalia (1993) look at the role of expertise in society, and discuss aspects linked to psychology, education and artificial intelligence.

References

Abbott, A. (1988). *The system of professions*. Chicago: University of Chicago Press.

Abbott, A. (1993). The sociology of work and occupations. *Annual Review of Sociology, 19*, 187–209.

Abbott, A. (2004). *Methods of discovery*: Heuristics for the social sciences. New York: Norton.

Abernethy, B. (1988). The effects of age and expertise upon perceptual skill development in a racquet sport. *International Journal of Sport Psychology, 22*, 189–210.

Abernethy, B., Farrow, D., & Berry, J. (2003). Constraints and issues in the development of a general theory of experts perceptual-motor performance. In J. L. Starkes & K. A. Ericsson (Eds.), *Expert performance in sport* (pp. 349–369). Champaign, IL: Human Kinetics.

Abernethy, B., Gill, D. P., Parks, S. L., & Packer, S. T. (2001). Expertise and the perception of kinematic and situational probability information. *Perception, 30*, 233–252.

Abernethy, B., Neal, R. J., & Konig, P. (1994). Visual–perceptual and cognitive differences between expert, intermediate and novice snooker players. *Applied Cognitive Psychology, 18*, 185–211.

Abernethy, B., & Russell, D. G. (1987). Expert-novice differences in an applied selective attention task. *Journal of Sport Psychology, 9*, 326–345.

Achter, J. A., Lubinski, D., & Benbow, C. P. (1996). Multipotentiality among the intellectually gifted: "It was never there and already it's vanishing". *Journal of Counseling Psychology, 43*, 65–76.

Ackerman, P. L., & Beier, M. E. (2006). Methods for studying the structure of expertise: Psychometric approaches. In K. A. Ericsson, N. Charness, P. Feltovich & R. R. Hoffman (Eds.), *Cambridge handbook of expertise and expert performance* (pp. 147–165). Cambridge: Cambridge University Press.

Aczel, A. D. (1996). *Fermat's last theorem*. London: Penguin.

Addis, M. (2013). Linguistic competence and expertise. *Phenomenology and the Cognitive Sciences, 12*, 327–336.

Addona, V., & Yates, P. A. (2010). A closer look at the relative age effect in the national hockey league. *Journal of Quantitative Analysis in Sports, 6.4*, Article 9.

Aglioti, S. M., Cesari, P., Romani, M., & Urgesi, C. (2008). Action anticipation and motor resonance in elite basketball players. *Nature Neuroscience, 11*, 1109–1116.

Ahmetov, I., & Fedotovskaya, O. (2012). Sports genomics: Current state of knowledge and future directions. *Cellular and Molecular Exercise Physiology, 1*, e1.

Alain, C., & Proteau, L. (1980). Decision making in sport. In C. H. Nadeau, W. R. Halliwell, G. C. Roberts & K. M. Newell (Eds.), *Psychology of motor behavior and sport* (pp. 465–477). Champaign, IL: Human Kinetics.

Alain, C., & Sarrazin, C. (1990). Study of decision-making in squash competition: A computer-simulation approach. *Canadian Journal of Sport Sciences, 15*, 193–200.

Alba, J. W., & Hasher, L. (1983). Is memory schematic? *Psychological Bulletin, 93*, 203–231.

Allard, F., Deakin, J., Parker, S., & Rodgers, W. (1993). Declarative knowledge in skilled motor performance: Byproduct or constituent? In J. L. Starkes & F. Allard (Eds.), *Cognitive issues in motor expertise* (pp. 95–107). Amsterdam: North-Holland.

Allard, F., Graham, S., & Paarsalu, M. E. (1980). Perception in sport: Basketball. *Journal of Sport Psychology, 2,* 22–30.

Allard, F., & Starkes, J. L. (1980). Perception in sport: Volleyball. *Journal of Sport Psychology, 2,* 22–33.

Allard, F., & Starkes, J. L. (1991). Motor-skill experts in sports, dance, and other domains. In K. A. Ericsson & J. Smith (Eds.), *Studies of expertise: Prospects and limits.* Cambridge: Cambridge University Press.

Allport, D. A., Antonis, B., & Reynolds, P. (1972). Division of attention: Disproof of single channel hypothesis. *Quarterly Journal of Experimental Psychology, 24,* 225–235.

Alquist, R., & Kilian, L. (2010). What do we learn from the price of crude oil futures? *Journal of Applied Econometrics, 25,* 539–573.

Amabile, T. M. (1996). *Creativity in context.* Boulder: Westview Press.

Anderson, J. R. (1982). Acquisition of cognitive skill. *Psychological Review, 89,* 369–406.

Anderson, J. R. (1993). *Rules of the mind.* Hillsdale, NJ: Erlbaum.

Anderson, J. R., Bothell, D., Byrne, M. D., Douglass, S., Lebiere, C., & Qin, Y. L. (2004). An integrated theory of the mind. *Psychological Review, 111,* 1036–1060.

Anderson, J. R., Corbett, A. T., Koedinger, K. R., & Pelletier, R. (1995). Cognitive tutors: Lessons learned. *The Journal of the Learning Sciences, 4,* 167–207.

Apkarian, A. V. (2008). Pain perception in relation to emotional learning. *Current Opinion in Neurobiology, 18,* 464–468.

Aristotle. (2011). *Nicomachean ethics* (R. C. Bartlett & S. D. Collins, Trans.). Chicago: University of Chicago Press.

Atkinson, R. C., & Raugh, M. R. (1975). An application of the mnemonic keyword method to the acquisition of Russian vocabulary. *Journal of Experimental Psychology: Human Learning and Memory, 104,* 126–133.

Baddeley, A. (1986). *Working memory.* Oxford: Clarendon Press.

Baddeley, A. (1990). *Human memory. Theory and practice.* Boston, MA: Allyn & Bacon.

Baker, J., Cobley, S., & Fraser-Thomas, J. (2009). What do we know about early sport specialization? Not much! *High Ability Studies, 20,* 77–89.

Baker, J., Cote, J., & Abernethy, B. (2003). Sport-specific practice and the development of expert decision-making in team ball sports. *Journal of Applied Sport Psychology, 15,* 12–25.

Baltes, P. B. (1993). The ageing mind: Potentials and limits. *The Gerontologist, 33,* 580–594.

Baltes, P. B., & Baltes, M. M. (1990). Psychological perspectives on successful aging: The model of selective optimization with compensation. In P. B. Baltes & M. M. Baltes (Eds.), *Successful aging: Perspectives from the behavioral sciences* (pp. 1–34). New York: Cambridge University Press.

Barker, V. E., & O'Connor, D. E. (1989). Expert systems for configuration at Digital: XCON and beyond. *Communications of the ACM, 32,* 298.

Barnes, J. (1985). Teaching experience and instruction. In T. Husen & T. Postlethwaite (Eds.), *The International Encyclopedia of Education, Vol. 9* (pp. 5124–5128). Oxford: Pergamon Press.

Baron-Cohen, S. (2009). Autism: The empathizing–systemizing (E-S) theory. *Annals of the New York Academy of Sciences, 1156,* 68–80.

Barron, F. (1963). *Creativity and psychological health.* Princeton, NJ: Van Nostrand.

Barron, F. X. (1969). *Creative person, creative process.* New York: Holt, Rinehart & Winston.

Barwick, J., Valentine, E., West, R., & Wilding, J. (1989). Relations between reading and musical abilities. *British Journal of Educational Psychology, 59,* 253–257.

Barynina, I. I., & Vaitsekhovskii, S. M. (1992). The aftermath of early sports specialization for highly qualified swimmers. *Fitness and Sports Review International, 27,* 132–133.

Bauer, M. W., & Bucchi, M. (2007). *Journalism, science and society: Science communication between news and public relations.* London: Taylor & Francis.

Baylor, G. W., & Simon, H. A. (1966). A chess mating combinations program. *1966 Spring Joint Computer Conference* (Vol. 28, pp. 431–447). Boston.

Beal, A. L. (1985). The skill of recognizing musical structures. *Memory & Cognition, 13,* 405–412.

Beals, K. A., & Manore, M. M. (1994). The prevalence and consequences of subclinical eating disorders in female athletes. *International Journal of Sport Nutrition, 4,* 175–195.

Bean, K. L. (1938). An experimental approach to the reading of music: The nature of the problem. *Psychological Monographs, 50,* 1–80.

Beasley, M. R., Datta, S., Kogelnik, H., & Kroemer, H. (2002). *Report of the investigation committee on the possibility of scientific misconduct in the work of Hendrik Schon and coauthors.* Murray Hill, NJ: Bell Labs.

Bechtel, W., & Abrahamsen, A. (1991). *Connectionism and the mind: An introduction to parallel processing in networks.* Cambridge, MA: Blackwell.

Becker, G. S. (1993). *Human capital* (3rd ed.). Chicago: University of Chicago Press.

Bell, E. T. (1965). *Men of mathematics.* New York: Simon and Schuster.

Benbow, C. P., Lubinski, D., Shea, D. L., & Eftekhari-Sanjani, H. (2000). Sex differences in mathematical reasoning ability at age 13: Their status 20 years later. *Psychological Science, 11,* 474–480.

Benbow, C. P., & Stanley, J. C. (1983). Sex differences in mathematical reasoning ability: More facts. *Science, 222,* 1029–1031.

Bengtsson, S. L., Nagy, Z., Skare, S., Forsman, L., Forssberg, H., & Ullén, F. (2005). Extensive piano practicing has regionally specific effects on white matter development. *Nature Neuroscience, 8,* 1148–1150.

Benner, P. (1984). *From novice to expert: Excellence and power in clinical nursing practice.* Menlo Park, CA: Addison-Wesley.

Benner, P., Tanner, C., & Chesla, C. (1996). *Expertise in nursing practice: Caring, clinical judgment, and ethics.* New York: Springer Publishing.

Berbaum, K. S. (2012). Satisfaction of search experiments in advanced imaging. *Proceedings of the SPIE, 82910V.*

Berbaum, K. S., Franken, E. A., Anderson, K. L., Dorfman, D. D., Erkonen, W. E., Farrar, G. P., et al. (1993). The influence of clinical history on visual-search with single and multiple abnormalities. *Investigative Radiology, 28,* 191–201.

Berbaum, K. S., Franken, E. A., Dorfman, D. D., Rooholamini, S. A., Coffman, C. E., Cornell, S. H., et al. (1991). Time course of satisfaction of search. *Investigative Radiology, 26,* 640–648.

Berbaum, K. S., Franken Jr, E. A., Dorfman, D. D., Miller, E. M., Caldwell, R. T., Kuehn, D. M., et al. (1998). Role of faulty visual search in the satisfaction of search effect in chest radiography. *Academic Radiology, 5,* 9–19.

Berbaum, K. S., Franken Jr, E. A., Dorfman, D. D., Miller, E. M., Krupinski, E. A., Kreinbring, K., et al. (1996). Cause of satisfaction of search effects in contrast studies of the abdomen. *Academic Radiology, 3*, 815–826.

Bereiter, C., & Scardamalia, M. (1993). *Surpassing ourselves.* Chicago, IL: Open Court.

Berlin, I. (1953). *The hedgehog and the fox: An essay on Tolstoy's view of history.* London: Weidenfeld & Nicolson.

Berliner, D. C. (1988). The development of expertise in pedagogy. Report #0-89333-053-1. American Association of Colleges for Teacher Education, Washington D. C.

Berliner, D. C. (2004). Expert teachers: Their characteristics, development and accomplishments. In R. Batllori i Obiols, A. E. Gomez Martinez, M. Oller i Freixa & J. Pages i Blanch (Eds.), *De la teoria….a l'aula: Formacio del professorat ensenyament de las ciències socials* (pp. 13–28). Barcelona: Universitat Autònoma de Barcelona.

Berliner, H. J. (1984). Search vs. knowledge: An analysis from the domain of games. In A. Elithorn & R. Banerji (Eds.), *Artificial and human intelligence* (pp. 105–117). New York: Elsevier.

Berliner, H. J., & Ebeling, C. (1989). Pattern knowledge and search: The SUPREM architecture. *Artificial Intelligence, 38*, 161–198.

Berman, Y., & North, K. N. (2010). A gene for speed: The emerging role of alpha-Actinin-3 in muscle metabolism. *Physiology, 25*, 250–259.

Berry, C. (1981). The Nobel scientists and the origins of scientific achievement. *British Journal of Sociology, 32*, 381–391.

Beyer, B. K. (1987). *Practical strategies for the teaching of thinking.* Boston, MA: Allyn and Bacon.

Bezzola, L., Merillat, S., Gaser, C., & Jancke, L. (2011). Training-induced neural plasticity in golf novices. *Journal of Neuroscience, 31*, 12444–12448.

Bhaskar, R., & Simon, H. A. (1977). Problem solving in semantically rich domains: An example from engineering thermodynamics. *Cognitive Science, 1*, 193–215.

Bigand, E. (2003). More about the musical expertise of musically untrained listeners. In G. Avanzini, C. Faienza, D. Minciacchi, L. Lopez & M. Majno (Eds.), *Neurosciences and music* (Vol. 999, pp. 304–312). New York: New York Academy of Sciences.

Bigand, E., & Poulin-Charronnat, B. (2006). Are we "experienced listeners"? A review of the musical capacities that do not depend on formal musical training. *Cognition, 100*, 100–130.

Bilalić, M., McLeod, P., & Gobet , F. (2007). Does chess need intelligence? A study with young chess players. *Intelligence, 35*, 457–470.

Bilalić, M., McLeod, P., & Gobet, F. (2008a). Expert and 'novice' problem solving strategies in chess – Sixty years of citing de Groot (1946/1965/1978). *Thinking and Reasoning, 14*, 395–408.

Bilalić, M., McLeod, P., & Gobet, F. (2008b). Inflexibility of experts: Reality or myth? Quantifying the Einstellung effect in chess masters. *Cognitive Psychology, 56*, 73–102.

Bilalić, M., McLeod, P., & Gobet, F. (2008c). Why good thoughts block better ones: The mechanism of the pernicious Einstellung (set) effect. *Cognition, 108*, 652–661.

Bilalić, M., McLeod, P., & Gobet, F. (2009). Specialization effect and its influence on memory and problem solving in expert chess players. *Cognitive Science, 33*, 1117–1143.

Bilalić, M., McLeod, P., & Gobet, F. (2010). The mechanism of the Einstellung (set) effect: A pervasive source of cognitive bias. *Current Directions in Psychological Science, 19*, 111–115.

Bilalić, M., Smallbone, K., Mcleod, P., & Gobet , F. (2009). Why are (the best) women so good at chess? Participation rates and gender differences in intellectual domains. *Proceedings of the Royal Society B, 276*, 1161–1165.

Binet, A., & Henri, V. (1896). La psychologie individuelle. *Année Psychologique, 2*, 411–465.

Binet, A., & Simon, T. (1905). Méthodes nouvelles pour le diagnostic du niveau intellectuel des anormaux (travaux de l'année 1904). *L'Année Psychologique, 11*, 191–244.

Birren, J. E., & Schaie, K. W. (Eds.). (1996). *Handbook of the psychology of aging* (Fourth ed.). San Diego, CA: Academic Press.

Bjerkedal, T., Kristensen, P., Skjeret, G. A., & Brevik, J. I. (2007). Intelligence test scores and birth order among young Norwegian men (conscripts) analyzed within and between families. *Intelligence, 35*, 503–514.

Blakemore, S. J., & Choudhury, S. (2006). Development of the adolescent brain: Implications for executive function and social cognition. *Journal of Child Psychology and Psychiatry, 47*, 296–312.

Blättler, C., Ferrari, V., Didierjean, A., & Marmèche, E. (2011). Representational momentum in aviation. *Journal of Experimental Psychology: Human Perception and Performance, 37*, 1569–1577.

Blättler, C., Ferrari, V., Didierjean, A., van Elslande, P., & Marmèche, E. (2010). Can expertise modulate representational momentum? *Visual Cognition, 18*, 1253–1273.

Bloom, B. S. (Ed.). (1985). *Developing talent in young people*. New York: Ballantine Books.

Blum, J. E., & Jarvik, L. F. (1974). Intellectual performance of octogenarians as a function of education and initial ability. *Human Development, 17*, 364–375.

Boden, M. (1990). *The creative mind*. New York: Basic Books.

Bonfadelli, H. (2002). The Internet and knowledge gaps: A theoretical and empirical investigation. *European Journal of Communication, 17*, 65–84.

Boot, W. R., Blakely, D. P., & Simons, D. J. (2011). Do action video games improve perception and cognition? *Frontiers in Psychology, 2*, 226.

Bornstein, R. F. (1990). Publication politics, experimenter bias and the replication process in social-science research. *Journal of Social Behavior and Personality, 5*, 71–81.

Boshuizen, H. P. A., & Schmidt, H. G. (1992). On the role of biomedical knowledge in clinical reasoning by experts, intermediates and novices. *Cognitive Science, 16*, 153–184.

Bossomaier, T., Traish, J., Gobet, F., & Lane, P. C. R. (2012). Neuro-cognitive model of move location in the game of Go. *International Joint Conference on Neural Networks (IJCNN 2012)* (pp. 1–7). New York: IEEE.

Bouchard, C. (2012). Genomic predictors of trainability. *Experimental Physiology, 97*, 347–352.

Bouchard, C., Gagnon, J., Pérusse, L., An, P., Rice, T., Rao, D. C., et al. (1999). Familial aggregation of V̇O2max response to exercise training: Results from the HERITAGE family study. *Journal of Applied Physiology, 87*, 1003–1008.

Bouchard, C., Sarzynski, M. A., Rankinen, T., Rice, T. K., Sung, Y. J., Rao, D. C., et al. (2011). Genomic predictors of the maximal O2 uptake response to standardized exercise training programs. *Journal of Applied Physiology, 110*, 1160–1170.

Boyd, D., & Addis, M. (2010). *Philosophy in construction: Understanding the development of expertise*. Paper presented at the Associated Schools of Construction Conference, Boston 7th–10th April.

Boyd, D., & Addis, M. (2011). *Moving from knowledge management to expertise management: A problem of contexts.* Centre for Environment and Society Research, Birmingham City University.

Boyer, P. (2002). *Religion explained.* New York: Basic Books.

Brady, P. T. (1970). Fixed-scale mechanism of absolute pitch. *Journal of the Acoustical Society of America, 48,* 883–887.

Bratko, D., Chamorro-Premuzic, T., & Saks, Z. (2006). Personality and school performance: Incremental validity of self- and peer-ratings over intelligence. *Personality and Individual Differences, 41,* 131–142.

Brewer, J., Balsom, P., Davis, J., & Ekblom, B. (1992). The influence of birth date and physical development on the selection of a male junior international soccer squad. *Journal of Sports Sciences, 10,* 561–562.

Brewer, S. (1998). Scientific expert testimony and intellectual due process. *Yale Law Journal, 107,* 1535–1681.

Broad, W., & Wade, N. (1983). *Betrayers of the truth.* New York: Simon & Schuster.

Brody, N. (1992). *Intelligence* (2nd ed.). San Diego, CA: Academic Press.

Bromme, R. (2001). Teacher expertise. In N. J. Smelser, P. B. Baltes & F. E. Weinert (Eds.), *International encyclopedia of the behavioral sciences: Education* (pp. 15459–15465). London: Pergamon.

Bronfenbrenner, U., & Ceci, S. J. (1994). Nature-nurture reconceptualized in developmental perspective: A bioecological model. *Psychological Review, 101,* 568–586.

Brown, A. L., Bransford, J. D., Ferrara, R. A., & Campione, J. D. (1983). Learning, remembering, and understanding. In P. H. Mussen (Ed.), *Handbook of Child Psychology, Vol. 3: Cognitive Development* (pp. 77–166). New York: Wiley.

Brown, J. R., & Goolsbee, A. (2002). Does the Internet make markets more competitive? Evidence from the life insurance industry. *Journal of Political Economy, 110,* 481–507.

Bruner, J. S., & Seymour, J. (2003). *Making stories: Law, literature, life.* Boston, MA: Harvard University Press.

Buchanan, B. G., & Shortliffe, E. H. (1984). *Rule-based expert systems: The MYCIN experiments of the Stanford heuristic programming project.* Reading, MA: Addison-Wesley.

Budd, J. M., Sievert, M. E., & Schultz, T. R. (1998). Phenomena of retraction: Reasons for retraction and citations to the publications. *JAMA-Journal of the American Medical Association, 280,* 296–297.

Burgess, N., Maguire, E. A., & O'Keefe, J. (2002). The human hippocampus and spatial and episodic memory. *Neuron, 35,* 625–641.

Cakic, V. (2009). Smart drugs for cognitive enhancement: Ethical and pragmatic considerations in the era of cosmetic neurology. *Journal of Medical Ethics, 35,* 611–615.

Calderwood, B., Klein, G. A., & Crandall, B. W. (1988). Time pressure, skill, and move quality in chess. *American Journal of Psychology, 101,* 481–493.

Campbell, D. T. (1960). Blind variation and selective retention in creative thought as in other knowledge processes. *Psychological Review, 67,* 380–400.

Campbell, M., Hoane, A. J., & Hsu, F. H. (2002). Deep Blue. *Artificial Intelligence, 134,* 57–83.

Campitelli, G., & Gobet, F. (2004). Adaptive expert decision making: Skilled chessplayers search more and deeper. *Journal of the International Computer Games Association, 27,* 209–216.

Campitelli, G., & Gobet, F. (2008). The role of practice in chess: A longitudinal study. *Learning and Individual Differences, 18*, 446–458.

Campitelli, G., & Gobet, F. (2010). Herbert Simon's decision-making approach: Investigation of cognitive processes in experts. *Review of General Psychology, 14*, 354–364.

Campitelli, G., Gobet, F., Head, K., Buckley, M., & Parker, A. (2007). Brain localisation of memory chunks in chessplayers. *International Journal of Neuroscience, 117*, 1641–1659.

Candy, E., Harri-Augstein, S., & Thomas, L. (1985). Reflection and the self-organized learner: A model of learning conversations. In D. Boud, R. Keogh & D. Walker (Eds.), *Reflection: Turning experience into learning* (pp. 100–115). New York: Nichols.

Carroll, J. S., & Payne, J. W. (1976). The psychology of parole decision processes: A joint application of attribution theory and information-processing psychology. In J. S. Carroll & J. W. Payne (Eds.), *Cognition and social psychology* (pp. 13–32). Hillsdale, NJ: Erlbaum.

Carter, K., Cushing, K., Sabers, D., Stein, P., Berliner, D., Carter, K., et al. (1988). Expert-novice differences in perceiving and processing visual classroom information. *Journal of Teacher Education, 39*, 25–31.

Case, R. (1985). *Intellectual development: Birth to adulthood.* New York: Academic Press.

Casey, B. J., Tottenham, N., Liston, C., & Durston, S. (2005). Imaging the developing brain: What have we learned about cognitive development? *TRENDS in Cognitive Science, 9*, 104–110.

Cash, K. (1995). Benner and expertise in nursing: A critique. *International Journal of Nursing Studies, 32*, 527–534.

Castellano, M. A., Krumhansl, C. L., & Bharucha, J. J. (1984). Tonal hierarchies in the music of North India. *Journal of Experimental Psychology: General, 113*, 394–412.

Cattell, R. B. (1971). *Abilities: Their structure, growth, and action.* New York: Houghton Mifflin.

Causer, J., Bennett, S. J., Holmes, P. S., Janelle, C. M., & Williams, A. M. (2010). Quiet eye duration and gun motion in elite shotgun shooting. *Medicine and Science in Sports and Exercise, 42*, 1599–1608.

Ceci, S. J., & Liker, J. K. (1986). A day at the races: A study of IQ, expertise, and cognitive complexity. *Journal of Experimental Psychology: General, 115*, 255–266.

Cerella, J. (1985). Information-processing rates in the elderly. *Psychological Bulletin, 98*, 67–83.

Cerf, C., & Navasky, V. (1998). *The experts speak.* New York: Villard.

Chaiken, S., & Trope, Y. (Eds.). (1999). *Dual-process theories in social psychology.* New York: Guildford Press.

Chambaz, B. (2011). *Marathon(s).* Paris: Seuil.

Champy, F. (2009). *La sociologie des professions.* Paris: PUF.

Chapin, F. S. (1928). A quantitative scale for rating the home and social environment of middle class families in an urban community. *Journal of Educational Psychology, 19*, 99–111.

Charness, N. (1974). *Memory for chess positions: The effects of interference and input modality.* Doctoral dissertation, Carnegie Mellon University, Pittsburgh, PA.

Charness, N. (1976). Memory for chess positions: Resistance to interference. *Journal of Experimental Psychology: Human Learning and Memory, 2*, 641–653.

Charness, N. (1979). Components of skill in bridge. *Canadian Journal of Psychology, 33*, 1–16.

Charness, N. (1981a). Aging and skilled problem solving. *Journal of Experimental Psychology: General, 110*, 21–38.

Charness, N. (1981b). Search in chess: Age and skill differences. *Journal of Experimental Psychology: Human Perception and Performance, 7*, 467–476.

Charness, N. (1981c). Visual short-term memory and aging in chess players. *Journal of Gerontology, 36*, 615–619.

Charness, N. (1988). The role of theories of cognitive aging: Comment on Salthouse. *Psychology and Aging, 3*, 17–21.

Charness, N. (1992). The impact of chess research on cognitive science. *Psychological Research, 54*, 4–9.

Charness, N., & Campbell, J. I. D. (1988). Acquiring skill at mental calculation in adulthood: A task decomposition. *Journal of Experimental Psychology: General, 117*, 115–129.

Charness, N., & Gerchak, Y. (1996). Participation rates and maximal performance: A log-linear explanation for group differences, such as Russian and male dominance in chess. *Psychological Science, 7*, 46–51.

Charness, N., Krampe, R., & Mayr, U. (1996). The role of practice and coaching in entrepreneurial skill domains: An international comparison of life-span chess skill acquisition. In K. A. Ericsson (Ed.), *The road to excellence* (pp. 51–80). Mahwah, NJ: Erlbaum.

Charness, N., Reingold, E. M., Pomplun, M., & Stampe, D. M. (2001). The perceptual aspect of skilled performance in chess: Evidence from eye movements. *Memory & Cognition, 29*, 1146–1152.

Charness, N., Tuffiash, M., Krampe, R., Reingold, E., & Vasyukova, E. (2005). The role of deliberate practice in chess expertise. *Applied Cognitive Psychology, 19*, 151–165.

Chase, W. G., & Ericsson, K. A. (1982). Skill and working memory. *The Psychology of Learning and Motivation, 16*, 1–58.

Chase, W. G., & Simon, H. A. (1973a). The mind's eye in chess. In W. G. Chase (Ed.), *Visual information processing* (pp. 215–281). New York: Academic Press.

Chase, W. G., & Simon, H. A. (1973b). Perception in chess. *Cognitive Psychology, 4*, 55–81.

Chassy, P., & Gobet, F. (2010). Speed of expertise acquisition depends upon inherited factors. *Talent Development and Excellence, 2*, 17–27.

Chassy, P., & Gobet, F. (2011a). A hypothesis about the biological basis of expert intuition. *Review of General Psychology, 15*, 198–212.

Chassy, P., & Gobet, F. (2011b). Measuring chess experts' single-use sequence knowledge: An archival study of departure from 'theoretical' openings. *PLoS One, 6*.

Chi, M. T. H. (1978). Knowledge structures and memory development. In R. S. Siegler (Ed.), *Children's thinking: What develops?* (pp. 73–96). Hillsdale, NJ: Erlbaum.

Chi, M. T. H., Feltovich, P. J., & Glaser, R. (1981). Categorization and representation of physics problems by experts and novices. *Cognitive Science, 5*, 121–152.

Chi, M. T. H., & Glaser, R. (1985). Problem solving ability. In R. J. Sternberg (Ed.), *Human abilities, an information-processing approach* (pp. 227–257). New York: Freeman.

Chi, M. T. H., Glaser, R., & Farr, M. J. (Eds.). (1988). *The nature of expertise*. Hillsdale, NJ: Erlbaum.

Chi, M. T. H., & Koeske, R. D. (1983). Network representation of a child's dinosaur knowledge. *Developmental Psychology, 19*, 29–39.

Chiesi, H. L., Spilich, G. J., & Voss, J. F. (1979). Acquisition of domain-related information in relation to high and low domain knowledge. *Journal of Verbal Learning and Verbal Behavior, 18*, 257–273.

Clark, P. (1956). The heritability of certain anthropometric characters as ascertained from measurements of twins. *American Journal of Human Genetics, 8*, 49–54.

Cleveland, A. A. (1907). The psychology of chess and of learning to play it. *The American Journal of Psychology, XVIII*, 269–308.

Close, F. (1990). *Too hot to handle: The story of the race for cold fusion*. London: W. H. Allen.

Coady, C. A. J. (1992). *Testimony: A philosophical study*. Oxford: Oxford University Press.

Cohen, A. A., & Shatzmiller, S. E. (1993). Structure design: An artificial intelligence-based method for the design of molecules under geometrical constraints. *Journal of Molecular Graphics, 11*, 166–173.

Cohen, H. (1981). On the modelling of creative behavior. Santa Monica, CA: RAND Corporation.

Cohen, K. S. (2008). *Expert witnessing and scientific testimony: Surviving in the courtroom*. London: CRC Press.

Cohen, P. R., & Feigenbaum, E. A. (1982). *The handbook of artificial intelligence* (Vol. 1). Los Altos, CA: Kaufmann.

Coiro, J. (2003). Exploring literacy on the Internet: Reading comprehension on the Internet. *Reading Teacher, 56*, 458–464.

Cole, J. R., & Zuckerman, H. (1987). Marriage, motherhood and research performance in science. *Scientific American, 256*, 119–125.

Collier, C. P. (2006). The expert on experts. Retrieved January 12th, 2014, from http://www.fastcompany.com/magazine/110/final-word.html

Collins, H. M., & Evans, R. (2007). *Rethinking expertise*. Chicago: University of Chicago Press.

Collins, H. M., & Pinch, T. (2005). *Dr Golem: How to think about medicine*. Chicago: University of Chicago Press.

Colvin, G. (2008). *Talent is overrated*. New York: Penguin.

Comte, A. (1830–1842). *Cours de philosophie positive (6 vols.)*. Paris: Rouen/Bachelier.

Cooke, N. J., Atlas, R. S., Lane, D. M., & Berger, R. C. (1993). Role of high-level knowledge in memory for chess positions. *American Journal of Psychology, 106*, 321–351.

Cooper, T., & Wogrin, N. (1988). *Rule-based programming with OPS5*. San Mateo, CA: Morgan Kaufmann.

Costa, P. T., Jr., & McCrae, R. R. (1992). *Revised NEO personality inventory (NEO-PI-R) and NEO five-factor inventory (NEO-FFI): Professional manual*. Odessa, FL: Psychological Assessment Resources.

Cote, J., Baker, J., & Abernethy, B. (2003). From play to practice. In J. L. Starkes & K. A. Ericsson (Eds.), *Expert performance in sports* (pp. 89–113). Champaign, IL: Human Kinetics.

Coughlin, L. D., & Patel, V. L. (1987). Processing of critical information by physicians and medical students. *Journal of Medical Education, 62*, 818–828.

Cowles, A. (1944). Stock market forecasting. *Econometrica, 12*, 206–214.

Cox, C. (1926). *The early mental traits of three hundred generations*. Stanford, CA: Stanford University Press.

Coyle, D. (2009). *The talent code*. New York: Bantam.

Cranberg, L., & Albert, M. L. (1988). The chess mind. In L. K. Obler & D. Fein (Eds.), *The exceptional brain* (pp. 156–190). New York: Guilford Press.

Crowdis, D. G., Shelley, S. M., & Wheeler, B. W. (1978). *Finite mathematics.* San Francisco, CA: Rinehart Press.

Csikszentmihalyi, M. (1990). *Flow: The psychology of optimal experience.* New York: Harper and Row.

Csikszentmihalyi, M. (1996). *Creativity: Flow and the psychology of discovery and invention.* New York: Harper Collins.

Dalton, S. E. (1992). Overuse injuries in adolescent athletes. *Sports Medicine, 13,* 58–70.

Davids, K. (2000). Skill acquisition and the theory of deliberate practice: It ain't what you do it's the way that you do it! *International Journal of Sport Psychology, 31,* 461–466.

Davies, J. (2006). *Semantic web technologies: Trends and research in ontology-based systems.* New York: Wiley.

Davison, A., Staszewski, J., & Boxley, G. (2001). Improving soldier performance with the AN/PSS12. *Engineer, 31,* 17–21.

Dawes, R. M. (1994). *House of cards: Psychology and psychotherapy built on myth.* New York: Free Press.

Dawson, N. V., Arkes, H. R., Siciliano, C., Blinkhorn, R., Lakshmanan, M., & Petrelli, M. (1988). Hindsight bias: An impediment to accurate probability estimation in clinicopathologic conferences. *Medical Decision Making, 8,* 259–264.

De Groot, A. D. (1965). *Thought and choice in chess (first Dutch edition in 1946).* The Hague: Mouton Publishers.

De Groot, A. D. (1969). *Methodology. Foundations of inference and research in the behavioral sciences.* The Hague: Mouton.

De Groot, A. D. (1978). *Thought and choice in chess* (2nd ed.). The Hague: Mouton Publishers.

De Groot, A. D. (1986). Intuition in chess. *Journal of the International Computer Chess Association, 9,* 67–75.

De Groot, A. D., & Gobet, F. (1996). *Perception and memory in chess.* Assen: Van Gorcum.

de la Chapelle, A., Traskelin, A. L., & Juvonen, E. (1993). Truncated erythropoietin receptor causes dominantly inherited benign human erythrocytosis. *Proceedings of the National Academy of Sciences of the United States of America, 90,* 4495–4499.

de Bono, E. (1968). *New Think: The use of lateral thinking in the generation of new ideas.* New York: Harper Collins.

Dellatolas, G., Annesi, I., Jallon, P., Chavance, M., & Lellouch, J. (1990). An epidemiological reconsideration of the Geschwind-Galaburda theory of cerebral lateralization. *Archives of Neurology, 47,* 778–782.

Delong, J. B., & Lang, K. (1992). Are all economic hypotheses false? *Journal of Political Economy, 100,* 1257–1272.

Derry, S. J., & Murphy, D. A. (1986). Designing systems that train learning ability: From theory to practice. *Review of Educational Research, 56,* 1–39.

Derry, S. J., Schunn, C. D., & Gernsbacher, M. A. (Eds.). (2005). *Interdisciplinary collaboration: An emerging cognitive science.* Mahwah, NJ: Erlbaum.

Deutsch, D. (1975). Two-channel listening to musical scales. *Journal of the Acoustical Society of America, 57,* 1156–1160.

Deutsch, D. (1987). Illusions for stereo headphones. *Audio Magazine, March,* 36–48.

Deutsch, D. (1999). Processing of pitch combinations. In D. Deutsch (Ed.), *The psychology of music, 2nd Edition* (pp. 349–412). New York: Academic Press.

Deutsch, D. (2013a). Absolute pitch. In D. Deutsch (Ed.), *The psychology of music, 3rd Edition* (pp. 141–182). San Diego, CA: Elsevier.

Deutsch, D. (2013b). *The psychology of music, 3rd edition.* San Diego, CA: Elsevier.

Dewar, K. M., Cuddy, L. L., & Mewhort, D. J. K. (1977). Recognition memory for single tones with and without context. *Journal of Experimental Psychology: Human Learning and Memory, 3*, 60–67.

Didierjean, A., & Gobet, F. (2008). Sherlock Holmes: An expert's view of expertise. *British Journal of Psychology, 99*, 109–125.

Didierjean, A., & Marmèche, E. (2005). Anticipatory representation of visual basketball scenes by novice and expert players. *Visual Cognition, 12*, 265–283.

Diehl, M., & Stroebe, W. (1987). Productivity loss in brainstorming groups: Toward the solution of a riddle. *Journal of Personality and Social Psychology, 53*, 497–509.

Diehl, M., & Stroebe, W. (1991). Productivity loss in idea-generating groups: Tracking down the blocking effect. *Journal of Personality and Social Psychology, 61*, 392–403.

Dijksterhuis, A., Bos, M. W., Nordgren, L. F., & van Baaren, R. B. (2006). On making the right choice: The deliberation-without-attention effect. *Science, 311*, 1005–1007.

Dingwall, R., & Lewis, P. (Eds.). (1983). *The sociology of the professions: Doctors, lawyers and others.* London: Macmillan.

Dippel, K. (1986). *Die Stellung des Sachverstaendigen im Strafprozeß.* Heidelberg (Germany): Decker's.

Djakow, I. N., Petrowski, N. W., & Rudik, P. A. (1927). *Psychologie des Schachspiels.* Berlin: de Gruyter.

Doll, J., & Mayr, U. (1987). Intelligenz und Schachleistung—Eine Untersuchung an Schachexperten. *Psychologische Beiträge, 29*, 270–289.

Draganski, B., Gaser, C., Busch, V., Schuierer, G., Bogdahn, U., & May, A. (2004). Neuroplasticity: Changes in grey matter induced by training. *Nature, 427*, 311–312.

Dreyfus, H. L. (1965). Alchemy and artificial intelligence. Santa Monica, CA: RAND Corporation, RAND Paper P-3244.

Dreyfus, H. L. (1972). *What computers can't do: A critique of artificial reason.* New York: Harper & Row.

Dreyfus, H. L., & Dreyfus, S. E. (1988). *Mind over machine: The power of human intuition and expertise in the era of the computer* (2nd ed.). New York: Free Press.

Dreyfus, H. L., & Dreyfus, S. E. (2005). Expertise in real world contexts. *Organization Studies, 26*, 779–792.

Dror, I., & Rosenthal, R. (2008). Meta-analytically quantifying the reliability and bias-ability of forensic experts. *Journal of Forensic Sciences, 53*, 900–903.

Dror, I. E., & Cole, S. A. (2010). The vision in "blind" justice: Expert perception, judgment, and visual cognition in forensic pattern recognition. *Psychonomic Bulletin & Review, 17*, 161–167.

Druva, C. A., & Anderson, R. D. (1983). Science teacher characteristics by teacher behavior and by student outcome: A meta-analysis of research. *Journal of Research in Science Teaching, 20*, 467–479.

Duckworth, A. L., Kirby, T. A., Tsukayama, E., Berstein, H., & Ericsson, K. A. (2011). Deliberate practice spells success: Why grittier competitors triumph at the National Spelling Bee. *Social Psychological and Personality Science, 2*, 174–181.

Duffy, L. J., Baluch, B., & Ericsson, K. A. (2004). Dart performance as a function of facets of practice amongst professional and amateur men and women players. *International Journal of Sport Psychology, 35*, 232–245.

Durkheim, E. (1922/1992). *Professional ethics and civic morals.* London: Routledge.

Dwyer, D. (2008). *The judicial assessment of expert evidence.* Cambridge: Cambridge University Press.

Ebbesen, E., & Konecni, V. (1975). Decision making and information integration in the courts: The setting of bail. *Journal of Personality and Social Psychology, 32*, 805–821.

Eberhard, J., Klomp, H. J., Foge, M., Hedderich, J., & Schmidt, H. G. (2009). The intermediate effect and the diagnostic accuracy in clinical case recall of students and experts in dental medicine. *European Journal of Dental Education, 13*, 128–134.

Edgar, S., & O'Donoghue, P. (2005). Season of birth distribution of elite tennis players. *Journal of Sports Sciences, 23*, 1013–1020.

Edwards, W. (1954). The theory of decision making. *Psychological Bulletin, 51*, 380–417.

Egan, D. E., & Schwartz, E. J. (1979). Chunking in recall of symbolic drawings. *Memory & Cognition, 7*, 149–158.

Ehlert, T., Simon, P., & Moser, D. (2013). Epigenetics in sports. *Sports Medicine, 43*, 93–110.

Ehrlich, P. (1968). *The population bomb: Population control or race oblivion.* New York: Ballantine.

Einhorn, H. J. (1974). Expert judgment: Some necessary conditions and an example. *Journal of Applied Psychology, 59*, 562–571.

Eisenstadt, M., & Kareev, Y. (1977). Perception in game playing: Internal representation and scanning of board positions. In P. N. Johnson-Laird & P. C. Wason (Eds.), *Thinking: Readings in cognitive science* (pp. 548–564). Cambridge: Cambridge University Press.

Elbert, T., Pantev, C., Wienbruch, C., Rockstroh, B., & Taub, E. (1995). Increased cortical representation of the fingers of the left hand in string players. *Science, 270*, 305–307.

Elga, A. (2007). Reflection and disagreement. *Noûs, 41*, 478–502.

Ellis, N. (1994). Vocabulary acquisition: The implicit ins and outs of explicit cognitive mediation. In N. Ellis. (Ed.), *Implicit and explicit learning of language* (pp. 211–282). London: Academic Press.

Elo, A. (1978). *The rating of chessplayers, past and present.* New York: Arco.

Elo, A. E. (1965). Age changes in master chess performances. *Journal of Gerontology, 20*, 289–299.

Engle, R. W., & Bukstel, L. (1978). Memory processes among bridge players of differing expertise. *American Journal of Psychology, 91*, 673–689.

English, I. (1993). Intuition as a function of the expert nurse: A critique of Benner's novice to expert model. *Journal of Advanced Nursing, 18*, 387–393.

Epstein, D. (2013). *The sports gene: What makes the perfect athlete.* London: Random House.

Epstein, S. (1996). *Impure science: AIDS, activism and the politics of knowledge.* Berkeley, CA: University of California Press.

Ericsson, K. A. (1996a). The acquisition of expert performance: An introduction to some of the issues. In K. A. Ericsson (Ed.), *The road to excellence* (pp. 1–50). Mahwah, NJ: Erlbaum.

Ericsson, K. A. (Ed.). (1996b). *The road to excellence.* Mahwah, NJ: Erlbaum.

Ericsson, K. A., & Charness, N. (1994). Expert performance: Its structure and acquisition. *American Psychologist, 49*, 725–747.

Ericsson, K. A., Charness, N., Feltovich, P. J., & Hoffman, R. R. (2006). *The Cambridge handbook of expertise and expert performance.* New York: Cambridge University Press.

Ericsson, K. A., Chase, W. G., & Faloon, S. (1980). Acquisition of a memory skill. *Science, 208,* 1181–1182.

Ericsson, K. A., & Faivre, I. A. (1988). What's exceptional about exceptional abilities? In L. K. Obler & D. Fein (Eds.), *The exceptional brain* (pp. 436–473). New York: Guilford Press.

Ericsson, K. A., & Kintsch, W. (1995). Long-term working memory. *Psychological Review, 102,* 211–245.

Ericsson, K. A., & Kintsch, W. (2000). Shortcomings of generic retrieval structures with slots of the type that Gobet (1993) proposed and modelled. *British Journal of Psychology, 91,* 571–590.

Ericsson, K. A., Krampe, R. T., & Tesch-Römer, C. (1993). The role of deliberate practice in the acquisition of expert performance. *Psychological Review, 100,* 363–406.

Ericsson, K. A., Patel, V. L., & Kintsch, W. (2000). How experts' adaptations to representative task demands account for the expertise effect in memory recall: Comment on Vicente and Wang (1998). *Psychological Review, 107,* 578–592.

Ericsson, K. A., & Polson, P. G. (1988). A cognitive analysis of exceptional memory for restaurant orders. In M. T. H. Chi, R. Glaser & M. J. Farr (Eds.), *The nature of expertise* (pp. 23–70). Hillsdale, NJ: Erlbaum.

Ericsson, K. A., & Smith, J. (1991a). Prospects and limits of the empirical study of expertise: An introduction. In K. A. Ericsson & J. Smith (Eds.), *Studies of expertise: Prospects and limits* (pp. 1–38). Cambridge: Cambridge University Press.

Ericsson, K. A., & Smith, J. (Eds.). (1991b). *Studies of expertise: Prospects and limits.* Cambridge: Cambridge University Press.

Ericsson, K. A., & Staszewski, J. J. (1989). Skilled memory and expertise: Mechanisms of exceptional performance. In D. K. Klahr, K. (Ed.), *Complex information processing: The impact of Herbert A. Simon* (pp. 235–267). Hillsdale, NJ: Erlbaum.

Ertmer, P. A., & Newby, T. J. (1996). The expert learner: Strategic, self-regulated, and reflective. *Instructional Science, 24,* 1–24.

Evans, J. S. B. T. (2003). In two minds: Dual process accounts of reasoning. *Trends in Cognitive Sciences, 7,* 454–459.

Evetts, J., Mieg, H. A., & Felt, U. (2006). Professionalization, scientific expertise, and elitism: A sociological perspective. In K. A. Ericsson, N. Charness, P. Feltovich & R. R. Hoffman (Eds.), *Cambridge handbook of expertise and expert performance* (pp. 105–123). Cambridge: Cambridge University Press.

Eynon, N., Alves, A. J., Sagiv, M., Yamin, C., Sagiv, M., & Meckel, Y. (2010). Interaction between SNPs in the NRF2 gene and elite endurance performance. *Physiological Genomics, 41,* 78–81.

Eysenck, H. (1986). The theory of intelligence and the psychophysiology of cognition. In R. J. Sternberg & D. K. Detterman (Eds.), *What is intelligence: Contemporary viewpoints on its nature and definition* (pp. 1–34). Norwood, NJ: Ablex.

Eysenck, H. J. (1995). *Genius: The natural history of creativity.* New York: Cambridge University Press.

Fanelli, D. (2009). How many scientists fabricate and falsify research? A systematic review and meta-analysis of survey data. *PLoS ONE, 4,* e5738.

Fantl, J. (2008). Knowing-how and knowing-that. *Philosophy Compass, 3,* 451–470.

Farnworth, P. (1969). *The social psychology of music.* Iowa: Iowa State University Press.

Farrow, D., & Abernethy, B. (2003). Do expertise and the degree of perception-action coupling affect natural anticipatory performance? *Perception, 32,* 1127–1139.

Feigenbaum, E. A., Buchanan, B. G., & Lederberg, J. (1971). On generality and problem solving: A case study using the DENDRAL program. In B. Meltzer & D. Michie (Eds.), *Machine Intelligence 6* (pp. 165–190). Edinburgh: Edinburgh University Press.

Feigenbaum, E. A., & Simon, H. A. (1962). A theory of the serial position effect. *British Journal of Psychology, 53,* 307–320.

Feigenbaum, E. A., & Simon, H. A. (1984). EPAM-like models of recognition and learning. *Cognitive Science, 8,* 305–336.

Fein, D., & Obler, L. K. (1988). Neuropsychological study of talent: A developing field. In L. K. Obler & D. Fein (Eds.), *The exceptional brain* (pp. 3–15). New York: Guilford Press.

Feingold, A. (1988). Cognitive gender differences are disappearing. *American Psychologist, 43,* 95–103.

Feldman, R. (2007). Reasonable religious disagreement. In L. Antony (Ed.), *Philosophers without gods* (pp. 194–214). Oxford: Oxford University Press.

Feltovich, P. J., Ford, K. M., & Hoffman, R. R. (Eds.). (1997). *Expertise in context.* Cambridge, MA: The MIT Press.

Ferrari, V., Didierjean, A., & Marmèche, E. (2006). Dynamic perception in chess. *Quarterly Journal of Experimental Psychology, 59,* 397–410.

Feyerabend, P. (1993). *Against method: Outline of an anarchistic theory of knowledge (First edition, 1975)* (3rd ed.). London: Verso.

Fitts, P. M. (1964). Perceptual-motor skill learning. In A. Melton (Ed.), *Categories of human learning* (pp. 243–285). New York: Academic Press.

Flavell, J. H. (1963). *The developmental psychology of Jean Piaget.* Princeton, NJ: Van Nostrand.

Flavell, J. H. (1976). Metacognitive aspects of problem solving. In L. B. Resnick (Ed.), *The nature of intelligence* (pp. 231–236). Hillsdale, NJ: Erlbaum.

Flavell, J. H., Beach, D. R., & Chinsky, J. M. (1966). Spontaneous verbal rehearsal in a memory task as a function of age. *Child Development, 37,* 283–299.

Folgman, E. C. (1933). An experimental study of composer-preference of four outstanding symphony orchestras. *Journal of Experimental Psychology, 16,* 709–724.

Fölsing, A. (1997). *Albert Einstein: A biography.* New York: Penguin Viking.

Fox, N. J., Ward, K. J., & O'Rourke, A. J. (2005). The 'expert patient': Empowerment or medical dominance? The case of weight loss, pharmaceutical drugs and the Internet. *Social Science and Medicine, 60,* 1299–1309.

Foxvog, D. (2010). Cyc. In R. Poli, M. Healy & A. Kameas (Eds.), *Theory and applications of ontology: Computer applications* (pp. 259–278). New York: Springer.

Freedman, D. H. (2010). *Wrong.* New York: Little, Brown and Co.

Frensch, P. A., & Sternberg, R. J. (1989). Expertise and intelligent thinking: When is it worse to know better? In R. J. Sternberg (Ed.), *Advances in the psychology of human intelligence* (Vol. 5, pp. 157–188). Hillsdale, NJ: Erlbaum.

Frensch, P. A., & Sternberg, R. J. (1991). Skill-related differences in game playing. In R. J. Sternberg & P. A. Frensch (Eds.), *Complex problem solving: Principles and mechanisms* (pp. 343–381). Hillsdale, NJ: Erlbaum.

Frey, M. C., & Detterman, D. K. (2004). Scholastic assessment or g? The relationship between the scholastic assessment test and general cognitive ability. *Psychological Science, 15,* 373–378.

Frey, P. W., & Adesman, P. (1976). Recall memory for visually presented chess positions. *Memory & Cognition, 4,* 541–547.

Freyhoff, H., Gruber, H., & Ziegler, A. (1992). Expertise and hierarchical knowledge representation in chess. *Psychological Research, 54*, 32–37.

Frijda, N. H., & de Groot, A. D. (Eds.). (1981). *Otto Selz: His contribution to psychology*. The Hague: Mouton.

Frydman, M., & Lynn, R. (1992). The general intelligence and spatial abilities of gifted young Belgian chess players. *British Journal of Psychology, 83*, 233–235.

Galton, F. (1869). *Hereditary genius: An inquiry into its laws and consequences*. London: MacMillan.

Garavan, H., Kelley, D., Rosen, A., Rao, S. M., & Stein, E. A. (2000). Practice-related functional activation changes in a working memory task. *Microscopy Research and Techniques, 51*, 54–63.

Gardner, D. (2011). *Future babble*. New York: Dutton.

Gardner, H. (1983). *Frames of mind: The theory of multiple intelligences*. New York: Basic Books.

Gardner, H. (1993). *Creating minds*. New York: Basic Books.

Gardner, M. (1957). *Fads and fallacies in the name of science*. New York: Dover.

Garland, D. J., & Barry, J. R. (1991). Cognitive advantage in sport: The nature of perceptual structures. *American Journal of Psychology, 104*, 211–228.

Gascoigne, N., & Thornton, T. (2013). *Tacit knowledge*. Cambridge: Acumen.

Gauthier, I., & Tarr, M. (1997). Orientation priming of novel shapes in the context of viewpoint dependent recognition. *Perception, 26*, 51–73.

Gauthier, I., Tarr, M. J., Anderson, A. W., Skudlarski, P., & Gore, J. C. (1999). Activation of the middle fusiform 'face area' increases with expertise in recognizing novel objects. *Nature Neuroscience, 2*, 568–573.

Gauthier, I., Tarr, M. J., & Bub, D. (2009). *Perceptual expertise: Bridging brain and behavior*. New York: Oxford University Press.

Geschwind, N., & Galaburda, A. M. (1987). *Cerebral lateralization*. Cambridge, MA: MIT Press.

Gibson, E. J. (1969). *Principles of perceptual learning and development*. New York: Appleton-Century.

Gibson, J. J. (1979). *The ecological approach to visual perception*. Boston, MA: Houghton-Mifflin.

Gibson, J. J., & Gibson, E. J. (1955). Perceptual learning: Differentiation or enrichment? *Psychological Review, 62*, 32–41.

Giddens, A. (1990). *The consequences of modernity*. Cambridge: Polity Press.

Gigerenzer, G. (1996). The psychology of good judgment: Frequency formats and simple algorithms. *Medical Decision Making, 16*, 273–280.

Gigerenzer, G. (2007). *Gut feelings*. London: Penguin.

Gigerenzer, G., & Gaissmaier, W. (2011). Heuristic decision making. *Annual Review of Psychology, 62*, 451–482.

Gigerenzer, G., & Goldstein, D. G. (1996). Reasoning the fast and frugal way: Models of bounded rationality. *Psychological Review, 103*, 650–669.

Gigerenzer, G., Todd, P. M., & the ABC Research Group (Eds.). (1999). *Simple heuristics that make us smart*. Oxford: Oxford University Press.

Ginther, D. K., & Kahn, S. (2009). Does science promote women? Evidence from Academia 1973–2001. In R. B. Freeman & D. L. Goroff (Eds.), *Science and engineering careers in the United States: An analysis of markets and employment* (pp. 163–194). Chicago: University of Chicago Press.

Gladwell, M. (2007). *Blink: The power of thinking without thinking.* New York: Back Bay Books.

Gladwell, M. (2008). *Outliers: The story of success.* New York: Little, Brown, and Co.

Glöckner, A., Heinen, T., Johnson, J. G., & Raab, M. (2012). Network approaches for expert decisions in sports. *Human Movement Science, 31,* 318–333.

Gobet, F. (1992). Learned helplessness in chess players: The importance of task similarity and the role of skill. *Psychological Research, 54,* 38–43.

Gobet, F. (1993a). A computer model of chess memory. In W. Kintsch (Ed.), *15th Annual Meeting of the Cognitive Science Society* (pp. 463–468). Boulder, CO: Erlbaum.

Gobet, F. (1993b). *Les mémoires d'un joueur d'échecs.* Fribourg (Switzerland): Editions Universitaires.

Gobet, F. (1997a). Can Deep Blue™ make us happy? Reflections on human and artificial expertise. In R. Morris (Ed.), *AAAI–97 Workshop: Deep Blue vs. Kasparov: The significance for artificial intelligence* (pp. 20–23). Menlo Park, CA: AAAI Press.

Gobet, F. (1997b). A pattern-recognition theory of search in expert problem solving. *Thinking and Reasoning, 3,* 291–313.

Gobet, F. (1998a). Chess thinking revisited. *Swiss Journal of Psychology, 57,* 18–32.

Gobet, F. (1998b). Expert memory: A comparison of four theories. *Cognition, 66,* 115–152.

Gobet, F. (2000a). Long-term working memory: A computational implementation for chess expertise. In N. Taatgen & J. Aasman (Eds.), *Proceedings of the Third International Conference on Cognitive Modelling* (pp. 150–157). Veenendaal, The Netherlands: Universal Press.

Gobet, F. (2000b). Retrieval structures and schemata: A brief reply to Ericsson and Kintsch. *British Journal of Psychology, 91,* 591–594.

Gobet, F. (2000c). Some shortcomings of long-term working memory. *British Journal of Psychology, 91,* 551–570.

Gobet, F. (2005). Chunking models of expertise: Implications for education. *Applied Cognitive Psychology, 19,* 183–204.

Gobet, F. (2009). Using a cognitive architecture for addressing the question of cognitive universals in cross-cultural psychology: The example of awalé. *Journal of Cross-Cultural Psychology 40,* 627–648.

Gobet, F. (2011). *Psychologie du talent et de l'expertise.* Bruxelles: De Boeck.

Gobet, F. (2012). Concepts without intuition lose the game: Commentary on Montero and Evans (2011). *Phenomenology and the Cognitive Sciences, 11,* 237–250.

Gobet, F. (2013a). Chunks and templates in semantic long-term memory: The importance of specialization. In J. J. Staszewski (Ed.), *Expertise and skill acquisition: The impact of William G. Chase* (pp. 117–146). New York: Psychology Press.

Gobet, F. (2013b). Expertise vs. talent. *Talent Development and Excellence, 5,* 75–86.

Gobet, F., & Borg, J. L. (2011). The intermediate effect in clinical case recall is present in musculoskeletal physiotherapy. *Manual Therapy, 16,* 327–331.

Gobet, F., & Campitelli, G. (2006). Education and chess: A critical review. In T. Redman (Ed.), *Chess and education: Selected essays from the Koltanowski conference* (pp. 124–143). Dallas, TX: Chess Program at the University of Texas at Dallas.

Gobet, F., & Campitelli, G. (2007). The role of domain-specific practice, handedness and starting age in chess. *Developmental Psychology, 43,* 159–172.

Gobet, F., Campitelli, G., & Lane, P. C. R. (2004). *Computational models of the development of perceptual expertise: Commentary on Palmeri et al. (2004).* Retrieved February 9 2014, from http://people.brunel.ac.uk/~hsstffg/papers/Computational models of the development of perceptual expertise.pdf

Gobet, F., Campitelli, G., & Waters, A. J. (2002). Rise of human intelligence: Comments on Howard (1999). *Intelligence, 30,* 303–311.

Gobet, F., & Chassy, P. (2008a). Season of birth and chess expertise. *Journal of Biosocial Science, 40,* 313–316.

Gobet, F., & Chassy, P. (2008b). Towards an alternative to Benner's theory of expert intuition in nursing: A discussion paper. *International Journal of Nursing Studies, 45,* 129–139.

Gobet, F., & Chassy, P. (2009). Expertise and intuition: A tale of three theories. *Minds & Machines, 19,* 151–180.

Gobet, F., Chassy, P., & Bilalić, M. (2011). *Foundations of cognitive psychology.* London: McGraw Hill.

Gobet, F., & Clarkson, G. (2004). Chunks in expert memory: Evidence for the magical number four... or is it two? *Memory, 12,* 732–747.

Gobet, F., & De Voogt, A. J. (submitted). Memory for draughts positions: The roles of age and expertise.

Gobet, F., de Voogt, A. J., & Retschitzki, J. (2004). *Moves in mind.* Hove: Psychology Press.

Gobet, F., & Jackson, S. (2002). In search of templates. *Cognitive Systems Research, 3,* 35–44.

Gobet, F., & Jansen, P. J. (1994). Towards a chess program based on a model of human memory. In H. J. van den Herik, I. S. Herschberg & J. W. H. M. Uiterwijk (Eds.), *Advances in Computer Chess 7* (pp. 35–60). Maastricht: University of Limburg Press.

Gobet, F., & Jansen, P. J. (2006). Training in chess: A scientific approach. In T. Redman (Ed.), *Chess and education: Selected essays from the Koltanowski Conference* (pp. 81–97). Dallas, TX: Chess Program at the University of Texas at Dallas.

Gobet, F., Johnston, S. J., Ferrufino, G., Jones, M. B., Johnston, M., Molyneux, A., et al. (2014). 'No Level Up!': No effects of video game specialization and expertise on cognitive performance. *Frontiers in Psychology, 5,* 1337.

Gobet, F., & Lane, P. C. R. (2010). The CHREST architecture of cognition: The role of perception in general intelligence. In E. Baum, M. Hutter & E. Kitzelmann (Eds.), *Proceedings of the Third Conference on Artificial General Intelligence* (pp. 7–12). Amsterdam: Atlantis Press.

Gobet, F., Lane, P. C. R., Croker, S., Cheng, P. C. H., Jones, G., Oliver, I., et al. (2001). Chunking mechanisms in human learning. *Trends in Cognitive Sciences, 5,* 236–243.

Gobet, F., & Oliver, I. (2002). A simulation of memory for computer programs. University of Nottingham (UK): Department of Psychology, ESRC Centre for Research in Development, Instruction and Training.

Gobet, F., Richman, H. B., Staszewski, J. J., & Simon, H. A. (1997). Goals, representations, and strategies in a concept attainment task: The EPAM model. *The Psychology of Learning and Motivation, 37,* 265–290.

Gobet, F., & Schiller, M. (Eds.). (2014). *Problem gambling: Cognition, prevention and treatment.* London: Palgrave.

Gobet, F., & Simon, H. A. (1996a). Recall of random and distorted positions. Implications for the theory of expertise. *Memory & Cognition, 24,* 493–503.

Gobet, F., & Simon, H. A. (1996b). Recall of rapidly presented random chess positions is a function of skill. *Psychonomic Bulletin & Review, 3,* 159–163.

Gobet, F., & Simon, H. A. (1996c). The roles of recognition processes and look-ahead search in time-constrained expert problem solving: Evidence from grandmaster level chess. *Psychological Science, 7,* 52–55.

Gobet, F., & Simon, H. A. (1996d). Templates in chess memory: A mechanism for recalling several boards. *Cognitive Psychology, 31,* 1–40.

Gobet, F., & Simon, H. A. (1998a). Expert chess memory: Revisiting the chunking hypothesis. *Memory, 6,* 225–255.

Gobet, F., & Simon, H. A. (1998b). Pattern recognition makes search possible: Comments on Holding (1992). *Psychological Research, 61,* 204–208.

Gobet, F., & Simon, H. A. (2000a). Five seconds or sixty? Presentation time in expert memory. *Cognitive Science, 24,* 651–682.

Gobet, F., & Simon, H. A. (2000b). Reply to Lassiter. *Psychological Science, 11,* 174.

Gobet, F., Snyder, A., Bossomaier, T., & Harre, M. (2014). Designing a "better" brain: Insights from experts and savants. *Frontiers in Psychology, 5,* 470.

Gobet, F., & Waters, A. J. (2003). The role of constraints in expert memory. *Journal of Experimental Psychology: Learning, Memory and Cognition, 29,* 1082–1094.

Gobet, F., & Wood, D. J. (1999). Expertise models of learning and computer-based tutoring. *Computers and Education, 33,* 189–207.

Gobet , F., & Yousaf, O. (submitted). Pattern of option generation predicts quality of decision in experts and non-experts.

Goertzel, M. G., Goertzel, V., & Goertzel, T. G. (1978). *300 eminent personalities: A psychosocial analysis of the famous.* San Francisco: Jossey-Bass.

Gold, A., & Opwis, K. (1992). Methoden zur empirischen Analyse von Chunks beim Reproduzieren von Schachstellungen. *Sprache & Kognition, 11,* 1–13.

Goldstone, R. (1994). Influences of categorization on perceptual discrimination. *Journal of Experimental Psychology: General, 123,* 178–200.

Goldstone, R. L. (1998). Perceptual learning. *Annual Review of Psychology, 49,* 585–612.

Gordon, S. E. (1992). Implications of cognitive theory for knowledge acquisition. In R. R. Hoffman (Ed.), *The psychology of expertise: Cognitive research and empirical AI.* New York: Springer-Verlag.

Gould, D. (2010). Early sport specialization: A psychological perspective. *JOPERD: The Journal of Physical Education, Recreation & Dance, 81,* 33–37.

Gould, S. J. (1981). *The mismeasure of man.* New York: Norton.

Goulet, C., Fleury, M., Bard, C., Yerles, M., Michaud, D., & Lemire, L. (1988). Analysis of visual-patterns during preparation for returning tennis-serves. *Canadian Journal of Sport Sciences, 13,* 79–87.

Gouvier, W. D., Uddo-Crane, M., & Brown, L. M. (1988). Base rates of post-concussional symptoms. *Archives of Clinical Neuropsychology, 3,* 273–278.

Grabner, R. H., Stern, E., & Neubauer, A. C. (2007). Individual differences in chess expertise: A psychometric investigation. *Acta Psychologica, 124,* 398–420.

Green, C. S., Li, R. J., & Bavelier, D. (2009). Perceptual learning during action video game playing. *Topics in Cognitive Science, 2,* 202–216.

Green, C. S., Pouget, A., & Bavelier, D. (2010). Improved probabilistic inference as a general learning mechanism with action video games. *Current Biology, 20,* 1573–1579.

Greeno, J. G., & Simon, H. A. (1988). Problem solving and reasoning. In R. C. Atkinson, R. Herrnstein, G. Lindzey & R. D. Luce (Eds.), *Stevens' handbook of experimental psychology (rev. ed.).* New York: Wiley.

Groopman, J. (2007). *How doctors think.* Boston, MA: Houghton Mifflin.

Grove, W. M., Zald, D. H., Hallberg, A. M., Lebow, B., Snitz, E., & Nelson, C. (2000). Clinical versus mechanical prediction: A meta-analysis. *Psychological Assessment, 12*, 19–30.

Gruber, H. (1991). *Qualitative Aspekte von Expertise im Schach.* Aachen: Feenschach.

Gruber, H., & Ziegler, A. (1990). Expertisegrad und Wissensbasis. Eine Untersuchung bei Schachspielern. *Psychologische Beiträge, 32*, 163–185.

Guida, A., Gobet, F., Tardieu, H., & Nicolas, S. (2012). How chunks, long-term working memory and templates offer a cognitive explanation for neuroimaging data on expertise acquisition: A two-stage framework. *Brain and Cognition, 79*, 221–244.

Guida, A., Tardieu, H., & Nicolas, S. (2009). The personalisation method applied to a working memory task: Evidence of long-term working memory effects. *European Journal of Cognitive Psychology, 21*, 862–896.

Guilford, J. P. (1967). *The nature of human intelligence.* New York: McGraw-Hill.

Guilford, J. P. (1982). Cognitive psychology's ambiguities: Some suggested remedies. *Psychological Review, 89*, 48–59.

Gutting, G. (1982). *Religious belief and religious skepticism.* Notre Dame, IN: University of Notre Dame Press.

Halpern, A. R., & Bower, G. H. (1982). Musical expertise and melodic structure in memory for musical notation. *American Journal of Psychology, 95*, 31–50.

Halpern, D. F. (2013). *Sex differences in cognitive abilities (4th ed.).* New York: Psychology Press.

Halpern, D. F., Benbow, C. P., Geary, D. C., Gur, R. C., Hyde, J. S., & Gernsbacher, M. A. (2007). The science of sex differences in science and mathematics. *Psychological Science in the Public Interest, 8*, 1–51.

Halpern, D. F., & Wai, J. (2007). The world of competitive Scrabble: Novice and expert differences in visuospatial and verbal abilities. *Journal of Experimental Psychology: Applied, 13*, 79–94.

Hambrick, D. Z., Oswald, F. L., Altmann, E. M., Meinz, E. J., Gobet, F., & Campitelli, G. (2014a). Accounting for expert performance: The devil is in the details. *Intelligence, 45*, 112–114.

Hambrick, D. Z., Oswald, F. L., Altmann, E. M., Meinz, E. J., Gobet, F., & Campitelli, G. (2014b). Deliberate practice: Is that all it takes to become an expert? *Intelligence, 45*, 34–45.

Hamel, G. P., & Breen, B. (2007). *The future of management.* Boston, MA: Harvard Business School Press.

Hammond, K. R. (1955). Probabilistic functioning and the clinical method. *Psychological Review, 62*, 251–262.

Harel, A., Kravitz, D., & Baker, C. I. (2013). Beyond perceptual expertise: Revisiting the neural substrates of expert object recognition. *Frontiers in Human Neuroscience, 7*, 885.

Hargittai, E., & Hinnant, A. (2008). Digital inequality: Differences in young adults' use of the Internet. *Communication Research, 35*, 602–621.

Harrington, A. (2004). *Art and social theory: Sociological arguments in aesthetics.* New York: Wiley.

Hartley, G., & Karinch, M. (2008). *How to become an expert on anything in 2 hours.* New York: Amacom.

Hassler, M. (1989). Musical talent and human spatial ability. *Canadian Music Educator, Research Edition, 30*, 39–45.

Hatano, G., & Inagaki, K. (1986). Two courses of expertise. In H. Stevenson, H. Azuma & K. Hakuta (Eds.), *Child development and education in Japan* (pp. 262–272). New York: Freeman.

Hatfield, B. D., & Hillman, C. H. (2001). The psychophysiology of sport: A mechanistic understanding of the psychology of superior performance. In R. N. Singer, H. A. Hausenblas & C. M. Janelle (Eds.), *Handbook of Sport Psychology* (pp. 362–386). New York: Wiley & Sons.

Hattie, J. (2003). *Teachers make a difference: What is the research evidence?* Paper presented at the Australian Council for Educational Research Annual Conference on Building Teacher Quality, Melbourne.

Hattie, J. A. (2009). *Visible learning: A synthesis of over 800 meta-analyses relating to achievement.* New York: Routledge.

Hayes, J. R. (1989a). Cognitive processes in creativity. In J. A. Glover, R. R. Ronning & C. R. Reynolds (Eds.), *Handbook of creativity* (pp. 135–145). New York: Plenum Press.

Hayes, J. R. (1989b). Writing research: The analysis of a very complex task. In D. Klahr & K. Kotovski (Eds.), *Complex information processing: The impact of Herbert A. Simon* (pp. 209–234). Hillsdale, NJ: Erlbaum.

Hecht, H., & Proffitt, D. R. (1995). The price of expertise: Effects of experience on the water–level task. *Psychological Science, 6*, 90–95.

Hedges, L. V., & Nowell, A. (1995). Sex differences in mental test scores, variability, and numbers of high–scoring individuals. *Science, 269*, 41–45.

Hedge, T., & Deakin, J. M. (1998). Deliberate practice and expertise in the martial arts: The role of context in motor recall. *Journal of Sport & Exercise Psychology, 20*, 260–279.

Heidegger, M. (1927/1962). *Being and time* (J. Macquarrie & E. Robinson, Trans.). London: SCM Press.

Heller, K. A., & Ziegler, A. (1996). Gender differences in mathematics and the sciences: Can attributional retraining improve the performance of gifted females? *Gifted Child Quarterly, 40*, 200–210.

Helsen, W., & Pauwels, J. M. (1993). The relationship between expertise and visual information processing in sport. In J. L. Starkes & F. Allard (Eds.), *Cognitive issues in motor expertise* (pp. 109–134). Amsterdam: North-Holland.

Helsen, W. F., Hodges, N. J., Van Winckel, J., & Starkes, J. L. (2000). The roles of talent, physical precocity and practice in the development of soccer expertise. *Journal of Sports Sciences, 18*, 727–736.

Helsen, W. F., & Starkes, J. L. (1999). A multidimensional approach to skilled perception and performance in sport. *Applied Cognitive Psychology, 13*, 1–27.

Helsen, W. F., Starkes, J. L., & Hodges, N. J. (1998). Team sports and the theory of deliberate practice. *Journal of Sport & Exercise Psychology, 20*, 12–34.

Hempel, A., Giesel, F. L., Caraballo, N. M. G., Amann, M., Meyer, H., Wüstenberg, T., et al. (2004). Plasticity of cortical activation related to working memory during training. *The American Journal of Psychiatry, 161*, 745–747.

Herlitz, A., Nilsson, L.-G., & Bäckman, L. (1997). Gender differences in episodic memory. *Memory & Cognition, 25*, 801–811.

Herman, D. (2013). *Storytelling and the sciences of mind.* Cambridge: MIT Press.

Higbee, K. L. (1988). *Your memory: How it works and how to improve it.* Englewood Cliffs, NJ: Prentice-Hall.

Hill, N. M., & Schneider, W. (2006). Brain changes in the development of expertise: Neurological evidence on skill-based adaptations. In K. A. Ericsson, N. Charness, P. Feltovich & R. Hoffman (Eds.), *Cambridge handbook of expertise and expert performance* (pp. 653–682). New York: Cambridge University.

Hill, R. (2004). Multiple sudden infant deaths: Coincidence or beyond coincidence? *Paediatric and Perinatal Epidemiology, 18,* 320–326.

Hinton, G. H., & Anderson, J. A. (1989). *Parallel models of associative memory.* Hillsdale, NJ: Erlbaum.

Hodges, N., Starkes, J., & MacMahon, C. (2006). Expert performance in sport. In K. A. Ericsson, N. Charness, P. Feltovich, & R. Hoffman (Eds.), *Cambridge handbook of expertise and expert performance* (pp. 471–488). New York: Cambridge University Press.

Hoffman, R. R. (1992). *The psychology of expertise: Cognitive research and empirical AI.* New York: Springer-Verlag.

Hoffman, R. R., Shadbolt, N. R., Burton, A. M., & Klein, G. (1995). Eliciting knowledge from experts: A methodological analysis. *Organizational Behavior and Human Decision Processes, 62,* 129–158.

Hoffrage, U., Lindsey, S., Hertwig, R., & Gigerenzer, G. (2000). Communicating statistical information. *Science, 290,* 2261–2262.

Holding, D. H. (1979). The evaluation of chess positions. *Simulation and Games,* 207–221.

Holding, D. H. (1985). *The psychology of chess skill.* Hillsdale, NJ: Erlbaum.

Holding, D. H. (1992). Theories of chess skill. *Psychological Research, 54,* 10–16.

Holding, D. H., & Pfau, H. D. (1985). Thinking ahead in chess. *American Journal of Psychology, 98,* 271–282.

Holding, D. H., & Reynolds, R. I. (1982). Recall or evaluation of chess positions as determinants of chess skill. *Memory & Cognition, 10,* 237–242.

Holohan, C. K., & Sears, R. R. (1995). *The gifted group in later maturity.* Stanford, CA: Stanford University Press.

Holyoak, K. J. (1991). Symbolic connectionism: Toward third-generation theories of expertise. In K. A. Ericsson & J. Smith (Eds.), *Studies of expertise: Prospects and limits* (pp. 301–335). Cambridge: Cambridge University Press.

Horgan, D. D., & Morgan, D. (1990). Chess expertise in children. *Applied Cognitive Psychology, 4,* 109–128.

Horner, M. S. (1972). Toward an understanding of achievement-related conflicts in women. *Journal of Social Issues, 28,* 157–175.

Houtsma, A. J. M., Durlach, N. I., & Horowitz, D. M. (1987). Comparative learning of pitch and loudness identification. *The Journal of the Acoustical Society of America, 81,* 129–132.

Hoving, T. (1997). *False impressions: The hunt for big-time art fakes.* New York: Simon and Schuster.

Howe, M. J. A., Davidson, J. W., & Sloboda, J. A. (1998). Innate talents: Reality or myth? *Behavioral and Brain Sciences, 21,* 399–442.

Howson, C., & Urbach, P. (1989). *Scientific reasoning. The Bayesian approach.* La Salle, IL: Open Court.

Hu, Y., Ericsson, K. A., Yang, D., & Lu, C. (2009). Superior self-paced memorization of digits in spite of a normal digit span: The structure of a memorist's skill. *Journal of Experimental Psychology: Learning, Memory and Cognition, 35,* 1426–1442.

Huettel, S. A., Song, A. W., & McCarthy, G. (2004). *Functional magnetic resonance imaging.* Sunderland, MA: Sinauer.

Hughes, E. C. (1958). *Men and their work*. New York: Free Press.

Hunt, E. (2011). *Human intelligence*. Cambridge: Cambridge University Press.

Hunter, J. E., & Hunter, R. F. (1984). Validity and utility of alternative predictors of job-performance. *Psychological Bulletin, 96*, 72–98.

Huntsinger, C. S., & Jose, P. E. (1991). A test of Gardner's modularity theory: A comparison of short-term memory for digits and tones. *Psychomusicology, 10*, 3–16.

Husserl, E. (1900/1973). *Logical investigations* (J. N. Findlay, Trans.). London: Routledge.

Hutchins, E. (1983). Understanding Micronesian navigation. In D. Gentner & A. Stevens (Eds.), *Mental Models* (pp. 191–225): Erlbaum.

Hyde, J. S., Fennema, E., & Lamon, S. J. (1990). Gender differences in mathematics performance: A meta-analysis. *Psychological Bulletin, 107*, 139–155.

Inzlicht, M., & Ben-Zeev, T. (2000). A threatening intellectual environment: Why females are susceptible to experiencing problem-solving deficits in the presence of males. *Psychological Science, 11*, 365–371.

Ioannidis, J. P. A. (2005). Contradicted and initially stronger effects in highly cited clinical research. *JAMA-Journal of the American Medical Association, 294*, 218–228.

Jackson, P. (1999). *Introduction to expert systems* (3rd ed.). Harlow: Addison Wesley.

Jackson, R. C., Warren, S., & Abernethy, B. (2006). Anticipation skill and susceptibility to deceptive movement. *Acta Psychologica, 123*, 355–371.

Jacob, F. (1988). *The statue within: An autobiography*. New York: Basic Books.

Jacobs, J., & Weisz, V. (1994). Gender stereotypes: Implications for gifted education. *Roeper Review, 16*, 152–155.

Jain, H. K. (2010). *Green revolution: History, impact and future*. Houston, TX: Studium Press.

Jamison, K. R. (1989). Mood disorders and patterns of creativity in British writers and artists. *Psychiatry, 52*, 125–134.

Jamison, K. R. (1993). *Touched with fire: Manic-depressive illness and the artistic temperament*. New York: The Free Press.

Jancke, L., Shah, N. J., & Peters, M. (2000). Cortical activations in primary and secondary motor areas for complex bimanual movements in professional pianists. *Brain Research: Cognitive Brain Research, 10*, 177–183.

Janis, I. L. (1982). *Groupthink: Psychological studies of policy decisions and fiascoes*. Boston, MA: Houghton Mifflin.

Janowsky, J. S. (1989). Sexual dimorphism in the human brain: Dispelling the myths. *Developmental Medicine and Child Neurology, 31*, 257–263.

Jastrzembski, T. S., Charness, N., & Vasyukova, C. (2006). Expertise and age effects on knowledge activation in chess. *Psychology and Aging, 21*, 401–405.

Jeffries, R., Turner, A., Polson, P., & Atwood, M. (1981). The processes involved in designing software. In J. R. Anderson (Ed.), *Cognitive skills and their acquisition* (pp. 255–283). Hillsdale, NJ: Erlbaum.

Johnson, J. G., & Raab, M. (2003). Take the first: Option-generation and resulting choices. *Organizational Behavior and Human Decision Processes, 91*, 215–229.

Johnson, K. E., & Mervis, C. B. (1997). Effects of varying levels of expertise on the basic level of categorization. *Journal of Experimental Psychology: General, 126*, 248–277.

Jones, A. M. (2002). Running economy is negatively related to sit-and-reach test performance in international-standard distance runners. *International Journal of Sports Medicine, 23*, 40–43.

Jones, C. M., & Miles, T. R. (1978). Use of advance cues in predicting the flight of a lawn tennis ball. *Journal of Human Movement Studies, 4,* 231–235.

Jones, G., Gobet, F., Freudenthal, D., & Pine, J. M. (submitted). Digit span measures knowledge in long-term memory and not the capacity of short-term memory.

Kahneman, D. (2011). *Thinking, fast and slow.* New York: Allen Lane.

Kahneman, D., & Frederick, S. (2002). Representativeness revisited: Attribute substitution in intuitive judgement. In T. Gilovich, D. Griffin & D. Kahneman (Eds.), *Heuristics and biases: The psychology of intuitive judgement* (pp. 49–81). Cambridge: Cambridge University Press.

Kahneman, D., Slovic, P., & Tversky, A. (Eds.). (1982). *Judgments under uncertainty: Heuristics and biases.* Cambridge: Cambridge University Press.

Kahneman, D., & Tversky, A. (1979). Prospect theory: An analysis of decision under risk. *Econometrica, XLVII,* 263–291.

Kalyuga, S. (2007). Expertise reversal effect and its implications for learner-tailored instruction. *Educational Psychology Review, 19,* 509–539.

Kane, M. J., Hambrick, D. Z., & Conway, A. R. A. (2005). Working memory capacity and fluid intelligence are strongly related constructs: Comment on Ackerman, Beier, and Boyle (2005). *Psychological Bulletin, 131,* 66–71.

Kanwisher, N., McDermott, J., & Chun, M. M. (1997). The fusiform face area: A module in human extrastriate cortex specialized for face perception. *Journal of Neuroscience, 17,* 4302–4311.

Kaplan, C. A., & Simon, H. A. (1990). In search of insight. *Cognitive Psychology, 22,* 374–419.

Keil, F. C. (1989). *Concepts, kinds, and cognitive development.* Cambridge, MA: MIT Press.

Kelly, T. (2005). The epistemic significance of disagreement. In J. Hawthorne & T. Gendler (Eds.), *Oxford studies in epistemology* (Vol. 1, pp. 167–196). Oxford: Oxford University Press.

Kemeny, J. G., Mirkil, H., Snell, J. L., & Thompson, G. L. (1960). *Finite mathematical structures.* Englewood Cliffs, NJ: Prentice Hall.

Kerr, J. M., & Hunter, R. (1993). *Inside RAD: How to build a fully functional system in 90 days or less.* New York: McGraw-Hill.

King, R. D., Whelan, K. E., Jones, F. M., Reiser, P. G. K., Bryant, C. H., Muggleton, S. H., et al. (2004). Functional genomic hypothesis generation and experimentation by a robot scientist. *Nature, 427,* 247–252.

Kintsch, W. (1970). *Learning, memory, and conceptual processes.* New York: John Wiley.

Kirk, S. A., & Kutchins, H. (1992). *The selling of DSM: The rhetoric of science in psychiatry.* Hawthorne, NY: de Gruyter.

Kirnaskaya, D. (2009). *The natural musician: On abilities, giftedness and talent.* Oxford: Oxford University Press.

Kitzinger, J., & Reilly, J. (1997). The rise and fall of risk reporting: Media coverage of human genetics research, 'false memory syndrome' and 'mad cow disease'. *European Journal of Communication, 12,* 319–350.

Klahr, D., & Kotovsky, K. (Eds.). (1989). *Complex information processing: The impact of Herbert A. Simon.* Hillsdale, NJ: Erlbaum.

Klahr, D., & Simon, H. A. (1999). Studies of scientific discovery: Complementary approaches and convergent findings. *Psychological Bulletin, 125,* 524–543.

Klein, G. A. (1989). Recognition-primed decisions. In W. Rouse (Ed.), *Advances in man-machine systems research* (Vol. 5, pp. 47–92). Greenwich, CT: JAI Press.

Klein, G. A. (1998). *Sources of power: How people make decisions.* Cambridge, MA: MIT Press.

Klein, G. A. (2003). *Intuition at work.* New York: Currency and Doubleday.

Klein, G. A., Orasanu, J., Calderwood, R., & Zsambok, C. E. (1993). *Decision making in action: Models and methods.* Norwood, NJ: Ablex Publishing Corporation.

Klein, G. A., & Peio, K. J. (1989). Use of a prediction paradigm to evaluate proficient decision making. *American Journal of Psychology, 102,* 321–331.

Klein, G. A., Wolf, S., Militello, L., & Zsambok, C. (1995). Characteristics of skilled option generation in chess. *Organizational Behavior and Human Decision Processes, 62,* 63–69.

Kline, P. (2000). *Handbook of psychological testing (2nd ed.).* London: Routledge.

Knapp, M. (2010). Are participation rates sufficient to explain gender differences in chess performance? *Proceedings of the Royal Society B: Biological Sciences, 277,* 2269–2270.

Knoblich, G., Ohlsson, S., Haider, H., & Rhenius, D. (1999). Constraint relaxation and chunk decomposition in insight problem solving. *Journal of Experimental Psychology: Learning, Memory and Cognition, 25,* 1543–1555.

Knopf, M., Preussler, W., & Stefanek, J. (1995). "18, 20, 2..." — Kann Expertise im Skatspiel Defizite des Arbeitsgedächtnisses älterer Menschen kompensieren? *Swiss Journal of Psychology, 54,* 225–236.

Kobasigawa, A. (1974). Utilization of retrieval cues by children in recall. *Child Development, 45,* 127–134.

Kocak, E., Ober, J., Berme, N., & Melvin, W. S. (2005). Eye motion parameters correlate with level of experience in video-assisted surgery: Objective testing of three tasks. *Journal of Laparoendoscopic & Advanced Surgical Techniques, 15,* 575–580.

Koedinger, K. R., & Anderson, J. R. (1990). Abstract planning and perceptual chunks: Elements of expertise in geometry. *Cognitive Science, 14,* 511–550.

Koedinger, K. R., Corbett, A. T., & Perfetti, C. (2012). The knowledge-learning-instruction framework: Bridging the science-practice chasm to enhance robust student learning. *Cognitive Science, 36,* 757–798.

Kotov, A. (1971). *Think like a grandmaster.* London: Batsford.

Krampe, R. T., & Charness, N. (2006). Aging and expertise. In K. A. Ericsson, N. Charness, P. Feltovich & R. R. Hoffman (Eds.), *Cambridge handbook of expertise and expert performance* (pp. 723–742). Cambridge: Cambridge University Press.

Krampe, R. T., & Ericsson, K. A. (1996). Maintaining excellence: Deliberate practice and elite performance in young and older pianists. *Journal of Experimental Psychology: General, 125,* 331–359.

Krupinski, E. A. (1996). Visual scanning patterns of radiologists searching mammograms. *Academic Radiology, 3,* 137–144.

Krupinski, E. A., Tillack, A. A., Richter, L., Henderson, J. T., Bhattacharyya, A. K., Scott, K. M., et al. (2006). Eye-movement study and human performance using telepathology virtual slides. Implications for medical education and differences with experience. *Human Pathology, 37,* 1543–1556.

Kuhn, T. S. (1970). *The structure of scientific revolutions.* Chicago: University of Chicago Press.

Kulkarni, D., & Simon, H. A. (1988). The processes of scientific discovery: The strategy of experimentation. *Cognitive Science, 12,* 139–176.

Kundel, H. L., & Nodine, C. F. (1975). Interpreting chest radiographs without visual search. *Radiology, 116,* 527–532.

Kundel, H. L., Nodine, C. F., Conant, E. F., & Weinstein, S. P. (2007). Holistic component of image perception in mammogram interpretation: Gaze-tracking study. *Radiology, 242*, 396–402.

Kundel, H. L., Nodine, C. F., & Toto, L. (1984). Eye movements and the detection of lung tumors in chest images. In A. G. Gale & F. Johnson (Eds.), *Theoretical and applied aspects of eye movement research* (pp. 297–304). Amsterdam: Elsevier.

Kundel, H. L., Nodine, C. F., & Toto, L. (1991). Searching for lung nodules: The guidance of visual scanning. *Investigative Radiology, 26*, 777–781.

Kundel, H. L., & Wright, D. J. (1969). Influence of prior knowledge on visual search strategies during viewing of chest radiographs. *Radiology, 93*, 315–320.

Laby, D. M., Rosenbaum, A. L., Kirschen, D. G., Davidson, J. L., & et al. (1996). The visual function of professional baseball players. *American Journal of Ophthalmology, 122*, 476.

Lakatos, I. (1970). Falsification and the methodology of scientific research programs. In I. Lakatos & A. Musgrave (Eds.), *Criticism and the growth of knowledge* (pp. 91–196). Cambridge: Cambridge University Press.

Lane, P. C. R., & Gobet, F. (2011). Perception in chess and beyond: Commentary on Linhares and Freitas (2010). *New Ideas in Psychology, 29*, 156–161.

Lane, P. C. R., Gobet, F., & Cheng, P. C. H. (2000). Learning-based constraints on schemata. *Proceedings of the Twenty Second Annual Meeting of the Cognitive Science Society* (pp. 776–781). Philadelphia, USA: Erlbaum.

Langer, E. J. (1975). The illusion of control. *Journal of Personality and Social Psychology, 32*, 311–328.

Langley, P., Simon, H. A., Bradshaw, G. L., & Zytkow, J. M. (1987). *Scientific discovery*. Cambridge, MA: MIT press.

Larkin, J. H., McDermott, J., Simon, D. P., & Simon, H. A. (1980a). Expert and novice performance in solving physics problems. *Science, 208*, 1335–1342.

Larkin, J. H., McDermott, J., Simon, D. P., & Simon, H. A. (1980b). Models of competence in solving physics problems. *Cognitive Science, 4*, 317–345.

Larkin, J. H., & Simon, H. A. (1987). Why a diagram is (sometimes) worth 10,000 words. *Cognitive Science, 11*, 65–99.

Larsen, H. B. (2003). Kenyan dominance in distance running. *Comparative Biochemistry and Physiology A: Molecular & Integrative Physiology, 136*, 161–170.

Lassiter, G. D. (2000). The relative contributions of recognition and search-evaluation processes to high-level chess performance: Comment on Gobet and Simon. *Psychological Science, 11*, 172–173.

Latour, B., & Woolgar, S. (1979). *Laboratory life: The social construction of scientific facts*. Los Angeles, CA: Sage.

Laudan, L. (1990). *Science and relativism: Some key controversies in the philosophy of science*. Cambridge: Cambridge University Press.

Lavallee, D., Kremer, J., Moran, A. P., & Williams, M. (2012). *Sport psychology: Contemporary themes* (2nd ed.). London: Palgrave-Macmillan.

Lave, J. (1988). *Cognition in practice*. New York: Cambridge University Press.

Law, M. P., Cote, J., & Ericsson, K. A. (2007). Characteristics of expert development in rhythmic gymnastics: A retrospective study. *International Journal of Sport & Exercise Psychology, 5*, 82–103.

Lehman, H. C. (1953). *Age and achievements*. Princeton, NJ: Princeton University Press.

Leinhardt, G., & Greeno, J. G. (1986). The cognitive skill of teaching. *Journal of Educational Psychology, 78*, 75–95.

Lenat, D., & Guha, R. V. (1990). *Building large knowledge-based systems.* New York: Addison-Wesley.

Levelt Committee, Noort Committee, & Drenth Committee. (2013). *Joint Tilburg/ Groningen/ Amsterdam investigation of the publications by Mr. Stapel.* Retrieved 13 January 2013, from https://www.commissielevelt.nl/

Levitin, D. J. (1994). Absolute memory for musical pitch: Evidence from the production of learned melodies. *Perception and Psychophysics, 56,* 414–423.

Levitin, D. J. (2006). *This is your brain on music.* London: Atlantic Books.

Lewin, C., & Herlitz, A. (2002). Sex differences in face recognition: Women's faces make the difference. *Brain and Cognition, 50,* 121–128.

Lindberg, S. M., Hyde, J. S., Petersen, J. L., & Linn, M. C. (2010). New trends in gender and mathematics performance: A meta-analysis. *Psychological Bulletin, 136,* 1123–1135.

Lindner, R. W., & Harris, B. (1993). Self-regulated learning: Its assessment and instructional implications. *Educational Research Quarterly, 16,* 29–37.

Lindsay, R. K., Buchanan, B. G., Feigenbaum, E. A., & Lederberg, J. (1993). DENDRAL: A case study of the first expert system for scientific hypothesis formation. *Artificial Intelligence, 61,* 209–261.

Linhares, A., & Freitas, A. E. T. A. (2010). Questioning Chase and Simon's (1973) "Perception in chess": The "experience recognition" hypothesis. *New Ideas in Psychology, 28,* 64–78.

Linley, P. A., Joseph, S., Harrington, S., & Wood, A. M. (2006). Positive psychology: Past, present, and (possible) future. *The Journal of Positive Psychology, 1,* 3–16.

Lippi, G., Longo, U. G., & Maffulli, N. (2010). Genetics and sports. *British Medical Bulletin, 93,* 27–47.

Lubinski, D. (2009). Exceptional cognitive ability: The phenotype. *Behavior Genetics, 39,* 350–358.

Lubinski, D., & Benbow, C. P. (2006). Study of mathematically precocious youth after 35 years: Uncovering antecedents for the development of math-science expertise. *Perspectives on Psychological Science, 1,* 316–345.

Luchins, A. S. (1942). Mechanization in problem solving: The effect of Einstellung. *Psychological Monographs, 54.*

Luck, S. J. (2005). *An introduction to the event-related potential technique.* Cambridge, MA: The MIT Press.

Luhmann, N. (1979). *Trust and power.* New York: Wiley.

Luhmann, N. (1995). *Social systems.* Stanford, CA: Stanford University Press.

Lum, G. (2012). Two concepts of assessment. *Journal of Philosophy of Education, 46,* 589–602.

Lum, G. (2014). *The assessment of professional knowledge.* King's College, London: Workshop on cross-disciplinary perspectives on expertise, know-how and professional education.

Luria, A. R. (1968). *The mind of a mnemonist.* New York: Avon.

Maass, A., D'Ettole, C., & Cadinu, M. (2008). Checkmate? The role of gender stereotypes in the ultimate intellectual sport. *European Journal of Social Psychology, 38,* 231–245.

MacCoun, R. J. (1998). Biases in the interpretation and use of research results. *Annual Review of Psychology, 49,* 259–287.

Mackintosh, N. (Ed.). (1995). *Cyril Burt: Fraud or framed?* New York: Oxford University Press.

Mackintosh, N. J. (1998). *IQ and human intelligence*. Oxford: Oxford University Press.

Maguire, E. A., Gadian, D. G., Johnsrude, I. S., Good, C. D., Ashburner, J., Frackowiak, R. S. J., et al. (2000). Navigation-related structural change in the hippocampi of taxi drivers. *Proceedings of the National Academy of Sciences of the United States of America, 97,* 4398–4403.

Maguire, E. A., Valentine, E. R., Wilding, J. M., & Kapur, N. (2003). Routes to remembering: The brains behind superior memory. *Nature Neuroscience, 6,* 90–95.

Maltby, J., Day, L., & Macaskill, A. (2010). *Personality, individual differences and intelligence* (2nd ed.). Harlow: Pearson.

Manning, D., Ethell, S., Donovan, T., & Crawford, T. (2006). How do radiologists do it? The influence of experience and training on searching for chest nodules. *Radiography, 12,* 134–142.

Marko, P., & Haworth, G. M. (1999). The Kasparov–World Match. *ICCA Journal, 22,* 236–238.

Martinson, B. C., Anderson, M. S., & de Vries, R. (2005). Scientists behaving badly. *Nature, 435,* 737–738.

Masters, M. S., & Sanders, B. (1993). Is the gender difference in mental rotation disappearing? *Behavior Genetics, 23,* 337–341.

Masunaga, H., & Horn, J. (2001). Expertise and age-related changes in components of intelligence. *Psychology and Aging, 16,* 293–311.

McKeithen, K. B., Reitman, J. S., Rueter, H. H., & Hirtle, S. C. (1981). Knowledge organisation and skill differences in computer programmers. *Cognitive Psychology, 13,* 307–325.

McCabe, S. E., Knight, J. R., Teter, C. J., & Wechsler, H. (2005). Non-medical use of prescription stimulants among US college students: Prevalence and correlates from a national survey. *Addiction, 100,* 96–106.

McClelland, D. C., Atkinson, J. W., Clark, R. A., & Lowell, E. L. (1953). *The achievement motive*. New York: Appleton-Century-Crofts.

McCorduck, P. (1979). *Machines who think*. San Francisco, CA: Freeman.

McCormack, B. (1993). Intuition: Concept analysis and application to curriculum development. *Journal of Clinical Nursing, 2,* 11–17.

McCutcheon, H. H. I., & Pincombe, J. (2001). Intuition: An important tool in the practice of nursing. *Journal of Advanced Nursing, 35,* 342–348.

McDowell, J. (1994). *Mind and world*. Cambridge: Harvard University Press.

McEvoy, G. M., & Cascio, W. F. (1989). Cumulative evidence of the relationship between employee age and job performance. *Journal of Applied Psychology, 74,* 11–17.

McGregor, S. J., & Howes, A. (2002). The role of attack and defense semantics in skilled players' memory for chess positions. *Memory & Cognition, 30,* 707–717.

McGuire, W. J. (1997). Creative hypothesis generating in psychology: Some useful heuristics. *Annual Review of Psychology, 48,* 1–30.

McNeil, B. J., Pauker, S. G., Sox, H. C., & Tversky, A. (1982). On the elicitation of preferences for alternative therapies. *New England Journal of Medicine, 306,* 1259–1262.

McRobert, A. P., Ward, P., Eccles, D. W., & Williams, A. M. (2011). The effect of manipulating context-specific information on perceptual-cognitive processes during a simulated anticipation task. *British Journal of Psychology, 102,* 519–534.

Meadow, R. (1977). Munchausen syndrome by proxy: The hinterland of child-abuse. *Lancet, 2,* 343–345.

Meadow, R. (1997). *ABC of child abuse*. London: BMJ books.

Medin, D. L., & Smith, E. E. (1981). Strategies and classification learning. *Journal of Experimental Psychology: Human Learning and Memory, 7*, 241–253.

Mednick, S. A. (1962). The associative basis of the creative process. *Psychological Review, 69*, 220–232.

Meehl, P. E. (1954). *Clinical versus statistical prediction: A theoretical analysis and a review of the evidence*. Minneapolis, MN: University of Minneapolis Press.

Meinz, E., & Hambrick, D. (2010). Deliberate practice is necessary but not sufficient to explain individual differences in piano sight-reading skill: The role of working memory capacity. *Psychological Science, 21*, 914 –919.

Meinz, E. J. (2000). Experience-based attenuation of age-related differences in music cognition tasks. *Psychology and Aging, 15*, 297–312.

Merton, R. K. (1968). The Matthew effect in science. *Science, 159*, 56–63.

Mieg, H. A. (2001). *The social psychology of expertise*. Mahwah, NJ: Erlbaum.

Mieg, H. A. (2006). Social and sociological factors in the development of expertise. In K. A. Ericsson, N. Charness, P. Feltovich & R. R. Hoffman (Eds.), *Cambridge handbook of expertise and expert performance* (pp. 743–760). Cambridge: Cambridge University Press.

Milgram, S. (1974). *Obedience to authority: An experimental view*. New York: Harper & Row.

Miller, D., & Hartwick, J. (2002). Spotting management fads. *Harvard Business Review, 80*, 26–27.

Miller, G. A. (1956). The magical number seven, plus or minus two: Some limits on our capacity for processing information. *Psychological Review, 63*, 81–97.

Milton, J., Solodkin, A., Hluštík, P., & Small, S. L. (2007). The mind of expert motor performance is cool and focused. *Neuroimage, 35*, 804–813.

Mireles, D. E., & Charness, N. (2002). Computational explorations of the influence of structured knowledge on age-related cognitive decline. *Psychology and Aging, 17*, 245–259.

Mitchell, T. (1997). *Machine learning*. New York: McGraw-Hill.

Moles, A. (1968). *Information theory and aesthetic perception*. Urbana, IL: University of Illinois Press.

Montero, B., & Evans, C. D. A. (2011). Intuitions without concepts lose the game: Mindedness in the art of chess. *Phenomenology and the Cognitive Sciences, 10*, 175–194.

Moses, J. (2012). Macsyma: A personal history. *Journal of Symbolic Computation, 47*, 123–130.

Moynihan, R., Bero, L., Ross-Degnan, D., Henry, D., Lee, K., Watkins, J., et al. (2000). Coverage by the news media of the benefits and risks of medications. *New England Journal of Medicine, 342*, 1645–1650.

Mueller, S., Abernethy, B., & Farrow, D. (2006). How do world-class cricket batsmen anticipate a bowler's intention? *Quarterly Journal of Experimental Psychology, 59*, 2162–2186.

Müller, U., Steffenhagen, N., Regenthal, R., & Bublak, P. (2004). Effects of modafinil on working memory processes in humans. *Psychopharmacology, 177*, 161–169.

Münzer, S., Berti, S., & Pechmann, T. (2002). Encoding timbre, speech, and tones: Musicians vs. non-musicians. *Psychologische Beiträge, 44*, 187–202.

Murphy, G. L. (2002). *The big book of concepts*. Cambridge, MA: The MIT Press.

Murphy, R. (1988). *Social closure: The theory of monopolization and exclusion*. Oxford: Clarendon Press.

National Science Foundation (2010). Land of plenty: Diversity as America's competitive edge in science, engineering and technology. Retrieved 27 January 2014, from http://www.nsf.gov/publications/pub_summ.jsp?ods_key=cawmset0409

Nee, C., & Meenaghan, A. (2006). Expert decision making in burglars. *British Journal of Criminology, 46*, 935–949.

Nettelbeck, T., & Lalley, M. (1976). Inspection time and measured intelligence. *British Journal of Psychology, 67*, 17–22.

Newell, A. (1990). *Unified theories of cognition.* Cambridge, MA: Harvard University Press.

Newell, A., Shaw, J. C., & Simon, H. A. (1958a). Chess-playing programs and the problem of complexity. *IBM Journal of Research and Development, 2*, 320–335.

Newell, A., Shaw, J. C., & Simon, H. A. (1958b). Elements of a theory of human problem solving. *Psychological Review, 65*, 151–166.

Newell, A., Shaw, J. C., & Simon, H. A. (1962). The process of creative thinking. In H. E. Gruber, G. Terrell & Werheimer (Eds.), *Contemporary approaches to creative thinking* (Vol. 3, pp. 63–119). New York: Atherton Press.

Newell, A., & Simon, H. A. (1965). An example of human chess play in the light of chess-playing programs. In N. Weiner & J. P. Schade (Eds.), *Progress in Biocybernetics* (pp. 19–75). Amsterdam: Elsevier.

Newell, A., & Simon, H. A. (1972). *Human problem solving.* Englewood Cliffs, NJ: Prentice-Hall.

Nickerson, R. S. (1998). Confirmation bias: A ubiquitous phenomenon in many guises. *Review of General Psychology, 2*, 175.

Nielsen, D., & McGown, C. (1985). Information-processing as a predictor of offensive ability in baseball. *Perceptual and Motor Skills, 60*, 775–781.

NIH. (2012). Findings of research misconduct: Press release. Retrieved 13 January 2013, from http://grants.nih.gov/grants/guide/notice-files/NOT-OD-12-149.html

Nilsson, N. (1998). *Artificial intelligence: A new synthesis.* San Francisco, CA: Morgan Kaufmann Publishers.

Noakes, T. (2003). *The lore of running (4th edition).* Oxford: Oxford University Press.

Nodine, C. F., & Kundel, H. L. (1987). The cognitive side of visual search in radiology. In J. K. O'Regan & A. Lévy-Schoen (Eds.), *Eye movements: From physiology to cognition.* Amsterdam: Elsevier-North Holland.

Nordin, S. M., Cumming, J., Vincent, J., & McGrory, S. (2006). Mental practice or spontaneous play? Examining which types of imagery constitute deliberate practice in sport. *Journal of Applied Sport Psychology, 18*, 345–362.

Okada, T., Schunn, C. D., Crowley, K., Oshima, J., Miwa, K., Aoki, T., et al. (1995). *Collaborative scientific research: Analyses of historical and interview data.* Paper presented at the 12th Annual Conference of the Japanese Cognitive Science Society.

Okada, T., & Simon, H. A. (1997). Collaborative discovery in a scientific domain. *Cognitive Science, 21*, 109–146.

Oliver, J. E. (1991). *The incomplete guide to the art of discovery.* New York: Columbia University Press.

Ornstein, P. A., Naus, M. J., & Liberty, C. (1975). Rehearsal and organizational processes in children's memory. *Child Development, 46*, 818–830.

Osborn, A. F. (1963). *Applied imagination: Principles and procedures of creative problem solving.* New York: Charles Scribner's Sons.

Osborne, J. W. (2007). Linking stereotype threat and anxiety. *Educational Psychology, 27*, 135–154.

Osborne, W. (1994). "You sound like a ladies' orchestra": A case history of sexism against Abbie Conant in the Munich Philharmonic. Retrieved 27 January 2014, from http://www.osborne-conant.org/ladies.htm

Otway, H., & von Winterfeldt, D. (1992). Expert judgment in risk analysis and management: Process, context, and pitfalls. *Risk Analysis, 12*, 83–93.

Oxford Talking Dictionary (1998). London: The Listening Company.

Paige, J. M., & Simon, H. A. (1966). Cognitive processes in solving algebra word problems. In B. Kleinmuntz (Ed.), *Problem solving, research, method and theory* (pp. 51–119). New York: Krieger.

Pais, A. (1982). *Subtle is the Lord: The science and the life of Albert Einstein.* Oxford: Oxford University Press.

Papert, S. (1968). The artificial intelligence of Hubert L. Dreyfus. Artificial Intelligence Memo No. 154. Project MAC. Cambridge, MA: MIT.

Parsons, T. (1939). The professions and social structure. *Social Forces, 17*, 457–467.

Parsons, T. (1951). *The social system.* New York: Free Press.

Pascual-Leone, J. A. (1970). A mathematical model for transition in Piaget's developmental stages. *Acta Psychologica, 32*, 301–345.

Patel, V. L., & Groen, G. J. (1986). Knowledge based solution strategies in medical reasoning. *Cognitive Science, 10*, 91–116.

Paull, G., & Glencross, D. (1997). Expert perception and decision making in baseball. *International Journal of Sport Psychology, 28*, 35–56.

Pearce, A. J., Thickbroom, G. W., Byrnes, M. L., & Mastaglia, F. L. (2000). Functional reorganisation of the corticomotor projection to the hand in skilled racquet players. *Experimental Brain Research, 130*, 238–243.

Peretz, I., & Zatorre, R. J. (Eds.). (2003). *The cognitive neuroscience of music.* New York: Oxford University Press.

Perkins, D. N. (1988). Creativity and the quest for mechanism. In R. J. Sternberg & E. E. Smith (Eds.), *The psychology of human thought* (pp. 309–336). Cambridge: Cambridge University Press.

Pesenti, M., Zago, L., Crivello, F., Mellet, E., Samson, D., Duroux, B., et al. (2001). Mental calculation in a prodigy is sustained by right prefrontal and medial temporal areas. *Nature Neuroscience, 4*, 103–107.

Peters, T. J., & Waterman, R. H. (1982). *In search for excellence: Lessons from America's best-run companies.* New York: Harper and Row.

Piaget, J., & Inhelder, B. (1956). *The child's conception of space.* London: Routledge and Kegan Paul.

Piedmont, R. L. (1988). An interactional model of achievement motivation and fear of success. *Sex Roles, 19*, 467–490.

Pintrich, P., Boekaerts, M., & Seidner, M. (Eds.). (2001). *Handbook of self-regulation.* Orlando, FL: Academic Press.

Pitt, M. A., & Crowder, R. G. (1992). The role of spectral and dynamic cues in imagery for musical timbre. *Journal of Experimental Psychology: Human Perception and Performance, 18*, 728–738.

Plomin, R., DeFries, J. C., McClearn, G. E., & McGuffin, P. (2012). *Behavioral genetics (6th Edition).* New York: Worth Publishers.

Plomin, R., & Petrill, S. A. (1997). Genetics and intelligence: What is new? *Intelligence, 24*, 53–78.

Poincaré, H. (1913). *The foundations of science* (G. H. Halstead, Trans.). New York: Science Press.

Polanyi, M. (1958). *Personal knowledge: Towards a post-critical philosophy.* London: Routledge.

Polanyi, M. (1966). *The tacit dimension.* Chicago: University of Chicago Press.

Popper, K. (1959). *The logic of scientific discovery.* New York: Basic Books.

Poropat, A. E. (2009). A meta-analysis of the Five-Factor model of personality and academic performance. *Psychological Bulletin, 135,* 322–338.

Post, F. (1994). Creativity and psychopathology: A study of 291 world-famous men. *British Journal of Psychiatry, 165,* 22–34.

Posthumus, M., Schwellnus, M. P., & Collins, M. (2011). The COL5A1 gene: A novel marker of endurance running performance. *Medicine and Science in Sports and Exercise, 43,* 584–589.

Poulin-Charronnat, B., Bigand, E., Lalitte, P., Madurell, F., Vieillard, S., & McAdams, S. (2004). Effects of a change in instrumentation on the recognition of musical materials. *Music Perception, 22,* 239–263.

Price, D. J. S. (1963). *Little science, big science.* New York: Columbia University Press.

Prietula, M. J., & Simon, H. A. (1989). The experts in your midst. *Harvard Business Review, Jan-Feb,* 120–124.

Puthucheary, Z., Skipworth, J. R. A., Rawal, J., Loosemore, M., Someren, K. V., & Montgomery, H. E. (2011). Genetic influences in sport and physical performance. *Sports Medicine, 41,* 845–859.

Qin, Y., & Simon, H. A. (1990). Laboratory replication of scientific discovery processes. *Cognitive Science, 14,* 281–312.

Raab, M., & Johnson, J. G. (2007). Expertise-based differences in search and option-generation strategies. *Journal of Experimental Psychology: Applied, 13,* 158–170.

Radford, J. (1990). *Child prodigies and exceptional early achievers.* New York: Harvester Wheatsheaf.

Ragert, P., Schmidt, A., Altenmüller, E., & Dinse, H. R. (2004). Superior tactile performance and learning in professional pianists: Evidence for meta-plasticity in musicians. *European Journal of Neuroscience, 19,* 473–478.

Raufaste, E., Eyrolle, H., & Mariné, C. (1998). Pertinence generation in radiological diagnosis: Spreading activation and the nature of expertise. *Cognitive Science, 22,* 517–546.

Rauscher, F. H., & Hinton, S. C. (2003). Type of music training selectively influences perceptual processing. In R. Kopiez, A. Lehmann, I. Wolther & C. Wolf (Eds.), *Proceedings of the 5th Triennial Conference of the European Society for the Cognitive Sciences of Music* (pp. 89–92). Hannover: University of Music and Drama.

Reber, A. S. (1993). *Implicit learning and tacit knowledge* (Vol. 19). Oxford: Oxford University Press.

Reed, T. E. (1984). Mechanism for heritability of intelligence. *Nature, 311,* 417–417.

Reimanna, F., Gribble, F. M., Cox, J. J., Woods, C. G., Belfer, I., Dai, F., et al. (2010). Pain perception is altered by a nucleotide polymorphism in SCN9A. *Proceedings of the National Academy of Sciences of the United States of America, 107,* 5148–5153.

Reingold, E. M., Charness, N., Pomplun, M., & Stampe, D. M. (2001). Visual span in expert chess players: Evidence from eye movements. *Psychological Science, 12,* 48–55.

Reingold, E. M., & Sheridan, H. (2011). Eye movements and visual expertise in chess and medicine. In S. P. Liversedge, I. D. Gilchrist & S. Everling (Eds.), *Oxford handbook on eye movements* (pp. 767–786). Oxford: Oxford University Press.

Reis, S. M., & Callahan, C. M. (1989). Gifted females: They've come a long way – or have they? *Journal for the Education of the Gifted, 12*, 99–117.

Reitman, J. S. (1976). Skilled perception in go: Deducing memory structures from inter-response times. *Cognitive Psychology, 8*, 336–356.

Reitman Olson, J., & Biolsi, K. (1991). Techniques for representing expert knowledge. In K. A. Ericsson & J. Smith (Eds.), *Studies of expertise: Prospects and limits* (pp. 240–285). Cambridge: Cambridge University Press.

Rensink, R. A., O'Regan, K., & Clark, J. (1997). To see or not to see: The need for attention to perceive changes in scenes. *Psychological Science, 8*, 368–373.

Retschitzki, J. (1990). *Stratégies des joueurs d'awélé*. Paris: L'Harmattan.

Reynolds, R. I. (1982). Search heuristics of chess players of different calibers. *American Journal of Psychology, 95*, 383–392.

Richman, H. B., Gobet, F., Staszewski, J. J., & Simon, H. A. (1996). Perceptual and memory processes in the acquisition of expert performance: The EPAM model. In K. A. Ericsson (Ed.), *The road to excellence* (pp. 167–187). Mahwah, NJ: Erlbaum.

Richman, H. B., Staszewski, J. J., & Simon, H. A. (1995). Simulation of expert memory with EPAM IV. *Psychological Review, 102*, 305–330.

Rikers, R. M. J. P., Schmidt, H. G., & Boshuizen, H. P. A. (2000). Knowledge encapsulation and the intermediate effect. *Contemporary Educational Psychology, 25*, 150–166.

Rikers, R. M. J. P., Schmidt, H. G., & Boshuizen, H. P. A. (2002). On the constraints of encapsulated knowledge: Clinical case representations by medical experts and sub-experts. *Cognition and Instruction, 20*, 27–45.

Rikers, R. M. J. P., Schmidt, H. G., Boshuizen, H. P. A., Linssen, G. C. M., Wesseling, G., & Paas, F. G. W. C. (2002). The robustness of medical expertise: Clinical case processing by medical experts and subexperts. *American Journal of Psychology, 115*, 609–629.

Rizzolatti, G., & Craighero, L. (2004). The mirror-neuron system. *Annual Review of Neuroscience, 27*, 169–192.

Roe, A. (1951). A study of imagery in research scientists. *Journal of Personality, 19*, 459–470.

Rosen, D. M. (2008). *Dope: A history of performance enhancement in sports from the nineteenth century to today*. London: Praeger.

Rosenthal, R. (1979). An introduction to the file drawer problem. *Psychological Bulletin, 86*, 638–641.

Rossi, F. F. (1991). Introduction. In F. F. Rossi (Ed.), *Expert witnesses* (pp. 3–10). Chicago: American Bar Association.

Royce, W. (1970). Managing the development of large software systems. *Proceedings of IEEE WESCON, 26*, 1–9.

Ruelle, D. (1991). *Chance and chaos*. Princeton, NJ: Princeton University Press.

Rumfitt, I. (2003). Savoir faire. *Journal of Philosophy, 100*, 158–166.

Runco, M. A. (2014). *Creativity theories and themes: Research, development, and practice*. New York: Academic Press.

Russell, S. J., & Norvig, P. (2009). *Artificial intelligence: A modern approach (3rd edition)*. Upper Saddle River, NJ: Prentice Hall.

Russell, Y. I., & Gobet, F. (2013). What is counterintuitive? Religious cognition and natural expectation. *Review of Philosophy and Psychology, 4*, 715–749.

Ryle, G. (1946). Knowing how and knowing that: The presidential address. *Proceedings of the Aristotelian Society, 46*, 1–16.

Ryle, G. (1949). *The concept of mind*. New York: Barnes & Noble.

Saariluoma, P. (1984). *Coding problem spaces in chess: A psychological study*. Turku: Societas Scientiarum Fennica.

Saariluoma, P. (1990). Apperception and restructuring in chess players' problem solving. In K. J. Gilhooly, M. T. G. Keane, R. H. Logie & G. Erdos (Eds.), *Lines of thought: Reflections on the psychology of thinking* (Vol. 2, pp. 41–57). New York: John Wiley & Sons Ltd.

Saariluoma, P. (1992). Error in chess: The apperception-restructuring view. *Psychological Research, 54*, 17–26.

Saariluoma, P. (1994). Location coding in chess. *The Quarterly Journal of Experimental Psychology, 47A*, 607–630.

Saariluoma, P. (1995). *Chess players' thinking: A cognitive psychological approach*. London: Routledge.

Saariluoma, P., & Hohlfeld, M. (1994). Apperception in chess players' long-range planning. *European Journal of Cognitive Psychology, 6*, 1–22.

Sabers, D. S., Cushing, K. S., & Berliner, D. C. (1991). Differences among teachers in a task characterized by simultaneity, multidimensionality, and immediacy. *American Educational Research Journal, 28*, 63–88.

Salas, E., & Klein, G. (Eds.). (2001). *Linking expertise and naturalistic decision making*. Mahwah, NJ: Erlbaum.

Salgado, J. F. (2003). Predicting job performance using FFM and non-FFM personality measures. *Journal of Occupational and Organizational Psychology, 76*, 323–346.

Salthouse, T. A. (1991). Expertise as the circumvention of human processing limitations. In K. A. Ericsson & J. Smith (Eds.), *Studies of expertise: Prospects and Limits* (pp. 286–300). Cambridge: Cambridge University Press.

Salthouse, T. A., Babcock, R. L., Skovronek, E., Mitchell, D. R. D., & Palmon, R. (1990). Age and experience effects in spatial visualization. *Developmental Psychology, 26*, 128–136.

Savulescu, J., Foddy, B., & Clayton, M. (2004). Why we should allow performance enhancing drugs in sport. *British Journal of Sports Medicine, 38*, 666–670.

Schacter, D. L., Chiu, C. Y. P., & Ochsner, K. N. (1993). Implicit memory: A selective review. *Annual Review of Neuroscience, 16*, 159–182.

Schlaug, G., Jancke, L., Huang, Y. X., & Steinmetz, H. (1995). In-vivo evidence of structural brain asymmetry in musicians. *Science, 267*, 699–701.

Schmidt, F. L., & Hunter, J. E. (1998). The validity and utility of selection methods in personnel psychology: Practical and theoretical implications of 85 years of research findings. *Psychological Bulletin, 124*, 262–274.

Schmidt, F. L., Outerbridge, A. N., Hunter, J. E., & Goff, S. (1988). Joint relation of experience and ability with job-performance: Test of 3 hypotheses. *Journal of Applied Psychology, 73*, 46–57.

Schmidt, H. G., & Boshuizen, H. P. A. (1993). On the origin of intermediate effects in clinical case recall. *Memory & Cognition, 21*, 338–351.

Schmidt, H. G., & Rikers, R. (2007). How expertise develops in medicine: Knowledge encapsulation and illness script formation. *Medical Education, 41*, 1133–1139.

Schmidt, R. A. (1975). Schema theory of discrete motor skill learning. *Psychological Review, 82*, 225–260.

Schneider, P., Scherg, M., Dosch, H. G., Specht, H. J., Gutschalk, A., & Rupp, A. (2002). Morphology of Heschl's gyrus reflects enhanced activation in the auditory cortex of musicians. *Nature Neuroscience, 5*, 688–694.

Schneider, W., Gruber, H., Gold, A., & Opwis, K. (1993). Chess expertise and memory for chess positions in children and adults. *Journal of Experimental Child Psychology, 56*, 328–349.

Schneiderman, B. (1976). Exploratory experiments in programmer behavior. *International Journal of Computer and Information Sciences, 5*, 123–143.

Schulz, R., & Salthouse, T. A. (1999). *Adult development and aging (Third edition)*. Upper Saddle River, NJ: Prentice Hall.

Schunn, C. D., & Anderson, J. R. (1999). The generality/specificity of expertise in scientific reasoning. *Cognitive Science, 23*, 337–370.

Schyns, P. (1998). Diagnostic recognition: Task constraints, object information, and their interactions. *Cognition, 67*, 147–179.

Selfe, L. (1977). *Nadia: A case of extraordinary drawing ability in an autistic child*. New York: Academic Press.

Seligman, M. E. P. (1975). *Learned helplessness*. New York: W. H. Freeman & Co.

Seligman, M. E. P., & Csikszentmihalyi, M. (2000). Positive psychology: An introduction. *American Psychologist, 55*, 5–14.

Selinger, E. (2011). *Expertise: Philosophical reflections*. Birkerød, DK: Automatic Press.

Selinger, E., & Crease, R. (Eds.). (2006). *The philosophy of expertise*. New York: Columbia University Press.

Selz, O. (1922). *Zur Psychologie des produktiven Denkens und des Irrtums*. Bonn: Friedrich Cohen.

Sententia, W. (2004). Neuroethical considerations: Cognitive liberty and converging technologies for improving human cognition. *Annals of the New York Academy of Sciences, 1013*, 221.

Shadbolt, N. R., & O'Hara, K. (1997). Model-based expert systems and the explanation of expertise. In P. J. Feltovich, K. M. Ford & R. R. Hoffman (Eds.), *Expertise in context* (pp. 315–337). Menlo Park, CA: AAAI Press / The MIT Press.

Shannon, C. E. (1948). A mathematical theory of communication. *Bell System Technical Journal, 27*, 379–423 and 623–656.

Shanteau, J. (1992a). Competence in experts: The role of task characteristics. *Organizational Behavior and Human Decision Processes, 53*, 252–266.

Shanteau, J. (1992b). How much relevant information does an expert use? Is it relevant? *Acta Psychologica, 81*, 75–86.

Shanteau, J. (2001). What does it mean when experts disagree? In E. Salas & G. Klein (Eds.), *Linking expertise and naturalistic decision making* (pp. 229–244). Mahwah, NJ: Erlbaum.

Sharp, C., & Benefield, P. (1995). *Research into season of birth and school achievement: A selected annotated bibliography*. Slough: NFER.

Shavinina, L. V. (Ed.). (2009). *International handbook on giftedness*. New York: Springer.

Shea, J. B., & Paull, G. (1996). Capturing expertise in sports. In K. A. Ericsson (Ed.), *The road to excellence: The acquisition of expert performance in the arts and sciences, sports, and games* (pp. 321–335). Mahwah, NJ: Erlbaum.

Shenk, D. (2010). *The genius in all of us*. New York: Doubleday.

Shepherd, J. C. (1973). Relations with the expert witnesses. In G. W. Holmes (Ed.), *Experts in litigation* (pp. 19–24). Ann Arbor: Institute of Continuing Legal Education.

Shuter-Dyson, R., & Gabriel, C. (1982). *The psychology of musical ability (2nd edition)*. London: Methuen.

Siegel, J. A. (1974). Sensory and verbal coding strategies in subjects with absolute pitch. *Journal of Experimental Psychology, 103,* 37–44.

Siegler, R. S. (1986). *Children's thinking.* Englewood Cliffs, NJ: Prentice-Hall.

Simon, D. P., & Simon, H. A. (1978). Individual differences in solving physics problems. In R. S. Siegler (Ed.), *Children's thinking: What develops?* (pp. 323–348). Hillsdale, NJ: Erlbaum.

Simon, H. A. (1955). A behavioral model of rational choice. *Quarterly Journal of Economics, 69,* 99–118.

Simon, H. A. (1956). Rational choice and the structure of the environment. *Psychological Review, 63,* 129–138.

Simon, H. A. (1966). Scientific discovery and the psychology of problem solving. In R. Colodny (Ed.), *Mind and Cosmos* (pp. 22–40). Pittsburgh, PA: University of Pittsburgh Press.

Simon, H. A. (1969). *The sciences of the artificial.* Cambridge, MA: MIT Press.

Simon, H. A. (1973). The structure of ill-structured problems. *Artificial Intelligence, 4,* 181–201.

Simon, H. A. (1976). *Administrative behavior.* New York: The Free Press.

Simon, H. A. (1977). *Models of discovery and other topics in the methods of science.* Dordrecht: Reidel.

Simon, H. A. (1979). *Models of thought* (Vol. 1). New Haven, CT: Yale University Press.

Simon, H. A. (1982). *Models of bounded rationality: Behavioral economics and business organization.* Cambridge, MA: The MIT Press.

Simon, H. A. (1989). *Models of thought* (Vol II). New Haven, CT: Yale University Press.

Simon, H. A. (1995). Explaining the ineffable: AI on the topics of intuition, insight and inspiration *Proceedings of the Fourteenth International Joint Conference on Artificial Intelligence* (pp. 939–948).

Simon, H. A., & Barenfeld, M. (1969). Information processing analysis of perceptual processes in problem solving. *Psychological Review, 7,* 473–483.

Simon, H. A., & Chase, W. G. (1973). Skill in chess. *American Scientist, 61,* 393–403.

Simon, H. A., & Gilmartin, K. J. (1973). A simulation of memory for chess positions. *Cognitive Psychology, 5,* 29–46.

Simon, H. A., & Gobet, F. (2000). Expertise effects in memory recall: Comments on Vicente an Wang (1998). *Psychological Review, 107,* 593–600.

Simon, H. A., Smithburg, D. W., & Thompson, A. V. (1950). *Public administration.* New York: Knopf.

Simonton, D. K. (1984). *Genius, creativity, and leadership: Historiometric enquiries.* Cambridge, MA: Harvard University Press.

Simonton, D. K. (1991). Emergence and realization of genius: The lives and works of 120 classical composers. *Journal of Personality and Social Psychology, 61,* 829.

Simonton, D. K. (1996). Creative expertise: A life-span developmental perspective. In K. A. Ericsson (Ed.), *The road to excellence* (pp. 319–335). Mahwah, NJ: Erlbaum.

Simonton, D. K. (1997). Creative productivity. *Psychological Review, 104,* 66–89.

Simonton, D. K. (1999). *Origins of genius.* Oxford: Oxford University Press.

Simonton, D. K. (2006). Historiometric methods. In K. A. Ericsson, N. Charness, P. Feltovich & R. R. Hoffman (Eds.), *Cambridge handbook of expertise and expert performance* (pp. 319–335). Cambridge: Cambridge University Press.

Simonton, D. K. (Ed.). (2014). *The Wiley-Blackwell handbook of genius.* Oxford: Wiley-Blackwell.

Singer, R. N., Williams, A. M., Frehlich, S. G., Janelle, C. M., Radlo, S. J., Barba, D. A., et al. (1998). New frontiers in visual search: An exploratory study in live tennis situations. *Research Quarterly for Exercise and Sport, 69*, 290–296.

Sio, U. N., & Ormerod, T. C. (2009). Does incubation enhance problem solving? A meta-analytic review. *Psychological Bulletin, 135*, 94–120.

Skinner, B. F. (1948). "Superstition" in the pigeon. *Journal of Experimental Psychology, 38*, 168–172.

Sloboda, J. A. (1974). The eye-hand span: An approach to the study of sight reading. *Psychology of Music, 2*, 4–10.

Sloboda, J. A. (1976a). Effect of item position on likelihood of identification by inference in prose reading and music reading. *Canadian Journal of Psychology, 30*, 228–237.

Sloboda, J. A. (1976b). Visual perception of musical notation: Registering pitch symbols in memory. *Quarterly Journal of Experimental Psychology, 28*, 1–16.

Sloboda, J. A. (1977). Phrase units as determinants of visual processing in music reading. *British Journal of Psychology, 68*, 117–124.

Sloboda, J. A. (1978). Perception of contour in music reading. *Perception, 7*, 323–331.

Sloboda, J. A. (1984). Experimental studies of music-reading: A review. *Music Perception, 2*, 222–236.

Sloboda, J. A. (1985). *The musical mind: The cognitive psychology of music.* Oxford: Oxford University Press.

Smith, J., Hausfeld, S., Power, R. P., & Gorta, A. (1982). Ambiguous musical figures and auditory streaming. *Perception and Psychophysics, 32*, 454–464.

Smith, J. F., & Kida, T. (1991). Heuristics and biases: Expertise and task realism in auditing. *Psychological Bulletin, 109*, 472–489.

Smith, L., Lane, P. C. R., & Gobet, F. (2008). Modelling the relationship between visual short-term memory capacity and recall ability. *European Modelling Symposium 2008 (EMS2008)*: Institute of Electrical and Electronics Engineers.

Smith, M. E., & Farah, M. J. (2011). Are prescription stimulants "smart pills"? The epidemiology and cognitive neuroscience of prescription stimulant use by normal healthy individuals. *Psychological Bulletin, 137*, 717–741.

Snowdon, P. (2004). Knowing how and knowing that: A distinction reconsidered. *Aristotelian Society, 104*, 1–29.

Spearman, C. (1927). *The abilities of man.* London: Macmillan.

Spencer, S. J., Steele, C. M., & Quinn, D. M. (1999). Stereotype threat and women's math performance. *Journal of Experimental Social Psychology, 35*, 4–28.

Staff, T., Gobet, F., & Parton, A. (in preparation, a). *Deliberate practice, early talent identification and the expertise specific optimal learning hypothesis: A study of Team GB Cycling at London 2012.*

Staff, T., Gobet, F., & Parton, A. (in preparation, b). *Expertise, talent or trained: An investigation into Team GB 2012 track and field Olympic athletes through the parameters of deliberate practice.*

Stanley, J., & Williamson, T. (2001). Knowing how. *Journal of Philosophy, 98*, 411–444.

Starkes, J. L. (1987). Skill in field hockey: The nature of the cognitive advantage. *Journal of Sport Psychology, 9*, 146–160.

Starkes, J. L., Deakin, J. M., Allard, F., Hodges, N. J., & Hayes, A. (1996). Deliberate practice in sports: What is it anyway? In K. A. Ericsson (Ed.), *The road to excellence* (pp. 51–80). Mahwah, NJ: Erlbaum.

Starkes, J. L., Edwards, P., Dissanayake, P., & Dunn, T. (1995). A new technology and field test of advance cue usage in volleyball. *Research Quarterly for Exercise and Sport, 65*, 1–6.

Starkes, J. L., & Ericsson, K. A. (Eds.). (2003). *Expert performance in sports.* Champaign, IL: Human Kinetics.

Staszewski, J. (Ed.). (2013a). *Expertise and skill acquisition: The impact of William G. Chase.* New York: Psychology Press.

Staszewski, J. J. (1988). Skilled memory and expert mental calculation. In M. T. H. Chi, R. Glaser & M. J. Farr (Eds.), *The nature of expertise* (pp. 71–128). Hillsdale, NJ: Erlbaum.

Staszewski, J. J. (1990). Exceptional memory: The influence of practice and knowledge on the development of elaborative encoding strategies. In F. E. Weinert & W. Schneider (Eds.), *Interactions among aptitudes, strategies, and knowledge in cognitive performance* (pp. 252–285). New York: Springer.

Staszewski, J. J. (2013b). Cognitive engineering based on expert skill. In J. J. Staszewski (Ed.), *Expertise and skill acquisition: The impact of William G. Chase* (pp. 29–57). New York: Psychology Press.

Stefik, M. (1995). *Introduction to knowledge systems.* San Francisco, CA: Morgan Kaufmann.

Stein, E. W. (1997). A look at expertise from a social perspective. In P. J. Feltovich, K. M. Ford & R. R. Hoffman (Eds.), *Expertise in context* (pp. 181–194). Menlo Park, CA: AAAI Press / The MIT Press.

Stern, W. (1912). *The psychological methods of intelligence testing* (G. Whipple, Trans.). Baltimore: Warwick and York.

Sternberg, R. J. (1996). Costs of expertise. In K. A. Ericsson (Ed.), *The road to excellence* (pp. 347–354). Mahwah, NJ: Erlbaum.

Sternberg, R. J. (1997). Cognitive conceptions of expertise. In P. J. Feltovich, K. M. Ford & R. R. Hoffman (Eds.), *Expertise in context* (pp. 149–162). Menlo Park, CA: AAAI Press / The MIT Press.

Sternberg, R. J., & Grigorenko, E. (1997). *Intelligence, heredity and environment.* New York: Cambridge University Press.

Sternberg, R. J., Wagner, R. K., Williams, W. M., & Horvath, J. A. (1995). Testing common-sense. *American Psychologist, 50*, 912–927.

Stewart, M. (2009). *The management myth: Why the "experts" keep getting it wrong.* New York: Norton.

Stoet, G., & Geary, D. C. (2013). Sex differences in mathematics and reading achievement are inversely related: Within- and across-nation assessment of 10 Years of PISA data. *PLoS ONE, 8*, e57988.

Stove, D. C. (2000). *Scientific irrationalism: Origins of a postmodern cult.* Piscataway, NJ: Transaction Publishers.

Strevens, M. (2013). Herding and the quest for credit. *Journal of Economic Methodology, 20*, 19–34.

Surowiecki, J. (2005). *The wisdom of crowds.* New York: Anchor.

Swensson, R. G. (1980). A 2-stage detection model applied to skilled visual-search by radiologists. *Perception and Psychophysics, 27*, 11–16.

Syed, M. (2011). *Bounce.* London: Fourth Estate.

Tabachnek-Schijf, H. J. M., Leonardo, A. M., & Simon, H. A. (1997). CaMeRa: A computational model of multiple representations. *Cognitive Science, 21*, 305–350.

Takeuchi, A. H., & Hulse, S. H. (1993). Absolute pitch. *Psychological Bulletin, 113*, 345–361.

Tanaka, J. M., & Taylor, M. (1991). Object categories and expertise: Is the basic level in the eye of the beholder? *Cognitive Psychology, 23*, 457–482.

Taylor, P. M. (2007). A review of research into the development of radiologic expertise: Implications for computer-based training. *Academic Radiology, 14*, 1252–1263.

Tenenbaum, G. (2003). Expert athletes: An integrated approach to decision-making. In J. Starkes & K. Ericsson (Eds.), *Expert Performance in sports* (pp. 192–218). Champaign, IL: Human Kinetics.

Terman, L. M. (1916). *The measurement of intelligence.* Boston, MA: Houghton Mifflin.

Terman, L. M. (1925–1959). *Genetic studies of genius (5 vols.).* Stanford, CA: Stanford University Press.

Tesauro, G. (1992). Practical issues in temporal difference learning. *Machine Learning, 8*, 257–277.

Tetlock, P. E. (2005). *Expert political judgment.* Princeton, NJ: Princeton University Press.

Thomsen, M., & Resnik, D. (1995). The effectiveness of the erratum in avoiding error propagation in physics. *Science and Engineering Ethics, 1*, 231–240.

Thorndike, E. L., & Woodworth, R. S. (1901). The influence of improvement in one mental function upon the efficiency of other functions. *Psychological Review, 9*, 374–382.

Thurstone, L. L. (1935). *The vectors of mind.* Chicago: University of Chicago Press.

Tikhomirov, O. K., & Poznyanskaya, E. D. (1966). An investigation of visual search as a means of analyzing heuristics. *Soviet Psychology, 5*, 2–15.

Torrance, E. P. (1972). Predictive validity of the Torrance test of creative thinking. *Journal of Creative Behavior, 6*, 236–252.

Torrance, E. P. (1974). *Torrance tests of creative thinking.* Scholastic Testing Service.

Tracey, T. J. G., Wampold, B. E., Lichtenberg, J. W., & Goodyear, R. K. (2014). Expertise in psychotherapy: An elusive goal? *American Psychologist, 69*, 218–229.

Tuddenham, W. J. (1962). Visual search, image organization and reader error in Roentgen diagnosis. *Radiology, 78*, 694–704.

Tuffiash, M., Roring, R. W., & Ericsson, K. A. (2007). Expert performance in SCRABBLE: Implications for the study of the structure and acquisition of complex skills. *Journal of Experimental Psychology: Applied, 13*, 124–134.

Turner, M. E., & Pratkanis, A. R. (1998). Twenty-five years of groupthink theory and research: Lessons from the evaluation of a theory. *Organizational Behavior and Human Decision Processes 73*, 105–115.

Turner, S. (2001). What is the problem with experts? *Social Studies of Science, 31*, 123–149.

Tversky, A., & Kahneman, D. (1974). Judgment under uncertainty: Heuristics and biases. *Science, 185*, 1124–1131.

Tversky, A., & Kahneman, D. (1981). The framing of decisions and the psychology of choice. *Science, 211*, 453–458.

Tversky, A., & Kahneman, D. (1992). Advances in prospect theory: Cumulative representation of uncertainty. *Journal of Risk and Uncertainty 5*, 297–323.

U.S. Glass Ceiling Commission. (1995). *A solid investment: Making full use of the nation's human capital.* Retrieved 27 January 2014, from http://digitalcommons.ilr.cornell.edu/key_workplace/120

Underwood, G., & Waters, A. J. (1998). Eye movements in a simple music reading task: A study of expert and novice musicians. *Psychology of Music, 26*, 46–60.

Ungerleider, S. (2001). *Faust's gold: Inside the East German doping machine.* New York: St. Martin's Press.

University and College Union. (2013). The position of women and BME staff in professorial roles in UK HEIs. Retrieved 28 January 2014, from http://www.ucu.org.uk/bmewomenreport

Unterrainer, J. M., Kaller, C. P., Halsband, U., & Rahm, B. (2006). Planning abilities and chess: A comparison of chess and non-chess players on the Tower of London task. *British Journal of Psychology, 97*, 299–311.

Unterrainer, J. M., Kaller, C. P., Leonhart, R., & Rahm, B. (2011). Revising superior planning performance in chess players: The impact of time restriction and motivation aspects. *American Journal of Psychology, 124*, 213–225.

Uttal, W. R. (2011). *Mind and brain: A critical appraisal of cognitive neuroscience.* Cambridge: MIT Press.

Valdés-Pérez, R. E. (1995). Machine discovery in chemistry: New results. *Artificial Intelligence, 74*, 191–201.

van de Wiel, M. W. J., Schmidt, H. G., & Boshuizen, H. P. A. (1998). A failure to reproduce the intermediate effect in clinical case recall. *Academic Medicine, 73*, 894–900.

Vera, A. H., & Simon, H. A. (1993). Situated action: A symbolic interpretation. *Cognitive Science, 17*, 7–48.

Vernon, P. A., Wickett, J. C., Bazana, P. G., & Stelmack., R. M. (2000). The neuropsychology and psychophysiology of human intelligence. In R. J. Sternberg (Ed.), *Handbook of Intelligence* (pp. 245–264). Cambridge: Cambridge University Press.

Vicente, K. J., & Wang, J. H. (1998). An ecological theory of expertise effects in memory recall. *Psychological Review, 105*, 33–57.

Vickers, J. N. (1996). Visual control when aiming at a far target. *Journal of Experimental Psychology: Human Perception and Performance, 22*, 342–354.

Voss, J. F., & Post, T. A. (1988). On the solving of ill-structured problems. In M. T. H. Chi, R. Glaser & M. J. Farr (Eds.), *The nature of expertise* (pp. 261–285). Hillsdale, NJ: Erlbaum.

Walberg, H. J., Rasher, S. P., & Parkerson, J. (1980). Childhood and eminence. *Journal of Creative Behavior, 13*, 225–231.

Wallach, M. A. (1970). Creativity. In P. H. Mussen (Ed.), *Carmichael's manual of child psychology* (pp. 1273–1365). New York: Wiley.

Wallas, G. (1926). *The art of thought.* New York: Harcourt Brace.

Ward, P., Ericsson, K. A., & Williams, A. M. (2013). Complex perceptual-cognitive expertise in a simulated task environment. *Journal of Cognitive Engineering and Decision Making, 7*, 231–254.

Ward, P., Hodges, N. J., Starkes, J. L., & Williams, A. M. (2007). The road to excellence: Deliberate practice and the development of expertise. *High Ability Studies, 18*, 119–153.

Ward, P., Suss, J., Eccles, D. W., Williams, A. M., & Harris, K. R. (2011). Skill-based differences in option generation in a complex task: A verbal protocol analysis. *Cognitive Processing, 12*, 289–300.

Ward, P., & Williams, A. M. (2003). Perceptual and cognitive skill development in soccer: The multidimensional nature of expert performance. *Journal of Sport & Exercise Psychology, 25*, 93–111.

Ward, W. D. (1999). Absolute pitch. In D. Deutsch (Ed.), *The psychology of music (Second Edition)* (pp. 265–298). San Diego: Academic Press.

Waterhouse, L. (2006). Inadequate evidence for Multiple Intelligences, Mozart Effect, and Emotional Intelligence theories. *Educational Psychologist, 41*, 247–255.

Waters, A. J., & Gobet, F. (2008). Mental imagery and chunks: Empirical and computational findings. *Memory & Cognition, 36*, 505–517.

Waters, A. J., Gobet, F., & Leyden, G. (2002). Visuo-spatial abilities in chess players. *British Journal of Psychology, 30*, 303–311.

Watson, J. B. (1925). *Behaviorism* (revised ed.). London: Kegan.

Watson, J. D. (1969). *The double helix.* New York: Mentor.

Weaver, H. E. (1943). Studies of ocular behavior in music reading I: A survey of visual processes in reading differently constructed musical selections. *Psychological Monographs, 55*, 1–30.

Weber, M. (1922/1979). *Economy and society.* Berkeley, CA: University of California Press.

Wedgwood, R. (2007). *The nature of normativity.* Oxford: Oxford University Press.

Weisberg, R. W. (1999). Creativity and knowledge: A challenge to theories. In R. J. Sternberg (Ed.), *Handbook of creativity* (pp. 226–250). Cambridge: Cambridge University Press.

Weisberg, R. W. (2006). *Creativity.* New York: Wiley.

White, A. (1982). *The nature of knowledge*: Totowa, NJ: Rowan and Littlefield.

Whitehead, A. N. (1929). *The aims of education.* New York: Macmillan.

Wiersma, L. D. (2000). Risks and benefits of youth sport specialization: Perspectives and recommendations. *Pediatric Exercise Science, 12*, 13.

Wilber, R. L., & Pitsiladis, Y. P. (2012). Kenyan and Ethiopian distance runners: What makes them so good? *International Journal of Sports Physiology & Performance, 7*, 92–102.

Wilensky, H. L. (1964). The professionalization of everyone? *The American Journal of Sociology, 70*, 137–158.

Wiley, J. (1998). Expertise as mental set: The effects of domain knowledge in creative problem solving. *Memory & Cognition, 26*, 716–730.

Williams, M., Davids, K., Burwitz, L., & Williams, J. (1993). Cognitive knowledge and soccer performance. *Perceptual and Motor Skills, 76*, 579–593.

Willis, S. L., & Dubin, S. S. (1990). *Maintaining professional competence.* San Francisco, CA: Jossey-Bass.

Wiltshire, S. (1989). *Cities.* London: Dent.

Winch, C. (2009). Ryle on knowing how and the possibility of vocational education. *Journal of Applied Philosophy, 26*, 88–101.

Winch, C. (2010). *Dimensions of expertise: A conceptual exploration of vocational knowledge.* London: Continuum.

Winkler, R. L. (2003). *An introduction to Bayesian inference and decision* (2nd ed.). Gainesville, FL: Probabilistic Publishing.

Winner, E. (1996). *Gifted children: Myths and realities.* New York: Basic Books.

Witten, I. H., Frank, E., & Hall, M. A. (2011). *Data mining* (3rd ed.). Burlington, MA: Morgan Kaufmann.

Wittgenstein, L. (1984). *Philosophical investigations.* Oxford: Blackwell.

Wolff, A. S., Mitchell, D. H., & Frey, P. W. (1984). Perceptual skill in the game of Othello. *Journal of Psychology, 118*, 7–16.

Wood, D. J. (1998). *How children think and learn* (2nd ed.). Oxford: Blackwell.

Worrall, J. (1991). Feyerabend and the facts. In G. Munevar (Ed.), *Beyond reason: Essays on the philosophy of Paul Feyerabend* (pp. 329–353). Dordrecht: Kluwer.

Worthen, J. B., & Hunt, R. R. (2011). *Mnemonology: Mnemonics for the 21st century.* New York: Psychology Press.

Wright, M. J., Bishop, D. T., Jackson, R. C., & Abernethy, B. (2010). Functional MRI reveals expert-novice differences during sport-related anticipation. *NeuroReport, 21*, 94–98.

Wright, M. J., Bishop, D. T., Jackson, R. C., & Abernethy, B. (2011). Cortical fMRI activation to opponents' body kinematics in sport-related anticipation: Expert-novice differences with normal and point-light video. *Neuroscience Letters, 500*, 216–221.

Wright, M. J., Gobet, F., Chassy, P., & Ramchandani, P. N. (2013). ERP to chess stimuli reveal expert-novice differences in the amplitudes of N2 and P3 components. *Psychophysiology, 50*, 1023–1033.

Wright, M. J., & Jackson, R. C. (2007). Brain regions concerned with perceptual skills in tennis: An fMRI study. *International Journal of Psychophysiology, 63*, 214–220.

Wynne, B. (1989). Sheepfarming after Chernobyl. *Environment, 31*, 10–39.

Wynne, B. (1993). Public uptake of science: A case for institutional reflexivity. *Public Understanding of Science 2*, 321–337.

Yates, F. A. (1966). *The art of memory.* Chicago: University of Chicago Press.

Yoshikawa, A., Kojima, T., & Saito, Y. (1999). Relations between skill and the use of terms: An analysis of protocols of the game of Go. In H. J. van den Herik & H. Iida (Eds.), *Computers and games. Proceedings of the First International Conference on Computers and Games (CG'98)* (Vol. 1558, pp. 211–227). Berlin: Springer.

Yu, L. (2011). *A developer's guide to the semantic web.* New York: Springer.

Zhang, S. L., & Duke, N. K. (2008). Strategies for Internet reading with different reading purposes: A descriptive study of twelve good Internet readers. *Journal of Literacy Research, 40*, 128–162.

Zhu, D., & Simon, H. A. (1988). Learning mathematics from examples and by doing. *Cognition and Instruction, 4*, 137–166.

Zhu, X., Lee, Y., Simon, H. A., & Zhu, D. (1996). Cue recognition and cue elaboration in learning from examples. *Proceedings of the National Academy of Sciences, 93*, 1346–1351.

Ziebland, S. (2004). The importance of being expert: The quest for cancer information on the Internet. *Social Science and Medicine, 59*, 1783–1793.

Zsambok, C. E., & Klein, G. A. (Eds.). (1997). *Naturalistic decision making.* Mahwah, NJ: Erlbaum.

Zubieta, J.-K., Heitzeg, M. M., Smith, Y. R., Bueller, J. A., Xu, K., Xu, Y., et al. (2003). COMT $val^{158}met$ genotype affects m-opioid neurotransmitter responses to a pain stressor. *Science*, 1240.

Zuckerman, H. (1977). *Scientific elite.* New York: Free Press.

Index

In this index *f* represents figure and *t* represents table.